BY A River, ON A Hill

BY A
River,
ON A
Hill

JOHN DURBIN HUSHER

LitPrime
"Your story is our priority"

LitPrime Solutions
21250 Hawthorne Blvd
Suite 500, Torrance, CA 90503
www.litprime.com
Phone: 1 (209) 788-3500

Published by LitPrime Solutions   04/14/2021

ISBN: 978-1-954886-41-4(sc)
ISBN: 978-1-954886-42-1(hc)
ISBN: 978-1-954886-43-8(e)

Contents

1

The Beginning

January 29, 1932

There was a nice hum in the brick building called the Pump House. The pumps were run by motors that turned them to an almost-melodious tune. Kneeling over one of the large pumps that had been pulled offline for repair was a nice-looking young man with bright red hair. The badge on his shirt indicated that he was John E. Husher. The badge number was 5345, dated July 10, 1930. As he worked on the pump, he was startled by the loud shout of a co-worker who had just entered the building.

"Hi, Red!" the man shouted. "How's the wife?"

"Big as a house," Red answered.

"Maybe she's going to have twins," the other man retorted.

"No, she's just a little woman ready to have a baby," Red answered.

With that, the man continued on his way through another door. As Red knelt to pull the bearing of the large pump from the shaft, he thought about Hon, his wife. She was having a hard time carrying this baby in the middle of the Depression that surrounded the country. He knew he had been fortunate to gain this job during these hard times. He was only eighteen in 1930 and had just graduated from Monessen

High School in Pennsylvania, when a close friend had told him about the job opening that he could get him here in the mill.

The Monessen steel mill was about three miles away from home, and he had received the lowest-paying job in the mill—twenty-six cents an hour—but it was a job. He had gladly taken it, since it had allowed him to marry Hon. They had gotten married when Red began the job in the Pump House at Pittsburgh Steel in Monessen. They had found a small apartment in Monessen that cost $6 a month. Even if Hon had to walk up three flights of stairs, it was a light chore, she had said. For a moment his mind returned him to the job and he continued to pull on the bearing. But, then he began thinking about Hon walking up those stairs and it brought her disability to his mind.

Hon's real name was Virginia Cecil Ray Corrick, and that's what she had been called before their marriage two years ago. Now he called her Hon because that was what she was to him. He couldn't love a person more. She had long, black hair and dark eyes that seemed to look through you. She was beautifully shaped. His mother hadn't wanted him to marry Virginia, since she was crippled. During her birth, the doctor had used forceps to extract her from her mother's womb. This had caused some damage and she had been left with a noticeable limp in her leg and a dropped wrist, both on the left side. She walked with a limp, but he thought she was beautiful. If she hadn't had the affliction, she could probably have been a model or movie star—and he probably wouldn't have had the chance to marry her.

Hon never seemed to consider that she was crippled. She went about everything simply. She cooked and kept the house in order. Keeping house was a bigger chore now that she was carrying the baby, but she was happy to do it for the baby and Red. Meals were on time, the house was always clean, his clothes were always clean, and he always went to work feeling strong and alive. Red liked to watch her hold a potato between her breast and wrist of her lame arm and peel away the skin with a knife in her good hand. The peels flew into the air, and she would quickly turn the potato into its next position against the breast with her right hand. She could peel a potato faster than anyone.

It had not taken long before she was pregnant, about a year after they were married. But there was an issue, and Red didn't know whether to be completely excited or not. The doctors had said that Virginia should not have any children with her affliction. There was a possibility that she would die during childbirth. But she had wanted children, and now she had gone more than eight months. She had made it this far. Any day now she should have the child, and he prayed each night that she would make it through the birth. He pulled a tool out of his tool cabinet and continued to work on the pump. He smiled to himself. She was so big in the stomach and so small in body that it looked like the child could fall out any time now. He was proud. Any day now, she would give birth. Yes, she was as big as a house.

As he continued to work, he thought about their good fortune. Practically everyone he knew was out of work. The Depression had hit the steel industry, just as it had hit most businesses. The demand for steel was a third of what it had been, and many men had been dropped from the mill. There were long lines everywhere. There were lines for food and lines with over a hundred men who were all competing for one job opening. But at least there was a job for someone, and he appreciated the people standing in that line for one job opening. Many people were trying to get their young ones to earn some money, maybe twenty five cents a day—something to keep food in the house.

Times were tough. With his take-home pay of about $20 every two weeks, he was able to rent an apartment for Hon and their expected baby. He knew that the job in the Pump House was limited. There was no way to get a promotion or to make more money. But the pumps had to keep running even if the mill was closed for a strike or a reduction in the work force, so he did have some job security. If the pumps didn't keep running during a strike, algae would grow in the pipes and would make them ineffective over time. The pumps forced cooling water from the river to the machines, the blast furnace, the open hearth, the rod mill, the wire mill, and the nail mill. This water was life for the mill, as it ran like blood to all the major centers of the mill. It cooled the motors, the engines, and the hot lines and completed its journey by returning to the river—waste and all.

Red stirred from his thoughts and realized it was 7:30 in the evening.

It was time for his break. He was working the four to twelve o'clock shift that week. He walked out of the Pump House and onto the bank of the river. It was pleasant to light up a cigarette and have a smoke while looking out over the river. It was dark out except for the light from the moon and the lights off in the distance. It was hard to see anything except the soft ripples of water reflecting from the moonlight. Too bad this river was polluted and there were no fish living in the river. He thought it would be fun to take Hon fishing on the river with his son—or daughter. He wondered which it would be.

It was quite cool at the end of January and Red felt the cool breeze coming down the river. The breeze smelled like the steel mill. He had grown to like the smell. It smelled like work. The jacket he wore kept him warm on nights like this, and it was a necessity to keep him warm in the Pump House, where the only heat was given off by the motors and pumps. He looked down at the river below and thought about how it provided him his work and much of the work for others in the mill.

He took a deep breath and thought about going home that night. Hon always had a bowl of cooked cereal or a fried egg for him to eat. Next week he would be on the midnight shift, working from twelve to eight in the morning. He liked that shift least of all. When he worked the midnight shift, he never got to sleep with Hon. He worked all night, came home, ate breakfast, and went to bed alone. He awoke around four when Hon called him to eat supper. But at least he was working, "It's good to work, no matter what hours" he thought and with that thought he flipped his cigarette down into the river and went back into the Pump House to finish repairing the bearing. It couldn't wait. He picked up his tool and bent over to begin working on the pump while continuing his thoughts. Tomorrow, another pump might have a problem, and a spare must always be available. He could almost repair the equipment in his sleep, but he never ceased being grateful for the work. But even better than that—soon he would see his Hon.

A Surprise—Twins

Red left work at 8:00 on Tuesday morning, the second of February, having worked the midnight shift. This was his second day of the workweek, and he was beginning to get used to the strange hours of work and sleep. As he walked along in the morning light, he thought about Hon. He could hardly wait to get home to see her. He was tired from working eight hours, but he felt quite refreshed knowing he was free until midnight, unless Hon had something for him to do before he hit the rack and getting a few hours of sleep..

When he got to the apartment steps, he thought it would be nice if their child were born this morning. That way he could be of help, and he wouldn't miss any work. He mounted the stairs to their apartment, and Hon was waiting for him. She had made a bowl of soft-boiled eggs and mixed them with toast and butter. It was one of his favorites.

Hon was radiant in her pregnancy. He had always thought she was beautiful, but now she was even more so. He gave her a big hug and kiss and sat down to eat. He described his day at work, and she, her day running the home.

After eating, Red went to bed, only to be wakened several hours later by Hon saying she was having labor pains. He hurriedly rolled out of bed and began to pace. He thought he had had it all figured out, but now he was confused as to what to do next. Hon shouted for him to call the doctor. Now he knew what he needed to do—call the doctor!

Red hurried down the stairs and ran to the store down the street and used their phone to call Doctor Heater and his nurse. He hurried back to his Hon, thinking that one day they would have a phone. He hurried up the three flights of steps, wondering what he would find when he reached the bedroom.

Hon was standing at the end of the bed, rocking and moaning. He could do nothing but wipe her brow with a cool damp washcloth.

Time passed slowly." Where was the doctor?" "Will he be on time, or would I have to deliver the baby myself?" All these thoughts went through Red's head. How could Hon put up with this torture? Was it like this way for all mothers, or is Hon's pain a result of her being so small and her physical problems?" "Red, get me another wet towel." Hon cries out. He hurries to the kitchen and picks up a small towel and shoves it under the cold water facet and returns with the cool towel. Hon yells for him to keep rubbing the back of her neck and across her forehead with the cool towel.

Red notices the veins in her neck popping out. He wondered how such delicate skin could withstand the pressure of those bulging vessels. He held her right hand and let her squeeze his hand as much as she wanted. He felt the grip of her right hand, which had gained strength through continuous use, since she couldn't use her crippled left arm. He was glad to feel her strength but knew it was due to the pain she was feeling.

Tears run down Red's face, as he suffers with her, hoping to relieve her pain in some way. Surely the doctor and nurse should be here now. Hon's shouting and moaning over the past hour were so loud that everyone in the neighborhood must know that her time has come. Maybe someone will come to their aid soon. "Where's the doctor?" Red shouts out at no one in particular. Then he hears footsteps coming up the steps. Maybe it was a neighbor coming to help. The door opened, and Doctor Heater and his nurse stepped inside. "Doctor Heater is here!" Red shouted to Hon. "It's OK, Hon. He'll take care of you and the baby."

The time between Hon's contractions was short. Doctor Heater told Red to fill a bowl with hot water, and he handed Red some large white towels. Red nervously wrung hot water from the towels and supplied them to the nurse, and Hon stretched across the bed with her knees up, pain written on her face.

As he continued wringing the towels, Red wondered what they would call the baby. If they had a boy, they might name him John, after me. If they had a girl, they might call her Cecile, Hon's middle name. Now he only hoped the pain would cease and the baby would be born in good health, whatever the gender.

Red held Hon's good right hand while the torture went on for almost two hours, and then Red heard the doctor quietly say, "Here it is, a healthy little boy." The doctor whacked the baby on the rear, and he began to cry, a sound that Red was happy to hear.

"It's over," he said. "And my Hon is in good shape."

The doctor handed the baby over to his nurse to clean while he cleaned his hands in the sink. He grabbed his bag and began packing. As he packed his bag, Hon broke the news: "Doctor, I think there's another one in there." The doctor was shocked. He checked, and he couldn't believe it, but she was correct. How could he have missed that? He became quite concerned that a second baby might involve complications that he wasn't prepared for. But, sixteen minutes later, a second son was born to Virginia and John Husher. Twins! They were both big children.

The doctor asked the nurse to bring the scale and to weigh the two boys. One weighed 9 pounds 8 ounces, and the other 9 pounds 10 ounces. He looked at Virginia in astonishment. "I was concerned that with your affliction you would have a hard time carrying a baby the full nine months. You not only carried one baby nine months, you carried two large boys. I'm amazed that a little thing like you could give birth to twin boys this size." Hon felt good enough to smile back at doctor Heater.

Red was so excited he couldn't stop breathing rapidly. He was hyperventilating at the turn of events. The doctor and nurse were almost as excited as Red. Dr. Heater grinned from ear to ear. "This is only the second set of twins I've delivered," he said. "This is wonderful, and they look so healthy." He turned to the nurse and said, "We need to mark these babies to ensure we keep their proper order of birth."

The nurse opened another bag and removed some ribbons and small, one-inch square leather pieces. She marked a number on each of the leather pieces, and she threaded the ribbon through a leather piece marked one. She wrapped the ribbon around the wrist of the baby born first. Then she took another ribbon and threaded it through the second leather piece marked two. She wrapped it neatly around the wrist of the baby born second. "There," she said, "now you can tell them apart."

Hon and Red smiled at their two packages, each tied up with a ribbon. "Maybe we can call them One and Two," Red said with a laugh.

"Let me hold Number One first," he cried as he lifted the firstborn from the bed. Red looked down at his miracle and couldn't stop the tears from running down his face. "I'm so happy for you, Number One, and for your mother, who brought you to us." Red turned and sat the baby back on the bed and lifted the second baby in his arms. He smiled down on the little baby and said, "And you came along as an extra gift to your mother and me. What a wonderful surprise." And again the tears slipped down his face, and he had to use his sleeve to keep them from falling on the baby. "You don't look like your brother." And with that remark, he turned to the doctor and said, "I thought twins looked alike."

The doctor replied, "When they come from the same egg that splits in the mother's womb, they look alike. But when twins are born from two different fertilized eggs, they don't look alike. These are called fraternal twins." Red leans down and places number two by number one and say, "I don't care if you came from one egg or two, you are beautiful."

Meanwhile, Hon was filled with pride as she watched Red dote over his two sons. She asked, "Don't I get a kiss or something for my part in this?"

Red turned and hugged and kissed his wife. "You did great," he said softly. "We have a big load to take care of, but it'll be worth it."

The doctor and nurse began to pack their things. The doctor and nurse gave Red instructions on how to care for his wife and what to watch for, and then they left. Red listened to their footsteps as they moved down the stairs, and he thought about what had happened since he had first heard their footsteps coming up those stairs. In that short time, he had become a father not once, but twice.

It was quiet and still in the apartment, like being left alone after a riot. It was still confusing to the couple that such a big event could happen in such a short time. Yesterday there had been work, Hon, and some small things to take care of. Now, twin boys had been added to the list. Red wondered how Hon will be able to handle two children while he was at work.

But he decided not to worry and turned his attention to Hon and the babies next to her. Red told Hon how proud he was of her.

"It's easy when it's for you," she said. "Now I have three men in my family, and now, Red Husher, we must think about what to name these two boys." She began to ramble on about names for boys or girls. She told Red about all the names she had been thinking of. "But now I have come up with two names for our boys."

The oldest, Hon wanted to name Lee after the husband of the nurse who had delivered her babies; with a middle name of Kenneth after Red's uncle. She had always liked that name. "The youngest we'll call John," she said, "after you, my beautiful husband. But I want to call him Jay, because I like that name. We'll give him the middle name of Durbin after my great grandfather's last name." "It's nice to give some tradition to the family."

Red listened to Hon as if they were directions. He had not thought much about a name , much less two names, and he was more than willing to go along with her wishes. Red thought about what she had said and spoke those names out loud. "Lee Kenneth and John Durbin," he repeated. "Lee Kenneth and John Durbin, I like the sound of those names."

And so began the lives of Lee Kenneth (Kenny) and John Durbin (Jay) Husher.

"Please call my mom and see if she can come over and help me. I know she will be excited about the twins."

Red walked across the street again and phoned his mother-in-law, Mom Corrick, to tell her that Hon had given birth to twins. The conversation was long, but Red eventually asked her if she would come that evening and watch Hon and the babies, because he had to go to work at midnight.

"No problem," she replies. "I'll be there in an hour, after feeding Dad dinner."

Soon Mom Corrick arrived and Red felt relieved. It was always good to see her because she was always upbeat. She was full of life and always seems to joke, even when times were tough. It didn't take her long to get the twins cleaned up and to cook something for Hon to eat.

Mom loved the names they had picked out. Right away, she picked up Ken and called him Kenny. She held him up in the air at arms length and looked him over. "Look at that, Kenny, you are born and flying on the same day." Next, she picked up Jay, held him above her head, and said, "You look fine, Jay Boy, and you get to fly on your first day too." She called Jay that for the rest of her life. Next, she looked down at Hon in the bed and said, "You did great. I can't believe how big they are."

Red was worn out and went to lie down for a couple of hours before going to work. He hit the bed thinking that he wouldn't be able to sleep because he was so excited, but as soon as he hit the bed, he was asleep. He couldn't believe he had slept that long when Mom called him to get ready for work. He was confused again. He walked out of the bedroom and looked to see if Hon had really had two babies or if he had been dreaming all this. But there they were: Hon and the two bundles of joy lying next to her. Goosebumps went up and down his spine, and the hair on his arms stood straight up. He wanted to jump up and down and shout, but Mom Corrick would think he was nuts.

Mom Corrick had made something for him to eat. He sat down but kept getting up and looking at his sons as though they were miracles that he had dreamed. They were miracles, but not just while he was sleeping—they were real.

"Hon and I did a good job," he thought. "Now it's Hon, me, and the twins." " No, not just the twins, but twins with names that end in Husher." It was too bad that he had to go to work. He would like to stay around and spend time with them.

Red thought about the name of Husher. He had been born a bastard, not knowing his real father or his true last name. His mother's name was Harriet Pearl Bolin. When he was two, Charles Husher had accepted his mother and him into his home. His sister Marguerite was not accepted and went and stayed with Mother Miller who had raised his mother. Charles Husher only accepted him on the condition that when he got old enough – sixteen or so, that he would work in the coal mines with him. With these conditions he was adopted by him and acquired his last name of Husher. With these two sons the name of Husher would be carried on.

Soon, he would be on his way to earn a living. Things had sure changed since he had gotten home this morning. He still found it hard to believe that only a few hours ago he had come home from work and hoped Hon would have the babies during the day. It seemed like a week ago.

Red went to work that evening disappointed that he would not be able to tell any of the guys at work about his twin boys, since they were working the day shift or second shift when he was on the third shift. There were only three workers to cover the three shifts and they rotated their work shifts every week. There was a foreman on the first shift that covered other areas of the plant as well. He could hardly wait until next week when he would be on first shift when most of the workers in the other parts of the plant are working and could tell everyone about his twin sons. He would take cigars to give to people at work and to his boss. He could hardly wait. He was so proud of his little woman and his two sons. Many of his coworkers didn't have sons, and none of them had twin sons. "Kenny and Jay," he kept saying to himself.

He continued on his way to work, which was about a mile from the apartment. Maybe it was better for him to be working the midnight shift that week. Hon would get some sleep, and her mom would be there to help. She would spend the week at their place to help with the babies.

As he approached the mill, he thought about the hard time he had gone through that day. There had been lots of things to do, even with Mom Corrick there to help. Maybe his mother would come and see the twins this week. She would be proud too. "I better call her when I get off work tomorrow morning," he said to himself.

He reached the mill and went to his locker to put on his work shoes and pick up his safety glasses. Red noticed a paper stuck to the front of his locker. On the paper was a drawing of a naked man with two penises hanging between his legs. Below the picture was written: "Red Husher, the man with the double barrel." He laughed out loud. It felt good to laugh. He hadn't realized how much pent-up emotion he had. "So, they had already heard about his good fortune and the twins, he thought out loud.". He wondered how they could have found out so fast. Maybe the doctor had told someone. It was funny, that drawing.

He smiled and could hardly wait to take it home to show Hon in the morning.

He began his work, but his mind was on the two sons he now had. "It's a miracle," he kept saying to himself as the night wore on. He was lucky that he could do his work in his sleep, since he was focused on going home and seeing his wife and sons. Red knew he had to keep busy so the time would go faster.

During his break that night, he smoked a cigarette as he stood above the river and thanked the Lord for delivering his sons and keeping Hon in good health. He looked across the river toward Charleroi and thought about the hospital there. He hoped that the next child could be born in a hospital. It would be easier on both of them.

The moon on the water reminded him of the water running off the twins as they were washed by the nurse. Their bodies had been shiny in some places and wrinkled in others. He wondered how long it would take for them to lose all their wrinkles and look like other kids.

He decided to treat himself to another cigarette to celebrate the twins. He lit up a second cigarette and said out loud, "Thank you, Lord, for the twin sons you have brought Hon and me. May they be blessed as Hon and I have been blessed." He finished the cigarette and flipped it into the river below. He had thrown two cigarettes into the river tonight to celebrate his two sons. Then he went back into the Pump House to continue his work.

He thought about the funny drawing that had been on his locker when he had come to work. He reached into his pocket, looked at it again, and laughed another time. So, they had already heard about the twins. He wonders how they could have found out so fast. Maybe the doctor told someone. It was funny, that drawing. He smiled and could hardly wait to show it to Hon. He left to go home and for some reason the world seemed different. His foot steps felt lighter and he wanted to shout out loud about his good fortune.

The Town—Monessen and Pittsburgh Steel

It's important to understand something about this town to which these twins were born. It was a tough steel mill town and each of the twins would grow up in this surrounding learning how to compete and be "street wise." They would spend most of their early lives growing up in this atmosphere, and it would pay dividends for them in their future.

The town of Monessen built its steel mill just after the turn of the century when the Industrial Revolution was in its early stages. This valley was made for this type of industry. Its name even reflected its destiny. The town of Monessen was named after the Monongahela River that passed through the town and after the town of Essen in Germany. Essen was the steel center of Germany. Cars had just been invented, and trains transported people and materials. The mill flourished around the time of World War I, when large motors were perfected and steel mills became something other than the makers of steel. Rolling mills were installed that allowed the mills to produce rods, sheet metal, wire, nails, and many types of castings.

The small town of Monessen drew Italians, Slovaks, Poles, Russians, Irish, English, Dutch, Swedes, and many other nationalities during this growth period. It was a godsend to the people of the valley. This valley was made for this type of industry. Its name even reflected its pre-ordained destiny. The town of Monessen was named after the Monongahela River that passed along its total length, and after the town of Essen in Germany. Essen was the steel mill center of Germany. Here in the valley, the river provided the perfect passage for carrying coal, iron ore, lime, steel scrap, and other natural resources. Raw material was carried across the Great Lakes down the many rivers to cities such as Monessen in western Pennsylvania. These boats had lives of their own and were treated like capital ships as they paddled along the river, pushing the loaded barges that carried the raw resources to the mills. Much of the coal came from as close as West Virginia, only thirty or forty miles away.

These waterways transported the raw materials and completed materials throughout the country. These waterways were an advantage that countries like Australia lacked, and they rapidly fell behind this country that was so blessed. But it wasn't only the waterways that differentiated the United States from Australia. Here, there were the raw resources—scarcely tapped—rich materials from Canada and all along the Great Lakes.

The paddle-wheel boats brought raw resources down the Monongahela River to the Monessen mill, where they were unloaded by large cranes, and either put in large piles or loaded on freight trains. The trains carried the resources to different locations in the steel mill where they were dumped or unloaded into trucks. The material was carried from boats to trains, from trains to trucks, from trucks to wheelbarrows, and eventually into the shovel of a steel mill worker.

Much of the material from these sources went to Monessen and some of the other steel mills further along the Monongahela River. Locks were located on these river ways to allow these boats to be lowered or raised to the different levels of the rivers. These boats had lives of their own and were treated like capital ships as they paddled their way along the river pushing the loaded barges in front that were carrying the raw resources to the mills.

They were handled like carriers of mercy along with their loads— lifted or lowered to the varying levels of the rivers so gently like they were babies being carried to church like a mother's milk to her child. Surely this was the food that provided the steel mills with the raw material to work and supply finished parts of various sorts. It was hard to think of them as big and brawny. Yet big and brawny they were, and still they paddled rather quietly back and forth on the rivers like ants carrying food to their lair and returning for more. You could not hear them moving quietly along their way unless you were down on the river where you'd see their paddles gliding through the water as smooth as silk. Yet, if you looked up and saw one you stopped to watch them parade by. These waterways and paddleboats were the pipelines that fortified the mills along the way.

Like a baton carrier in a relay race, the paddle-wheel boats brought the raw resources to a point on the banks of the Monongahela River next to the Monessen mill where they were unloaded by large cranes and either put in large piles or loaded on freight trains that were there especially for supplying the steel mill. The trains picked up the baton, continued the relay race and carried the resources to different locations in the steel mill where they were dumped or unloaded into trucks; and the run with the baton carried on. The material was carried from boats to trains, from trains to trucks, from trucks to wheelbarrows, and eventually into the shovel of a steel mill worker.

The town of Monessen prospered from this mass movement of resources into its womb. Like a child within a woman's womb that builds it structure and energy from a mother's provided resources; the town shaped up and built up from these outside resources. Stores were built, cars began to stir around this town that contained only a couple of streets paved with bricks, and even a bus and electric "street cars" were available for transportation in 1932. And the town, its people, and its mill did their part to repay the world. From raw resources it added value and shipped finished products or material cast or machined into a preferred shape for the next performers in the states or the other parts of the world.

From these raw resources, coal was sent to the coke ovens to be converted into a higher-heat capacity in the form of coke. Coke was needed to provide the hot temperatures required for making steel.

The town of Monessen prospered from this mass movement of resources into its mill. The town developed and prospered from these outside resources. Stores were built, cars began to appear, and a bus and electric streetcars were available for transportation in 1932.

Then this flourishing town was hit with the great Depression in 1929 and things slowed down to a crawl. The Monessen Steel Mill (Pittsburgh Steel) laid off many workers as this great depression sucked away the demand for its steel products.

It was in this tough environment that the twin boys were born, with resourceful parents to raise them and teach them how to cope.

2

The Depression

Sam Pool and Buck Shutterly

At the time that Hon and Red had twins and expected great things, the country experienced just the opposite. The Depression, which had started in the late twenties, had made an impact by 1932. Young people graduating from high school couldn't get any jobs. This free time had its impact on many young people. Some were glad not to have to work, but were restricted in what they could do because of a lack of money. Gasoline was almost free, costing between ten and twelve cents a gallon. Cigarettes were only five or six cents a pack. Whiskey was less than fifty cents a fifth. Young people began having get-togethers.

A teen would have access to a car, and four or five friends would have the combined amount it took to buy the fifth of whiskey. They picked cigarettes out of their parent's pants or coats. They would drink and drive. The only thing that inhibited these get-togethers were flat tires, which happened often in those days.

These events began to affect the whole country. There were leaders, and there were followers. A sense of urgency was lost. What was the hurry? There was little money and less work, especially for the young. The parents would tell their children to look for a job, but they left the house with no desire to find work. It was easier to go join with others their own and age and lose themselves in happiness and self-pity.

To make things worse, many parents were not working, which made it hard for the parents to provide leadership, direction, or discipline. Some parents even joined in the drunken journeys from one town to the next. Gangs trashed buildings, broke windows, raided vegetable gardens, stole liquor, and caroused.

Somehow though, the crème does rise to the top. Eventually, the ones with the most ambition made it out of this malaise. Sam Pool and Frank (Buck) Shutterly were both bright young men who were inquisitive enough to search for an out. Both had gone to Pittsburgh Steel and American Chain and Cable, which manufactured wire, and signed up for employment. Both were met with the same reply: "No work."

Sam was an avid reader and continued to fill his mind with new ideas. But he could find no doors open. Fortunately, his father was working and provided a good home for him, his two younger brothers, and one sister in a little rented apartment up on the hill. They ate well, since his mother knew how to manage the little money that did come in. More income would have made it into the family, but Sam's father was an alcoholic.

Interesting enough, Sam and Buck met at one of these get-togethers. They talked about their ambitions and the stonewalling they were receiving in seeking employment. They soon found they had much in common. Sam and Buck were both good with mechanics and worked on cars for a hobby—whenever they could find a car to work on.

Buck was powerfully built and prone to fighting. Sam was tall, of medium build and not violent. Yet Sam found he had more in common with Buck than not, and they continued to pal around with each other. Sometimes they worked together on Buck's motorcycle, or they worked together fixing someone's car.

They met and discussed what each had tried and how they had failed in the way of getting jobs. One evening they discussed the possibility of going west, maybe to California or Colorado. They had heard that work was available for the young and ambitious out that way. In Pennsylvania, much of the available work that was available was controlled by the unions, and neither belonged to a union. Their mental picture of the West was one where there were no unions. It was first-come, first-served in their imaginations. Perhaps this was the way to go. They would think about it.

About that time Sam met a girl named Peg Foertsch at one of these get-togethers. She came from a German family, just as Sam had. She was dark haired, beautiful, tall, and slim. He found her a great drinking partner as well as a bright woman. Peg and Sam looked like a match. She was bright and could discuss things with Sam that many other men could not. Peg picked up on many of the discussions her father had about cars, machines, and tools. This fit perfectly with Sam's interests. Together they would scrape up enough money for a gallon of gas and borrow Peg's father's car. Her father worked in the zinc works in Donora, just across the river from Monessen. He worked many shifts, and there were times when his car was available while he was at work.

Peg's father, Fred, was an extraordinary mechanic and machinist. He had a cellar full of tools to repair cars and machine parts. What he couldn't machine there, he took to work and machined. A story goes that one night during the midnight to eight shift Fred got a call from a friend who had wrecked his dad's car and wanted to know if Fred could repair it before the father saw it. Fred told him to bring it to the mill gate, which he did. Fred took the car inside, and when morning came he drove it out to his friend's house. There was little—if any—evidence of the wreck. Fred had a friend for life!

So Sam and Peg made it to many gatherings and soon split off into a smaller group of Peg and Sam along with Buck and one of his girlfriends. They would ride, talk, and laugh. They would go to dances, but Sam didn't dance. He just watched. He loved to watch Peg, who was full of energy and completely taken up with the music.

Day by day this union grew to the point where Sam didn't need to look, nor Buck. They were always together. It was obvious that Sam and Peg were in love, but they couldn't do anything about it. There was no work on which to form a good basis for a marriage and the start of a family. It became more obvious as the days wore on that he had to find work. He had to be able to make enough money to do the things he wanted to do. He needed some type of closure on his aspirations. He was longing to advance himself. He read every magazine he could find. He looked up every word in the dictionary that was new to him. He saw things in the magazines that he could build, but they all cost money. He knew now that he could not delay his pent-up desire any longer. It was even greater than his love for Peg at that moment.

Meanwhile Buck became interested in electrical things. He read magazines on how to wire a house. He would drop in the stores that carried magazines and would read sections out of them. He began going to the library and reading about other electrical installations. He talked to Sam about this and it turned out that Sam had also been reading articles about electricity and was very interested in discussing this. The two of them would meet once a week to discuss things like cars, car repair, troubleshooting of car problems, house wiring, the differences between 120 volt applications and 240 volt applications. This common understanding between the two grew and when they were together Peg sometimes couldn't get a word in. This built up desire to put what they had learned to test wasn't being relieved by the lack of employment in the area. It was with background that they finally decided to try their luck out west.

Heading West on a Motorcycle

Early in June 1932 Sam and Buck decided to make the journey to the West. Together they had $16. It was not much, but it was enough if they traveled on Buck's motorcycle. They figured that at fifty miles per gallon, it would take them forty or so gallons to get to Colorado on his motorcycle. At twelve cents a gallon, this would cost between five or six dollars for the trip. They felt they could make it to Colorado in three days. If they each kept their eating to a minimum, they figured they could make it on $1 a day for food. This was $3 for the entire trip. So if nothing bad happened they could make it to Colorado for between $8 and $10. This time of the year the weather was good, and they could sleep along the roadside. Each would have to take turns staying awake to ensure their safety and prevent robbery.

It was tough for Sam to tell Peg. She was concerned at his leaving, but she understood. He promised her when he found work he would send for her. She told Sam that he was the only person in her life and he hugged her and kissed her and told her he didn't know how he could get along without her, but without a job to earn a living there was no alternative. Peg told him if he got a job to let her know immediately and she would find a way to come to him. On July 12, 1932, each of their parents gave them food, and Peg pitched in. They bundled the food along with some blankets, and off Sam and Buck went, each with a lump in his throat, not knowing what the next few days would bring, let alone their future. They made good time the first day but were surprised at how much riding long distance took out of them. It wasn't like riding in a car. The wind was sometimes brutal, and their hands and feet would get numb from the chill of the night air. They knew they could not travel like that in the winter, and this made them apprehensive of any trip home that might not be in the middle of summer.

That first evening, they got off Route 70 and found a little stand that was selling sausages just outside Indianapolis, Indiana. It was a bit of luck finding this little stand, which ended up serving two purposes. It gave them a cheap meal, and the old gentleman at the stand said they could sleep next to the stand during that night. They had intended to make it to St. Louis but were weary from the motorcycle ride. Much of the ride was over dirt roads. They had thought that the roads would be better than they were. Eating dust all day on the road sure makes one weary, they mentioned to each other. Yes, it was a bit of luck finding this little stand, and after eating and talking with the gentleman for a half hour they drove and pushed the big cycle up into a field and ended up sleeping in a wheat field next to some hog pens.

The next day of travel took them to St. Louis and across the Mississippi. They stopped and spent an hour looking around. They were both excited and dismayed. They were excited that they had made it this far and had seen what none of the people back home had ever seen, but they were dismayed because the river was muddy and didn't look much different than the Monongahela River back home. And so they got back on the bike and tried to reach Topeka, Kansas, that night and Colorado the next day.

However, they only got a few miles down the road when suddenly Sam felt the bike jerk and pull roughly to one side. He knew right away that they had had a blowout of one of the tires. He had been through this kind of thing before. Luckily, Buck was strong and experienced on the bike and soon had it under control. He headed toward the side of the dirt road. But now what? They didn't have a spare inner tube for the tire. They figured that one of them would stay with the bike and the other would go back toward one of the small towns and find a garage. They knew an inner tube would cost them at least a dollar. Sam would go back and get the tube. So Sam stuck out his hand and tried to hitch a ride.

Several cars went by, and no one stopped. It was pretty hot and dusty, and Sam could appreciate how the bike had kept him cool with the wind pounding at his front. Then a man in a small-paneled truck saw Sam. The truck pulled over to the side of the road and the man got out. A big fellow with slightly gray hair walked up to where the bike sat. He towered over Buck and Sam.

"See you have a problem. That's not uncommon around here. There are a lot of nails along this road," he said. "Well, at least it's the front tire. They're easier to pull off than the back wheel," he continued. "What do you want to do now?"

Sam told him that he was trying to go back toward St. Louis and find a place where he could get an inner tube for the tire.

The man nodded. "My name's Mel," he said.

Sam and Buck responded with their names and told him about their trip to the West to look for jobs.

Mel let out a large, hearty laugh. "Not likely to get a job out here anywhere," he said. "Many guys went east towards Detroit and Pittsburgh to try and find work," he said. "How about you getting your cycle up on my truck, and I'll take you to a town about ten miles back that might have an inner tube for this bike."

Before long they were back on the road. Sure enough they turned off on another dirt road about ten miles down the road, went about a mile, and hit a cluster of homes and stores. There was a gas station and a sign that read, "White's Truck and Car Repair." They pulled in, and it wasn't long until they had a tube. The man stuffed it in the tire, filled it with air from a large compressor, and mounted the wheel back on the bike. Mel bought them each a soda pop to drink and cool them down.

As they got back on the road, Buck could only think what a gentleman that big man had been. "We sure were lucky," he hollered to Sam over the roar of the engine. Sam nodded, and Buck pushed the bike a little harder, intent on getting to Topeka, Kansas, that day if possible. It was dark when they went through the fairly large town. They only went about ten miles farther and decided to pull off the road and try to get some rest. The day had been longer than they had expected. They were down to only a few dollars and hoped nothing else would come up. They couldn't afford anything else.

They found some apple trees along the road, and Buck held the bike while Sam reached up and took a handful of apples. They were green and sour, but they had eaten apples like that before and were glad to have them. They knew that the next day they would have to find a place to eat breakfast. They needed some food to carry them the rest of the way.

Early the next morning, they were up at the crack of dawn, riding along Route 70 and looking for a small town where they could eat breakfast. They found a small town south of Limon, Colorado. . They ate breakfast in this small town at a place where they got two eggs, toast, and coffee for twenty-one cents. The food tasted great, and the hot coffee refreshed them. Then they were on their way again They were soon on the road and traveling at about 50 to 60 miles per hour, trying to reach Limon Colorado which is 450 miles north of Topeka. They knew that when they got to Limon they would have to turn off of Route 70 to get to the town of Littleton, Colorado, where Buck had an aunt.

They arrived in Limon at about 4:30 and took the road that said Castlerock. Now they had only about eighty miles to go. However, while traveling Sam felt moisture on his face, put his hand up, and saw oil. He shoved Buck in the back and showed him the oil. They pulled over. Sure enough the oil line had broken, and they had no way of fixing it. They had to get to the small town in Colorado where Buck's aunt lived, but they had run low on money. They couldn't even pay to get the bike repaired if they found someplace to repair it. They were seventy or eighty miles from Littleton, Colorado, with little hope of getting there. They sat down on the ground next to the cycle and the puddle of oil and each held their head between their hands. Each was in shock. They both mumbled a few cuss words and looked into the sky, as if looking for an answer. It was sort of a crude prayer.

Like an angel answering their prayers, along came a car driven by an older, gray-haired woman. She stopped and asked them if there was anything she could do. If she drove them to a town with a garage, they didn't have the money to have the bike fixed. If she drove them to Littleton, (where she happened to be going) they would have to leave the bike. Without the bike, they were dead in the water. Either way they went, they had to leave the bike here since the lady had no place to carry it.

Then the answer came. Buck told the lady that he believed he could hold on to the window bar in her car and ride on the motorcycle while holding on. Would she let him try that? She said, "We can give it a try, but only for a short distance and if it doesn't work, what then?"

Sam thought out loud. "Buck, you can't hold on to the car for eighty miles. Your arm will fall off." Buck said, "I don't know that we have any other alternative." "Let's give it a try." If I can't handle it, I will yell out."

But there wasn't another alternative. So Sam rolled down the windows on the passenger's side and jumped in the backseat. Buck grabbed the window bar on the right side of the car, and they began this part of the journey. Sam looked out at the muscular forearm of Buck as he grabbed the bar between the front and back open windows of the car.

Slowly, the ride began and soon they were doing thirty or thirty-five miles per hour. "Amazing," Sam thought. Lucky it's not me that has to hold on for several hours with Buck held on with his left hand

and his right held the handlebars of the cycle to keep it in control and close to the side of the car. Meanwhile, Sam kept his right hand on Bucks hand to help support him.

The lady kept the speed fairly constant and the car moving as straight as she could. Fortunately, this part of the road was fairly flat and not as bumpy as some of the other dirt roads they had been on. Dust kept flying in the window, and Buck had a large handkerchief wrapped over his face so that he could keep the dust out of his nose. He wore big goggles to keep his eyes safe.

They had gone about forty miles when Buck hollered for her to stop, and slowly the lady brought the car to the edge of the road. Buck said he needed a break and had to relieve himself. Sam was glad for that since he had been holding his water for about an hour now. He didn't want to stop while they were making good progress. Soon they were back on the road, and Sam seemed more relaxed now, knowing that Buck could accomplish this tough task. If nothing else happened, they would make it to Littleton.

It seemed like an entire day, but sure enough they pulled into Littleton at 7:30, just as the sun was starting to set. They had come around 500 miles in twelve hours on the road that day. They looked at each other and Buck said "pretty good time considering the last 80 miles was hitching a ride with an elderly lady." Sam jumped out of the car and helped Buck push the big cycle over to the gas station. Buck said, "I told you I could get you here, Sam." And he let out a big yell, grabbed Sam, and leaped up and down. They had made it. They had made it to the town of Littleton. They each hugged the lady and thanked her till she had to tell them to stop. "You will be in our thoughts and prayers," the two of them said to the lady. "Without you, we were dead in the water." They got the lady's address and phone number and promised her they would keep in touch. With that, and a big smile on her face, the lady left them at a gas station.

Between them they still had a dollar and ten cents of their original $16. They had to eat before calling Buck's aunt. Down the street was a small bar and grill. They went in, and each had two hamburgers and a cup of coffee.

Buck called his aunt. She was surprised to hear his voice. Buck's mother had called her and said they were trying to make it to California and would stop in Colorado. She hadn't seen him other than pictures she had received from Buck's parents over the years.

She welcomed them, and that night Buck and Sam shared her only spare bed. They were happy to be there but didn't know what to do about fixing the motorcycle. They pulled the change they had left in their pockets. Between them they had 17 cents. But that was tomorrow's problem, they thought. They crawled into bed.

"Boy, is it good to get in a bed again," Buck said.

"Man, we were lucky," Sam said. "Every time we had a problem, someone would save us." It made them feel good that people out here were also having problems but sharing what they did have.

The next day the two began to read newspapers and look for employment. This place was beginning to look like back home with no jobs available. The want ads were non existent.

After several days they decided to try to hitch a ride to Denver to look for work. They were successful in hitching a ride but found little success in Denver. Each of them had done chores here and there to earn fifty cents—enough to get them food, but not enough to do any kind of business.

After two days of looking in Denver and no money left, they hitched a ride back to Littleton. They described their ventures to Buck's aunt. She gave them $5 to hold them over. This went on for weeks. Sam or Buck would get a small job and earn a dollar or two, enough to keep them going. However, sometimes days went by without anything, and Buck's aunt would give them another $5. From what they heard, California was not any better. They decided to stick it out in Colorado and find a job.

Meanwhile, Sam had written to his parents and Peg almost everyday, to keep them aware of their turmoil. Stamps were three cents in 1931, lowered to two cents in 1932 and then rose back to three cents this past month. Penny postcards were a penny in both years.

After a week and a half, Sam received a letter from Peg and the next day one from his mother. He began to receive mail daily from Peg, and he would spend an evening reading her letter over and over before he wrote her back. It relieved him to read her letters, and it relieved him to sit down and write her. It was relaxing. He was in love, and now he was lovesick, lonesome, and homesick. Peg's letter were like a double sword, on the one hand he was happy to receive them, on the other hand her letters expressed her love for him and her yearning to see him and this made him more homesick. But he continued to seek a job.

There were more places around there than back home, but they were small businesses and didn't employ many.

One day, they saw a bread line and joined the line. It was hot, but they moved slowly toward the portioning area. When they got to the portioning area, they were given a bowl and a cup. Next there was a ladle of soup put in the bowl, and they were allowed to take two pieces of bread. Each got a cup of coffee, but there was no milk or sugar—still they were glad to receive what they had. They sat down to eat their food. As they sat there and talked, it became evident to Sam that he wanted to return home. He mentioned this to Buck. Buck frowned and nodded his head. They would talk about it one of these days, he said. It was obvious that Buck was going to try instead of going back home. Besides, his cycle needed to be fixed first.

The next day they split up and looked at places that Buck's aunt said they might try. She had talked to her friends, and they had suggested a couple of places. That night, Sam came back to the house, disappointed that he had found nothing.

Later that evening, Buck came home in a good mood. He had met a girl, she had taken him home, and he had eaten a good meal. She had a job working in her dad's grocery store.

July and August soon passed made up with a lot of walking, small jobs, and letters from home to each of them, and letters from Peg. Sam kept writing, and he always signed it, "Sammy and Buck." So it always looked like Buck was communicating also. Sometimes Sam only sent a postcard because it was cheaper. Sometimes he sent two postcards with the one continuing where he had left off on the other. Every once in a while they had to get another $5.00 from Buck's aunt.

Sam talked with Buck about going back home, and it their

conversation always ended with a delayed decision. Buck had a girlfriend, and he didn't seem in a hurry to leave. Meanwhile, they made some extra money and were able to take Buck's motorcycle to a garage. They didn't have enough to pay for fixing the cycle, but they left it. The man said he would start on the repair, but they couldn't get it back until it was paid for. Sam offered to work on the cycle so they would only have to pay for the parts and something to the garage owner. With Sam doing most of the work it got started. He was able to tear the bike down, but the garage didn't have the parts to repair it. It would be weeks until the parts would arrive. They had to order them. So, this slowed everything down. The garage owner didn't want to order any more than he had to, and things dragged on. Working on the bike kept Sam busy, and the garage owner gave him something to eat while he was working. Meanwhile, Buck earned a buck or so every couple of days on odd jobs.

They took a couple more sojourns to Denver and stayed overnight on both occasions. They slept in a big barracks that was opened for people who were out of work. Once in a while, they would get a free meal there or in another bread line. But everything was still as tight as a drum when it came to openings for jobs.

Finally, in September Sam decided that he was going back home. He was going to try to hitch a ride on a freight train. He wrote to Peg and told her of his intentions. Soon, he got a letter back, telling him not to try to hitch a ride on the trains. They have train detectives and yard marshals that patrol those trains and put people in jail if they get a hold of them. Also, the people he might meet on these ventures, unsavory characters, might do him harm. So he delayed and wrote her again. He told her that if he didn't find a job by the end of September, that he would have to try hitching a freight car ride back. Any later in the year, and he stood a good chance of meeting terrible weather. "Winter weather starts early back here," he wrote. Sometimes there were bad snowstorms in early November. So he wrote, "I'll take off in the last week of September, hopefully hitching a ride to Chicago on one of the freight trains that go from Denver to Chicago." If he could get to Chicago, he knew he would find many freight trains heading toward Pittsburgh. That was his plan. He knew he wouldn't receive a letter back from Peg before he put his plan into effect.

Sam Pool and the Return Home

So early one morning in the last week of September, Buck drove Sam to Denver in a car he was able to borrow. The plan was for Sam to eat in Denver that evening and then to sneak into the train yards after dark and look for a train headed to Chicago. Buck had checked around and found the different freight lines and where they were located in the yard. Best is to get an empty train that was going to Chicago to pick up a load, or one partially full.

That night Sam climbed over the chain-link fence and entered the train yards. He knew he had to find a train that was being loaded and climb aboard when it was starting to move. Or he might find one with the engine running, telling him it was on its way. He headed to the area that Buck had checked out as the most likely to have a train headed for Chicago. There were many cars in the yard and not many engines, so this led him to seven that were candidates.

He began sneaking alongside of the empty cars that set like abandoned children in the yard until he saw some activity on a large train with many cars attached and smoke pouring from its engine. He laid quietly under one of the empty, untended cars, waiting for movement from the freight train. He had visually picked out one that looked like he could get on and hide in the open car among some large boxes.

As Sam lay there, his heart beat at about twice its normal rate. He already missed Buck. They had been together for months, and he was a source of strength in a way. They had helped one another. If it weren't for Buck's aunt he didn't know what they would have done. Now he was on his way home to Peg. His thoughts then switched to thinking of Peg and this relaxed him, and his heart slowed down a little.

He was happy that he had not seen anyone around this part of the yard, and he began to think about what was in store for him once he got aboard the train car. He was suddenly alerted by a sudden jerk of the train he was watching and realizing that the train he was to board was starting to slowly move. Now his heart really began to pound it out, not only fast but hard beats. He leaped with his rolled-up bag of clothes and belongings and ran toward the freight car. It was like a delusion to him; he kept seeing the freight car and almost at the same time saw Buck's face as he raced to the car. He threw his roll into the car and climbed up the end of the car and into position beside the large wooden boxes. He grabbed his roll, tucked himself next to the box, and waited anxiously to see what would happen next.

The train moved a little faster and then began to slow. Each time Sam's heart beat a different beat. Now they were moving past the yard offices, and he kept close to the floor of the car, up against that wooden box. He held the roll over his face and body so as to not see what was going on.

He knew this would be the most difficult place to get past on his journey. "If only I could make it out of the yards, if only I could make it out of the yards," he thought over and over. And then he realized he was saying this to himself at a faster clip; keeping up with the sound of the metal wheels again the rails. Faster and faster he repeated, "If only I can make it out the yards." He then realized that he was repeating it so fast that the train was now traveling about thirty or forty miles an hour. He must be out of the yard. He took the roll from his face and peered at the open sky. Luckily it was dark, he thought. And then he relaxed and thought about Peg.

Many hours passed, and they seemed like days to him. Was he on the right train? Was it going to get to Chicago before sunrise? If so, how would he now hide when the train entered the yard?

And then it became light. It was the morning, and the train kept clipping along at a nice rate. Sam ventured a look at the land around him. Soon he passed over a bridge, and there was a river below. He wondered what river it might be. He wished he had had enough money before he left to buy a map and try to guess where he was.

"Boy, the United States is big," he said.

Every so often, they would pass a town, and he could see it go by in the distance. Every so often the train would slow its pace, and they would move closer to humanity. He would curl back into a ball next to the wooden box with the roll over him. He was cold during the night, but it was all right now. A little cool but he could handle it. He was hungry, and he took out an apple that Buck's aunt had given him. It tasted good.

The train kept moving, and eventually it became dark again. He stood up in the car, confident that no one would see him in the darkness. There, off in the distance, he could see the lights of a big town—or a bunch of towns.

"I wonder if that's Chicago," he said out loud. He was feeling like he was getting closer to home, and he relaxed and thought about Peg. He began to sing to himself the song that reminded him of her—"Peg o' My Heart, I love you," it went on.

Now he was getting close to a big metropolitan area, and he knew it must be Chicago or the outskirts of Chicago. He didn't know if the trains going to Chicago went just outside or to the middle of the city. He tucked himself next to the big wooden box and put the roll of clothes over his face and as much of his body as he could. Now the train was slowing down, and he was glad it was dark. Soon, they entered the main yard of a big train station. He knew he would have to get off soon, and his heart began to race. He grabbed the roll of clothes with the belt buckled around them and began to look for several things: the train to stop, empty cars in the yard, lights, flashlights, any sign of life. Fortunately, he was far enough from the engine that wherever it stopped he would probably be out of view.

And then the train stopped, and he leaped to the edge of the car, threw his roll over, and climbed down. He lifted his roll and ran toward some boxcars that were obviously not going anywhere. Still, he looked for flashlights and any signs of guards or company security men. As he hid under a car, he heard voices. and his heart beat even faster than before. He could hardly breathe. Sam held his breath and listened. They were laughing about something. He continued to listen and finally figured it was other men hiding under a car two cars up on the other track. Then he saw a cigarette being lit. He knew he couldn't stay there all night. He had to find out how to get to Pittsburgh. What to do? What to do?

He took a deep breath and crawled out from under the car and toward the cigarette. When he got about twenty feet away, he called out softly, "Hey, hello there." Then he waited. All was quiet. He called out again, "I need help." It was still quiet. "I need help," Sam again shouted, only a little louder.

"Come over here," a voice said.

Sam took all the nerve he had left and crawled toward the cigarette. It kept waving in the night and moved in a circular motion as if waving him on. Finally, he got about five feet away. He saw two colored guys curled up under a freight car.

"What's your problem?" they asked.

"I'm trying to get to Pittsburgh," Sam answered. "Do you know which part of the yard I should go to hitch a ride?"

They smiled and said, "You call that a problem?"

"Yes," Sam replied. "I've never done this, and I have to get back home."

They seemed friendly, and he spent a few minutes telling them about looking for a job and not finding anything in Colorado. They also were in the same predicament and were headed toward Detroit—their home. They had been looking for jobs for the past two years and had gotten used to traveling in this manner. They told Sam that he would have to go to the southern part of the yards to catch a freight to Pittsburgh. They told him the lines that went that way, such as the Baltimore and Ohio, and a few others.

"Look for trains full of coal or boxes of power equipment. Many times they' are going to Gary, Indiana, or Pittsburgh." They pointed to where the southern part of the yards were and gave him some pointers on what to watch out for.

Sam thanked them and headed out. As he continued along, he became more and more apprehensive about being able to find a train. He had been lucky so far and began to feel his luck would not continue to pan out. He began to sweat as he proceeded. He didn't realize how huge these yards were.

It seemed like it took him forever going at a fairly good pace, sometimes running, sometimes crawling, sometimes just hiding when something passed or when he saw a light and hid. Every once in a while he would see flashlights and hide. It took him the good part of almost an hour for him to make it to the southern part of the yard. There he looked as the two men had directed him for signs of a train that was loading and about to take off, or a train that was dropping off a couple of cars before it continued to the next town on its stop.

He saw a freight train that looked like it was ready to go and had equipment being boarded on some of the cars in the rear. He saw the name of Westinghouse on the sides of some of the boxes, and he thought that they were either going to Westinghouse or coming from Westinghouse. There were several Westinghouse plants in Pennsylvania, so maybe that was where they were headed. Should he chance it? What other alternatives did he have? Not any that he could see. But this train had no open cars on them like the one he had rode from Denver. How would he ride it?

Soon, the men working on the loading train were walking down the track towards where he was located. It was light enough now that he could see them. It must be six in the morning, he thought. It was still somewhat dark out and sort of foggy. He hid behind one of the large wheels of a freight car. Soon, he could hear them talking and passing by. He could smell their cigarettes. Boy, he'd give anything for a cigarette. But he didn't even have one, and he hadn't asked those two colored guys for one.

Sam knew he had to go for this train and hoped it headed toward Pittsburgh. He thought about Buck. He hoped his cycle stayed in good shape, or he could trade it for money to get back home. Maybe he would find a job. He had a girlfriend, and that would probably hold him. She was at least working. She wasn't making much, but it could hold her and maybe him until he could find something.

Boy, it was lonely lying next to a boxcar. It was quiet except every now and then when a whistle would blow or he could hear trains banging against each other. He thought a car was probably hooking up to another car to make up a train to go somewhere. How amazing that so much could happen where boxcars lay dormant and trains were asleep; waiting for something to be tied to their back end. Like a dog sled where the dogs are there and just waiting to be hooked up to a sled and be off and running. Sam had hallucinations about trains having a life of their own. Like big animals that get fed coal to make their stomachs churn and their wheels to come to life and have the energy to move. The only problem was they had to wait for man to make the first move. Once he got them in action they were off and running; like an animal coming back to life. And each time they went to a different place, had a different load, a different number of cars, a heavy or light load, go by day or go by night, sometimes slow, sometimes fast. And when in these yards, they rested.

He thought on but was shocked by the sound of a jerk on the train he had been watching. Yes, it was starting to move slowly. He didn't know whether to jump up and run now or wait. What to do, what to do, what to do? And then like answering his question to himself he found his legs lifting his body and beginning to run, faster and faster, and then he met the slow- moving train. He didn't even look to see if there was anyone who could see him. He was committed. He had slipped the belt on his roll over his shoulder, and it flapped on his back as he ran. And now he was reaching up and grabbing a metal ladder on the side of one of the cars. Up he went. How hard to make those climbing steps when your heart is pounding away. "Boy," he thought, "those guys who do this for a living must be used to this." It's a hard job, and he didn't know if he was going to make it. Somehow, he was then on top of the car and breathing hard. He had to grab something, or he would slide back down. He stretched and reached a piece of metal and pulled himself to the top.

He had thought about what he would do once on top. He would take the roll, and stick his hand in the belt, and grab something so that the roll was on top of his hand, which would help protect him and give his hand some warmth. He did this and was happy to realize it worked. He had his hand between the roll and the train roof, with the roll reaching down over his shoulders to help keep that part of him warm. It was cool, and he knew he needed this. How long would it take and would he be able to hold it the whole time of the trip? He thought about Buck on his motorcycle, holding the woman's window brace on her car for eighty miles. Now he was in somewhat the same predicament. Could he hold on long? Could he hold while the train was going fast? Would they see him on top of the freight train? Luckily it was still not quite daylight. This would help him get out of the yards without being seen. Does this train take him toward Pittsburgh? Does this train stop at some other place on its way? He hoped not," he thought. Getting out of the train yards without being caught would be hard enough. Again his heart began to thump. Thump against the metal top of the train. It seemed like a drum, like the train was amplifying his heartbeat. Now the train was going about ten miles an hour. He was glad the roll covered his face so he couldn't see if anyone saw him. Ignorance is bliss. His knees, pressed against the hard metal, were already hurting. He would have to find a better position as he went along.

The train was running smoother. Like its lift of speed gave it a more liquid flow of the wheels against track; it also helped to make Sam's body feel more comfortable, bumping less against the top of the metal roof. Now the train was going at least thirty miles an hour. That meant they were out of the train yards, and he was on his way—to where, he would soon find out.

As the sun rose, lighting the sky, he felt a little warmer. Sam welcomed the bright sun. It made him feel safe. He was in the open and could see the trees go by, and sometimes houses in the distance. The train was going fifty or sixty and made him feel like a bird must feel when it takes off for the south during the wintertime; knowing it had a long trip but knowing it was free and flying. He thought about the small wooden planes he had made when he could get the wood and the glue.

He had to change hands now. His hand holding the metal was numb and tired. His arm felt the pull of the train against his grip. The other hand was also holding on, but it seemed colder than the other hand. If he could now shift the roll to the other hand and release the left from the load of the roll, it would help to keep it warm. Why did it feel so heavy? It hadn't been heavy when he had been in the yard, but here it felt like a load. He now had his right hand under the belt. He gripped the piece of metal and allowed the roll to go free from his left hand. He took the chance to move his left hand under his left hip. That felt better. He must have had a cramp in that arm, and it had been cold. It might have been from the lack of blood flow in that arm the way it was positioned. He reminded himself to shift the weight on his right hand and arm to not have this happen again.

He was more confident that he didn't have to hold it as long with the right hand and could shift the load back and forth without being scared of losing his grip and flying off the train, as long as the train continued at a fairly constant speed. He had thought it would be harder to hold on when the train was going fast, but it was easier than when it was going slow and jerking along. At the higher speed, when constant, it was almost like lying on some floors he had laid on during his life, the only difference being the wind. He found he could almost relax and release his hand from holding on, if not for the wind.

His imagination would play tricks on him. He felt his legs slide toward the side, ready to fall off, but when he moved his legs to right them, they were exactly where they had been. Maybe he had been in the same position too long.

He must have been on the train for six or eight hours now. He couldn't chance a look at his watch. He might fall. He knew he must remain calm and hope he was on his way to Pittsburgh; or somewhere in that direction. And then it happened.! He saw a sign on the roadside as he passed by, and it said Akron, Ohio. He knew he was at least going in the right direction. Even if the train were to stop in Akron, he would be able to hitch a car ride from Akron to Pittsburgh. But the train moved on.

It started to cool down as the sun became lower in the sky and darkness became evident. There were no lights on yet, but he knew it wouldn't be long. He wondered if he would be able to see anything when it got dark. He knew it was important to be able to get off this train in a few hours. He was beginning to feel confident about the direction he was going and how close he was to Pittsburgh. It must only be about a hundred and fifty miles to Pittsburgh from Akron,

Ohio. Again, he wished for a map before he left. Should he get off at a town that didn't go all the way to Pittsburgh and into those train yards that still scared him?

"We'll see," he thought and shifted the roll from the one hand to the other. It was an easy chore now, and he shifted his body weight to allow some form of relief. "One day, I'll be able to afford to pay to ride a train," he thought. "I wonder if it will be this exciting. I know it will be a lot more comfortable—and I would be able to eat." But that only reminded him of how hungry he was. He had only eaten that apple back in Colorado. He wished he had an apple now, or a hamburger, or a sausage, or anything. But then he remembered that he wouldn't be able to eat it anyhow. He couldn't afford to let go of the piece of metal that he clung to, so how could he eat?

This thought made him even hungrier, and now it was getting cold. It was dark, and lights were rapidly going by. He squinted against the wind and tried to make out signs, but it was impossible at this speed and with the little light available. He wished he had taken his cycle goggles out of his bag before getting on this train. He needed a big town and hoped to make out some signs.

Sam heard a whistle in the distance, and it blew again. He could tell it was coming closer. He remembered reading about how a whistle got higher and higher in tone as it approached, and he knew this one was approaching. And now he knew it was coming toward him from the front. "I hope no one sees me on that train and sends a message to the train I'm on," he worried. And then the whistle was not only deeper in tone but very loud as it swept past him on the left. He kept his head under the roll and tried to look as small as possible. Soon the train had passed, and he could hear the tones become lower and lower. Eventually, it was far off in the distance. Funny how much he always liked that sound of a train whistle in the distance. Now he liked it even more so. Then it occurred to him that passing a train may mean he was getting close to a big city where trains come down the line fairly often.

He hadn't heard a train for hours now. Again, he peered out to see if he could see signs to tell him where he was. Sometimes he got whiffs of smoke from the train and it made him cough. Now it seemed to be coming more often. Seemed that the train was slowing down; and he thought it was probably doing about forty now— and maybe coming toward a town. Yes, he could see lights up ahead and off to the right. Maybe he could make something out if he looked harder. Then he heard another whistle blowing and it was his train. Off in the distance, he heard another train coming this way. Maybe that's why they are slowing down. It gets scary when you think that maybe another train may be on the same track you are on. But it did mean he had to hide under the roll as much as possible again, and he knew he might miss the name of the town.

As he rolled his head so as to lean on the left side of his head under the roll, his eyes spotted a big, red-printed sign on the side of a large wooden building. It said "Butler Fertilizer and Feed." "This must be Butler, Pennsylvania," he thought. That's only about fifty miles or so from Pittsburgh. Now he knew he was close. Again his thoughts reviewed his options: if the trains slowed down near one of these towns, maybe he should get off instead of waiting all the way until Pittsburgh where he might be spotted—. even though it would make his hitchhiking trip longer, since Monessen was south of Pittsburgh.

He convinced himself that hitching was the safest way. Hitchhiking at night is kind of questionable, though. There's less traffic on the road, especially in these hard times. Maybe he would be picked up by one of the groups he had been associated with in their "togetherness" meetings. Maybe they didn't have them anymore. Maybe those gatherings were only close to Monessen. Out in the rural areas, there probably weren't any of those meetings.

His mind rolled these thoughts over and over. Boy, how hungry I am now, he thought. He had two dollars and some change on him. Maybe if he got off he could buy something. Then again, who would be open at this time of night? All the little stores that are in business closed at six in the evening, he thought.

"No chance of getting anything to eat tonight," he thought to himself.

Hopefully, if things went right, he'd be able to eat at home tomorrow. Soon he saw signs that led him to believe he was by Aliquippa and his heart began to pound. He knew he had to get off soon, or he would be in Pittsburgh. If only the train would slow down. So far it had not slowed enough for him to get off, no matter his thoughts and desires. He was stuck. There were lights along the way, and he knew he was passing one small town after another. Funny, he thought how each seemed to have lights of their own, like you could tell you were going from one town to another. He knew this must be his imagination, or because he was cold, or because he was hungry, or because he was getting more and more tenuous about what his decision would be. He knew it would have to be spontaneous—without much thought of details and all foreign to him. It was like when he took his first engine apart and didn't know what to expect until it appeared before him. He had been lucky in those cases and got to the position where he wasn't afraid of any engine when taking them apart. But this was different; how would he handle it? And then the train began to slow, and he heard a loud whistle. He looked at the lights and tried to make out where he was. He decided to lift his body slightly to see what was ahead. He could see many lights ahead, both on the side and in front of him on both sides. It looked like the train was going through a small town and had to slow down, he thought. This looked like his best chance. If only it would go a little slower. It was still moving too fast for him to jump off. And then the train jerked as it slowed down further, and he almost got thrown from the train.

Without thinking, he freed his hand holding the roll and threw the roll off to his right. He slid to that side, grabbed the rail on top of the metal ladder, and let himself down. He held his breath and jumped. He hit landed on his hands and knees and it hurt, but when he hit the ground he immediately rolled forward and down slightly. Soon, he stopped. He knew he was bruised, but nothing felt broken and he only had a small cut on his left hand. He slowly got up and watched as the train moved by. He didn't realized how long the train had been. It seemed to take ten minutes for it to pass. He then dusted himself off and headed back to find his roll. He walked about thirty feet to where he thought it would be, and he couldn't find it. He thought maybe it is might be down further down, and he walked another fifteen to twenty feet and looked everywhere around him and up and down the small bank of dirt and weeds. No roll. Maybe someone had seen him get off and had grabbed it. He continued looking down the track.

He decided he would go as far as the roll could possibly be while staying close to the track. If he couldn't find it, he would double back at the lower level and look again. He counted his paces. Ten paces, thirty feet, and still no roll. Another ten paces, and still no roll. He must be a hundred feet from where he had landed by now. He knew it was only a roll of clothes and things that he had brought back with him, but they seemed to have some quality that made them feel like a partner or close friend. He was overwhelmed with loneliness, along with being cold and hungry. He slid down the dirt bank that was lit by the moonlight and some of the lights from the city he was close to. As he slid, his feet hit a soft obstacle. He reached down and felt his roll. What luck! He never thought it would be back this far. He grabbed the roll and hugged it close to him. It made him feel warm again. He almost cried, and then began to laugh, thinking about how he thought of the roll as a friend.

He was safe, near Pittsburgh, and off the train. There were no yard police to avoid. "Now how do I get to the town from here?" he thought. There was a chain-link fence running along the rails, separating the tracks from a road alongside the fence. He knew he could climb the fence, but resisted the urge and walked in the direction the train had been going. He came to the spot where he thought he had landed, and he continued on. He then came to a place where the ground was a little higher next to the fence, and he decided that was where he would get over. He threw the roll over the fence and proceeded to climb over.

He was on a road not far from what looked like an active part of a small town. After walking a good distance, he turned up a street that looked like it might be occupied. So far he had not seen a single person. It was 10:15 at night when he had first looked at his pocket watch. He saw an old man sitting on a bench by what looked like the police station. He asked the man what town this was.

"Ambridge, young man," came the answer. "Don't tell me you are so screwed up that you don't know what town you are in?" he retorted.

Sam told him he was coming from Denver, Colorado, and was trying to make it home to Monessen.

"Monessen is about forty to fifty miles away," said the old man. "Go down two blocks, and you'll come to a bridge. Go over the bridge and another block, then you'll come to the main road that leads south, which will take you toward your destination. You might be able to catch a ride there, though there's not much traffic this time of night."

Sam walked in that direction and soon came to the bridge. It was a long bridge. He crossed, and it took about fifteen minutes to get to the other side. As the man had said, he walked another block and saw a sign that said Route 51. He knew this route went close to where he was headed. But there was no traffic.

He waited. About twenty-five minutes went by and no car came by. He wondered if he should try to find a place to sleep and wait until morning. As he stood there thinking about it, he realized how tired he was. He was almost asleep on his feet when he realized there were lights coming down the road. He stuck out his right arm with thumb extended, and he waved it to attract the attention of the driver. It was a truck, and it was not going too fast. He could see the driver in the cab, and his eyes lit up when he could hear the brakes being applied and the tires skidding to a stop. "Thank God," he thought, as he ran toward the big vehicle, jumped up on the running board, and opened the door.

"Where you headed this time of the night?" the driver shouted

"South," Sam said, "toward Monessen."

"No problem," the man said and motioned him in. "I'm headed toward Donora. Is that the way you're going?"

Sam jumped inside and his heart would jump out of his body with glee if it could. "Donora is right in the back pocket of Monessen," he said. He had walked the three miles from Donora to Monessen many times. Donora was where Peg lived. "This can't be true," he said to himself.

The man said his name was Jake and asked where he was coming from, and Sam told him some of the details. The man was quite surprised that he had made it this far in so short a time, and that he was going to take him almost to his doorstep. Sam was happy to feel warm again.

He had noticed how warm the cab was when he got in, and now the heat had soaked into his bones and made him feel at home. It also felt good to bend his legs.

He was so tired that it wasn't long before he fell fast asleep. While sleeping, he was conscious of the sounds of the truck, and it threw him from side to side. He kept correcting his position. It seemed like only ten minutes, and Jake was shoving his shoulder and telling him they were there.

Sam looked up, hardly believing they were in Donora already. He knew it would take at least an hour and a half. He looked up and saw a familiar site. There was Page Mill in the distance. "But this is Monessen," Sam said.

Jake said, "Yeah, I thought I'd take you that last three miles. I can always go back and still be in time for my delivery. It's almost two in the morning, and you would have a hard time making that last three miles."

Sam could have hugged him. "What a gentleman," he thought, as he jumped down from the cab seat. "So long and have a good trip," he shouted to Jake, and then the truck was gone. Sam stood there in amazement. It had been miraculous that he had made it from Denver to where he stood. He knew that looking for a job at home would now be easier. It had to be better than what he had been through.

"I'm blessed," he thought, as he strode down the dirt street toward his parent's place on Athalia Avenue. They lived on the second floor of an old apartment building. About six families lived there. He hadn't paid much attention to them but decided as he walked that he would in the future. He had learned from this trip to trust in people. He was euphoric as he walked along that night. Even though he was in Monessen, he still had a long walk to Athalia Avenue, where his folks lived. He had to walk the distance of the city, which was about two miles and up the hill about another three quarters of a mile. But he felt good as he headed toward his parents' home.

Tomorrow he'd get up and go to see Peggy in Donora, even if he had to walk all the way. "Life is good," he thought. He thought about Buck and hoped he was OK. But tomorrow he would see Peg.

Building the Golden Gate Bridge

And now it was late in 1932, and Sam was surprised that the time had passed so fast in the two months since he had come home. He had heard that they might start hiring at the Page Mill. It was part of American Chain and Cable, and everyone was talking about a bridge they might build in San Francisco. Page Mill might get the order to provide some of the wires or cables, and he put in his name for any job that might open. They had him take a written test in the middle of December to see how well he scored against the other potential candidates. He scored well and hoped that meant something. Surely if they got some kind of business he would get some type of job. He didn't care what.

If he got a job, he and Peg had decided they would get married. First the job, and then borrow a car and head for Cumberland, Maryland, to get married. They could get married in one day there. They didn't need a blood test or anyone to sign for them since they were over eighteen.

The *Monessen Daily Independent newspaper* said that the bridge might get approved in San Francisco. The state of California had spent years planning and lobbying for federal support. The state intended to pass a bond issue to support the cost of the bridge. It was supposed to cost about $30 million dollars to build, which would make it the costliest bridge to date. They were to build at the entrance to the bay in San Francisco, where the ocean comes into the bay. From what Sam read, it took four hours to go by car from San Francisco to the land on the other side in Marin County. When the bridge was eventually built, it would only take fifteen to twenty minutes to walk across. At night when he went to bed, Sam prayed for that bridge.

And then it happened; the bridge was approved. They were going to start working on it around January 10, 1933. Sam had written to Buck and told him to come back, and he came back around Christmas of '32. He made it on his motorcycle, but it was tough in colder weather.

Bridge Materials Relieve Pennsylvania

On January 8, 1933, the paper said that the American Chain and Cable had gotten the contract to build all the cables for the Golden Gate Bridge in San Francisco, and American Chain and Cable (Page Mill) was to supply that cable. But it didn't stop there: the state of Pennsylvania was to supply almost all the materials to make the bridge. The basic steel, the machined parts, the cast parts, the cable, and some of the ancillary equipment were to be supplied from Pennsylvania. The architect firm responsible for the bridge had sent drawings and specifications of all the parts to firms in Pennsylvania for quotes on cost and delivery about a year before, and suppliers had been selected. Each of these firms had to meet specifications so that, when fabricated in Pennsylvania, the parts would fit the bridge being built in San Francisco. All the cables and steel would be transported east to Philadelphia, and large freighters, or ships with barges, would carry these completed parts down the Atlantic coast to the Panama Canal, then over to the Pacific Ocean and up to San Francisco.

The city was abuzz. The state was abuzz. A bridge being built in Pennsylvania would be put in place on the other side of the country. Sam immediately went to the Page employment office to check his status, and they said he would be hired and start the following week. With his test grades, he qualified as an assistant foreman, making fifty-two cents an hour. This was terrific, he thought, as he leaped all the way down the street to his home. Only 10 days passed and Sam and Peg borrowed a car and drove to Cumberland, Maryland and got married.

Meanwhile, Pittsburgh Steel Company in Monessen would be making a lot of the steel for the bridge. The Golden Gate Bridge was golden to the town of Monessen. The Depression hung over the country like a huge blanket: no work, bread lines for about 25 percent of the people in the country, and about 50 percent of the other three quarters were only working part-time. Yet, here in Monessen, and in San Francisco, there was a little peephole in that blanket of grief.

It would take at least four years to build the bridge—maybe more from what everyone could tell. It was a huge project. It would be the largest suspension bridge in the United States—maybe in the world. So, that little peephole in the blanket their relief should last at least this length of time. Sam thought that maybe if Buck and he had made it to California, they would be celebrating in San Francisco. One day, he'd take Peg to San Francisco.

And so it started. He went to work each day at Page Mill. During the first several months, he learned about the equipment. Much of it would be changed or added to. They knew they had to do a good job on this contract; that was so visible to the whole country. They had made wire and cables before, but these were huge cables made of a special new alloy. It was wonderful to know where the wire and cable you were making was going. The mill knew that they were building the Golden Gate Bridge in San Francisco. Hearts were high. The pay still wasn't all that good, but it was much better than this area had seen for four or five years.

New equipment for stringing the cables started coming into the factory. American Chain and Cable (the parent company of Page Mill) must have been pretty sure they would get this job, because they made a commitment at least a year ago for these cable machines to come early in the program.

Many nights, Sam didn't go straight home. After handling his job of making wire to the right diameter, keeping the machines working, and fixing them when they went down, he would watch them twist the cable on huge machines set up to do this. He would watch for a quarter of an hour and then go home to Peg.

Life was good.

Each day as Sam went to work and spent time looking at the cable headed to the West Coast, he thought about that bridge. "One day I will go out to San Francisco and see that bridge when it's done. It's amazing that the parts for a bridge can be made in Pennsylvania and put together in San Francisco. If it was just a normal bridge, it would be something, but this bridge is going to be the longest suspension bridge ever built. Yes, I will have to go and see this one day."

3

The Twins' Early Years

The Early Years

It was a bright summer day in July 1933, and Red was working the four to eight shift, so he and Hon had the morning to themselves and took a walk with the stroller and the twins. They couldn't afford two strollers or a double stroller, but a friend of Hon's offered the one she had. It was in good shape. Red did a little work on it, and it was fit. It was kind of tight for the two kids, but that was the best they could do.

As they walked along on this bright and clear day, everyone wanted to see the twins, who were now eighteen months old. It was like the whole town seemed to know about the twins, and this, Red could see, made Hon sparkle. As they walked along, she told him it was like a dream. Having twins was tough during their first year while he was at work, and when one hadn't been breast-feeding, the other one had been. And when one hadn't been crying, the other one had been. And during the night one would wake up and she would just get him settled, and the other one would be awake and making a racket.

On weekends they took turns getting up during the night, but during the weekdays Hon always got up to make sure Red had enough sleep. She didn't like the midnight shift either. It was lonely with him

45

at work. The twins kept her company, but, when they were cranky, it was difficult for her. She wasn't getting the right amount of sleep, and then she wasn't very nice when Red came home from work.

That particular day as they walked along, they stopped and let the twins out. They could walk now, and were happy when allowed out of their stroller. When Red and Hon were around the apartment, they let the two tykes walk around, and the neighbors were always helpful in playing with them and bringing them goodies to eat. As they walked, Hon mentioned to Red that Ken was bigger than Jay. He was longer and heavier. She wondered if anything was wrong with Jay. It was obvious that Jay wasn't the size of Ken.

"Maybe it was because he's so active," she said. Ken was heavier and seemed to be more content.

"You're just looking for problems," Red replied. "Jay is eating OK, so he must be OK."

They were also happy about the bridge being built in Pennsylvania and San Francisco: the Golden Gate Bridge. Hon said how much she liked that name and to the people in Monessen it was golden. Red had gotten a raise and now made about $50.00 every two weeks after taxes and other deductions. The little extra seemed to be taken up easily with things the kids needed. The morale of the city seemed to be much better now with Page Mill doing the big job of making all the cables for the Golden Gate Bridge. Pictures had been in the Monessen *Daily News* about what it was supposed to look like when it was done. They read where it would be dangerous to put the bridge up. It was going to be high and the winds that come through that opening from the ocean to the bay could be very harsh. Men were going to be high in the air doing this work with heavy equipment, and the winds could cause problems. One person had already been killed, and they were only putting in concrete on one side of the bridge. They hoped everything would go OK and that the work on the bridge would continue.

Hon said she hoped people didn't think them selfish to be worrying more about the work staying than people getting hurt. Red said that it was normal to think of work since many people were suffering without jobs. Someone will always get hurt to make progress, he mentioned.

Every once in a while, during these walks, they would sometimes meet Sam and Peg Pool walking down the street towards town. The Pools lived up on Motheral Avenue in an apartment that wasn't very far away from them, maybe two blocks. Sam and Peg were a couple of years younger than Hon and one year younger than Red, so they were aware of each other and became speaking friends during these walks. The Pools had just been married not too long ago and were always excited to see the twins in their stroller. Sam and Red talked about work at the wire mill and steel mill. Sam had mentioned how hard it had been to get a job until this bridge in "Frisco" came along. He told Red a little about the trip west and back again to this area. These talks made Red and Hon happy that the wire mill was able to put these people and others like them to work, and they talked about it later in the day after being home and reminiscing about their talks with the Pools. Now life was good for others besides them and the twins.

This part of Pennsylvania was very fortunate for the people and their having chances at jobs while much of the country was still in bread lines. Franklin Delano Roosevelt was the president and had set up with Congress many projects to help put people to work. Some projects were still in the early stages of planning but included building many large dams that would not only help put people to work but would provide major advantages in providing power to parts of the country that had a shortage of power. Some would provide water to areas that were arid, with plans to raise these levels to farming land. In other places it would provide water for population growth. It was going to take some time, but there were plans that had a chance of taking the country out of the Depression. For now, Hon and Red had their two young sons to feed, clothe, and take care of. This provided enough of a challenge. Hopefully the country would meet its own challenge.

As the first couple of years went by, there were events that occurred, both good and bad. Jay had pneumonia when he was about twenty months old, and by the time he recovered he had to learn to walk all over again. Red would put a towel under Jay's arms and around his chest and hold it up in the air like a harness. This took the weight off Jay's legs and allowed him to take steps. After a month, he was walking on his own again. When they were almost two in January 1934, Red took their picture out in the snow with their snowsuits on and their cheeks red from the cold. Hon showed it to someone, and they told her to submit it to the roto section of the *Sunday Sun Telegraph newspapeer* out of Pittsburgh. Sure enough the picture was picked, and their picture was printed in color in the roto section one Sunday. They were proud as peacocks, and they bought many papers and sent them to their friends. And the Sun *Telegraph* framed the picture and sent it to the Hushers with a nice letter.

When the twins were three, the family moved to a different apartment. This one was much better. It was at 209 Rostraver Street, and the apartments went horizontally next to each other, being side by side instead of being stacked on top of each other. It was more like living in a house because no one lived above or below them. Each apartment was two stories high, but there was another story below them that was used for small businesses. But it didn't seem like there was a floor below the apartments, because they were not connected. To get in the apartments, they went around to the back. In back, there were only two levels, the first being at ground level with the second floor above this level. Four apartments were attached side by side. They all were fronted on the main street of Schoonmaker, and the people walking on this main street could be seen from the front windows.

There were two main streets in Monessen: Donner Avenue and Schoonmaker Avenue. Donner Avenue took traffic one direction—south. Schoonmaker took the traffic north. As you went along Schoonmaker it took you from the high street numbers towards lower street numbers that crossed Schoonmaker. They proceeded from sixth to fifth to fourth to third and then Rostraver and then second and then first. So Rostraver was the only one of those streets that didn't have a street number. It was also the only street that stopped at Schoonmaker. All the other cross streets completed the transition from Schoonmaker to Donner.

To get to the apartments from the Schoonmaker street level, you had to take a right from the sidewalk and walk up the elevated steps on Rostraver Street. Rostraver Street was so steep that cars could not make it up during the summer or during the winter. These steps were about ten feet wide and four feet deep and then split into steps that were five feet wide continuing up Rostraver and five feet wide that branched off to the right to the backsides of the apartments. This led to a concrete walk that proceeded behind the four apartments. So, there were no front entrances to these four apartments, only this rear entrance.

The first apartment was rented by the Icavangelo family, who were Italian. Next was the Elias family, who were Syrian; followed by the D'Alonzo family, who were Italian; and then the Husher family. It was nice because there was a large backyard behind all four and contiguous to each other. The first three apartments had a two-level yard for the first three apartments, with one level being on the same level as the entrance to the apartments and then a wall and then the second level of yard. This was great since the kids could play in the backyard and not worry about any traffic. Rostraver Street was so steep that cars could not make it up during the summer or during the winter. It was constructed of bricks and was piped off at the bottom about fifteen feet before you got to Schoonmaker Ave. with a big five-inch diameter pipe about twenty-five feet across that was about three feet in the air and supported on each end by an iron beam that was concreted into the ground. Each of the first three families had a backyard that was about twenty feet deep to the wall that was about five feet high and then the rest of the yard continued from that height and sloped up about ten feet as it went back about another fifty feet and ended where Situ's (Grandma in Syrian, who was the grandmother of the Elias family) driveway began. Red and Hon's backyard of the fourth apartment didn't have that wall and was fairly flat all the way back to where the others ended—about seventy feet.

However at that point there was a "sort of" cave that went under a concrete driveway above. This cave was naturally formed due to the concrete driveway that extended over the back part of the Husher's yard – hanging out like an unsupported cantilever. This cave was about thirty-five feet deep and twenty-five feet wide and made a great place for the kids to play games and let their imaginations make all kinds of things out of the cave. Sometimes it was an Indian hut, a gold mine, a coal mine, or a hideout, or whatever their minds would make it. And there was no traffic to worry about because Rostraver was traffic free. The sloped yard, off to the left of the Husher backyard, was where the families took turns hanging up their weekly washing. There were long clothesline ropes going from one end of this elevated yard to the other end where they terminated on each end with what looked like football goal posts. These also ended up being places the kids also played: climbing the goal posts and walking across on the beam, which was only four inches wide. Many kids got hurt on them over the years. The kids had this big-sloped yard, the flat yard, and the cave to play games.

When summer came and it was hot, Hon sat out back and sprayed them with the garden hose. All the kids in the neighborhood and the colored kids from Third Street, which was right next to this area, would play for hours in the water sprayed on them in their underwear. It was lucky they had this nice yard because they didn't have any money to do anything else.

The rent was now $12 a month, and the kids needed new clothes as they grew up. Hon was a good manager of the funds. She was the boss of the family. Whatever she said was the last word. The kids each had two pairs of socks. They would wear one pair while the other pair was being washed. She felt superior because she had their large backyard, Red could plant some vegetables. They never grew very well because nothing grew very well anywhere because of the mill dust. Most of the cars on the streets were rusty from the steel mill air, and trees didn't grow very well around the towns for miles. In Donora, which was only three miles up the river, there were no trees or grass as a result of the zinc mill air.

But this backyard was their little world, and that was all they needed. The front of these apartments was above the street level by one story. The story below the four apartments was made up of warehouses for storage and fronted on Schoonmaker Avenue. This sort of made it nice since there was a small, metal front porch sticking out from each of the apartments above the sidewalk and beyond the stores below. When there was a Halloween parade, they would sit out on the porch and watch it go by. When the twins were five, Red and Hon entered them in the Halloween parade as "Ike and Mike, they look alike" (even though they didn't), and they won a prize and every year after that till they were fourteen. Hon would paint their faces and give them old hats to wear and small wooden canes to strut along the parade.

In the winter, it was tough to keep the apartment warm. It was a small apartment with two bedrooms and the only bathroom upstairs. Downstairs, on the main floor, there was a small kitchen, a small dining room, and the living room, which led to the porch hanging over the street below. The place wasn't insulated, and it was heated by a small coal stove called a Heatrola that sat in the middle of the living room. Each night Red would bank the Heatrola by covering the hot coals with a layer of new coal. This would essentially smother the fire, but it acted as an insulator that kept the hot coals hot. Each morning Red would get up first in the morning, stoke the Heatrola to expose the hot coals, get the flame started, put some new coal in it, and then make the twins cooked cereal on the gas stove in the kitchen. He would leave the kitchen stove on until it started to get warm in the kitchen. Then he would get everyone up.

Ken and Jay kept their clothes next to their bed and put their clothes on under the covers because it was too cold to get out and put them on. They would come downstairs, get their cereal, and stand by the gas stove to warm up.

New Brother

On September 2, 1938, Hon gave birth to another son. His name was David Lynn and everyone loved him. When he was two, he was either at Mrs. D'Lonzo's next door with a bowl of spaghetti that he carried around or at Mrs. Elias's with a small, flat loaf of Syrian bread. He was always eating these gifts from the neighbors.

Ken and Jay loved him. This close feeling led to a problem. The twins had measles when they were nine, and David would crawl into bed with them with their fevers. Shortly after, David got sick. He had measles, and the measles failed to show up on his skin. The doctor gave him different medicines to make him sweat, but still no measles to show. The neighbors gave David special tea to make him sweat, but still no measles.

Finally, some appeared on his forehead but none on the rest of his body. Some of the neighbors brought old very ripe bananas to feed him. They said that would help the little guy. Ken and Jay remember their mother screaming, "Red, come up here. David is dead!" Red ran up the steps two at a time (the only time he ever hurried in his life). When he came down a few minutes later, he gave each of us ten cents and told us to go to the movies.

When we came back, there were a lot of people there, and everyone was crying. I cried for hours and days. Every time I thought about David over the next several years, a lump formed in my throat. My mother never did get over it.

When Ken and I were ten years old, we each got a job carrying newspapers. We carried papers everyday, and on the weekends each of us stood on different corners and sold Sunday papers. Between us, we were making almost half of what Pap (Red) made at the mill. Ken and I did whatever was needed to help.

When coal was delivered in the winter, the coal truck delivered it to the corner of Rostraver and Schoonmaker, below the steps leading to the back of the apartments. Ken and I helped Pap to carry it up in buckets and carry it back to the cave. Pap would order whatever amount of coal Mother told him to order, depending on whatever they could afford at the time. It took about all day to carry the coal. We only stopped to eat and deliver our newspapers. Even with the coal stove to warm the winter it got very cold during the night. Ken always took a glass of water with him and set it beside the bed so if he got thirsty during the night he wouldn't have to get out of the bed.

One morning, when we got up, the water had frozen and broken the glass. Mother said that was the last time he would carry water to bed; she didn't want her one set of glasses broken.

Ken and I carried the papers, and eventually we each had the biggest route in the city when we were ten years old. My route went up the Fourth Street steps, which, like Rostraver Street, was so steep it was blocked off to keep cars from trying to make it up. There were seventy-eight steps up to McKee Avenue, the second street above Schoonmaker. I carried the total load of papers up those steps before I started delivering. Once I got to the top, I stopped and took a deep breath, happy that I was past those steps. The rest of the way was fairly flat. I worked my way down McKee Avenue back and forth from one side of the street to the other. As time went on, I learned how to fold the papers and throw them the fifty feet or so up to the porches. About halfway through the route, the papers finally began to feel light, and at the end of McKee I went up Sixth Street for two blocks up to Knox Avenue and delivered the papers all the way back to the Fourth Street steps. It sure was a lot easier going down than coming up. It took about an hour to deliver on a normal day. If I was in a hurry, I almost ran and threw most of the papers to the porches. There were times (later when I had to go to baseball practice) when I could make the run in a half hour.

During this period, my mother told Ken and me how life begins, why it was bad to smoke cigarettes, and about some men who liked little boys. "Beware of them," she said. She told us about girls and how they were different than boys. She also told us how messing with girls could get us into trouble. But one day, she said it would be OK and that things would work out between some girls and us.

She also was the taskmaster of the family. She set up the schedules for Pap, Ken, and I. She gave out the punishment when punishment was due (according to her). She sat and talked to Ken and me about life. Ken and I carried the things she told us for the rest of our lives. She gave us confidence. She had a superior attitude and as she directed our young lives, without our knowing it, she was setting the groundwork for when Ken and I would be adults and have to live our own lives. No one could say the Husher twins were backward or introverted—just the opposite. Those early lessons our mother taught us stuck.

Pap was quiet, but when he said something it was important and instructive. Ken and I were lucky to have this early parental guidance, even though we didn't know it at the time. Subconsciously, we took these inputs and stored them for later use.

Twins' Experiences during the War

When Ken and I were almost ten, we had a very scary time. It was December seventh and the Japanese bombed Pearl Harbor in Hawaii. I remembered listening to the radio in the living room with Ken, my mother, and Pap. There was President Roosevelt declaring war against Japan. I had been following what was happening in Europe before this. We had been sending Liberty ships over to help England and Russia even before America was at war. Many of these ships had been sunk by the German navy. We were concerned now that we would be bombed like the people had in England. We were also scared that the Japanese would invade California and drive their armies into the United States as they had in China.

I became scared, because I thought they would take my dad to fight in the Army. What would we do if he had to go? How would we eat? Dad told us he probably wouldn't have to go because they were taking men without families first. Also, his job in the mill was considered important to the war effort. This calmed me a little, but each day while delivering the papers, I was reading the headlines and many of my customers were talking about this war.

Many of our ships had been sunk, and many lives lost. Pap always called me a worry wart. I worried about what would happen if the mill closed. How would all the people in the town eat? Now there was another worry. They had stopped making cars. Food was rationed.

Women went to work in factories to help make things for the war while men went off to war. Each day I listened to the radio and read what I was able, at that age, to ascertain. Mostly I looked at the pictures and my mother or dad read aloud the areas of the paper too difficult for me to read. We lost Bataan in the Philippines, then Corregidor, General Macarthur escaped, and then we were defeated in other battles.

You could not believe how excited Ken and I were when the Navy defeated the Japanese navy at Midway Islands only about six months after Pearl Harbor. I couldn't believe it; the papers said the Japanese navy was so badly hurt that it would no longer be a force in the war.

Then General Doolittle led a squadron of B24 bombers taking off from an aircraft carrier and bombed Japan. After the bombing raid, the planes had to keep flying until they ran out of fuel and crash-landed in China. This was a complete surprise to the Japanese people, who felt they would never be bombed by U.S. planes. The newspapers read, "Bombs fall on Japan." This was an exciting realization that we were taking the offensive and the papers were full of exclamations about this unexpected feat.

The newspapers also showed what the Japanese papers were saying about this unexpected offensive threat on their country. "They were too far away from Japan to bomb us," were the comments as the newspapers framed what the Japanese people were saying about this unexpected event. They didn't realize that the planes had come from an aircraft carrier, since bombers were not supposed to be able to take off on that short a runway (the aircraft carrier's runway) were some of the comments I read. I felt the difference delivering papers. The morale suddenly had been boosted, and people were talking freely about the war as I made my way along the route. It sure felt good to win for a change.

The war changed many things: butter, sugar, coffee, meat, gasoline, cigarettes, and tobacco were all rationed, along with many other things. My mother gave Ken and me each a dollar to carry in our pockets in case we ever saw any rationed goods being sold anywhere. I would see a line of people standing outside a store and hurriedly ask what the line was for. "Butter," someone would say. I immediately jumped in line for about an hour and was able to buy a quarter pound of butter. Then I ran home so excited I could hardly breathe. I showed my mother, and everyone was happy. No one liked the fake butter called Oleo. It came in a package and looked like lard with food coloring mixed in to make it look like butter. I couldn't stand it.

Sometimes I found a line and they were selling Mail Pouch tobacco. I bought the one they allotted per person and hurried home with this treasure. My dad would roll cigarettes out of it. Both Pap and Mother smoked at the time.

Another thing that was scarce was aluminum, because it was used to build airplanes. Every so often there would be an aluminum drive in Monessen. If we brought an aluminum pan or anything made of aluminum to the fire station, we got a free ticket to a movie. We could also go to the movies and give them a pan and they would let us in the movie free. All of the collected aluminum was sent by trucks to Detroit, where it was recycled for use in airplanes. Ken and I went around looking for aluminum things. We went to houses where they didn't have any kids and asked for pieces of aluminum. We did well, and we never had to pay for a movie for several years.

It became exciting to deliver papers, and the headlines told about the effort in the Pacific and across the Atlantic in Europe. Island by island, the American forces bombed and then invaded the islands. I couldn't wait to read the successes and felt bad when I read about the number of men we were losing.

Meanwhile, I was completely taken up in reading about the air fights over England. Early on, many planes were lost to the Nazis over England, where the early air battles were fought. As time progressed, the United States supplied England with faster and better airplanes, and the battle over England began to change. Then, week by week, bombers flew out of England and bombed German industrial towns. But we were losing many airplanes, pilots, and crews during the trips into Germany. The fighters could only escort the bombers so far from England and then had to turn back because of their limited range before running out of fuel.

After a couple of years, I was taken up by reading about the American Lockheed P-38 Lockheed Lightning and the P-51 Mustangs when they arrived in England to provide for bomber escort. Previously, the Germans would wait until the fighter escort for the bombers had to turn around and then attack the bombers. This, I found, was the reason so many bombers were lost. The fighter escort, the British Spitfires and American P-40s, could only go so far on a full tank of gas and had to turn around because of their limited flying distance. With the arrival of the U.S.-supplied Lockheed P-38 Lockheed Lightning, followed a little later by P-51 Mustang, the air war changed. The flying distance of these two fighters was almost twice that of the escort planes they replaced. So they never turned back and escorted the bombers all the way to their targets.

The German planes kept waiting for them to turn around and leave the bombers, but they didn't. Soon, German planes were running out of gas, and American planes were shooting them down. It was like reading a true adventure story. I could hardly wait to hear the news on the radio, read the papers I delivered, or hear my customers explain what they read that I couldn't. Then the papers showed bombers going over to bomb Dresden and pictures in the paper showed them and described that there were so many that they darkened the sky. Day after day, a different city was hit in Nazi Germany.

"Looks like we're starting to win," Ken would say to me.

"Yes, and now we are bombing Germany, and the bombing of England had almost stopped."

The Allies invaded northern Africa. Heavy fighting was shown in the newsreels at the movies. It showed the Nazi general Rommel, who seemed to be undefeatable, and sometimes it looked like we were going to lose. And then some hero would pop up, and we wouldn't lose. Montgomery of the British was fantastic. Patton of the U.S. Army was unbelievable.

Patton soon defeated Rommel's tank troops in northern Africa. Then we invaded Sicily, and Patton was again victorious. Then Italy was invaded, and the Italian troops pushed back. There was heavy fighting and casualties at Casino, with a large monastery being used as a fortress at the top of one of the hills. It took many days for the allied troops to smash this fortress and to capture the hill.

It was actually an exiting time for the country and for kids like Ken and me. It was like a movie. One day you would read about conquests in Europe or northern Africa, and the next about taking an island in the South Pacific. I remember seeing several newsreels at the movies talking about the genius of the American technical people. Hitler had said America could never win a war because the Japanese would cut off our supply of materials for making rubber that were located in the Far East. "An army could not fight a war without tires," said Hitler. We had our silk cut off from Asia and France. No more cork. Major fuel supplies cut off. Many of the supply ships had been sunk by the German navy, both during our help to Britain and Russia before we were in the war and after we were in the war. We had lost much of our fleet at Pearl Harbor.

Quinine, for fighting Malaria, came from the trees in Java and had been cut off by the Japanese. Java made 95 percent of the world's supply of quinine, and most of the war in the Pacific was fought on islands and land where mosquitoes and heat were prevalent. Malaria was as formidable a foe as the Japanese soldier.

But American ingenuity responded rapidly. Synthetic rubber was developed to take the place of rubber. Nylon was invented by DuPont and took the place of silk. Soldiers were now using nylon to help defeat the enemy by using it for parachutes or ingredients in the synthetic tires, or for barter in the form of women's nylons traded to foreign women to find out enemy secrets. Substitutes were developed to take the place of cork.

Henry Kaiser set up a ship-building empire in California that built a ship a day. They were launched out of the bay in San Francisco where the Golden Gate Bridge stood. Out under this bridge they would proceed to be used as supply ships, or some were converted to small Jeep aircraft carriers. They were called Jeep carriers because they were only about half the length of a standard carrier and reminded one of the small Jeep vehicle developed for the war. Women took the place of men in the factories, and they manufactured ships. Also, since all the automobile plants had been converted for war use, out popped tanks, guns, Jeeps, and airplanes. The war was exciting.

Within a year of our country entering the war, we had developed synthetic quinine from trees in South America that proved to be better than quinine from the trees of Java. Spam was developed to feed the troops. Its claim to fame was that it could keep for years. Open up a can of Spam and eat it all. It was not to be wasted, but you never had to worry about it wasting if the can remained sealed.

New types of weapons were developed. Some of the sea battles took place fifty miles from where our ships were located. People had high morale because they were active in helping the war effort, and they were seeing on film or in the paper or hearing on the radio that we were winning. Everyone in the United States belonged to some organization that supported the war effort. My dad was an auxiliary fireman. He learned how to fight fires and how to help people who were injured. He went to classes twice a week. People gave blood. Blood plasma was developed that could be successfully used in the battlefield was developed. Some men were auxiliary police and learned how to handle issues in case they were needed here in the United States. Women learned how to be auxiliary nurses to help wherever they might be needed.

We had air raid drills in every city. Some evenings the sirens went off at the fire station (new, special-built ones that were louder than the old ones), some evenings and you had to turn out all the lights, draw the curtains or drapes, and stay inside. There were designated air-raid shelters for those who were somewhere remote when the sirens went off, and they would scurry to the shelters nearest them. All of these shelters were marked with large letters. We were lucky since our shelter was the fire department building, which was only about a tenth of a mile away.

Even the movies were better. When you could go to a movie it was likely to be a war movie and showed some hero like John Wayne, Dick Powell, Gary Cooper, and many more. There was a movie about the escape from Corregidor, or taking back Bataan, or the Battle of Midway, or Humphrey Bogart in northern Africa. There were movies about the French underground and how they helped the Allies, and movies about heroes from Norway or Denmark. Ken and I saw them all. Wherever you saw me, you would see Ken; and wherever you saw Ken, you would see me. We still dressed alike. Mother always insisted we dress like twins, even though Ken was about six inches taller than me. He would be on his street corner selling papers on a Saturday evening or Sunday morning and me on my corners. And when we came together at the end of the day to turn in our money to the Paper Boss; he or she would always say, "Here come the twins." We dressed alike, but we were fraternal twins and did not look alike. You could probably tell we were brothers, but not twins, except for the similar clothes. Ken was tall and thin; I was short and stocky. But we both liked those war movies!

There were bad times. Many people were killed, and some from our hometown. Each window in the city had a special star for each of the number of soldiers in their family. Some had one star, but some had three or four. Then there were the sad stars. When a soldier who lived in Monessen was killed, their star had a dark background. When I saw one of these in a window, I was saddened because I knew the people inside were sad. I saw in the paper that General Patton had slapped a soldier. Here was a hero that you had learned to love from his heroics in the war. People took sides as to whether they thought he was right in what he had done or not. They thought he had earned the right to do it if the soldier had had it coming to him. I went to bed at night and wondered.

And then things got good again, and the Allies landed in Normandy, France. The invasion was on. Ken and I sold more papers and got more tips. After many battles and it looked like we were headed for Berlin and the war was going to end, but we heard about the Battle of the Bulge. Many American and British soldiers were caught in a trap during a counterattack by the German army and tank troops just before Christmas. This went on for days. But then you read that Patton's army had made it to the Bulge and freed the troops. And then it was on to Berlin. Reading about these heroics was exciting for two young boys.

VE day—Victory in Europe. The headlines shouted out. There were pictures showing the excitement in New York City and many of the other places in the country and across the world. This was fantastic for two twelve-and-a-half-year-old twins. Many were excited, like the war was completely over, instead of the war being only half over—the war continued in the South Pacific. Ken and I continued to sell a lot more papers and get a lot more tips. Mothers were happy because many of them had sons in the war in Europe. Now they would come home. But maybe they would have to go to the Pacific war. The war with Japan was not over. We kept taking islands, but it was hard to take an island. Ships shelled the island for days before our troops went ashore, and still the Japs would be there. They hid in caves and came out when the invasion started. They fought until the end. They were very tough and knew how to improvise. There was no mass surrendering like there had been in Europe. And this went on.

Then one day when I picked up my pile of papers, the headlines said, "Atom Bomb: America Develops a New Secret Weapon." Below, in smaller print, it described how this secret weapon had been developed. It described a bomb that was the equivalent of the all the bombs dropped on the major cities in Germany. This bomb was dropped on Hiroshima in Japan.

I sat down, a thirteen,-and-a-half-year-old paperboy, and I read the article over and over. At my age, I could not comprehend a weapon like this. At that time I thought it was wonderful that the United States had developed this before the Germans or the Japanese. Here were some new heroes for me—these scientists that had made this. We dropped the bomb over Hiroshima in Japan. Over the next few weeks, I read about the number of people who were killed in this attack. It was hard to believe. It was like science fiction. I read about how the land was poisoned with radiation from the bomb, and people would not be able to live there for years. It was scary!

Ken was glad and I guess I was too at the time. Glad that we had developed this capability rather than Japan or Germany. "Better them than us," we used to say. And then not long afterward another atomic bomb was dropped on another Japanese city, Nagasaki. And now you read that the papers said this was done to end the war. Truman believed the Japanese people would never surrender, having seen how they fought on the islands we took back from them. It was his hope this would persuade them. His hope was of ending the war early to save lives on both sides. And eventually it did.

Soon, there was VJ day—Victory in Japan. The war was over, and Ken and I sold even more newspapers and got good tips. It might seem cruel to think of making money off of something like this war, but Ken and I had worked for years to help the family, and each bit of money was appreciated. It was great to go home at the end of the day and show Mother and Pap the money we had made.

Second Set of Twin Boys Born

About the time of the Battle of the Bulge, my mother had a battle of her own bulge. She had been carrying twins again for months and was looking quite large. This time the doctor knew she was going to have twins, and everyone was prepared for it. On December 4, 1945, however, she gave up the bulge and had twin boys once again. They were Terry Max (Terry, after the comic hero in *Terry and the Pirates*, and Max, after Doctor Max Heater, who had been the family doctor for years) and Cary Noel (After Cary Grant, the actor, and Noel because it was close to Christmas), and she had them at Charleroi-Monessen Hospital. This time she had to have a Cesarean birth. Terry was in good health, but Cary had some minor medical problem. They kept Cary in the medical ward, and eventually he was doing well. Then one day (it is claimed he was left by an open window by a nurse in the hospital) he developed pneumonia and passed away. This was a sad time in our family, but we were happy to have Mother back home and our new brother, Terry.

Terry was an interesting brother. He was much younger than Ken and I, and as he grew up he said things that were funny. He was always in trouble. We wondered if he would ever settle down, but the things he did were cute and I used to laugh. Sometimes when I went to bed I would think about the funny things he had said or did that day and a smile would cross my face as I fell asleep.

Early Teen years

The war was over, and it was amazing how fast people fell back into their old habits. Those were the learning years, not only at school but at home, and wherever Ken and I went. Ken and I used to sneak off and go down to the river—the river that was contaminated and had no fish could live in this water due to pollution, and nothing survived in it—and swim in the nude. We had started to do this when we were about twelve, and here now we were fourteen years old and able to swim quite well. No one was allowed to swim in the river due to pollution, but we would sneak down anyhow. There we would meet our friends swimming. Those were the learning years, not only at school but at home and wherever Ken and I went. This was where the mill pumped out its waste and where all the sewers from the towns around dumped their wastes. We saw almost anything floating in the river.

We went to one of two places most of the time. One was located about two miles from home down river, or and the other was up river about a mile towards Charleroi, where we could leap off the high concrete walls that were along side of the locks (Lock #4 on the river).

One day we were swimming in the river, and Doctor Heater (our family doctor) called Mother and told her he heard we had gone swimming in the river. Mother told Pap to go find the boys (we were about fourteen then) and to whip their asses every step of the way home. He always did what she said. He found us, made us put our clothes on (we always swam naked), and he whacked one of us on the ass on one step and the other on the ass the next step of the way home. This went on, for about two miles home. When we got home and Mother sent us up to our bedroom for the rest of the day, we heard Pap crying and saying to Mother, "There, I did what you said, but I will never whip them again," and he never did. It was the one and only time he gave us physical punishment.

Ken and I continued delivering papers. The only time we missed was when we were sick or once every couple of years when Aunt Marguerite (Pap's sister) took us with Uncle Ferd on vacation for about three days. During that time, Pap delivered the papers. He knew each of our routes. We always planned went with our aunt when Pap worked the morning shift. That way he could come out of work, go home, eat, and then take the papers. He had no car, so taking two routes was really tough after a day in the mill. We never missed selling papers on the weekend because we earned five cents for every paper we sold instead of one cent for the every day paper. So Pap never had to handle weekends, and my aunt would bring us back before the weekend.

Those were special times for us when we went to Aunt Marguerite's. She and Uncle Ferd worked in Pittsburgh and had good jobs. Being devoted professional people left them no time for children, so we were told. We went to work with Aunt Marguerite and waited for her to finish. She gave us money to go to the movie sometimes while she was working.

When they took us back to their house at the end of the workday, Uncle Ferd fed his chickens and turkeys. We were always excited to help feed the animals, including their large German shepherd, Duke. One day, while we were out feeding the turkeys, a hawk came down and tried to grab a chicken. I ran and got a broom. The next time the hawk came down, as it passed over the yard, I swung the broom in the air and hit it. Duke pounced on it and shook it to death. I was so proud. My uncle praised me over and over.

One time they took us to New York to see the Statue of Liberty. We walked up as far as they let you at the time. Then Aunt Marguerite and Uncle Ferd took us to the Empire State Building. We went to the top and looked out over the world—as I thought of the world at the time.

Another time they took us to Lake Erie to go swimming. The day before, I made a blowgun by reaming the pulp out of the middle of a reed to make a hollow tube. I put berries in my mouth and pushed the berries with my tongue to the front of the tube in my mouth and blew hard. It popped the berries out like a native blow gun. Uncle Ferd heard what I was doing and came out and said, "That berry is some kind of poison berry." I didn't believe him. He said, "OK, we'll see."

Well, the next day on our way to Lake Erie my face, neck, and mouth got all swollen. My aunt stopped in a little town, and got some calamine lotion, and put it all over me. We went to the Lake, and from my neck to the top of my head was swollen and itchy. I was in bad shape, and but the water from Lake Erie made it feel somewhat better., but at the end of the day, my aunt decided we should go home and have me taken care of by a doctor, what a disappointment. Ken was mad at me for days. He felt I had taken some of his vacation from him.

Between the ages of twelve and eighteen Ken and I played with about a dozen different kids on the block and the back alley between Donner and Schoonmaker Avenue along with about ten of the colored boys from Third Street. We would either play or fight. I didn't believe anyone could fight me and win. I was always getting into fights to prove it, even though I was smaller than most. My mother taught us confidence. She didn't think there was anything we couldn't do, and Ken and I were out to prove she was right. We lost many times. When some of the kids got angry with Ken or me, they chased us and we ran home to the backyard, but they chased us there. Pap would come out and say, "Do you want to fight?" If they said yes, he'd say wait until he got the boxing gloves out, and then they could fight me. On would go the boxing gloves and we'd fight until one of us gave up. I never gave up, sometimes fighting until both of us were too tired to go anymore. Sometimes I had to fight one and when that was done fight another of the kids.

Ken's best friend and mine was Vince Notaurangelo, the Icavangelo's nephew. Vince lived on third street which was less than a block away. Wherever we were, he was with us. He was a year older, but he didn't seem to mind and enjoyed the same things we did. One day, he came running into the yard with Ike Crable chasing him. Ike was the meanest of the colored kids from Third Street. My dad asked him if he wanted to fight. Ike said, "No, I guess I just want to make friends." My dad told them to shake hands and make up. When they went to shake hands, Ike pulled Vince's hand down and brought his knee into Vince's face. It flattened Vince's nose and blood squirted everywhere. Ike Crable ran out of the yard. We knew never to shake hands again in that kind of situation.

When we were about fifteen, we had street fights with the kids on the block and the colored kids from Third Street. It was a war. It usually started out fun, but then it got serious. These were the kids we played football and softball with—our friends. But once our fights got serious, the friendship stopped for about a week. We filled small canvas bags with one or two pounds of sand and put them in strategic places where we thought one of the fights might lead us. We placed some on top of the billboard across from the Keystone bakery. These billboards were twenty to twenty-five feet high and had framework in back that we rapidly climbed to the top of the billboard. Another key place was the second floor alley behind Ernie's woodworking store on Schoonmaker Avenue. During these wars, when one of the colored kids came along, we dropped these bags onto their heads, backs, legs—or missed altogether. I remember being on top of the billboard with Ike chasing Ken below. I dropped a bag, and it hit him right on the head.

Down he went. Then I got scared and took him to my house, and we put ice on his head. He never even cried. But after that, our wars seemed to stop; maybe we were getting older and learning the value of a person and their friendship.

My mother taught us about everything. She'd look us in the eye and tell us there were men in this world that would try to play with a boy's gentiles. "Never let that happen," she said. "Kick him in the balls, and then run." She would tell us how babies were made, and, if we didn't watch out, we could get into trouble putting that thing where it didn't belong.

I also remember coming home after a fight at school. I told her that this one kid, Jack Moskola, who was in my class but about a half foot taller than me, said he was going to get me during the lunch hour. I had gone out to meet with him and try to find out what the problem was. While I was talking to him, he hit me right in the face, and the fight began, but the whole time I was dizzy. When someone broke up the fight and we went back into school, I was dizzy for about an hour. Mother told me, "Never let the other guy hit you first." "If it's certain that there's going to be a fight, hit him first. Always get the advantage." This paid off for me several times in my life.

My mother made sure we did our homework for school and always pushed us to be better than the other kids. She also passed out the punishment when we did something wrong. As teenagers, she normally punished us by not allowing us to do something we really wanted to do. However, on one occasion while eating dinner, Ken made me laugh, and I couldn't stop laughing. Mother said, "Stop it, Jay, and eat your dinner." But, I couldn't stop laughing. She reached down with her good hand and lifted the dining table over on me and all of the meal with it. Then she said, "Laugh now. See that mustard on the wall? Well, you're going to use your allowance to buy new wallpaper, and you're going to paper the whole kitchen all by yourself." Needless to say, I didn't laugh at the table any more. Mother was strict about certain and forgiving about many others. She believed you should have good table manners and keep the house looking neat. Later, after giving some tough advice or something like the incident of laughing at the table, she would apologize for the way she acted and advise us against losing our cool. She would hug you and make you feel good. She also would have my Dad help we do the wallpaper job on the kitchen.

When we were fifteen, Ken and I went down to a place called Wild Cat Hollow, which was a woody area at the north end of town. We went about a mile up the woods to a creek, where we built a dam and made a swimming hole. Ken and I, along with Vince and a few of our buddies, hung a large bull rope from a tree. We used to swing out on it and let loose and land in the water (like in the Tarzan movies we had seen). The water was from underground streams that came from the underground mines around that area and was yellow from sulfur. We used to come home with red eyes. Mother would punch us with that strong right arm and knocked us across the room. That settled us down for about three weeks, and then we would sneak up to the creek again. We learned how to keep our eyes from getting red. We would keep our heads above water as much as possible and we never opened our eyes under water.

Then we started to go back down to the river. I liked to swim there, but Ken loved it. As the paddleboats went by, he swam out to catch the first wave after the paddle before any of the other guys could get to that wave. This was dangerous, and he made bets with the other kids that he would get the first wave before them. I never saw anyone beat him. He was a terrific swimmer and could swim all day without touching ground. I swam for a while, then came ashore and sat in the sun for a while, and then swam out again. We got grease all over us from the river. We found a green-leaved plant that would suds up if you rubbed it against you and it took away all the grease and dirt when we rubbed it against us. It was like soap. We made sure we did this treatment before going home. We didn't want Mother to know we had been in the river.

One day, after swimming for several hours, Ken and I were getting soaped up and getting ready to go home. Before leaving, we sat there and talked. Ken said, "When I grow up, I want a house along the river. I always want to be near the river."

"Not me," I said. "I want to live on a high hill so I can see all of the world."

And then we got up and headed home, happy with our swimming and happy to relate to each of our goals in life: *By a River, On a Hill.*

Late Teen Years

The years from fifteen to eighteen were exciting years for me. I'd say that four things stuck out as the main parts of those years:

1. School
2. Baseball
3. The girl I met
4. The cellar people

When we were fourteen, Ken and I belonged to the First Street Ramblers Little League baseball team. It was made up of all the kids who played softball on the lot at First and Schoonmaker. The empty lot was just big enough to play softball. The left fielder played in the middle of First Street, so we had to make sure a ball was pitched when no cars were going down First Street. I played second base.

When the First Street Ramblers baseball team was started, I began to pitch. By the time the first year was over, I had developed a fast pitch. I found if I rotated my right hand inward in a counterclockwise motion as my arm came down, the ball not only went faster but it broke in on a right-handed batter.

Later, I found out it was known as a screwball. This opened a new world for me. Now instead of relying on a curve or slider to get people out, I had a fastball. This was unexpected from someone as small as I was, at 5 feet 7 1/2 inches and 147 pounds. As I delivered my newspapers, I threw the papers about fifty feet to the porches. This accomplished two things: not only did I finish faster, but it built up my throwing arm. By the time I was sixteen, I was known for my good fastball, and, when I tried out for the high school baseball team, I made it. They gave me two pairs of white athletic socks. I couldn't wait to get home to show my folks. Two pairs of neat, white athletic socks! This meant I now had four pairs of socks, counting the ones my mother washed daily. Baseball practice started every day during the week at 4:30. I got out of school at 3:45, so I hurried to pick up my papers and ran along the route. I usually got to practice about 5:00.

The High School Burns Down

When Ken and I started high school, we attended the school in the middle of my paper route. Near the end of ninth grade, there was great commotion one day as I approached the high school delivering papers. I couldn't believe I was seeing smoke billowing out of the top of the school. I joined the crowd of about a thousand people watching the high school burn down. From then on, we attended high school at the junior high, which was adjacent to the high school. There was not enough space in the junior high to handle the number of students from seventh to twelfth grade, so we went to school on half days. The first half of the day was for students in the seventh to ninth grades, and the second half for students in the tenth to the twelfth grades. Classes were jam packed. This city of about 20,000 had a hard time coping with students from junior and senior high attending crowded classes.

Ken and I looked for jobs to help out at home. While delivering my newspapers one day, I noticed that people took out their ashes every Wednesday night and they were picked up on Thursday morning. The ashes were the residue out of the bottom of the furnaces. Ashes left over from trash burned or sometimes of incomplete burning of the coal. I watched the following week, and sure enough there were bushel baskets of ashes out on the curbs. I thought collecting ashes would be a good way to earn money. So that Saturday while I was collecting money from my paper customers, I asked them if they needed someone to take out their ashes each Wednesday. Sure enough there were eighteen customers signed up. At twenty-five cents a bushel, I did very well each week. Some houses had two bushels, and each week I took out about twenty-five bushels and earned an extra $6.25 per week.

One weekend, I dropped in on the confectionary store next to the apartment we lived in on Fourth and Schoonmaker to get a Coke. They asked me if I wanted a job scrubbing their floors once a week. I told them I did. Well, the first time I was down on my knees scrubbing the floor, I heard this clump, clump sound of footsteps that only my mother made. By the time I looked up, she had grabbed me by the neck and pulled me out of the store and told me in no uncertain terms: "You don't scrub floors for anyone." My mother was a proud lady.

I had to take Latin during the ninth and tenth grades. At first I thought I would hate it, but I had a great teacher, Mrs. Haninen. She convinced me that Latin was exciting if you got involved with the story. It was mainly about Caesar and the wars he fought. She was right. She also told me that many English words were derived from Latin and that this might help me one day. As I read through the book in her class, I got so interested that I went to the library to read more stories in Latin about Caesar. Needless to say, I got an A in Latin every report period. Little did I know how much learning Latin would influence my life. I was to learn this several years later.)

Needless to say I got an "A" every report period in Latin. Later in life I was to realize how much Mrs. Haninen affected my life. My second grade teacher's pushing me on arithmetic also affected my life positively as the years went by. (Later in life I would reflect upon the impact one person can have on another's life. Of course your parents can have a major impact on your life, as they should. However, separate from one's parents, you can never tell who might have an impact on your life; it might be a teacher, an athlete, a friend, an enemy, an individual event, a co-worker, or a co-student and the list goes on.)

Time was pretty well taken up with school, baseball, and delivering papers. However, Ken and I took drum lessons and were soon playing in the high school band and orchestra. In the orchestra, I played the kettledrums or timpani. This got us interested in the Belle Vernon Drum and Bugle Corp, which was known all over the East as one of the best. By the time we were juniors in high school, we had been accepted into the Belle Vernon Drum and Bugle Corp. The town of Belle Vernon was only about four miles from Monessen. Ken and I hitchhiked or walked to get there. The Corp played all over Pennsylvania, and one year we played at the Cherry Blossom Festival in Winchester, Virginia, where we won first prize.

Ken and I had many good times in Belle Vernon. We both had girlfriends there at one time or another. When we marched in the Corp, the girlfriends followed the parade and met us afterward. Many a hot time was had after the parades, normal boy-girl stuff including sexual encounters.

I Meet Peggy Pool

When I was seventeen, a friend of mine, Corky Reese, called me on the phone and asked if I wanted to go to the fair in Rostraver, which was the next town over from Monessen. His parents had a car, and he was allowed to drive it every once in a while. We drove the few miles to Rostraver and parked. We walked to a place called Pricedale, located about a quarter of a mile from the school. We stood there a while and watched the people coming up the hill from the fair. After about a half hour, I noticed two girls coming up the hill, and one of them I couldn't take my eyes off of. I asked Corky, "Who is that girl with the bright blue eyes?" He said her name was Peggy and her last name was Pool. (Remember Sam Pool riding the motorcycle with Buck Shutterly out West during the depression). She had a pink sweater on, and the combination of the pink sweater and her blue eyes caused me to say out loud, "She looks like a beautiful bunny rabbit." Little did I know her long-term effect on me. We stopped them and talked for about a half hour. I asked Peggy what she did on certain days and she mentioned that she went to the Monessen Junior High gym to a dance every Saturday evening at 7:00. When they continued on their way, I told Corky that I was going to see that girl again as soon as I could. He told me that she was a few years younger than me, but it didn't matter.

A couple of weeks after the first meeting with Peggy, I happened to be downtown in one of the stores, and low and behold there she was. We talked a while, and she said her mother was going to take her to the dance on Saturday. I told her I would meet her there. I told her I enjoyed meeting her the other day and she said that she liked meeting me. We did some small talk and it was obvious that that we wanted to talk more but since we had just met there wasn't anything we could think of to talk about. She had to leave and meet her mother who was shopping.

That Saturday could not come fast enough. The dance started at 7:00, and I arrived at 7:30. It didn't take me long to find her. She tried to get me to dance, but I told her that dancing was for sissies. (I changed my mind later in life.)

But every Saturday I went and sat there with her, except when she was dancing. Afterward, her mother picked her up outside the school. She had been named after her mother, who always came with a Dalmatian dog in the backseat. He was ferocious. When I got close to the car, he attacked the side windows, and slobber, from his teeth gnashing against the window, ran down the window. Needless to say, I never got a ride home.

When summer came and school was out, I would walk to the north end of town, to Wild Cat Hollow , and go up through the woods to where Peg lived. It was about a three-mile walk to her house. I loved to go there, not only to see her; her mother and father were great to me. They had a beautiful house on top of the hill across from the city park. It had a cellar, main floor, and upper floor. I'd only be on the main floor for a few minutes, and then I went down in the cellar. There, her dad, Sam, (Remember Sam Pool riding the bike out West during the Depression?) worked on large model airplanes that he built from scratch. There was anywhere from four to fifteen guys down there making planes and getting advice from Sam. The planes Sam made had wingspans of about six to eight feet. He covered the wings with silk he had delivered from Japan. He then coated the silk with clear varnish like dope. After drying them, he lightly sanded the silk and applied another coat of the clear dope. This was done fifteen or twenty times, until the silk made a ping sound when you snapped your fingers on the wings. It sounded just like metal.

The thing that impressed me the most was the technical skill of the "cellar people," - those. people who hung out in the cellar with

Sam. There was always some problem to be solved—mechanically or electrically—and they found ways to solve them. If they couldn't buy a part, Sam would make it on the lathe he had or on other tools. Sam Pool was the most skilled teacher I ever had, and day after day I went there and watched and learned. I believe this began my eventual career, but I didn't recognize it at the time.

During the ages of sixteen to eighteen, there were three things that drew most of my time and attention: Peg, baseball and the "cellar people." Pitching was now a love. I often thought about how to throw the ball a different way. I had small hands, which, along with my small physique, worked against me as a pitcher. But the long stride I took, plus the unorthodox method of releasing the ball out of the opposite side of my hand (in a counterclockwise motion instead of the typical clockwise for a right-hander) found the ball going at a very high velocity and breaking in toward a right-hand batter. When I held the ball almost the same way and released it out of the normal side of the hand (toward the thumb) it rolled off with a snap and broke the opposite way—a slider. If I released it with a more horizontal rotation of my arm, it gave me a wide-sliding curveball. But probably the best pitch, other than my screwball, was a pitch like a knuckleball that I used as a change of pace. Since my hand was small, I couldn't hold the ball like a normal knuckleball pitcher did. There was another pitcher on the team named John Galven who threw this sort of knuckleball, and I asked him how he did it. With John's method the whole hand was used to hold and deliver the ball. The ball was placed such that it rested on the fingernails of my three bent middle fingers while my little finger and my thumb gripped the ball. When throwing this pitch, during the release, the three middle fingers pushed their fingernails forward against the ball while the arm was being thrust forward, and the thumb and little finger gripped the ball tightly. Just when the two outside fingers released the ball by the two outside fingers, the nails of the three middle fingers snapped against the leather of the ball, thrusting it in a non-twisting motion. The ball went about fifteen miles an hour slower than my fast pitch, and dropped at home plate. This proved to be an excellent change of pace pitch. (Later in life, in the eighties, pitchers in the majors started to use a split-finger fastball by holding the ball between the spread fingers of the index finger and the middle finger. It had the same result as my pitch.} The way I held the ball and released it served the same purpose with my outside thumb and little finger serving as their long fingers. The added touch was the three middle fingers and their release. Depending on how I pushed the nails of these three fingers against the ball on release, it provided a different action of the ball as it neared home plate.)

It was always interesting to see a batter who had my fastball zip past him, followed by this pitch. He normally swung too early and usually over the top of the ball. He either missed it or fouled it along the third base line. When a left-handed batter was at the plate, he threw the screwball at him, and it broke down and over the inside corner of the plate. Most of the time, the batter pulled away, thinking the ball was going to hit him.

So my summers between the age of sixteen and eighteen were spent pitching baseball, seeing Peg, or watching the cellar people do their things. Ken's summers were spent visiting girlfriends in the nearby towns of Belle Vernon or Bentleyville or playing drums in a dance band. He was a better drummer than I and loved playing at dances. He was also a better dancer than I was, and he did it to charm the girls. And charm them he did.

Ken and Me

During school I was always excited about learning, and I participated in many activities. Ken and I had different feelings about school. Ken went there because he had to. He didn't care if he got good grades or not. He liked playing the drums, running with his friends, or seeing different girls. He was excited about life and enjoyed it to the fullest. School was a place to see his friends and girlfriends, and learning came last. No matter how much my parents pushed him, he set his own pace, and it wasn't to study. He never failed any subjects because he was naturally intelligent, but he just passed them. A "B" was outstanding as far as he was concerned, and he was happy with a C. But to me, he was the greatest. I loved him. Guys could say what they wanted about me, but they couldn't say anything derogatory about Ken while I was around. If we went anywhere and anyone gave him a hard time, I stepped in, and there would be a fight.

I remember going to a Friday football game, and we had good seats. Near the middle of the game, Ken and I went to the men's room. Upon arriving at our seats there was another boy in Ken's seat. Ken told him that it was his seat, and he told Ken to find another one. I told him,"Either give him the seat, or we go outside and determine who gets the seat." "Let's go outside." He said. And out we went, along with Ken and a few other guys. I fought the kid, and Ken watched. After that was over, we went back in and got our seats back. No one could talk to my brother like that and get away with it.

Ken and I fought each other like we were going to kill each other, but it always stopped at some judicious point. I thought twins fighting were normal. Later in life I learned that twins either couldn't stand each other or they loved each other. He was my best friend, and I loved him. We were such good friends that I didn't gain many close friends as a young boy; as long as Ken was around, I was happy.

I did well at school, not because I was smart, but because I wanted to learn and was persistent. I took all courses needed to go to college, even though I knew my folks couldn't afford college. It was hard enough just making it from one month to the next. But when I learned something I went home from school happy. Sometimes while delivering papers or playing baseball, I thought about something I had learned that day. It pepped me up.

In my junior and senior years, I was vice president of the class. Each year the president of the class was an outstanding student for some athletic reason or for his high intellect. My junior year, the president was Jim Mandarino, who, after receiving his law degree, rose to be the second highest political power in Pennsylvania. He did a great deal for the communities and industry in western Pennsylvania, and when it was obvious he would be the next governor of Pennsylvania; he died at the young age of forty-one. Later, a highway was built in western Pennsylvania named the James Mandarino Highway.

My senior year, the president of the class was Jim Ralston. He was a great football player and was on the All-American High School football team. He received scholarships from about every school in the country. He chose Yale and was an outstanding player but a better student. He got his degree in chemical engineering and managed several key factories before retiring at fifty, only to pass away at the early age of fifty-three.

So, while at school I studied to maybe one day have the chance to go to college. When school was out, it was off to my paper route, then to baseball during the baseball season, then to dinner, and then to Peg's house and the cellar people.

When I was a senior, the school in Monongahela (where Joe Montana would later attend) couldn't handle all its students. So some students were sent to Monessen High. One of them became a good friend of mine and added several highlights to my life. His name was Ron Neciai. He was a tall guy and played first base on our team our senior year. He was a great hitter and fielder, and we won enough games to get in the WPIAL playoffs in western Pennsylvania. We were great friends, but that summer, my last summer, (my last year in school having been completed) I played for the Monessen American Legion baseball team, and he played for the Monongahela Legion team. We both won our championships in our respective legion areas, and eventually we played each other for the Western Pennsylvania American Legion Baseball Championship.

It was a three-game playoff series. In the first game, they were ahead by three to one in the seventh inning, and the coach sent me in to pitch the last three innings. The first guy up to bat was Ron, a tremendous hitter (later a member of the Pittsburgh Pirates), and I was excited to pitch against him. I threw my best pitches at him, and the count was two and two. I threw the screwball, and he filed it off. I threw the knuckleball, and he filed it off. I threw a roundhouse curve, and he filed it off. I looked past the coach to my dad cheering like mad in the stands, and I knew I had to throw something special to get him out. I waved off several calls by the catcher and finally agreed on the slider. It was probably the best slider I ever threw. It broke down and away and ended up at ankle level in the catcher's hand and past the swing of Ron.

I leaped in the air as if I had just won the championship. This sticks in my mind to this day. I held them for the rest of the game, but it ended at three to one. The coach was so impressed with those three innings that he started me the next day at their field. Some guys could pitch two days in a row. I found out I couldn't. My arm was stiff, and I couldn't throw anything that required me to snap my wrist. So I told the catcher to just give me targets outside and low on each batter, and I would try to keep it down and away from their power. This worked for three innings, but they finally began to pound the pitches. I was out of the game, and our team lost to Monongahela.

I would later watch the career of Ron Nechai as he continued his minor league career.

It turned out he couldn't hit the curve ball in the minors either, but he could throw the ball so hard that they made him a pitcher. Later he would come up to the Pirates, and he had a great first season. During the second season, he hurt his shoulder and never could return to form. Forty years later, I received my copy of *Sports Illustrated,* and the cover had the face of someone that I thought I knew. The cover said, "Only happened once." I opened the magazine and read the article. It was about Ron Neciai. While in the minor leagues, he had done something while pitching for Memphis that no one had ever done and still has never done. He struck out twenty-seven batters in a game. Every batter that came to the plate in nine innings went down on strikes. It was not just a perfect game, but a *truly* perfect game—he struck every batter out! I read the article, and all I could remember was my dad looking at me before I put one past Ron when I was eighteen years old).

My final year of school ended in June of 1950. I had a scholarship to go to a small college in West Virginia based on my relatively good grades and high school activities. It wasn't that far from home, but far enough away that I couldn't commute. I had no money to stay there, or money for books or food. Worst of all, I didn't know what I wanted to study in college. I knew if I stayed at home I needed to get a job to help the family. I liked the idea of staying around, seeing Peg and the cellar people, and running around with Ken while we played in the Belle Vernon Drum and Bugle Corp.

Ken and I searched for jobs and finally started to work for the local natural gas company as laborers. We dug ditches and laid pipelines. It wasn't bad work. We were paid sixty-five cents an hour. Between us we provided a nice sum of money for the family. About that time, the war with Korea broke out. There was talk about being drafted, and as the summer moved on I kept thinking of where my life was going. Ken and I talked with Vince Notaurangelo, our best friend growing up, about going to the Navy. It was casual talk, nothing serious.

Vince was a year older than Ken and Me and lived only a block away from our place. We had grown up together and he was Ken's and my best friend. He would travel to Belle Vernon with Ken most of the time. He worked with us digging ditches for the gas company. That summer Vince and Ken bought an old Chevy Coupe for $50 from Vince's uncle, and the three of us used to drive all over the valley together. It had a rumble seat in the back, so we could stuff three people in the front seat and two or three in the rumble seat. Ken drove me up to Peg's house many times and took off to see his girlfriend. Life was fun, but we were going nowhere. Digging ditches tired us out, but as soon as we ate supper and took a bath, our energy was back and away we went to have a fun evening.

And so the summer of '50 was soon over, and we continued digging ditches. One evening, the three of us, along with Jerry Simmons and Rich Marrino, decided to drive to Wheeling, West Virginia, to the whorehouse to get some. We checked our money and between us we had about $21. We thought that would get us there, and we could make our hit and come home. I drove. We got about five miles from

Wheeling when a cop named Mac stopped us for speeding. He said the fine was $15, or I could stay in jail all night. I told the guys to take off, that I would stay in jail and they could pick me up on the way back in the morning. The cop took me back to the cell and was about to open it when another cop told him to let me go. The boys had paid the $15. So, on the way back I drove, but this time toward home with only a couple bucks among us. We used to laugh that we were in smelling distance when stopped by a big Mac. If any of us saw the others in a crowd, we hollered out, "Hey, Mac," and the other person looked around and laughed.

And so we were back to the ditches through September and October. Then one day in late October we were digging ditches in the rain. It was a miserable day to work, and the foreman started to give Ken hell about something. Ken leaped up and said, "Hell, I'm going to join the Navy." I came out of the ditch with him, and along with me came Vince. We went down to the recruitment office and signed up. Then we went home and told Mother and Dad. They were distraught. Their twin boys, who they had proudly raised and loved, were about to leave them.

It was not fun. We were to take a bus to Pittsburgh on the morning of November 2, 1950, and be sworn in. Then we would take the train to Chicago and from there to Great Lakes, Wisconsin, to boot camp. This gave me about ten days to get ready, visit with friends, see the cellar people, and spend time with Peg. She felt bad that I was going away, but perhaps her folks felt worse about it than she did. She was young and enjoying life.

4

The Navy

Navy, Here We Come

On the first of November, the day before leaving, Ken and Vince said I could use the car. Two guys from Belle Vernon had decided to go to the Navy with us—Sonny Marrino and Ralph Manderino. They were going to go with me to a dance in a town called Hermanie about twenty miles from Monessen. We went that night and had a good time. We were leaving the dance at about 1:00 AM when Sonny asked me if he could drive the car. I said, "OK, but remember this is a small car. It's not like your dad's."

By this time, it was raining lightly. We were headed back home to catch that bus at 7:00 that morning, and, as we rounded a bend in the road, I felt the car slipping. All I could see was a telegraph pole coming toward me. I woke up on the road. Ralph was lying in a ditch with a bone sticking out of his leg. There was a cover in the rumble seat, and I got it out and laid it over him. Sonny was walking around in a field, and I asked him if he was OK. He said yes and collapsed. I dragged him to the side of the road and kept thinking I was lucky that nothing had happened to me. Then my left eye and forehead felt itchy. I reached up and thought, "My God, I have a hole in my head. I better lie down."

About five minutes passed, and a woman driver came by, saw us, and said she would get someone from the hospital to come out. Another twenty minutes went by, and an ambulance arrived and took us to the hospital.

———— ⁓⦿⦿⦿⦿⦿⦿⁓ ————

Both Ralph and Sonny were kept in the hospital. They were scheduled to go to the Navy with Vince, Ken, and me, but it turned out that neither one would ever go to the service due to their injuries. It took several years for Ralph's leg to respond to treatment. Sonny had headaches for several years. Oddly enough, I never saw them again in my life.

———— ⁓⦿⦿⦿⦿⦿⦿⁓ ————

I was told I would have to be admitted to the hospital to repair a broken cheekbone, a hole next to my left eyebrow, and a hole in my kneecap. I told them I had to leave, since I wanted to go to the Navy with my twin brother. In the end, I had to sign papers refusing treatment. I walked out of the hospital around 2:00 AM. Before long, the ambulance driver came along and told me to jump in. He drove me to Monessen, right to my door. I knocked on the door and heard my mother upstairs hollering, "Red, it's Jay. I know something's wrong." Pap opened the door and couldn't believe what he saw. I climbed the stairs, and there was Ken. He looked at me and began to cry. My mother was ready to faint. Soon I had them feeling better, since I still felt no pain. The bus was coming by in a couple of hours, and Ken and I were off to Pittsburgh to catch the train to Chicago and Great Lakes Naval Training Center.

When I was getting on the train in Pittsburgh, my face and leg began to hurt. An older woman saw me and had the porter put me in her berth. They put ice packs on my face and leg. By the time we had made Chicago and then to Great Lakes, the pain was bad even with four aspirin in me.

Boot Camp and Recognition

At Great Lakes, the Navy doctors didn't want to accept me. I begged them because of my twin brother and finally they gave in. Later they asked me if a dentist could work on my cheekbone. They said they could do it without a scar on my cheek. I was in no condition to argue with them one way or the other, and so they decided on this way. The dentist made a cut above my teeth between my cheek and gums and put his hand in this slot and moved the cheekbone in place. Afterwards, they put a mask on my face to hold this it in place. Meanwhile, they sewed the hole next to my eye and stitched the hole in my kneecap.

While I was recovering from this, they kept Ken to work on his teeth. He came and saw me each day, went to the dental office, and awaited dental care. For about a week they didn't do anything to him but had him work around the dental ward cleaning things while I was getting better. Then, the day I was released from medical, I went to see him, and he was laid up in a bed. They had pulled three teeth and filled eleven—all in one sitting. He was in pain. Fortunately, we lived through this, and we were off in training for the next three months. A funny thing happened to me. They cut everyone's hair off in a crew cut, but since I had these straps around my head to hold the brace on my face, they could only do a partial haircut. When I got out of boot camp several months later and they had taken the brace off, I had hair that was half an inch on some of my head and about four inches on the rest of my head. The picture on my ID card was something to behold.

Boot camp was an interesting experience. We learned about the Navy, and we gained other experiences. They had athletic activities such as swimming, running, boxing, learning how to shoot a rifle, target practice, marching, and how to handle a four-hour duty watch—better known as guard duty. Ken and I used to laugh about the watches at Great Lakes. Some nights we had a four-hour watch where all we did was guard some garbage cans with the temperature around zero and the wind blowing in from the lake. This was to teach us discipline. It sure did, especially if we happened to not be doing it the day the officer made his rounds and caught us sloughing off. Fortunately, this never happened to Ken or me.

A wonderful thing happened for me at the conclusion of boot camp. I was named Honor Man of Company 395. Scoring the highest on the tests taken during the twelve weeks of training made me a candidate. Out of five candidates, the Chief, and two other chiefs, then evaluated the activities we were involved in during boot camp. I had been on the swim team, and the boxing team (not long), and had scored well at the rifle shooting range. Each activity gave me so many points. The last twenty-five of a hundred points came from the 120 guys in the company and the chief petty officer running the group, who voted for the candidate they preferred. They must have felt sorry for me and my face and leg issues.

As Honor Man, the Navy paid for my mother and father to fly up to Great Lakes for the graduation ceremony, including a stay at a nice hotel. My mother was too scared to fly, so my dad and Aunt Marguerite came to see me graduate. During the graduation ceremony, I marched with the flag at the front of the company, and they presented me a nice silver bracelet with the inscription: "Honor Man Company 395" on the front of the silver bar and my name and serial number on the back. They gave my dad a cigarette lighter with an inscription that read: "U.S. Navy."

During the last couple of weeks of boot camp, the commanding officers tried to determine where we were best suited to serve the Navy. During my interview, I asked the interviewee what his rating was. He said he was a personnel man, and this included such duties as training, education of others, personnel records, recruiting, and others tasks, such as the job he was doing there. I told him that personnel sounded good to me. Because of my Honor Man selection, I was given a high choice of any of the schools offered and left boot camp for Norfolk, Virginia, and personnel school. Ken was sent to the naval air station at Patuxent River, Maryland, with Air Transport Squadron One (VR1).

Navy School and Waiting For My Ship

Personnel school had thirty naval personnel attending. There were twenty-nine men and one woman named Virginia Sellers, who sat next to me. She had graduated out of North Carolina University that year and had decided to join the Navy. She was a tall, nice-looking girl and was excited about being in the school. The first day, the chief petty officer administering the classes asked for people who could type fifty words a minute or more to raise their hands. Sellers was the only one who raised her hand. He went on, asking for hands on forty words a minute, thirty words a minute, and then twenty words a minute. The chief then said that that should take care of the class, and I raised my hand and told him I didn't know how to type. He asked me how I had gotten in the school, since one of the requirements was being able to type a minimum of twenty words a minute. The requirement was based on the skill of typing needed to send or receive code by telegraph key. He had me pick up a big mechanical typewriter and took me to the back of the class. He gave me a book on typing and told me to read it and to practice one hour each day during the typing class, which met three days a week. He told me not to look at the keys and to make sure I practiced hitting the numbers without looking. After three weeks of this, I felt like I was doing quite well and should be up with the rest of the class.

One day up there, and I knew I wasn't ready. When they had the typing test, my fingers were hitting the keys at the same rate as Sellers was hitting the return arm to start the next line. So back I went. After another two weeks, I started to like typing and brought in the newspaper in the evening and typed articles out of the paper. I was then moved up with the rest of the class. I had already been attending all the other classes, so it was only the typing that I had to catch up on. By the time I graduated the thirteen weeks of school, I was the second fastest typist behind Sellers, mainly because there was a lot of numbers in the final typing test, and I was able to hit numbers without looking. Many of my classmates couldn't.

Upon completion of school, I was assigned to the Jeep aircraft carrier CVE 122, the USS *Palau*. The problem was that it was not in port, and I had to go to the Norfolk receiving station mess hall and perform duty as a mess hall setup server until it arrived in port. The mess hall fed the station personnel plus any ship that came into port for repairs and other short-term reasons. This meant several thousand mouths to be fed each day.

Each day, they awoke me at 4:30 AM, and I went to roll call for those whose ship was in port. Then they advised us as to when we could go aboard. If the ship was not in, we went to the chow hall and performed whatever duties we were assigned. Each day, my ship was not in. So each day I went to the chow hall and carried large food containers to set up the chow line for the cooks and serving personnel. After they had completed their breakfast, the doors would be opened to feed other personnel. This continued all day. I got to eat only as I carried the large containers back and forth. This continued until about 7:00 PM, and then I was allowed to go back to the barracks where I was staying. The USS *Palau* still wasn't in port, so I went about my duties in the chow hall. This went on for about a week, and it was very demoralizing. I felt like I was in jail serving a sentence.

Easter weekend came, and steak and turkey were the main meal. At the end of the day, we took the unused food out back and piled it up next to a chain-link fence to be carried away. Because it was Easter and they had wanted to make sure there was enough for everyone who came into the receiving station, they had overcooked. There was a very large pile of steaks and turkey meat being piled up outside. The piles of turkey and steak were about ten feet high, and each covered an area of about a four hundred square feet. Civilian workers who were on the station were climbing the fence and getting out steaks and turkey in bushel baskets. I never saw so much food piled in one place, and so many people trying to carry it away. Normally they would not be permitted over the fence, but on Easter they let it go, as long as there was a guard present and no one was being harassed. So a lot of people ate Easter dinner that day thanks to the Navy. I was happy for them.

Finally, after about another five days at roll call, they called my name and said the USS *Palau* was due in port in three days. I was so happy knowing I only had three days of the grueling work in the chow hall that those three days seemed like nothing to me.

Aboard Ship, Aircraft Carrier USS *Palau* CVE 122

While reporting aboard the USS *Palau*, the officer of the day asked for my papers and my ID card. He looked at the picture on the ID and said that it didn't look like me, since it had been taken at boot camp and my hair was all different lengths. He took out scissors and cut the card in two, and then he took his cigarette lighter and burned the card as I tried to explain to him that this was the only picture from boot camp and I had wanted to save it. He instructed me to get a new picture taken the next day at the ship's service center.

There were many exciting days aboard the ship, but I didn't like this duty at all. I had always lived under extraordinary conditions growing up. Even though I had only had two pairs of socks, my mother would wash one pair one day and the other the next day. The same was true of everything at home. My mother, crippled as she was, always worked to keep the house and our clothes clean. Onboard the ship, I couldn't get used to my clothes being in a sea bag or in a very small locker. Each night, I rolled up the pants and tops I had worn that day and put them in an eighteen-by-eighteen-inch locker that was three feet deep. I removed them the next morning to wear that day. They always smelled musty to me. Between the use of the ships laundry and the shower, I kept the clothes as clean as I could, but they always smelled sour.

The most exciting part about living aboard the ship was seeing the planes take off from the ship. It was exciting to see the planes take off from the ship. Since the ship was shorter than a normal aircraft carrier, it had to catapult the planes in takeoff. Each plane took off with an explosion. It was exciting to see the planes landing on the ship's deck and catching on the steel cable across the landing deck. This was especially true when I had the watch in the Coning tower high above the deck. The TBM (torpedo bomber medium) bomber fighters used to land with a loud crunch and sort of jump in the air before being securely held and then released by the long cable as it moved into position to receive the next incoming plane. The USS *Palau* and these planes served on hunter/killer duty, looking for foreign submarines in the waters along the East Coast. The *Palau* also served as a refueling ship for Navy blimps (helium-filled air ships). The blimps dropped a long refueling line down to the surface of the ship, and fuel was pumped up to the blimp above.

One day, while serving on watch in the high superstructure of the ship during landing maneuvers, I watched as planes were hitting their wheels on the deck with regularity and taking off immediately. The planes couldn't take off from this short a carrier—it was only about 600 feet long and converted during WWII from tanker hulls to fight in the Pacific—without a large catapult system to provide a powerful launching for the planes. However, on this day when they were landing and taking off immediately, the catch cable was only used in emergencies. The planes hit with their wheels just touching and immediately took off with the momentum built up by the plane. These landing practices went on for a whole day, and sometimes two days, without stopping to give the pilots practice on landing the heavy TBM aircraft on this short carrier. I would fall asleep at night with the "thump thump" of the planes landing and taking off echoing in my head.

A signalman at the receiving end of the flight deck signaled the planes coming in, waving his flags to the position of the wings relative to the receiving deck. If the pilots looked like they were not going to be in proper position to make a landing, the signalman waved his flags above his head as a wave off, and the planes applied power and flew over the flight deck. If the signalman liked the attitude of the plane, he gave a wave-through signal, and the pilot hit the deck at full throttle and took off for another fly-through practice.

One day, while on watch in the conning tower, the planes were actually landing, being caught by the steel cable, and then being placed forward on the flight deck out of the way of the next plane coming in. On this day, one of the planes coming in looked good until the last moment, and the signalman gave the wave-off sign. The pilot didn't see the signal until it was too late, and he had already got down to the level of the flight deck before he began to power his plane to take off.

Meanwhile, the hook on the tail of his plane caught the steel cable, and the plane bounced up and down like a tiger caught by the tail and smashed the radar cone on the bottom of his plane. The plane veered to the left, and the one landing wheel caught the steel deck that surrounded the flight deck about eight feet below. The pilot was thrown through the glass and into the ocean. The plane hung there hopelessly like a bird caught with nowhere to escape. Helicopters were immediately dispensed from one of the other ships accompanying the *Palau*, and they picked up the pilot and brought him back aboard the *Palau*. He was banged up a little, but he was in pretty good condition considering.

Another episode occurred about a month later. The ship was cruising in the Caribbean off the coast of Cuba in search of possible submarines. The weather was hot, about a hundred degrees Fahrenheit and very hot below decks. The word came over the loudspeaker that anyone wanting to sleep on the flight deck that night could do so if they took their bedding up by 2000 hours (8:00 PM) and returned it to their bedding site by 0600 hours (6:00 AM). About half the crew took their bedding up that night. I took mine and fell asleep in the evening breeze. It was much nicer than sleeping below. I fell asleep within half an hour only to have the main alarms go off sometime in the middle of the night. "Man overboard, man overboard!" was announced over the loudspeaker.

We are trained to go to muster (roll call) during this type of emergency, except for the crew on duty. This at least provided information as to whether someone was missing and who. We were part of a small force of ships made up of two destroyers: an escort destroyer and the *Palau*. The huge floodlights of these ships lit up the night as the ships circled the area. The *Palau* sent up a couple of helicopters, as well as one small one from one of the destroyers. We searched for two hours with lights, and eventually it was light enough to continue our search—but it was in vain. The name of the person was determined. It was surmised that he had sleepwalked right off the edge of the flight deck and fell across the catwalk.

The next anxious moment occurred about two months later. We were up near Newfoundland when a storm hit us. The announcement was made at about 1600 (4:00 PM) for everyone to batten down and close all the hatches, which meant to tie down and secure all equipment. This was done to prevent material from sliding around in the heavy sea and causing some type of accident, as well as keeping water from entering certain areas. The weather continued to be very rough, and the announcement was made at around 1900 that a movie would be shown at 2000 hours on the hangar deck; this was the deck below the flight deck and contained much of the equipment for maintaining the aircraft. This was also the location of the elevator shaft, which raised planes to and from the hangar deck to the flight deck. This shaft went down about another fifty feet below the hangar deck and had a large piece of the metal deck attached to the top of it so that when the elevator was all the way up, it was a part of the flight deck. During bad weather and rough seas, the shaft was up and the deck was locked into the flight deck. This prevented weather from entering the hangar deck from above. In addition, there were four large corrugated metal doors—two on a side—that went up and down much like old garage doors. These openings were used to bring supplies and material aboard the *Palau*. These doors were down at the time to block the hangar deck from the rough sea and weather. When they were open, it was a twenty-five-foot drop to the ocean from the hangar deck. Deck chairs placed on the hangar deck accommodated about three hundred people to watch the movie. To prevent anyone from falling down the elevator shaft to the metal floor below, this area was roped off and tied to stanchions.

The movie started on time and was a John Wayne movie. Everyone was sitting in the dark watching the movie, when suddenly a huge rush of water blasted into the hangar area. The pressure of the water was terrific, and it threw the chairs around like leaves in the wind. All I could hear was, "We're rammed, we're rammed!" or "We've been hit by a torpedo!" I was crawling around in the darkness on the steel deck, thinking that I had to get out of that place or die. Bodies shoved against me, and others were running over me. The chairs were being thrown as I crawled to where I thought the garage doors would be, and hopefully to where the chains to the roll-up doors were located. I thought that the place was being flooded, and I was going to make it to the side doors and jump out. I was not thinking at the time that a person could only live a very short time in the cold Atlantic water around Newfoundland. Blindly, I got to the side of the ship and felt around for the chain, when suddenly the lights came on in the hangar deck.

It became apparent what was happening. The water was from the large water hoses surrounding the hangar deck, which were used to put out fires in the hangar deck. Someone had thrown the emergency flooding switch. These hoses could provide a blast of water that would easily throw a person thirty or forty feet. Finally, the hoses were turned off and the damage assessed. There were injured men lying all around on the deck, and others walked aimlessly like they had been through a bad nightmare. Chairs were everywhere—over injured bodies, in puddles of water, and at the bottom of the elevator shaft along with six bodies.

Later, I heard that one person was killed and several sustained concussions, while others had bruises and cuts of one type or another. They never determined who had caused the tragic situation. It remained in my mind for years after, and I have never truly forgotten it.

During my stay on the *Palau*, my mother wrote letters to the Pennsylvania senators that her twin boys should be together, but no action was taken. Finally, she sent a letter to the chief of naval operations in Washington DC, requesting that I be transferred to Ken's location in Patuxent River, Maryland. She explained that she had been born a cripple and that when Ken and I went to the Navy she had suffered from an additional illness that brought about depression and other side effects. She explained that if I were transferred to Maryland, I could return home every so often to see her, and this would relieve some of her stress and allow her some help around the house. One day, my chief petty officer called me to see him and showed me a copy of the letter that had been sent to the chief of naval operations. He felt there would be some action taken. I only hoped they wouldn't assign Ken aboard the ship. I didn't like ship duty and I thought it would cramp Ken's style. Well, to my good fortune, a week passed, and orders came to transfer me to Air Transport Squadron One in Patuxent River, Maryland. The *Palau* was sitting in port just outside of Norfolk, Virginia. I was told to get my gear together and be ready for transfer the next day.

The next day, the captain's gig was lowered into the Chesapeake

Bay, and I was placed aboard for transfer to shore. I remember riding the waves away from the *Palau* and thinking about my experiences while aboard. I thought, "I was only aboard the ship for four months. It's hard to believe that so much could be experienced in that short a time." Then I remember looking back and saying, "Good-bye, you iron bastard." Some people love sea duty. I didn't.

Patuxent Naval Air Station: Early Troubles

Upon arriving at the gate to the naval station, Ken was there to meet me. He had a Navy van pick me up, and we rode about a mile to the barracks where I met most of his friends. They had a hard time believing I was his twin brother—me, of five feet, seven and a half inches in height and him about six feet, two inches or so. There was some kidding around, and then Ken asked me if I would like to go get a beer. It was a warm August evening, and white uniforms were the dress code for this time of the year. We changed to our dress white uniforms and started for the gate. As we approached the gate, we could see two marines in the glass-enclosed guard shack that guarded the entrance and exit to and from the base. One marine checked IDs of personnel going out the gate, and one checked those coming into the base.

We got about five feet from the gate when one marine said to Ken, "Square that hat away, sailor."

The white, navy cap was supposed to be worn with the front sitting on the forehead just above the eyes. Ken had the hat sitting on the back of his head. He took the hat, sat it straight up on the top of his head (sort of like a dunce cap), and said, "Do you like it this way better?"

The marine said, "You're a wise guy," and stuck his index finger in Ken's chest.

Ken glared. "Don't do that again."

The marine started to put his finger on Ken's chest again, and Ken threw him through the glass window of the guard shack. Before I knew what had happened, I was surrounded by marines punching me, and two marines had Ken by the arms. Out of the guard shack came the marine with blood on him, and he tried to hit Ken. Ken kicked him right back through the window and into the guard shack again.

Before I knew it, I was in the brig holding a garbage can, and Ken was wiping it down with two sponges. When my arms got tired, he held the can, and I sponged. After about an hour of this, they let us rest. It was about 9:00 PM and time to hit the rack for most on the base.

As I leaned against the brig wall, I turned to Ken and said, "What the hell have you been eating since I saw you last?" Here was my brother, who I had had to fight for whenever the time came, because he wouldn't. He just smiled at me and said, "Hey, Gort, (a nickname that I will describe later) let's get some rest. We need it after that."

We spent another day in the brig and then went to captain's mass the following day.

The Mass was headed up by a full lieutenant (equivalent to a captain in the Army, Marines, or Air Force). He had Ken give his version of what occurred at the gate, and then he heard mine. Next, he heard the version of the guard (marine private) who Ken had engaged. His version was quite different from ours.

Then he called in the marine sergeant of arms who was responsible for all the marines at the gate during his duty time. In walked the picture-perfect marine sergeant: he was sharply dressed with shiny shoes, and he snapped the shoes together, saluted the lieutenant, and stated his name and rank. The lieutenant asked him to give his version of what had occurred at the gate, and he told the same version as Ken and I had. He was immediately dismissed, and the marine private was called to the desk. The lieutenant sat and read through his record folder and then looked up.

He said, "I thought maybe you had just returned from duty in Korea and were uptight, but your record shows no record of hazardous duty anywhere. As a guard at the gate, you are responsible for not only ensuring our safety but also to see that armed service personnel passing through these gates are treated with respect. You did not do this. I am transferring you to six months duty on the ammunition dump starting tomorrow, after which you will go through an indoctrination period of one week on how to handle situations such as this. As for Seamen Husher and Husher, you will be confined to the base without liberty for one week, with the two days you have served in confinement to count as having served this one week. This incident will be removed from your records. You are free to go now."

And so that was how my first couple of days at Patuxent were served. I learned that Ken had completely changed. He had gone from a person with little confidence to one of complete confidence. I have always thought this was a result of two things: being away from our mother, who was very domineering, and being responsible for himself. What a great gift the Navy gave my brother. He had become a man.

My duties during the first year at the station consisted mostly of maintaining the records of the personnel in Air Transport Squadron (VR-1). This included all things that transpired within VR-1: a person's ranks and change in ranks, military schooling, medical records, leave accrual (leave is earned two weeks a year, and any taken leave must reduce the amount they accrue), any transfer from one station to another, any special actions such as special pay for married people living outside the base, special pay for flight duty (hazardous duty), dental records, special awards, medals won, letters of accommodation, pay records, advancement in pay, and any other miscellaneous happenings while in the service. For example, a copy of the letter my mother sent to the chief of naval operations was in my record. I advanced in rank as fast as one can advance in the Navy to third class petty officer and then to second class petty officer.

During this time there was an occurrence that I must mention. Ken had taken two weeks leave in late 1952. Upon returning from leave, a person had to report to the officer of the day in VR-1 and drop off leave papers, showing that he or she had returned at the time the leave expired. The officer of the day signed these papers were signed and recorded the hour and date of the person's return from leave. These papers were sent to me the next day, and I entered them into the person's leave record and subtracted the days taken from those he had accrued, showing the remaining valid vacation days on their record. This paperwork was then sent to the personnel officer for his signature. The personnel officer's name was Lieutenant Donald D. Stone. If a person was late, he was considered AWOL (absent without leave) for whatever time he was over his leave expiration time.

One day, I heard him holler, "Husher, come in here."

I went into the office, and he said, "I know your brother went on leave recently, but I've seen no record in here for me to sign. Did you discard his leave papers?"

I told him I hadn't. After further questioning, I told him I had intended to discard his papers, but they had never come from the officer of the day's office. They had evidently been misplaced. (If a person took fifteen days leave and their paperwork never was entered in his records, it would be like he never took leave and he would have fifteen days coming.)

He said, "Did you say you meant to discard his papers?"

I said yes. (I might commit fraud, but wouldn't lie)

He told me to get out of the office until he thought about what I had said. Out I went. Later, he beckoned me into his office and stated that he could dishonorably discharge me from the Navy, he could order me to be transferred to work detail, or he could restrict me to the base. He asked, "What do you think I should do?"

I answered, "You trusted me, and you know what I intended. I don't deserve your trust. You should do what you think is right based on my experience under your command and how you now feel about me."

He told me to get out of the office again.

Here was an officer who had been an enlisted man who was supposed to only advance as far as chief petty officer. In rare occasions, enlisted men may eventually be promoted to a warren officer's position. This is the first level of an officer and below that of an Ensign in the Navy but greatly respected for some outstanding service they performed to move up from an enlisted man's status to this officer level. Lieutenant Stone was two levels above warren officer, which indicated how much it took for him to reach this rank of mustang lieutenant. This was the kind of person who held my Navy life in his hands.

Later, he asked me back into his office. He said, "After considerable thought on the matter, the way in which you have served up to this time, I'm going to let you remain in your position; however, you do not have any off-base liberty (I had to hand in my liberty card), you may not take any leave, and if you have to piss while on duty you will come into this office and ask for permission to piss. This punishment will last until I decide to relieve it. Do you understand?"

I did, and I had to hand in my liberty card.

My days were spent on the base after that. I went to the base movie, which cost twelve cents. I went to the base photo shop, learned how to process film, took pictures I had, and made them into special layouts and enlargements. Once a week I went to the base golf course and learned to golf. On Saturdays Ken and I went to the enlisted men's club on the base for dancing. They had a small band playing music, and two or three busloads of women came down from Washington DC. It was great fun, and that was where I learned how to dance. I soon learned that dancing wasn't a sissy thing, as I had imagined in high school. Ken showed me how to dance.

Jay at Patuxent 1952

I met a girl named Jackie Knight and danced with her. She was beautiful and in high demand on the dance floor, but she liked to dance with me. She wanted to meet me outside the base and go to a movie or something but I told her I was not permitted to leave the base. So, all in all, the restriction to the base was a good learning period.

It was also during this period that I tried out for the base baseball team. The season was almost over, but they had lost a couple of pitchers through injury. I was in good shape, and the coach was impressed, particularly with the speed of my fastball. After a couple of weeks training with the team and pitching a couple of relief appearances, Coach Morgan gave me a start. It was near the end of the season, and there were only fourteen games left on the schedule. I started three games. At one point, I had gone nineteen straight innings without giving up a hit. Because of this, my brother and dad ended up giving me a nickname from the movie *The Day the Earth Stood Still*. This movie featured a robot named Gort. My dad and brother said I had an ass as hard as a robot's, and the fact that I had pitched like a robot (going nineteen innings with no hits) got me the moniker of Gort with the baseball team, which I carry to this day. My mother hated the name, but everyone else in the family sooner or later called me Gort (Ken, my dad, and later all Ken's children, their husbands, and Ken's grandchildren).

Another interesting thing happened on the baseball team. We had a new man out of boot camp who had been named to the all-New Jersey team as a pitcher before joining the Navy. His name was Joe Batiglia, and he was six feet, four inches tall and weighed about 240 pounds. He was ugly. He thought he was the cat's ass when it came to pitching. He was around less than a week bragging about how fast he could throw a fastball when something funny happened.

One day when we went to practice, Coach Morgan got tired of hearing him boast. He called him out. "Batiglia, come here. Husher, come here. Husher, take the backup catcher out to right field and show Batiglia how to throw a fastball."

Batiglia laughed as he looked at me and my size. When we arrived in right field, I told Batiglia to show me some pitches. Here was a guy that was about 6 feet 4 inches and 240 pounds and he threw a couple of warm ups and then I told him to show me his stuff. He reared back and threw about five pitches, which were pretty fast. Then he turned to me and said, "OK, shorty, let's see you throw a few." I took the ball and threw three fast screwballs. He said, "Wow, how can you throw that fast?" I told him I had found that I could throw the ball a lot faster if I took a long stride and used my body momentum to throw a screwball, which is to spin the hand in the opposite direction from normal. He asked me to show him how, and we were friends for life.

After about four months of working in the personnel office under restriction, I was called into Lieutenant Stone's office. He told me that the chief petty officer who headed up education for officers' training was being transferred to another base and I was the highest grade qualified petty officer to serve in that capacity until another chief was transferred to the squadron.

Providing Education for Officers

I began immediately. This was a very impressive function for a petty officer first class, and I was quite proud. The restriction to the base was removed. Lt. Stone's last comment to me was, "Husher, I'm going to be watching you. You better not screw this up." I saluted and was on my way to the other side of the hangar. (my station and Ken's was at the hanger that maintained VR-1 aircraft and officers and personnel for VR-1. The enlisted men had a barracks about a mile up through the woods near the mess hall. The officers had special quarters on base or off base if they were married.)

Upon arriving at my new position, I immediately reviewed the records of the ten people who reported to me and the records of officers who had been promoted over the years and those who hadn't. It was obvious to me that the education office was about a half year behind on preparing officers for advancement tests. The office people were called together, and I told them what I expected. I wanted VR-1 to have the best promotion record possible. I told them that if they performed at a certain accelerated level of preparation for the officers— including bringing them in and advising them of what was needed to pass for promotion each week and providing them special tests to prepare them for taking their final tests—that I would allow half of the office to take off on Friday for a long weekend of liberty, and the following week the same would apply to the other half. Everything was full speed ahead.

Day after day and week after week, the various officers (approximately sixty-seven of them) were brought up to speed to pass all the qualifying tests. These courses covered basic things like mechanics, engineering, flight regulations, weight limits on flights, procedures for auto landing, procedures for various flight patterns required for various landing fields, responsibilities of each rank, and other officer preparation. After ten months, the various officer candidates for promotion were qualified to take the service-wide tests for promotion. Of those qualified, 92 percent passed the advancement tests. From that point, the promotion was determined by several other things, for example flight training such as openings available in the rank, time in rank, grades versus others that were also qualified, recommendations by each officer's superior officers, and lastly—how their "twin" did.

It turns out that in the Navy each officer is assigned a twin. This person is unknown to him. This assignment comes out of the chief of Navy personnel's office in Washington D.C. The assignment can be an officer of lower or higher rank. If that person doesn't qualify for advancement for some reason, then his twin cannot be advanced. What this does is put pressure on all officers in the Navy to do what they can to make the other officers do better. If they notice a shortcoming in an officer they are expected to confront that officer and advise him how to improve. They don't know who their twin is, and therefore if they aren't doing everything they can to help their fellow officers, it may come about that the person they didn't help turns out to be their twin and they don't receive their promotion. (Later, when I was running production plants and had engineering reporting to me I thought this should be the way businesses should be run to ensure the development of personnel within their private business ranks.)

Meanwhile, Ken was attached to the Link Trainer Room on the second floor of the hangar. The Link Trainer Room consisted of four Link training cockpits. When you were in one, it was just like being the pilot enclosed in the cockpit of an aircraft. The inside controls were the same, and each Link Trainer could be controlled from outside to create different environments for the plane, like being in a storm, going through a low pressure area, dealing with cross winds, and so forth. Each pilot in VR-1 was required to spend a certain amount of hours per month piloting a plane or training inside the Link Trainer. Even if a pilot met his/her requirements of real airtime, they were required to go through a minimum number of hours in the trainer. Ken recorded their date of training and by reviewing their previous records determined what they were currently required to complete.

For example, upon entering the Link Trainer, a pilot was given an approach map for a naval airport in the United States, perhaps Oletha, Kansas. Upon entering the cockpit, the system was turned on, and the pilot was at a given height and distance from the Oletha, Kansas, airport, where he was to make a landing. The approach for every landing field is different, and requires a slightly different flight pattern for approaching for a landing. When following the required flight pattern, a monitor scope showed where he was relative to the field, and other equipment showed his attitude (the position of the plane relative to being parallel to the ground) as well as altitude of the plane relative to ground. It showed his air speed, and everything else he needed as he handled the controls.

Meanwhile, outside the Link Trainer, Ken pushed certain controls that changed the airflow (artificially generated) about the trainer. It could control a storm being simulated and the cockpit would be met with violent movement as if in a storm. Or it could change the crosswinds, which the pilot inside had to compensate for. Eventually, the pilot would land, and after exiting the Link Trainer he would be given a grade. The report went in his record and eventually provided information in his promotion reviews.

Those systems proved to be very valuable, since they provided the action and reactions required without the possibility of actually wrecking. These systems were set up for the two-engine and four-engine propeller planes that VR-1 flew. As different types of planes were introduced into VR-1, the programs were changed on the Link Trainers, or the Link Trainer would be replaced with a newer version.

Ken had several basic responsibilities. He was responsible for ensuring records were kept of the various pilots and the various programs each had completed. He administered the actual run" done by the various pilots that were scheduled; providing each with the landing pattern for a given air field that was synthesized during their flight. He was responsible for reviewing each pilot's training flight with them and providing input to improve their next flight. He was responsible for normal maintenance of the Link Trainer. If something went seriously wrong with the Trainers, they called in the companies who had sold the systems to the Navy for complete inspection.

My job in education was to receive the information and data from Ken's Link Trainer update, enter it into the officer's personal folder, review the Link training hours and results, and consult with each officer as to his status on qualifying for promotion. If he hadn't met his hours of Link training successfully or completed his required actual flying time to qualify for promotion, I would advise him on what he could do to catch up. The flying time and Link Trainer time were considered his empirical requirements. To qualify for promotion, each officer had to fulfill these empirical requirements, as well as taking the required academic courses and passing them successfully. In addition, the officer had to have his required number of years in his present rank, there had to be openings in his rank and rating (i.e., if he was a doctor, there had to be openings for a doctor in the rank he was seeking promotion. If he was a line officer, there had to be an opening for a line officer of the rank he wanted to be promoted to), he had to have better marks than other officers seeking promotion to this level, and his twin had to be qualified.

My job was to see that an officer met the qualifications for promotion and advise that person on where he or she was lacking and where he or she had completed the requirements. If an officer was passed over twice for promotion, he might be asked to leave the service.

Having been released from my restriction to the base, Ken and I went to the movies or to the bars. One day, when paying a cashier for a movie, the girl said, "Oh, you're Jackie Knight's boyfriend." I told her that I wasn't, and I couldn't wait to get out and call Jackie. On the phone I told her that we were not attached, and she was nice about it.

Later on, I started to date her on a regular basis. She was quite good looking and a great dancer. I was invited to her home for dinner, not knowing that her dad was Commander Knight, the captain of the base. Her mother had prepared spaghetti, and we sat down to eat when her dad arrived. As we were eating, he asked what I did on the base (he couldn't tell since I was wearing civilian clothes, which were permitted outside the base), and I told him.

He turned to Jackie and said, "Jackie, I told you that if you want to date anyone from the base, it must be an officer. I don't want you to date regular swabbies."

I looked up and said, "Mr. Knight, I will no longer come to your house, but I will date your daughter." And I got up and left.

So Jackie and I kept dating. The more I went out with her, the more I respected her. Eventually, she was competing in beauty pageants and won them. She was selected for Miss Southern Maryland and was to attend the pageant that would select Miss Maryland for the Miss America Beauty Pageant. She wanted me to be her escort and said she would not wear high-heel shoes so she would not be taller than me. I told her to wear the high heels, because she had beautiful legs and looked good with them. And so we went to the Miss Maryland pageant. She didn't get selected, but I was happy for her to get that far. The whole time I was dating her, I knew that I loved Peg back home. I kept trying to get Ken to date Jackie, but he had his own girlfriend.

I told him, "Ken, this is a beautiful girl, and she has her head screwed on right. She would be great for you." Meanwhile I knew that Peg was something special.

But, it didn't work. I dated Jackie when I was around the base. This went on for about two years. Her dad got promoted and transferred to the West Coast. We wrote to each other, but eventually it was over.

During the winter of 1952–53, I went to the gym almost daily with a friend, Ron Cherazzi, who caught my practice pitching. I worked on fastballs, curves, screwballs, and that special pitch I had developed that is similar to today's split-finger pitch. Ron and I spent about four months doing this every evening. I could hit the catcher's mitt wherever Dave held it, no matter which pitch I threw. We went for about forty-five minutes each evening. Sometimes my arm would be tired, and we missed a day. Or other times Ron would go home for a weekend liberty, and there was no pitching. I knew I would be ready for March when spring training began for the baseball team.

Commendation

As winter wore on, I was surprised by a letter of commendation from the captain of VR-1 for preparing VR-1's officers for their fiscal report and their promotional preparedness reports. This letter went in my personnel record file, and all the officers were sent copies. The letter went on to say that a higher percentage of officers met their requirements and were promoted than at any time previously. Of course I was proud, and one day while walking across the hangar deck I crossed the path of Lt. Stone. I saluted and was on my way when he said in his usually gruff voice, "Husher." I stopped dead in my tracks. I turned around and faced him—expecting to be reprimanded for something I had done wrong. He looked at me and said, "I heard you did an excellent job in the education office. Congratulations. How did you accomplish that?"

I told him about giving half the office the weekend off if they completed their accelerated goals each week, and he said, "I knew you were doing something wrong," and continued on his way across the hangar deck. I watched him go and thought he was proud of what I had done. I hoped so. The squadron benefited by these promotions.

My work provided me with information about all the various opportunities available in civilian life. I decided to be an engineer when I left the Navy. I sent away to the University of Oklahoma (because they had such a good football team) and took several USAFI courses in mathematics to better prepare myself for going to college when I got out. My work also impressed on me how officers lived versus enlisted men. Although my life in the Navy was great as an enlisted man, I could see its limitations. Being an officer was the only way I would ever come back.

Baseball

Finally, spring arrived, and baseball practice arrived. Practice was held each day after hours, meaning after we completed our day's duty. I felt great throwing the ball on the sidelines. My speed was good and control was good. I was ready to beat the world—or so I thought. Then one day the coach said we'd have an intra squad game, and I was to pitch the first two innings for my team. What a rush. I went out on the mound and threw my first pitch from this elevated position, and I heard a cracking sound. I had a hard time raising my arm. All winter I had practiced on flat surfaces, and, when I went to the mound and took the long stride to deliver the ball, my arm wasn't used to the elevated position and my rotator cuff gave out. I went to the sidelines, and each day I tried to throw, but the pain was unbearable. I rested for a week, and the same problem persisted. After another two weeks, the coach told me my arm was done.

So much for not working slowly on the mound to loosen my arm during spring training. I had outsmarted myself.

A Car for Our Parents

The years 1953 and 1954 were interesting years in the Navy. Ken and I decided to save our paycheck each month and buy our parents a car. No one in our family had ever had a car, and so we spent most of our time on the base during 1953.

Then I got some added help in saving money. When I was twelve years old, my parents couldn't afford to send me for a haircut. So, my dad cut Ken's and my hair. At the same time, he taught me how to cut his hair. Eventually, I cut Ken's hair and the other neighbor kids who couldn't afford to go to the barber. When I was about fifteen, my dad bought me a nice set of clippers that allowed me to cut hair faster and better; from then on I cut his hair.

Now, here I was in the Navy and wanting to earn some extra money. The barber for VR-1 was a man named Pat Pavone. Fortunately, he came from Pennsylvania, and we became friends. I learned that he had a barbershop outside the base that he ran in the evenings and on the weekends. I went to Pat and asked about cutting hair in his shop. He said he had plenty of business, and for every head I cut I'd get fifty cents and he'd get fifty cents. Since getting out of boot camp, I had cut my own hair by looking in a mirror and holding another mirror. I learned that you can see flaws in a mirror that do not show under normal conditions and normal lighting. That's why barbers have mirrors in their shops, so as they cut they can see the results in the mirror. I told Pat Pavone this, and he didn't know, even though he had been cutting hair for about fifteen years.

Anyhow, cutting hair outside the base was interesting. If a Navy guy came in for a haircut, it was because he didn't like the cuts he got on the base. These guys wanted a haircut that didn't look like they had just gotten a haircut. So they got a trim, and it cost them a buck (plus a tip).

On the other hand, the farmers and other civilians who came to the barbershop were just the opposite. They would say, "Cut it short, I don't want to come back for three months or more." So I just took out the electric clippers and had fun. They liked what they saw, but they didn't tip. When they came in again, they'd say, "Hi, Jay. I'm back. Same cut as last time, and see you in three months."

I earned about $50 a week at the shop. That was big money in 1953. This allowed me to save about $600 during the year, and, along with my Navy pay, I helped get the money we needed to buy our folks a car.

Ken and Jay visit home 1953

By the end of 1953, we had saved enough money to buy them a car. We went shopping, and new cars were coming out. We finally decided on a new 1954 Plymouth (which was available in October of 1953). It cost around $1,600, which we were able to pay off. Mother and Pap were surprised. Mother had become somewhat immobilized due to her limp, and this opened a new world for her and Pap. This allowed Pap to take her around the town and eventually to different towns in Pennsylvania. In 1954, Pap brought her down to Washington DC, where Ken and I met them. This was around a 240-mile trip each way. They came on a Friday evening, stayed at a motel that night and Saturday night, then headed home on Sunday. In one year's time of car rides with Pap, our mother looked ten years younger—and happier.

We continued saving our money, and I bought a new 1953 Ford. They wanted $1,800 for it. I pointed out that it had a blemish on the trunk from residue dirt prior to the paint job. So I got a new eight-cylinder Ford in November of '53 for $1,600. Ken got a 1953 red convertible with special mufflers that sounded great. His was a girly wagon—meaning the girls liked it.

By the time I got discharged in 1954, I had put 46,000 miles on my Ford. (Ken put a lot of miles on his car too, but he put more miles on girls than on the car.) Every time I had a chance, I drove up to Monessen to visit my folks, my young brother Terry, and Peg. I couldn't wait to get there. When I got on the Pennsylvania Turnpike, I felt I was home even though I was still about a hundred miles away. My love for Peg only grew as I saw her more often. I never felt the love was reciprocated, even though we got along great. To her, it was puppy love. She was going to college and I knew she was dating other guys, but I was persistent. She never told me she loved me, but every time I drove back after one of these weekends, I got homesick as soon as I left. I thought, "Maybe one day she'll feel my love."

On these visits home, I loved to take Terry around. He was only eight years old, and he looked up to Ken and me. He was always proud that we were in the Navy. I took him to the movies and sometimes up to Peg's house with me. Sometimes when I came home, Mother told me that some kid had beat Terry up. I found the kid and told him that if I came back and heard he had hit Terry again, I'd make sure he got hurt. I was just kidding, but it didn't take much to scare them. Terry thought I would look after him, and he later told me that I was his hero in life.

Through these weekend travels, I got a different perspective on what made the world tick. When I knew Peg wouldn't be home, I'd travel to some other big city and eat Italian food while touring the town. There was a dramatic difference between my hometown of 22,000 and places like New York, Virginia Beach, Atlantic City, Philadelphia, and Boston. I made a promise to myself that if I ever had children, when they were sixteen, I'd get them a vehicle. They would have no excuse for not being able to see the world, being exposed to other ways of life, and determining what they wanted to do in life. Also, they would have no excuses for not being home on time.

A Medical Problem

Early in '53 while walking with Ken down to the hangar, I had a sudden pain in my back and couldn't walk. I lay on the ground, and Ken ran to get help. Later in the medical ward, they checked my urine and found blood in it. I felt fine by then, but they said they needed to run some tests. They gave me a cystoscope examination, which consisted of sticking a bent metal tube about as thick as a pencil and a foot long up my penis and then jerking down on it to get the bent part past the sphincter muscle (the one you use to urinate) and up to my kidney. It hurt and I yelled, and the whole time they examined me, I held my breath. Afterwards the two technicians said, "You didn't yell as loud as the last guy."

The next morning the doctor came in and talked to me. He sort of smiled and drew what the normal kidney and urethra looked like, and then he drew what mine looked like. I had three kidneys and matching tubes to and from the kidneys. They decided to send me to Bethesda Maryland Naval Medical Center to have the situation analyzed.

At Bethesda, I went through the same procedure with the cystoscope, only this time they tore something while taking the tube out. I was in pain, and they gave me a shot that knocked me out until midday the next day. I had a hard time walking and urinating for a few days. Later I told my friends that my fingerprints had been permanently embedded on the chrome tubes that led to the urinal from me squeezing them while peeing in pain.

Two days past, and the doctor came and asked me if I could walk. I said yes. They told me that my kidneys and all the tubes looked normal and that everything should be OK. They felt that the pain I had previously felt may be due to a kidney stone or inflammation of the kidney, but there was no evidence of these problems at this time. This made me feel much better; then they shocked me. They told me they had scheduled me to play nine holes of golf the next morning around the course at the hospital. I told them I could *hardly* walk. They said I would be OK.

The next morning they woke me and had a young medical technician take me to the golf shop and provide me with a set of clubs to play. I limped along and still couldn't see how I would swing a golf club. Needless to say they were right. By the fourth hole, I had forgotten all about the problem. I was sent back to duty the next day.

A Transistor Radio Changes My Life

In late 1953, while going through the Navy base store (called the PX), I saw a transistor radio for the first time. I couldn't get over the fact that it was so small and turned on instantly when you threw the on switch. I was used to the large tube radios that were heavy and when you turned them on you had to wait about a minute for the tubes to heat up before you could listen to them. The batteries inside those radios were bigger than the total size of the transistor radio. I couldn't afford to buy the radio since I was saving for the car for Mother and Pap. But the transistors interested me. I decided to read about transistors wherever I could find information. This was going to be a turning point in my life. I read all the paperback magazines and newspaper articles about transistors and tried to understand them as much as possible.

This reading and understanding went on for the rest of my life. (I did not know at the time how much this hobby would benefit me, more than the formal education I was to later receive). By the time I got out of the Navy I was as up on transistors as one could be without a formal education.

5

College and Marriage

Discharged/Start College

Ken and I had enlisted in the Navy on November 2, 1950, with a four-year enlistment. This meant we would be discharged from the Navy on November 1, 1954. Because of Korean duty, all enlistments were reduced by two months. The war was now over in Korea.

This was a great break for Ken and me, since if we got out on the first of November we'd miss the fall semester of college and two months earlier allowed us to enroll for the fall semester. I had convinced Ken to go to college on the GI bill. We could go to college or a trade school and receive a monthly check to help pay the cost of school. I didn't have to do much convincing, since Ken also observed the advantages of an education. My main argument was that his high school grades wouldn't matter, and he could get good grades with his present attitude. The Navy had won again; it was the best thing that Ken and I could have done.

We both got honorable discharges on September 1, 1954, just in time to register for school. I enrolled at the University of Pittsburgh, and Ken enrolled at California State College in California, Pennsylvania. I enrolled in engineering, and Ken enrolled in industrial arts.

Originally, I was to be in mechanical engineering. I didn't like chemistry, but I did like mechanics. I thought electronics—other than transistors—was black magic. However, most of my second semester of physics dealt with electronics, and I really liked it. It was no longer black magic. So I changed my major from mechanical to electrical engineering. I thought I'd be able to pick up some technical information on transistors during those four years. I found out that there were no books yet approved for teaching transistors in college. It had only recently been invented, and no one was yet qualified to write a teaching book on the subject. So my education on transistors continued as a hobby.

There were a couple of happenings during the early part of my school year. The first day at lunchtime, I went to the cafeteria and picked a sandwich and something to drink. It came to one dollar. I said to myself, "I can't afford a dollar each day for lunch. So I'll have to eat a good breakfast to carry me over until I get home each day." This turned out to be a decision that affected my whole life. (I have never eaten lunch to this day.)

The other event related to a doctor at the University of Pittsburgh. Doctor Jonas Salk developed a cure for polio. I remember standing in line with several thousand students at the University of Pittsburgh and volunteering for polio shots, proud that someone from my school had made this tremendous contribution to mankind. In 1953, several hundred thousand people had contracted polio and had either become an invalid or died. Only three years later, polio was almost nonexistent as a result of the Salk vaccine.

During the school year, I got a part-time job in the atomic cyclotron at the University. I worked about four hours each day measuring atomic tracks that were generated by high-energy beams hitting certain materials and traces deflecting onto glass slides that left a track where the particle entered and ended in the glass. These atomic tracks were captured by the flight of these scatterings in and across the glass slides. The angle and length of the tracks provided information for the physicists about the material being bombarded. Each working student was expected to measure a certain number of tracks per hour. I got so good at measuring the tracks that I could spend half my time measuring the tracks and half the time doing my studies and still have more than my quota completed.

I got paid seventy-five cents an hour, which really helped out during the first year. I was receiving a monthly sum from the veteran's pay that was awarded to Korean veterans who went to college. Working cut down on the time I had to study, but I had good grades in everything except chemistry, where I carried a C.

When the school year ended, Ken and I went to Atlantic City to get jobs. I got a job as a swimming instructor at one of the large hotels, and Ken got a job bartending in one of the large hotels. I only worked a week and decided to try to get a job in the steel mills back home. I was paid well as an instructor, but the kids I trained were spoiled brats, and I couldn't stand being around them. I also wanted to see Peg, who had just graduated from a two-year college course at Thiel College in Pennsylvania. So I went back to Monessen to get a job in the steel mill.

I had no luck at the Monessen steel mill that summer, so I tried other places. Eventually I got a job as a laborer in the steel mill in Clairton Pennsylvania at $1 an hour. By that time, Ken was back, and he got a job there also. We were working in the open-hearth labor gang, and it was tough. I worked under high heat and kept saying to myself that I would work ten more minutes and quit. I worked the whole summer of 1955 that way.

Meanwhile, Ken had met Sherie Shutterly (remember Buck's Shutterly on the motorcycle ride out West during the depression?) from Monessen, and they were dating. I remember Ken came to me and said, "Guess who I dated?" and I asked him who.

He said, "Remember Sherie Shutterly, who used to have buck teeth when we were kids? Well, she was in a car accident and had her front teeth knocked out, and they replaced them. She no longer has buck teeth, and she's beautiful."

I laughed and said, "The Lord has funny ways."

Sherie was in nursing school while Ken attended the University of Pennsylvania at California (Located in California, Pennsylvania.) Sherie wasn't allowed to be married while in nursing school, but by summer's end they had run away and gotten married in Cumberland, Maryland. Sherie finished school the following year without others knowing about their marriage.

Meanwhile, I got to date Peg during that summer, and things were better than they had ever been. We went to dances every week and took in an outdoor movie every so often. We were made for each other. I knew she loved me now. Our romance had now become one of sexual pleasures and I realized that God must have created sex to show another how much you really love them. It sure beat kissing, although that was still a pleasure. It was interesting, I had spent three years and ten months in the Navy, and Peg was three years and ten months younger than me. The Navy time had prepared us for each other.

The second year of school started, and I worked at the steel mill in the evening. This was a tough schedule, since I had to drive thirty miles to school. When I got out in the afternoon, I drove fifteen miles to work. After four hours of work, I traveled home and studied a little during the week. I drank hot tea to keep me awake most of the time. On the weekends, I worked eight-hour shifts and spent as much time as I could with Peg.

Married to the Daughters of Sam and Buck

By December of 1955, Peg and I got engaged, intending to be married during my spring break in February of 1956. We felt that between the two of us working and my Veterans Korean benefits, we would do quite well and rented an apartment that was located between where she worked and where I went to school. We both had to travel about the same amount; me to school and her to work. Life was great. We got married on February 4, 1956, in the Lutheran church in Donora, Pennsylvania. The reception was at her parents' house in Monessen. One of the surprises at the reception was Ken's father-in-law, Buck Shutterly, spending most of the time with my father-in-law, Sam Pool., going over old times and the trip back west. The two men who had biked out to Denver in 1932 on Buck Shutterly's motorcycle were together again. They were quite surprised that each had one daughter, married to one of the Husher twins. So, even though this did not leave them related to each other, it was close. (Sherie and Peg became close and were to treat each other like sisters over the years).

Peg was the only child of the Pools, and Sherie was the only daughter of the Shutterlys. Through this marriage, Sam and Buck renewed a friendship that had begun years before. Sam was the superintendent of the wire mill of Page Wire and Steel, and Buck was the head electrician of Page Wire and Steel in Monessen. Each of them told stories to Ken and me about their growing up together.

My folks, Ken, Terry, my grandparents, and my aunts and uncles were at the reception and enjoyed the whole thing. My mother brought some of her homemade food to supplement the other goodies there to eat and drink.

Peg and her gown Feb. 4, 1956

Peg and Jay's reception

In the car on the way to honeymoon

As the evening wore on, Peg and I changed from our wedding clothes to everyday clothes. On a rainy night, we started for our honeymoon. Peg's uncle was a major in the Air Force and had invited us down to Cherry Point, North Carolina, to stay in the officer's barracks. We couldn't afford to go to a motel, so this was a great break. We drove through Cumberland, Maryland, and on to Cherry Point, where we stayed in a visitor's barracks for a couple of days. When we arrived, Peg started her monthly period. So, on the first night of our honeymoon, I went down to the receiving desk and talked to the woman marine on duty. I had to ask her where I could find some Kotex for my new wife. It was funny and not funny at the time. Peg and I laughed about it several times in later life. We found ways to get around that issue and still had a loving time. Being close to her was my dream from the time I first saw her walking up from the fair at Rostraver. It was love at first sight, and it stayed that way. We had a great time on our honeymoon. It was a break for Peg from work and a break for me from school and work. It relaxed us for what was ahead.

After the honeymoon, we went back to school, working and sharing a different time in our lives, sharing ourselves with each other. We rented an apartment that was located between where she worked and where I went to school. We both had to travel about the same amount: me to school and her to work. Life was great. Each day I couldn't wait to come home from work or school to be with her. Life was good.

Meanwhile, Sherie and Ken had been expecting their first child, and Lori Kim Husher was born at Charleroi-Monessen Hospital in the spring of 1956. We were at the hospital when she was born and couldn't believe how beautiful she was. We could see the excitement in both Sherie and Ken and how proud they were to have a healthy girl. Lori would bring them many happy moments in life.

The summer of 1956 was a tough one for me. I worked in the open-hearth labor gang of U.S. Steel in Clairton, Pennsylvania, during the whole summer. There were twelve open-hearth furnaces at this mill. Each could hold about 220 tons (440,000 pounds) of molten steel.

Working on the Open-Hearth Labor Gang

The open hearths were shaped like large cylinders with their ends cut off. Half of the cylinders were below ground, and half were above ground. The ends were closed and made up of firebricks to keep the heat in. The bottom half was below ground and provided the steel-making portion. The curved upper half served as a roof to retain the heat. The bottom half was locked down to a foundation made up of firebricks. The bricks also covered the steel frame that was above the work floor level, except for three large, hydraulically controlled doors on the work floor side. These doors, with quartz portal-like windows, worked off remote hydraulic systems to raise and lower them. The bricks on the bottom of the hearth pit were covered with dolomite stones, which were calcium/magnesium natural occurring stones, about one to two inches in diameter.

Below the furnace floor were the checkers. These served to take the ashes (mostly carbon) that were the residual of the flaming gas and molten steel, as well as reacting with the dolomite to form a slag. In front of the furnace, at the working floor level was a narrow-gauge train track that allowed dolly cars to pass in front of the furnace. When steel was first being made, the furnace was filled with about a hundred tons of crushed, recycled steel. It was mostly old cars that were crushed and brought to the front of the furnace doors in small, dolly boxcars riding on rails. These dollies were about five feet wide by five feet deep by twenty feet long, sitting on the train base perpendicular to the direction of movement. In this way, as they passed by the furnace, the ends were pointed toward the furnace. This made it easy for a charging machine to pick them up and shove the other end into an open furnace door. Once the charging machine had the box inside the furnace, the box was flipped upside down, and the load of crush steel was dumped into the empty furnace. The empty dolly was retracted from the furnace, and the next box was lifted, inserted, and dumped. This procedure was followed at each of the three doors until the furnace was filled with the required tonnage of crushed old steel. Later in the process, 120 tons of hot metal was delivered from the Blast furnace via an overhead crane, and was added to the melt via a large funnel that fit into the middle door. There were now approximately 220 tons of melt to be made into steel..

Where the melt meets the specifications required for that day, the first helper would shout, "This is close enough. Let's dump this thing." It was time to exorcise the melt to a huge ladle that sat low on the other side of the furnace. This ladle was about forty feet deep and thirty feet wide; it looks like a large cooking bowl. About five feet from the top of the ladle was a spout. Outside this ladle and next to the spout was another smaller ladle. This was called the slag ladle.

The first helper went to the microphone and called out, "Knocking the monkey on furnace number 7. Third helpers to furnace number 7. Clear the ladle side of all furnaces."

Almost immediately, the third helpers arrived at furnace number 7 and took hold of a long steel shaft that was about thirty feet in length and four inches in diameter. On the end of this shaft was a cylindrical steel head. It was about three feet long and had a diameter of approximately eight inches. The middle door was opened and closed in one movement, and the shaft was inserted and rested on the bottle sill of the middle door.

The first helper went to the portal window and viewed how the shaft lined up with the monkey—a clay insertion used to plug a hole on the far side of the furnace beneath the melt. He couldn't see the monkey, since it was below the surface of the furnace melt. He knew it was exactly in the middle, which was marked above the melt. He knew how far below the surface it was. When lined up to this mark, he raised his right arm, and the third helpers raised the long shaft, dropping the cylinder head below the melt on the far side. Then the first helper hollered out, "Charge!" The third helpers moved forward with a surge and, assuming the head was lined up with the monkey, pop the monkey out the other side of the furnace.

On the quiet side of the furnace there was a sudden explosion as the monkey flew out, and the hot, molten steel flew out in a lightning-like arch that extended to the ladle below. If there was any water left in the ladle, it exploded off this surface as the hot melt hit it. As the ladle filled, there was a coating of slag that formed on the top surface. This was the unwanted material that poured down the spout at the top of the ladle and into the smaller ladle beside it.

The 220 tons of hot steel began its journey through the other parts of the steel mill, converted into different forms of usable steel to be shipped to many parts of the world.

Labor Gang Repairing an Open-Hearth Furnace

I could go on to describe what happens to the steel after this point, but that is not my point of focus. With some familiarity with the furnace parts, my objective is to describe the work that a labor gang does on a furnace like number 7.

Each month, one of the twelve furnaces was put down and reworked. This gave each furnace eleven months of action, and then the furnace was reworked and the outside rebuilt to ensure efficiency over the following twelve months.

To prepare the furnace for rebuild, the train and its dolly cars were brought to the front of the furnace, and one by one the doors were opened and a dolly was lifted and placed inside the furnace with its open side up. This was continued until between ten to twelve dollies were inside the furnace. At this point, an overhead crane arrived, holding a large steel ball about eight feet in diameter. The ball was suspended above the furnace roof and then dropped. It crashed against the bricks that make up the arched roof. The ball was raised and dropped against the roof until the red-hot bricks began to fall from the roof into the dolly cars inside the furnace.

After an eight-hour shift, the roof had been completely destroyed, and the remains were inside the dolly boxes or on the floor of the furnace. Most of these bricks still glowed red from the heat they had been under day after day for about a year. Now the labor gang began its toughest task, which would last almost a month.

On the first day, the laborers would take steel bars that had been pounded into sharp blades and begin to hit the mortar between the bricks on the front wall. The object was to remove the first layer of bricks to get to the second layer of bricks. It was hot in front of the furnace, about 100 degrees Fahrenheit before this first layer of bricks were removed and the red-hot second layer was exposed. Now the temperature increased from the heat of the exposed bricks, and a laborer could only hit the bricks with the pry bars for a limited time (about fifteen minutes) before he ran out of energy from the heat and physical pounding against the wall of bricks. The laborers then moved about twenty-five feet from the furnace and were handed a piece of ice to chew and cool down. They would spend about five minutes cooling off, and then they would go back at it again and again. This went on twenty-four hours a day for about two days. As the first layer of bricks fell off, it exposed the bricks of the next layer, which were hot, and the temperature in front of the furnace was around 140 degrees. A worker was not permitted to work with any metal buttons on his shirt or pants, or he would sustain a burn.

A laborer could only spend about five minutes in front of these bricks before falling back for a piece of ice. On hot days, a bucket of water was dowsed on the laborer's head as he retreated from the wall. This continued for about three days on a twenty-four-hour basis.

The double layers of bricks were removed, and next came an even hotter task. Inside the furnace were the bricks that hadn't made it into the dolly boxes when the roof had been smashed. The laborers were given asbestos gloves and face shields. Special wood and metal shoes slipped over their own shoes that lifted them about six inches off the ground.

The laborers formed three lines: each in front of where the doors used to be, and now only a metal frame stood. The task was to run up to the doorframe and to rapidly leap onto the metal frame in one move, and then to leap inside the furnace with both feet to the furnace floor.

The laborers were now inside the furnace. They picked up bricks one at a time that surrounded the dolly boxes, threw them into the dolly boxes, turned, and jumped out of the furnace. They were only inside for about fifteen to twenty seconds, but all they could think of as they ran away from the furnace was how hot it was in there, and that they can finally breathe. They would flip the big gloves they wore, to the ground and ran awkwardly to the ice relief. At times, someone may have been waiting to throw a bucket of water on them, and then they were in line again to make their next pass at the 140 degree furnace.

This procedure went on until the foreman thought each person needed a break, usually after an hour. At that point, the laborers got a ten-minute break to cool off. They slipped off the extra six inches of hot boot that was attached to each shoe, but then it was back on with the shoe and back in line to take another rush toward the hot behemoth.

This procedure took about three days, and all the bricks were out of the furnace. The dolly boxes were removed the same way they were placed and carted away on the small train—still hot. At this point, the task that lay ahead was the hottest and loneliest of all the tasks in the rebuild. Usually there was a one-day break of doing other tasks before going to the next hot duty.

The laborers were led beneath the furnace in the cellar. At a point where furnace number 7 intersected the cellar, there was a round steel cover in the floor that looked like a manhole cover. The heavy metal manhole cover was removed, and the workers looked down a circular shaft that led to a floor about ten feet below. At the bottom of this shaft was a tunnel about five feet high and ten feet wide. The tunnel led about thirty feet to the checkers that collected the flue dust under the furnace.

A small wheelbarrow was on the tunnel floor, awaiting use. A ladder was dropped to the tunnel, and three men were sent down. The task of the three men was split into three parts: the lead person was to shovel the hot, black flue dust piled up in the checkers into the wheelbarrow;

a second person pulled the wheelbarrow to the ladder; and the third person scooped the flue dust from the wheelbarrow into a bucket that is pulled up, emptied, and lowered again. The maximum time the three could stay below was one minute, due to the high heat. The ladder had been removed during the whole procedure. The temperature in the dark tunnel and in the checkers was between 100 and 140 degrees Fahrenheit. Each of the workers had a mask and protective glasses over their face to keep the dust away from the eyes and from breathing it in. It was somewhat like being in a coal mine in West Virginia, but much hotter.

On one of these occasions, the first team of three laborers went down into the tunnel and immediately wanted out due to the high heat. A second group of three was sent down, and they were not in more than ten seconds and wanted the ladder dropped. Eventually, I was one of the three going down. I was on the wheelbarrow. I made the first excursion to the checkers, and the worker there cried that he couldn't stand it. I went back and told them to drop the ladder. The general foreman, Vince Brown, said, "Stay down a little longer."

I made a move toward the checkers with the wheelbarrow, and the man at the checkers was crying. I went back and hollered at the foreman to put down the ladder. Brown hollered for us to stay and get some flue dust first. I hollered back, "Drop the ladder, or, when I get out, I'll put a pick in your head."

The ladder was dropped, and the three of us made our escape. I hadn't planned to do anything more than get out and cool off. However, as I emerged from the hole, Brown said, "What happened? Did you get chicken?" I grabbed a pick handle and leaped toward Brown. The other workers grabbed me, and Brown told them to lead me to the superintendent's office. The super of the open-hearth operations was Gordon Strong.

The issue was described to Gordy, and we went back to the site of the incident. As we arrived in the dark cellar, the other workers were enjoying their time off and were sitting around talking. Upon our arrival they almost stood at attention. Gordy Strong had them lower the ladder and went below. He was back out within twenty seconds, and, as he got to the top of the ladder, he looked at Brown and said,

"If I ever catch you sending men into a hole that is that hot, I will see to it that you have worked your last day with U.S. Steel." He said this to a foreman who had been with the company for fourteen years. The temperature was approximately 150 degrees Fahrenheit without any air circulation to allow one to breathe.

That was the last time I was ever sent below to clean the checkers. Brown always gave me some other job, like working the hydraulic levers that raise and lower the doors in the front of the furnace. Cleaning the checkers was a long job and took about two weeks to complete. This was because of the conditions and the limited amount of flue dust that could be removed with each excursion. By the second week, the task became more routine, as the temperature cooled somewhat and the men got used to the tunnel. They knew it was a limited time, and then they were out of the hole for about four minutes while other groups of three went into the pit.

After the checkers, the next job was not so hot but felt hot because the work was more strenuous. The next job was to clean out the area between the large ladle and the underbelly of the furnace called the slag pit. This area would get slag and some runoff of steel during the filling of the ladle. By this time (approximately three weeks since the furnace was last used), the main areas of the furnace had been cleaned and upgraded, and the slag and metal had cooled and hardened in the slag pit. We had to go in with jackhammers and dynamite to clear out the slag pit. At any given time, there were three laborers using jackhammers to chip away at the steel. Sometimes large chips came loose, and these were picked up with a Cat (small caterpillar) and carried away.

However, most of this material was not that easy to remove and required holes to be chipped out of the metal with the jackhammers. Then dynamite was loaded in the holes, the area was cleared, and the dynamic was exploded. This chipping and exploding occurred twenty-four hours a day, seven days a week.

While this work was going on, there was the rebuilding of the furnace by bricklayers. They completely covered the steel framework with two layers of bricks, mortared just like a brick house. At the same time, the furnace bottom was rebuilt. At the end of this fourth week, the furnace and its surroundings had been cleared and rebuilt, and the furnace was ready for a preheat run. The preheat was merely the running of the heating gases as though there was steel being made. This heating fired the bricks and the mortar, resulting in a completely autonomous, sealed open-hearth furnace, ready for action.

Now that the furnace was completely checked out, it was time for the laborers to move to the next furnace that would receive the same treatment. This was a somewhat-depressing time, since we had just rebuilt a furnace and were left with the same arduous tasks that we had just left.

———————

Now that you have a feel for what type of work Ken and I endured while we were going to college, you can better appreciate our drive and motivation to better ourselves and our state of living, as well as improving the state of life for our families. It also provides one a picture of the amount of time and energy devoted to working, rather than studying. Later in life, I regretted the amount of schooling I missed and made a promise to help other students make their way through college. Eventually, I would find a way.

———————

Ken and I worked eight hours a day during the summer break. During school, I scheduled four or six hours a day during the week and eight hours each day on Saturday and Sunday. This usually added up to between thirty and thirty-six hours a week. Since the Clairton Steel Mill was located about twenty miles from our schools, we also spent a considerable amount of our time traveling to work or to school or to home at night.

A Chance at Being a Junior Electrical Engineer

But my luck was about to turn. After my junior year at college, I heard there was an opening for a junior electrical engineer at the Monessen Steel Works of Pittsburgh Steel. I applied for the job.

The day I went to be interviewed, I found fourteen applicants outside the chief engineer's office. I didn't know what number I was going in for the interview, but there were others before me and after me. It was an interesting interview. The chief engineer of Monessen Steel Mill was John Peth. He was around sixty with a gruff, loud voice. I handed him my application, and he told me to take a seat. He glanced at me and through my application. He then looked up at me. He gazed at me for a second and then said in the gruff voice, "This says you are working at Clairton in the open-hearth labor gang. Is that correct?"

I answered in the affirmative. He laid the application down on his desk and said, "Anyone who has worked in the open-hearth labor gang for this long and didn't quit can work for me. You have the job."

I could have jumped for pure joy. He was quiet for a few seconds and said, "My oldest son graduated from high school and didn't want to go to college. I got him a job in the open-hearth labor gang. He worked there for one week and phoned me and said he wanted to go to college. He said that he sure didn't want to work in the labor gang. He has a degree in chemical engineering. I had the same experience with my younger son, and he now has a master's degree in finance."

So that was how I got my last job in college. From a laborer to a junior engineer was like going from hell to Heaven in one day. That was what going to college buys you, and it sure beats the alternative.

College and a Little Rough Going for Ken

Peg and I rented an apartment in Whitehall, which was only about eight miles from where Peg worked and about the same distance to school for me. It was great having our own apartment away from other people in our lives and going though the stages of being a married couple.

It was fun being married and living with Peg in our rented apartment. Love between two people cannot be explained. Each day seemed like a new experience. We met many young people around the area and sometimes had time to have some fun between work and school.

Peg was working at the Westinghouse plant that designed the first atomic submarine in Large, Pennsylvania. We had fun watching our black and white television and making love several times a week. I was in heaven.

A funny thing happened one week. I visited my mother and Pap, and my mother made Halupkies, which are cabbage leaves rolled tightly around a mixture of ground hamburger, ground pork, and rice, all cooked in a tomato sauce. When I was leaving, my mother gave me a large quart jar full of them to eat during the school week.

When I got to the apartment, Peg asked me what those were and I told her. She said, "I don't like cooked cabbage." I thought that was unusual, since she was not picky about what she ate. I told her that was OK and that I would eat these for the next couple of dinners at home. I rationalized that this would relieve her from having to feed me for the next couple of days. Anyhow, I went to school the next morning, then to work, and then home. On my way home, my mouth was salivating thinking about those Halupkies. When I got home and looked for the large jar, I couldn't find it. I asked Peg where the Halupkies had gone. She said, sort of sheepishly, "They looked good, and I was hungry. I thought I'd take a bite before making something for myself. They tasted so good I couldn't stop eating them."

I laughed out loud. "You sure don't like cooked cabbage!"

After that, she called my mother and found out how to make them. She cooked these each week for about two months, and they tasted just like my mother's. Peg was not concerned about cooking something new and went about perfecting the food that she enjoyed. This trait carried on through our married lives, and everyone who came to visit us went away saying how good the meal was (and it wasn't always Halupkies).

I finished my second year at Pitt with good grades and began to work my second summer in the steel mill labor gang. At the end of summer, Ken came to me and said he had to quit school. He said that Sherie would have their second baby in October and that he couldn't afford to raise a family on the part-time job he had in the mill. It bothered me, and I went home and said to Peg, "Let's make sure there's no baby while I'm going to school." I felt bad about Ken and Sherie and wondered how they would get along. This was just the beginning of their married lives, and without a college degree I didn't know if Ken could rise above being a laborer in a steel mill. So Peg and I took precautions to avoid pregnancy until I got out of school.

This went on until the summer of 1957, and in July Peg said she was pregnant. I was happy, since the baby would be due about the time I would graduate with my electrical engineering degree. The summer of 1957 I also started my new job at Monessen Steel Mill (Pittsburgh Steel), so I had two things to be happy about: a baby Husher and a job as a junior engineer instead of working in the labor gang. I would have a more controlled work schedule and could be home with Peg. Life was good.

Junior Engineer Experiences

Working as an engineer was a revelation. Here, I could think. My first job was to go around the whole steel mill, search down the electrical wiring, and ensure it was correct on the steel mill drawings. Mr. Peth wanted to bring those drawing up-to-date. Some had been lost, some were never made, and he wasn't so sure the ones we had were accurate. This left me free to roam around the mill and acquaint myself with the operations while doing the job I was being paid for. I was making $2 an hour, just double what I had been making in the heat of the mill.

I had many experiences in the mill, but the one that sticks out the most occurred in the autumn of '57. I was in the wire mill checking out the wiring in the roof.

This job now provided me the opportunity to roam to the different parts of the steel mill and see how things progressed as the left the open hearths I had worked in. Metal poured out the back of the open hearth into a large ladle. From here the metal was poured into tall steel molds on a small train. The molds were about 20 feet high and five feet by five feet in cross section. Each was railed through heat soaking pits to anneal the steel and then sent to the rolling mill. Here each was released from it's mold and deposited on a large rolling mill and were carried back and forth through large rollers (like your mother when she took rolling pins over pie dough) to spread out the metal to a thickness of about four inches. From here they went to a rod mill where the steel was cut into long rods. These rods were either shipped out or sent to the wire mill where each was pulled through reducing dies until they reached the dimensions of wire they wanted for that day's production. This wire was either sent out in large spools of wire or some were sent to the nail mill to make nails of different sizes. Some of the large bars were sent to the Allenport Mill down the river about three miles to have them rolled into sheet metal. This was sent to places like Detroit where it was used to stamp out the body parts for various cars. So, from used old cars that were initially used to make the steel came these finished parts that ended up in new cars or were used by other factories to produce other demands by the world's market.

The making of wire in the wire mill is quite interesting. Rods come from the rod mill. They are about two inches square and twenty feet long. They are still a little red from the heat of going from thick steel sheets to rods. The rods go through rather small electrical furnaces and arrive rosy-red at the wire mill to be drawn into wire of various gauges. The brilliant red rod is drawn through a set of dies and reduced in diameter as it goes from one set of dies to the next. This is repeated until the rod is about as thick as a number two pencil. By this time this thick wire is about a hundred feet long and continues being drawn through smaller and smaller dies. Now, if you were to watch the operation, as I did one day, you would become mesmerized by the beauty of it.

The wire is now down to about the double thickness of the lead in a pencil and glows red with heat. In this state, it goes through the final set of dies, like a long piece of spaghetti.

It makes its way down a set of dies for about fifty feet, and a wire thrower catches the wire with long tongs and directs it into the next smaller set of dies that carry the wire back and parallel from which it came. If you were to view it from above it would look like a weaving motion with the wire getting smaller and smaller as it made its way through this set of dies. At the end of the first string of dies, the wire actually flies toward infinity, but the wire catcher grabs it with a set of long tongs and loops it around and redirects it back from which it came and into the next set of dies leading away from him. This forms a red-hot loop of wire that extends from the end of the first row of dies to the beginning of the next set of dies. This next set of dies may be the last set, depending on the thickness of wire specified for that day. If so, a machine cuts the wire at a given length, and it continues through a cooling medium prior to being spun onto spools. If the wire is to be made smaller, it continues on its way and is eventually led to another double die loop as before, and it continues its red-hot path and another wire catcher will swing the loop through the air and back to the direction from which it came.

This wire catcher has a potentially hazardous job swinging this flying loop of hot wire back into the second set of dies. He must catch it, or it will fly past him toward a steel wall. The catcher must push a foot pedal to stop the wire being drawn through the dies.

As I was in the wire mill checking the wiring in the roof, I made my way along the steel walkway that passes the catcher. I looked through the safety glass and admired the beauty of the work. I made my way past the point and began to open a steel door when I heard a high-pitched whirling sound. I turned and ran six feet, but where the catcher had stood was now vacant.

The wire was wrapped around a steel pole, and the catcher's shoes had flown off and his safety hat was still rattling along the steel floor. The wire had crushed him and cremated him all in one motion. The red-hot wire had slipped from the catcher's tongs and whipped through the air, taking him with it as it spun around the steel pole. I leaned over against the wall and emptied my stomach. This was the worse thing I had ever witnessed. Even so, the year I worked in this position was very educational, providing me with experience on motors, generators, wiring, switch gear, transformers, machinery, and wisdom from a very informed group of senior engineers.

Second Child Born to Sherie and Ken

Sherie gave birth to their second girl in mid-1957: Gaye Lynn Husher. Peg and I were at the hospital to see her on her day of birth, and she was a chubby little thing that was bigger than Lori and just as cute. They said this was the last child for a while, since two girls puts a load on Sherie's time and on Ken's budget.

"We shall see," I joked. "Sometimes that head between your legs has other ideas." They laughed and commented that love couldn't be stopped, but the results could be delayed if you were careful. It was hard for me to see Ken with two children and me still going to school to learn how to earn a living. I would go home and hope that they could handle things financially. I always worried about Ken, and now I had Sherie to also be concerned about—plus two nieces. Our family had grown!

As I entered 1958 and my final semester of school, I was excited about my future and what was in store for Peg and me and our new child to be. I knew with my experience that I would be able to pick the place I would work after school. Finally, I was going to have a good financial base. That drove me through the end of my naval experience and through four years of school. I wanted a house and a yard like Aunt Marguerite and Uncle Ferd had. I was to soon find that this personal drive might also spell the end of that dream.

Early in 1958, I began the final semester of my schooling and the final quarter of Peg's pregnancy. She was due in April, and she looked more beautiful than ever. Her blue eyes looked bluer, and from the rear view she didn't even look pregnant. She continued to work as a secretary at Westinghouse in Large, Pennsylvania, not far from our apartment. So between our paychecks and the military benefits for attending school, we were doing quite well and could afford a washing machine and dryer in our apartment.

Take a Lower Paying Job/We Have Our First Child

It was during this time that I began to interview with various companies for a position after graduation. By March, I had received offers as an electrical engineer. This began a period of anxiety for me that ended in the hospital. In early '58, the offers for graduating electrical engineers ran between $8,000 and $10,000 a year. With my experience in the steel mills and my self-taught knowledge of transistors, I was being considered for jobs in steel mills, as a field engineer for electrical power installations, and in electronics. The offers for the electronic positions ran between $9,000 and $10,000 a year, while at the same time, the particular offer of interest was as a field engineer with Westinghouse at $18,200 per year. Both were good pay for that time. If anyone bought a home in Monessen for $10,000, they were considered rich. Only doctors and lawyers owned those kinds of homes in Monessen.

———⁓∿∾·◌⌒◌·∾∿⁓———

To give the reader a frame of reference, Doctor Jonas Salk was paid about $3700 a year while developing the Flu Vaccine at the University of Michigan and then accepted a position at the University of Pittsburgh around 1950 where he developed the Salk Vaccine for Polio with a salary of approximately $7000 a year.

———⁓∿∾·◌⌒◌·∾∿⁓———

Each day my mind was torn between the obvious: take a job I was best suited for with the highest money or go into electronics where my experience was nil—my only experience was reading about transistors. Here I was, a young man who had grown up wanting a job that paid good money, and it was within my grasp. This is what I had lived for—to be somebody and to be able to afford the better things of life as I saw them. This was the best financial offer received by any of the graduating engineers in my class, including mechanical, electrical, and chemical engineering graduates. The offer was almost double what others were being offered, probably due to my experience in the steel mills and some maturity gained from the Navy.

As I drove, my mind gravitated to this decision. Should I go to the position that paid the most or to a position that revolved around my present interests?

Late in March, while studying in the library on the seventh floor of the engineering building, my head sagged onto the table, and I couldn't lift it.

Immediately, I thought, "My heart is not beating faster, my breathing is normal, I can remember everything I have read, I know what day it is. What's the matter with me?" My schoolmate sitting next to me asked me what was wrong, and I told him I couldn't lift my head. He said he would go tell the librarian to call the hospital, and I told him to wait a while. After about five minutes with no progress, he went and told the librarian.

Soon, I was in the hospital. They checked me out for the next several hours. After all the tests, a doctor asked me if I had been under a lot of stress lately. I explained the various things that were going on in my life: work, a baby, school graduation, and the job offers I had received.

He said, "You're worn out. You have to quit the job you have, or you won't see graduation in June. You're headed toward a nervous breakdown. Make a decision about your future and get on with it."

This struck me hard. I couldn't walk without falling, and he was warning me that I might not be able to reach the goals I had longed for all my life. He called Ken to come and get me. For the next two weeks, I spent the days in bed at Peg's parents' house. Peg called my work and told them I had to quit due to a medical problem.

Peg's family doctor came to the house, examined me, and asked a lot of questions. During the examination, he looked in my ears and said he was prescribing a nose spray because he saw something tilted in my ear during the examination. This could cause the dizziness and the balance problem, and a nose spray would relieve this. The nose spray arrived, and I was able to walk two hours later. However, I would be dizzy for the next year each time I turned my head too fast or turned my body too fast, but I ignored this and went about my business.

The first day I was able to drive to school, I saw a payphone. I pulled the car into a parking lot, called Westinghouse, and turned down the field engineer position. I called Bell Avionics in Buffalo, New York, and accepted their position as an electronics engineer in their components group. A big weight had been lifted from my shoulders.

On April twenty-fourth, Peg began her labor pains, and I drove her to the hospital in Charleroi. Each time I hit a bump, Peg moaned. When we got to the hospital, they took her away, and I sat nervously waiting. Then Peg Pool, my mother-in-law, came into the waiting room to keep me company.

After about an hour, a nurse came out and asked if I wanted to be with Peg. I said yes. I was taken into the room where she was lying, and her body was convulsing. I saw the muscles in her neck strain against the pain. I could only stand it for about half an hour, then I walked out of the room and asked her mother if she wanted to go in. She asked why. I told her that Peg was in terrible pain, and it made me hurt. "There's no sense in both of us being in labor," I said.

So Peg's mother went in. The labor lasted eight hours. Jay Durbin Husher was born on April 25, 1958, exactly forty-five years to the day that Sam Pool had been born. So it was easy to remember both of their birthdays, and we would celebrate them for many years together. I was breathless and excited. Peg was all right, and I had a son.

Two weeks after our son was born in early May, I had completed all my studies and took off for Buffalo and Bell Avionics. Peg and JayD. were to stay with her parents until I could find a place for my growing family to live. I didn't have time to attend my graduation. My BSEE diploma was sent to me by mail in June 1958.

6

The Twins Enter the Industrial World

An Electrical Engineer with Bell Avionics

Bell Avionics was an interesting place to start my career. It was the home of the designs of the fastest planes in the world. The Bell X series and subsequent developmental jet aircraft were designed and evolved here. The breaking of the sound barrier occurred with the planes designed here. When I arrived, they were working on an experimental aircraft call Dyna-soar. This evolved over time to the shuttle aircraft that would circle the globe and return to earth many years later. Unlike other satellites, it would land like an airplane and be used over and over.

My initial job was in the components group. Here, various components for use in the electronics of Bell's aircraft were tested and characterized. After passing certain high-temperature testing and life testing over 1,000 hours with successful results, the component would be placed on the qualified list of parts available and on the qualified vendor list. Some components were rejected as a result of the tests while others qualified, and the vendor, along with his product, was placed on the qualified vendor list.

It only took two months for the management of the components group to realize that I had a better understanding of solid state components like transistors and diodes than any of the older engineers and technicians in the group, and I was made supervisor responsible for the testing and qualification of all solid state elements (transistors and diodes). It was exciting to be recognized for my hobby more than my formal education.

Meanwhile, Peg visited Buffalo, and we looked for a place to rent. After about a week, we found a home with an Italian older couple. They had a big house and rented out the two upstairs apartments. Peg liked the place because it had a separate entrance, and the place was very clean. You could smell Italian food all the time, and it reminded me of my neighbors growing up. Peg took Jay in his stroller for walks each day. She met nice neighbors, and I met people our age at work. It didn't take long for us to make friends and to share our evenings with some of them, playing cards and other games or sharing a light dinner at our place or theirs.

It wasn't long before the snow in Buffalo became an obstacle. It would snow a foot overnight, and Peg and Jay would be snowed in, beginning in November. I went to the cellar and began to build a wooden sled. Since it was for an infant, I made a chair with arms like a baby's high chair, and screwed it onto the wooden platform. The sides of the sled were made of solid wood that curved up in the front to a hole on each front side to hold a rope for pulling. The bottom of each was sanded with fine sand paper to provide a very smooth surface. This was followed up by staining and varnishing the complete sled to make it waterproof. Then a cake of soap was run back and forth over the bottom edges to make them slide easier. I kept the sled small, only big enough for a young boy, so that it was easy to carry in and out the house.

When I went to work each morning, Peg spent time cleaning, and she would go out with the sled and Jay. She met many neighbors and their kids during these excursions and took pictures of Jay on the sled and the neighboring kids playing in the snow. Every couple of weeks, we had the pictures developed, and I got to enjoy them with Peg before sending some of them back home to our parents.

The work with Bell didn't last long. During that first winter, there were several work strikes by Bell's hourly employees. To get to work, I had to go in around 4:00 AM to avoid the picket line. Then I got a paycheck, and it was shorted. I went to the financial office, and they told me that I must have been late: anything between zero and six minutes lost one tenth of an hour in pay. I told them I worked more than forty hours every week, coming in often on the weekend to finish something I had been working on. I was a professional. As a result of this conflict, in early 1959, I decided to find a position with a company that was more professional. I was paid by the hour, and it became difficult to perform one's function under these conditions. The conditions being that I felt as a salaried person I should get a salaried pay. Also, I worked many hours over the normal quitting time, so I didn't expect for them to pay me on a forty hour week and drop pay for being late one day. We looked through the *New York Times* advertisements for engineers. There were many openings across the country. I finally sent my resume to three companies and was interviewed by all of them and offered a job with each. The one that stood out in our minds was the one in Youngwood, Pennsylvania, which was only twenty miles from my hometown, with Westinghouse and their Semiconductor Division. They made power transistors, power diodes, and power silicon-controlled rectifiers, and they offered me a job as a test design engineer. I had been interviewed by Doctor Herb Henkle, who was head of engineering and development in the Semiconductor Division. He was impressed with my knowledge of semiconductors and my energy level. So my hobby made a decision for us, and away we went. This would prove to be a remarkable decision.

Ken and Family Go to Argentina

The following section is pieced together from discussions I had with Ken or letters I received from Ken or Sherie from 1959 to 1962 to the best of my recollection. As such, they are my paraphrasing of those events.

Early in 1959, just before starting to work for Westinghouse in Youngwood, Pennsylvania, Ken came to see me. He said he had accepted a job to go to Argentina and work for Koppers, a German firm. They were going to build coke ovens and establish a coke byproducts plant there. Ken's five-year experience working as a laborer and being promoted provided him good experience and insight for this type of job. He felt it was his chance to break away from hard labor and become a salaried professional.

Ken and his family would be in Argentina for about three years. I asked him why he wanted to go , and he said, "Gort, I've done some neat things to improve the coke oven efficiency here by increasing their output with changes made to the ovens. I told engineering for a year that I knew how to improve their efficiency, and they finally tried it and it worked. They asked me how I knew to do this, and I told them I went home and made cardboard models of the ovens and figured out some improvements. They asked me where I had learned to make patterns with cardboard. I told them I took a course at California (Pennsylvania) State Teachers College on pattern making. Anyhow, an opening came up, and they didn't give it to me. They think I am too young at twenty-seven. So I'm going to Argentina to get more experience, and then maybe someone will eventually give me a shot at one of these openings."

I told him I could understand his feelings, but what about Sherie, Lori, and Gaye? He said they had talked it over, and they all agreed that this was a chance to gain experience for something better in the future. The timing was also good, because neither Lori nor Gaye were old enough to go to school. When they came back in 1962, Lori would be ready for school, and Gaye ready for preschool. So off they went in late 1959.

I went to the airport when Sherie, Ken, Lorie, and Gaye were to fly to Argentina—with a couple of stops in between Pittsburgh and Buenos Aires. Their first stop was New York City, which turned out to be the main flight. They left New York on a cool, autumn day in October on a propeller-driven plane—there were no commercial jet flights at the time—that took thirty-six hours to get to Argentina from

Miami. Ken carried a rifle on the plane, since he didn't know what he would get into down there, and he wanted to hunt. When they arrived in Buenos Aires, they began a real adventure, because hardly anyone spoke English. Fortunately, enough Americans had traveled that way for a vacation or had taken residence there, that the locals learned enough English for them to make out at the eating places and grocery stores.

Koppers had purchased a fairly large area for houses to be built to house the new team arriving, mainly from the States. There were also several Japanese who joined this experienced team of experts, all there to build a plant from the ground up. Ken, Sherie, and the two girls stayed in a small hotel for six months while their house was built. The hotel was located only two blocks from the Pink House, where the President of Argentina resided.

When they arrived they were so tired that they didn't mind the hotel and were just happy to be "at home" so to speak. They were tired from the long journey, from the excitement, and from the feeling of being "strange" in that new and foreign land. They just wanted to lie in bed and get some rest,. But rest wouldn't come immediately. as they spent the good part of a day unloading what they knew was needed for their hotel stay.

They also spent most of the first day meeting other Americans, along with their wives and children, who were housed in the hotel and who were part of the team of experts, along with their wives and children, who had arrived earlier. Buenos Aires and the local area are at latitude that is the same as southern Australia or northern New Zealand, and therefore they were surprised at the temperature when they arrived. They had left Pittsburgh in the beginning of the fall season, when the days were getting shorter, and in Buenos Aires it was spring, and the daylight hours were getting longer. It seemed like the perfect time to come to Argentina. They packed their winter clothes and pulled out their spring/summer wear.

They had shipped their refrigerator, dryer, and Hi-Fi system because Ken had heard these things were hard to come by in the area. They had also shipped their Opel station wagon, knowing that the roads were narrow. This small car would be ideal for transportation.

Ken was smart enough to find out before leaving home what was lacking. Some of the things they were short of in the area were air-conditioning, refrigeration, and Hi-Fi systems because they did not have the right voltage and power available. He found a transformer that worked off fifty cycles (instead of the sixty cycles used in the states) and could transform the frequency and voltage at the compound to the right voltage needed for a refrigerator, the washer and dryer, and the Hi-Fi. He had it sent to the barrio (the name of housing area where the management team would be housed) before leaving the States.

The transformer was there when they arrived, but the other packages came before the completion of the house they were to live in. The station wagon was there, and it was a happy sight. It just fit his whole family, but it was ideal for the small roads around the area. On the second day, they drove out to where the plant was to be built. An American came to meet them at the hotel, and after eating they drove out to the site of the steel mill, located outside the city of San Nicholas, which was about a four-hour drive from Buenos Aires, sort of out in the wilderness.

While they were living in the hotel, Ken went to where their house was being built and worked on hooking up the transformer and making everything ready for the day when the house would be finished.

Finally, after four months, their house was complete. It was a three-bedroom ranch house, which was common with the Americans there and provided by Koppers. This area of new homes was called a barrio, and all the homes were owned by Koppers and assigned to each family. Their home was built on a half acre and had a nice backyard for the kids to play in. Ken worked on the house the whole time he was there, making it more like their home back in the States. He started a garden and grew things they couldn't buy easily at the local fairs. There was no heat for the house, and it got cold in the wintertime (June, July, and August), so they traveled to Buenos Aires and found little heaters to heat the place.

The cooking stove had no temperature gauges on it, and Sherie burned a lot of meals until she found how to adjust the heat. She learned where the low, medium, and high were on the knob settings. Naturally, when they moved into the house, one of the first things Ken did was hook up the refrigerator, the washer and dryer, and the Hi-Fi (high fidelity which was the state of the art in record music playing at the time). Then they turned on the Hi-Fi, and the whole family danced around as the music played, and the refrigerator turned on and began its first cooling at the Husher house.

They were not the only ones to have a refrigerator in the area; the other Americans also thought ahead and had these types of things shipped to them. Having these pieces of equipment would prove to be invaluable while the family lived there.

While grocery shopping, everything was purchased in kilos (instead of pounds). One kilo was 2.25 pounds, and everything was wrapped in paper—even jelly—since there was no aluminum foil or paper bags to hold the food. In 1959, Argentina was about fifty years behind the United States when it came to almost all consumer items—no canned or boxed food.

The climate also made it a great ambiance for bugs and other small creatures. Sherie had to sift worms out of the flour, and those she didn't get out with the sifting she let float to the top of the water when cooking pasta.

When they bought beef, it was fresh off the hoof. It had to bleed for a few days before they could eat it. They only bought pork in the winter due to lack of refrigeration in the stores and for transporting the pork. Beef was bought at the butcher's, and flowers and vegetables were bought at the fair on Saturdays.

Ken found a Japanese store that had celery. He had to order it a week in advance. A stalk of celery cost more than a whole filet of mignon. There was a great deal of beef available but no ground beef. Ken built a grinder for Sherie to grind up the beef for hamburgers and other things. There was no soft bread. The big meal was at noon, so Ken had to work his schedule so he had an hour for lunch so he could drive home and sit down for dinner.

If you wanted to have chicken for a meal, you picked out a live chicken and they killed it for you. Chicken was the most expensive food to buy. Most people had to have the chicken killed the same day they ate it, since it would spoil rapidly without refrigeration. Fortunately, the Hushers and other Americans had a refrigerator. It was exciting to do something as mundane as filling your refrigerator. She was tickled when she had filled it. This had never excited her back in the States, but here it was a novelty. Nothing was refrigerated in the area, and the local people bought what they needed for that day and hurried home to put the meal together, or they went out into the local wilderness and shot their food for that day.

Eggs were green because the chickens ran wild and ate garlic and anything they could find. Not only were they not the same color as back in the States, they didn't taste the same, and the texture was tougher. Eventually, Sherie and Ken talked a farmer into caging chickens for them, and all the Americans took turns driving the twenty miles for fifty dozen eggs to be divided up by the American community.

Sherie actually had fun with her Argentine neighbors. She showed them around the house. Ken and Sherie were the youngest American couple, but this never deterred them from mixing with the others and making friends. For entertainment, since there were no drive-in movie theaters and no movies on TV, the Americans and some of the other expatriates had dances in their homes. The carpets would be rolled up, the Hi-Fi went on at the Hushers' house, and dancing began. It was like having a small hometown where everyone knew everyone else. Everyone knew what was going on with the others. It was a difficult to determine what they could make to feed their guests. They had to think several days in advance—due to the lack of selection or the lack of keeping it good—but they found a way to enjoy what they had. But their way of living built confidence in them every day.

Ken drove to the site of the steel mill and coke plant. The design for the steel mill had been completed twenty years before, and all the equipment had been ordered, arrived, and set in crates for eighteen years. The steel mill had been planned just before World War II, and the war had started about the time the equipment was being shipped. This left a large amount of equipment that hadn't arrived at the site until after the war. It was a sight to see all those huge crates sitting around and stacked on top of each other and looking very weathered.

Only recently had the local companies begun to uncrate them and started to assemble the huge parts that would made up a steel mill. This was to be the first steel mill in Argentina.

Argentina was a Communist country, and there were many soldiers walking around the perimeter with machine guns over their shoulders. The same was true at their home. It was odd for them to see two soldiers walking around the perimeter of their house with machine guns—ready for something; they knew not what.

There were a lot of things to do in that rough and wild environment. The hunting and fishing were great. There were no limits, and they could do either all year long. Ken went with several of the other team members and a few locals to great fishing sites: rivers, brooks, and if he wanted to make a four-hour trip to the ocean, he could fish there. Hunting was the same. Ken could drive two miles from home and hunt.

Both of these sports were well attended by all. Some only liked to fish, others only to hunt, and some did both. They were guaranteed to catch something in abundance in either of these ventures. Ken went along and wished his kids were old enough to enjoy it. Sherie didn't like to hunt or fish, but she was always excited to see what Ken brought back from his hunt.

Fortunately for Ken and the other team members, Koppers had ordered the coke plant equipment over the past two years. Some of it had arrived, and other pieces were arriving each day. So there were not many crates setting out in the elements, and only a few soldiers patrolled the perimeter of the soon-to-be coke plant.

While the coke plant would be built by Koppers on contract for the local company, the steel mill was contracted locally to many small companies in Argentina. They had begun building the steel mill just before Ken had arrived. He had found it interesting to watch its progress, but had been happy that he wasn't involved in that portion of work. The workers walked around in the steel mill malaise in their rubber thongs and with no helmets to protect their heads. There were no safety rules or signs.

Ken would ensure these mistakes wouldn't happen at the new coke plant. He would get them safety helmets and safety glasses, but the footgear was hard to come by. He would make them at least wear leather shoes to protect their feet. Ken knew a lot about the operation of coke ovens, but that was his first experience with building one from the ground up and putting it into operation. Thus began three years of this new and interesting experience.

Coke is essentially produced by burning coal at very high temperatures under certain controlled conditions where air is not allowed to contact the coal. This results in a material that looks like porous coal that is silver in color and has a lower density than coal.

Coke, when burned in this form, provides a much hotter gas output than coal and is used in blast furnaces and open hearths to make steel because of this higher-heat capacity. The byproducts of the coke-making process are derived from processing the gases that escape during the coke-making process.

As the basic coal burns and the temperature increases, the gas coming off contains different constituents, which are separated off at higher and higher temperatures. At even higher temperatures, other constituents can be separated off. Further processing these exhaust gases results in tar, benzene, toluene, xylenes, and naphthalene's, all valuable byproducts with many uses. Some people might think of the coke as the prime product of this operation, but others probably think the byproducts are more important. There is no doubt they all play a part in our in one form or another.

Although the building of the coke plant was managed by Koppers management team, the actual work was done by the locals under supervision. Workers came from as far as fifty miles away to work at the site each day. Some found tents they could live in, while others found trailers they could drag to the general site. These were poor conditions compared to the standards people live and work by in the States.

However, they find the work and pay there to be better than any they could find elsewhere. They were happy campers. Ken was paid a salary that allowed his family to live above these levels and with things they had not experienced before in the States. Before many days in the new house Sherie had a maid that took care of the kids and cleaned house. She was there every day except the weekends. If Ken and Sherie wanted to go somewhere on the weekends, they took the maid along like one of the family, and she helped with the two girls.

Altogether there were about forty members of this Management Team and their families. A few were from Japan, one from Germany, two from Spain, and the majority from the States.

Right off, Ken decided that Sherie and he should learn as much Spanish as is needed to get along around the area and when they went to the big city of Buenos Aires. Each weekend was exciting. Sometimes they took the kids and went into the high forest areas with beautiful views. It was fun to find fruit-bearing trees that were growing wild. They would stop and have a little picnic, eating cut-up portions of the fruit and some cheese they had brought with them.

Back at home, Ken worked on building a go-cart that he would race against the other members of the barrio, sometimes winning and sometimes losing. He worked on his go-cart in the evenings to pass his time, changing the steering or pepping up the small engine. He was a kid all over again, but this time he could afford things.

The work on the coke plant was exciting and included reviewing the blueprints for the foundation, erecting the steel structure that made up the skeletons of the large ovens, installing the high-temperature bricking that made up part of the structure, and the pouring of a special concrete-like material for some of the walls that took high temperatures. Day by day, these things came together, and the coke plant began to rise. It was beating the steel mill construction, which was OK, since they needed to have coke when the steel mill was ready to begin production.

After two years, the basic structures of the coke ovens were completed, and it was time to test out the structures. The ovens were lit up. The flames began to bake the inside of the systems. It was important to soak these bricks and the mortar that held them together in a high-temperature environment so they could reach the proper strength while maintaining their integrity at high temperatures. This baking was done gradually until eventually the highest temperatures were reached.

There were problems with some walls cracking as these temperatures rose, and they had to be demolished and rebuilt. They found that they would have to repair these walls with a slightly different compound. They had learned that a better material was available that could hold its integrity through temperature changes day after day, time after time.

This newly poured internal wall was allowed to harden for a week before the gases were turned on again, and the walls were baked at a low temperature for several days before the temperature was raised to the next level required to properly anneal these bricks. Eventually it was time to increase the temperature to check the system out again.

This was a nervous time for the workers. It took two days to get to the highest temperature, and then they backed off for a day and took it back up to temperature. This temperature cycling was done to create cracks—if any were to be created—with the hope that this wouldn't happen. This was the final test before inserting coal to be turned into coke. After each cycle, the supervisors (Ken was one of them) waited a couple of days and then went in and checked every inch of what could be checked.

After a week, they were confident they had met their requirements. They had singing, dancing, and wine to celebrate, and the bottles were passed around with a great exuberance. They knew the structure could take the temperature cycling.

The coal came from local mines and was one of the few materials indigenous to the area that related to the production of coke, thus insuring a continuous supply of the raw material as needed. This was probably one of the reasons the steel mill and coke plant had been built at this location.

Several months passed, and the day came when they charged the systems with coal and performed its primary function. Several small loads of coal had been introduced and processed over the preceding months to optimize all functions, and the day approached when they would fire up a full load. People came from miles around. The president of Argentina was there, and all the families of the consultants were given a tour. It takes time to make coke, so the process was initiated well before the banner event in order for the Americans to demonstrate the finished product.

Just like clockwork, coke was pushed out of the coke ovens when the president finished his speech. There was a big roar from the audience. At this point the coke was too hot to hand around, so some of the previously processed coke was passed around for the audience to see.

Ken even got goose bumps as he felt the energy of the crowd. And then the wine was passed around in small containers so the audience could be included in the celebration.

Sherie had brought the two girls. They were now four and five years old and joined with the Americans parading through the building. At times Sherie had to lift the girls over a small stream of molten steel that came from the steel mill adjacent to the coke plant. Among the splendor, it was crude in places.

Ken thought about the extreme levels of the technology he was witnessing—going from steel essentially leaking from the steel plant to the shiny and beautiful pieces of coke coming from his plant. He had learned a great deal during the building of this edifice, and there was still much to learn. He had to stay for about five months to teach new workers how to run the equipment and how to schedule the various materials needed to insure continuous operation and output of the plant.

The last five months in Argentina were exciting for the family. Ken was involved in teaching and debugging the operation for new hires. They had to train new hires to work on a three-shift basis. They also had to select workers (who had already proven themselves over the past six months) to be elevated to foremen to take over the day by day operations when the consultants left the site at the end of their contract.

Most of these selections worked out well, but a few had to be replaced. Some who he thought would never be able to cope proved they could, and other promising ones did not make the grade. It was hard to calibrate how people would perform when they were left to the task.

Those last five months were interesting from a work standpoint because problems Ken hadn't known how to handle as a laborer or a supervisor in the States became solvable. Having seen the system built from the ground up, he could now relate problems to some physical element he had seen go into the bowels of this system. Being able to relate to cause and effect was beneficial. It was the first time in this profession he had this advantage, and he was one of few wise enough to absorb this great lesson.

Those last six months were exciting for another reason: Sherie's father had had a massive heart attack, and she had had to return to the States with Lori and Gaye six months before Ken's contract was up. They were all excited, including Ken, because they were to fly back on a commercial jet.

The time came for Ken to see them off, and there was mixed feelings at the airport. The girls couldn't wait to see the grandparents they had hardly known and who they had a hard time remembering. Lori had been three and Gaye two, so they were now returning as a six- and a five–year-old. Lori would be starting school, and Gaye would start preschool.

They were excited because they knew they had changed a lot and would surprise their relatives. They knew a few Spanish words and could talk some Spanish between them while everyone looked on in surprise. On the other hand, they wouldn't see their dad for six months, and that part they didn't like. Sherie would miss the house they had lived in for two and a half years but would be glad to get back to civilization and be warm in the wintertime. She knew it would be awful without Ken. She would miss him every moment they weren't together. Of course, Ken would miss them terribly. It would be quiet and lonely around the house without them. The next six months without them made him long for them more each day.

Finally, the six months had passed, providing him with some exciting moments as problems popped up and left him with additional experience. The day arrived, and Ken was more than ready. He was excited to go back and use what he had learned, but he would miss the open wilderness. He had enjoyed the fishing and the hunting. He would miss the nearness of these sports and how you could go from working amidst the hardness of a Coke Plant or steel mill to the complete wilderness of the area in less than an hour. Or vice versa, go from the complete wilderness of being out in the brush to being in a shower and ready to go to the plant in no time.

He also would miss the plant where he had gone from seeing what had transformed from dirt to a complete new plant able to perform many functions. He knew that plant better than he knew almost anything. He would miss it, but he was excited about what the future had in store for him. Things would be different.

Fortunately, he did not have to sell the house since it belonged to Koppers, but he had to bring in locals to pack up the things to be shipped back to the States. Then they would have to look for a new home. These are the challenges all consultants (called ex-patriats since they did not give up their U.S. citizenships) face when they leave a foreign country and return to the States.

Returning, he flew in a jet, and it took six hours to fly to Miami with its sandy beaches and clean-looking buildings. He returned to Pittsburgh in September of 1962, ready to face the fall season just as when he had left.

I was working in Youngwood, Pennsylvania, and drove to the airport to meet him when he arrived. Ray Shutterly, Sherie's brother, was also there to drive him to Sherie's parents' home, where they were to stay until Ken determined where he was going to work.

I was surprised to see Ken come off the plane with slightly graying hair. He had at least achieved this I thought. He now looked old enough to hold high-level jobs. I couldn't hug him enough, and tears ran down our cheeks. I had seen the kids several months before, and I was surprised at how much they had changed. And Sherie looked great. I had worried about them the whole time they were gone, and now they were all safely back, looking the better for their venture into a foreign country.

Westinghouse—Youngwood, Pennsylvania:
My Invention without a Patent

I started at Youngwood in March of 1959 and began designing a tester to determine the power output of Westinghouse's highest frequency transistor. I was only there a couple of months when the engineer in charge of the engineering development line left. Dr. Herb Henkle promoted me to supervisor of this fabrication line, against my protestations. I told him chemistry was my worst subject in college and that this line required deep knowledge of chemistry. I told him that I didn't even know what water was composed of. But he was impressed with my knowledge of transistors and how to make them better. He told me to give it a try, and, if after several months it wasn't working out, he would replace me. This became one of the most productive times of my life. Each day became a learning experience on managing and learning how to make transistors.

Now, the fact that I didn't eat lunch began to pay off in wonderful ways. During my lunch hours, I experimented with the power transistors from the main production line. These devices were made on silicon wafers that were an inch in diameter and twenty thousandths of an inch thick. The silicon wafers had gallium diffused two microns deep (25 microns equals one thousandth of an inch, so the diffusion was only about one tenth of a thousandth of an inch deep) on the top surface, which eventually served as the p-type base of the transistor.

The base and emitter were made up of rings of doped gold alloyed into the top surface. The base ring was boron doped (p-type) and made ohmic contact to the p-type gallium, and the emitter ring was antimony doped (n-type) and was alloyed into the gallium and formed an n-type region that was the emitter of the transistor. These appeared on the top of the silicon wafer and a gold Antimony plate was fused to the bottom of the silicon wafer and represented the collector.. The emitter supplies electrons toward the collector, and the base determines how many electrons are supplied. The collector receives these electrons. With very little change in voltage and current on the base, it releases 100 to 1000 times as many electrons to be used by the collector in the form of current and the load it drives. An analogy is water flowing in a pipe from one point to another, controlled by a valve, which can be closed to stop the water flow or open and allow the water to flow at a higher rate, or the valve could be partially opened to allow some portion of water to be released.

One of the engineers and I wanted to know if we could get four transistors on each wafer—if we could somehow make a shallow cut through the gallium and two gold rings on this upper layer to isolate four islands of gallium diffusion and the gold rings from each other. Hopefully, this would separate the base and emitters on the surface with a common collector for the four transistors on the bottom of the wafer. If this worked, we should see four transistors each having different characteristics than the original transistor.

During the lunch break, I went to the machine shop and got a piece of stainless steel an eighth of an inch thick that was two inches square and milled a tenth of an inch groove through the material in the form of a cross, one and a half inches long and one and a half inches wide. I hoped this would provide a mask so that I could sandblast a cross through the thickness of the gallium layer and the gold rings on top of the power transistors and divide it into four independent transistors.

By placing the metal sheet on top of each of the four power transistors wafers that were taken off the production line, I could experiment on sand blasting the cross in a groove in each of the large transistor through the gallium layer. It took several lunch periods to complete this sand blasting on the four large transistor wafers with the hope of ending up with sixteen transistors remaining on the four, one-inch wafers. A visual inspection showed that a groove was cut through the gold and gallium, but now I had to test to see what I had.

Each of the quadrants was then tested. The excitement I received as I measured each of the quadrants was indescribable. One by one the quadrants responded with a good transistor—sixteen quadrants on the four transistors resulted in sixteen good transistors with characteristics that were similar to the large transistor but at lower currents.

For example, where the large initial transistors would have gains of about 50 at currents of 2 amps and 20 volts, these would have gains of 50 to 100 at currents of .5 amps and 20 volts. Each lunch period, I wrote notes describing these results in my patent notebook. There was an interesting side benefit of this procedure: not only did I have four isolated transistors, but the gallium layer had a sheet resistance of 200 ohms per square. I could use these to make resistors. The junction between the gallium and the silicon gave me a diode that could be used as a capacitor.

But, where to now? What could I now use these four transistors and resistors on a wafer for? Being the only electrical engineer, I had an advantage. I realized that I might now be able to connect the four transistors and resistors to form different circuit functions. I thought about the various combinations I could connect and the resultant function I expected from these circuits. I could also see how to form resistors, diodes, and some small capacitors within the wafer. But how would I interconnect them from one to the other?

At the time I had read where Bell Labs (inventors of the original transistor) had developed a method of wire bonding gold wire to various metals on transistors, such as gold and aluminum transistors. I went to Dr. Henkle and asked him if he could purchase some 2 mil (two thousandths of an inch in diameter, compared to a human hair, which is about 7 mils in diameter) gold wire so I could try to replicate the bonding described by Bell Labs.

At this time, gold was not legal tender, and one had to have a legitimate need for its use. It had to be ordered through federally-controlled warehouses that maintained the material. In addition, we had to keep perfect records to account for all the material purchased. The material was ordered and placed in a safe. Each day the gold wire was issued, it had to be weighed as it was withdrawn and weighed again upon return. An entry had to be recorded in a book as to the amount used and the use.

Meanwhile, I got a record-playing machine, and some glass capillaries (like the ones used in hypodermic needles), some hypodermic needles, and during my lunch hours I began to build a wire-bonding machine with the help of some of my friends in the machine shop. The gold wire was fed from spool of wire on top, like tread is fed from a spool on top of a sewing machine, and fed down through the capillary ready to be used as thread on a sewing machine. Meanwhile, alongside of the end of the capillary, was a hypodermic needle that had been hooked up to a source of hydrogen nitrogen gas. The gas flowing through the hypodermic needle was ignited and a sharp flame was sent out about a quarter of an inch in length. This served as a sort of mini- torch to cut the gold wire when a foot switch was released. Before any bonding was done, the foot switch was released to cut the end of the gold wire. This caused a gold ball to appear on the end of the wire. This gold ball was the part to be bonded to the transistors. Its size was about twice the size of the hole in the capillary holding the gold wire and prevented the gold wire from being pulled back from its original position. I practiced hitting a spot on some scrap silicon power transistors. At first it didn't bond to the gold metal on the transistor. After changing the temperature and the pressure several times, I finally got gold wires to bond on a regular basis.

When a bond was made, the position of the capillary was moved to where the end of that wire would be bonded. This movement pulled additional wire from the gold wire spool on top of the machine, just as thread would be pulled from the spool on a sewing machine. Once bonded, the foot switch was activated, and the hypodermic torch cut the gold wire, leaving a wire stitched from the first location to the second. Meanwhile, the cutting action of the torch formed a new gold ball on the end of the wire and awaited the next bond to take place. Using this method, wires could be bonded from one position on the wafer to another. This was a crude bonding machine, but it served my purpose. Soon after, the mechanical engineering group would make an elite machine.

The gallium that had been diffused into the surface of the original wafer and formed the base for the power transistor resulted in a sheet resistivity of 200 ohms per square. I found this could be used to form resistors. By placing apiazone wax over the area where I wanted a resistor to be and etching away the gallium diffusion on the unprotected portions, individual resistors could be formed in the protected areas. Since the resistivity was 200 ohms per square, I could form a resistor with the value desired by having the wax cover an area that was the length divided by the width times 200. An example would be apiazone wax being placed that resulted in the length being five times the width, and I would get a 1,000 ohm resistor. Now I not only had separate transistors on a wafer, but I also had separate isolated resistors. Prior to the transistors being made on the production line, I had them pull several wafers and place gold dots at positions on the wafer where I knew I would be forming these resistors. These gold dots allowed for wire bonding the resistors to other places within the four transistors on a wafer.

I spent each lunch hour etching resistors into the various places and bonding resistors to transistors to form different circuit functions.. Here my education as an electrical engineer really helped. I was schooled on circuits and their functions, whereas the people around me were chemists, chemical engineers, physicists, and people schooled in materials and processes. Every evening I thought about the different electrical functions I could form with my transistors, resistors, diodes, and some small capacitors. Then I went to work, and during the lunch hour I connected the circuits to form these different circuit functions.

For example, by using the common collectors of two transistors and wiring the emitter of one transistor to the base of a second transistor and wiring the emitter of the second transistor to ground and placing a wire on the base of the first transistor to serve as an input terminal, I ended up with a three-terminal device just like a transistor. However, instead of having gains of 50 like each of the two transistors, I now had a three-terminal device that had gains of 2,000. I wrote these results in my patent notebook. I called this circuit a "common collector, common emitter" device. (Later an engineer named Darlington would make this a common device that was commercially available called a Darlington transistor. If Westinghouse would have recognized that it was the same as one of my devices described in my patent notebook, they could have had the patent and retained royalties for its use).

Every couple of days there was a different function that I described in my notebook. I was able to tie many combinations of resistors and transistors together and then measure their functions. Typical circuits were an audio amplifier, and a video amplifier.

My Chips for Our Space Satellites

One afternoon, Dr. Henkle came down to where I was working and said, "I hear you've been doing some interesting things during your lunch hour. Have you been entering them in your patent notebook?" I told him I had, and he asked for my notebook and away he went.

He returned during work and pulled me into his office. He commented on the fact that our government was concerned that the Russians had put up a large satellite, and we didn't have the large rockets required to do this. So they wanted private U.S. companies to find ways of making circuits without the use of large transistors, large inductors, and large capacitors, and they were calling them microcircuits.

They would provide money for research on ideas that promoted the reduction of circuit size and weight. He said that Westinghouse Air Arm Division in Baltimore had been awarded millions of dollars to work on these unique approaches. He got really excited and said, "I'm going to call Arnold Palmer and see if he'll fly you and me up to Wright Patterson Air Force Base in Ohio tomorrow. Arnold is a friend of mine, and he has his own airplane. He flies out of Latrobe, Pennsylvania, Airport, which is only a few miles down the road."

A few hours later, he called me to his office and said that Palmer couldn't go but he would loan the plane and a pilot to take us to Wright Patterson in the morning. The next day's flight was quite interesting. Dr. Henkle kept exclaiming to me that the circuits I had done were just what our government was looking for.

We arrived and went to a meeting with the high-level people at Wright Patterson. Herb got up and explained how "Westinghouse had been working on a program to reduce circuit size and complexity. The approach is a monolithic (all function on one piece of silicon) approach on silicon, and Westinghouse was calling them function electronic blocks—FEBs." This was interesting to me, since Westinghouse didn't have a program on developing this approach. It was done personally by me on my lunch hour. I also was surprised that he gave the approach a name that I had never heard before. They were highly interested in his discussion, and they all had a great respect for Dr. Henkle.

On our flight home, Dr. Henkle couldn't contain himself. He told me that what I had done was wonderful and that he bet the military would give us funds to generate circuits via this method.

A couple of months passed and, sure enough, Westinghouse Youngwood was awarded a substantial amount of money (millions of dollars) to proceed on the development of these monolithic circuits called Functional Electronic Blocks. A new building was built behind the present building and was called Westinghouse MED (Molecular Electronics Division - my personal work had created a new Westinghouse Division.), and the search began to hire engineers, physicists, and material scientists to pursue this new electronic thrust. The program, awarded by Wright Patterson was to develop a 300-megacycle, triple-conversion transmitter/receiver for the military using the FEB approach.

Life would never be the same for anyone, as will be seen over the next forty-five years. Almost all circuits would be made using these techniques of putting the whole circuit on a single piece of silicon. They would be called integrated circuits or "chips" and all new computers would be dependent on these chips for their design. Things would improve on a continuous basis and these chips would be ubiquitous. Westinghouse did not get the credit due it. A fellow engineer at Texas Instruments and another at Fairchild would receive credit for inventing the integrated circuit. They did their work at the same time I was doing mine. The one at Texas Instruments didn't even invent monolithic circuits. His approach used many individual bars of silicon wired together to form a function. The one at Fairchild had written a paper on the use of oxide as a mask to form circuits inside silicon and monolithic circuits, and a circuit on a single piece of silicon had not been generated by Fairchild at the time Westinghouse's Monolithic devices were working. I had actually made circuits in a single piece of monolithic silicon.

Shortly after that Fairchild made some neat digital circuits using the oxide masking method in a monolithic approach. I hadn't even submitted our monolithic devices as patentable devices to the Westinghouse patent department, since I thought it was obvious what I had been doing. So here was a significant invention that was never submitted as an invention. The making of monolithic circuits at Youngwood, Pennsylvania, was never recognized for its major contribution toward the space program, and they never received a patent for these original circuits I had described in my patent notebook. Early in 1961 Dr. Herb Henkle died of a heart attack, at the age of thirty-nine, or he would have contested these others as the first integrated circuits. I would say that Fairchild should have received the credit due them in that their approach of using oxide as the mask for defining the various components in integrated circuits was more efficient and easier to manufacture than the way I was etching circuits. In 1960 we were using oxide masking (in place of our wax method), to generate our FEBs.

—————✦∿∿◦∿◦✦◦∿∿————

Later, in 1961, we started calling our circuits, integrated circuits (ICs) to conform to the accepted name. The industry that grew out of these developments was called the integrated-circuits industry, and it created a completely new form of electronics to form functions at lower power, higher complexity, and lower cost. The integrated circuit, or chip as others called them, became the major technical invention of the century.

As 1959 and 1960 progressed, Westinghouse gathered a great team of scientific people to work on these new techniques. We used the oxide masking technique introduced by Fairchild to define the various devices within a circuit rather than the slow method of using wax to mask areas; and hired engineers to develop optical techniques to form the various circuits. New approaches were invented that the industry still uses to this day. The approach pursued by Westinghouse was to use devices made using epitaxial, n- type silicon deposited on the p-channel silicon-starting wafer. We felt this would provide superior device characteristics.

This was later proved correct, and Texas Instruments and Fairchild changed to this method in 1962 and 1963. A buried layer (we called it the floating collector) was invented by Dr. Bernie Murphy, who Westinghouse had hired in 1960. He had written his doctorate thesis on gallstones and knew nothing about transistors when Dr. Henkle hired him. However, he read about them on the boat over to this country, and, in a couple of months, he was ahead of most people. His patent on the buried layer was excellent, since it was diffused in the Silicon prior to the epitaxial growth and served as the collector rather than the bottom of the wafer. This resulted in the high voltages of the epitaxial approach with the low collector resistances provided by this buried layer. Originally, the use of phosphorus as the buried layer didn't work well because the phosphorus diffused too fast and flooded the whole transistor instead of retaining its position.

Later, in 1960 or early 1961, Paul Kisinko and I introduced arsenic as the buried layer, and this proved to work quite well. I patented many of the things I discovered, but many I took for granted, including this use of arsenic for the buried layer. Soon, I invented the sinker that connected to the top surface to the buried layer, lowering the collector resistance as well as providing a place to bond the collector on the top surface. Still most, if not all, of the techniques are still used in making today's chips, such as the epitaxial layer, the Sinker, the Stopper Diode, the Buried Diode, the Gold-Stopping Diode (lifetime diode), which was used for pulling charge out of digital circuits to help turn them off; were my patents, along with Murphy's Buried Layer and are used in bipolar chips today.

During the development of a bipolar transistor approach for the 300-megacycle triple-conversion receiver, I gained patents on many circuit functions, including oscillators, AM detectors, FM detectors, tuned amplifiers, automatic amplitude control, automatic frequency control, IF amplifiers, Video amplifiers and many patents that were later replaced by improved versions that other engineers invented.

In 1960, Westinghouse began building a new building for MED

near Friendship International Airport in Maryland to house the growing division. It was to be completed in 1962 and would be made up of four buildings. Meanwhile, I was made the supervising engineer for the development group at Youngwood, and we were making great strides in developing ICs with higher gain and higher breakdown voltages.

Dr. Henkle hired Dr. Bill Hugle and his wife Frances, also a PHD, to learn how we make the circuits and to start up a development line in a new location at Caneo Park in Southern California. The Hugles worked about six months at Youngwood before heading out to California. During those six months, they were supposed to learn what I knew about ICs. There was a cartoon that appeared on the bulletin board showing the top of my head being lifted and Frances Hugle picking my brains. It was a time of great excitement.

We began development of NAND digital circuits for Univac of Minneapolis for use in the high-speed computer they were developing. Here again, my education as an EE paid dividends. I understood their needs and helped develop new, faster methods for forming their digital circuits including the use of push-pull output devices. Univace was the first computer company to design a computer around integrated NAND logic.

The First IC Radio/Dr. Henkle Dies

One day, Dr. Henkle came to me and said the president of Westinghouse was going to come to the plant the following Tuesday, and he wanted to know if I could make something special for his visit. I told him I could make a complete single-conversion radio receiver made up of several FEBs. He didn't think I could do that in such a short time, since it was Wednesday and only five days till his visit.

The next day, I figured out how I would do it, and Toti Unotso (a young Italian doctor of electrical engineering, who Henkle had hired the previous year) said he would work with me to complete this. We worked all day Friday, Saturday, Sunday, Monday, and got finished early Tuesday morning—all without leaving the plant or getting any sleep. Between adrenaline and hot tea, we stayed awake.

Meanwhile, they were putting an antenna on the roof. We hooked it up, and the radio operated as it should. I could dial in stations by changing the voltage applied to the circuit. Then I told Dr. Henkle I had to go home and sleep. He couldn't believe I wouldn't stay for the demonstration to the President of Westinghouse. I left, drove about five miles, pulled over to the edge of the road, and fell asleep. I drove almost home and had to pull over, and I fell asleep again. I finally made it home on the third try.

On Thursday, when I went in to the plant, Henkle came and saw me. He said, "The president loved the small radio. He said to mount the chips on a small board, and he would have another division make a beautiful chrome radio case for it. The speaker was three inches in diameter and much bigger than the receiver, and it was beautiful. The president of Westinghouse had the radio passed around the company to show what could be attained with this new technology. This was the first integrated radio receiver built.

And then Dr. Herb Henkle died of a heart attack at age thirty-nine. Here was our leader—gone. Westinghouse searched around for a replacement and hired Harry Knowles from Motorola in Phoenix, Arizona. Knowles had made a name for himself at Motorola in power transistors. Knowles was made vice president of MED and began to hire people from Motorola and the West Coast.

For a short time, this resulted in a form of demotion for me since Knowles thought the Univac line could be better produced at the California facility. However, within months he gave me a phone call from California and asked if I could make the Univac digital circuits at Youngwood. I said I could. I felt that digital circuits were much easier to produce than linear circuits. This proved to be correct. My team of people at Youngwood provided Univac with their circuits, which eventually was called the Westinghouse 200 series.

Family Life – circa 1960

Meanwhile, Peg and I were building a new house not far from the Youngwood plant. I had the GI Bill and was able to obtain low-interest loans to help pay for the house. Peg and I were also expecting a new child in the family. We moved into the new house in March of 1960 and our next child—a girl named Karen Lynn Husher, was born on June 12, 1960. What a fantastic day: not only did I have a son but now a daughter, who would grow up to be beautiful woman. A man couldn't ask for anymore.

We knew the baby would be born around June, so Peg stayed with her parents in late May. After a week, I also began to sleep there since I missed Peg. When the labor pains began, I wanted to take Peg to the hospital, but she said the doctor had previously told her to wait till she showed blood. So we waited and then rushed her to the hospital. The baby came so fast that the nurse almost had to deliver her, but Doctor Kregor arrived just in time. Afterward he asked, "Why did you wait so long?" I told him about waiting to show blood, and he said, "That's on the first baby. On the second one, you get them to the hospital as fast as you can." So that was a good lesson for me.

My mother had always wanted at least one girl because girls were closer to their mother than boys. Even after girls get married, they stay close to their mother. Well, I was happy because I had a beautiful daughter that Peg would have close to her for the rest of her life, and me too.

It was great fun for us to have a house of our own, and Peg and I worked to make it even better. Peg had an unsaturated amount of energy, and needed it with Jay being two and Karen a baby. She continued to work on the inside of the house. My love for her just kept growing until it was ready to burst. I thought she was the most beautiful woman I had ever seen and was always proud to take her to company functions and show her off. She was also easy to please, not caring about having the latest in clothing and such. She was more interested in things for the children and the house. I would see a dress in a store window, pick one her size, and bring it home. She would try it on, and if it fit she kept it, and if it didn't I took it back.

By Christmas of 1961, I had paneled the downstairs family room, and we had a big Christmas tree surrounded by gifts for Jay and Karen. Their eyes lit up as they came down the stairs to the family room. I have pictures of this that remind me of how great it was living in our first house and how much fun the kids had.

Later in 1961 Peg was with child again. Our third child, David Todd Husher, was born on April 7, 1962. During the week of April seventh, I pleaded with Peg. "Peg, you can't have the baby this weekend because the Masters Golf Tournament is on, and I want to watch Arnold Palmer win the tournament again."

Saturday came, and about 3:00 PM Peg said she was feeling a discomfort in her stomach. I had a neighbor watch Jay and Karen, and I took Peg to Doctor Macdad's office. and he sent us immediately to the hospital. We arrived in the Greensburg hospital about ten minutes later, and there was a woman waiting with a wheelchair. We ended up on the fourth floor, and they took Peg into the delivery room. As she was going in, Doctor Macdad asked, "Do you like pizza?" to which we nodded. He said he would have the nurse order one.

By this time the golf tournament was on, and I looked to see which floor had a TV so I could see the results—not expecting Peg to deliver for a few hours. I found the TV on the third floor and watched for about ten minutes. I was ready to go back up to the delivery room when a nurse called me. I asked her if Peg was still in the delivery room, and she said, "No, your wife has delivered and is in her room." I couldn't believe it, and I rushed to the room. There she was looking pretty good. Peg was so happy, that she didn't have to go the long hours it had taken to deliver Jay.

David Todd Husher was born on April 7, 1962. Palmer won the Masters championship.

The nurse who had met us at the entrance with the wheelchair came in to see Peg. She said, "When I saw your wife coming in to have a baby, I said to myself, 'This young girl thinks she's going to have a baby today. She isn't going to have a baby any more than I am.' I was surprised when I heard she had already had two and had already delivered the third."

Just as she was saying this, the doctor came in with a pizza. Peg, the doctor, the nurse, and I each had a piece. I said I had better go and see how the kids were at home.

Later, when I came back, the lady in the next bed said, "I can't believe your wife. I've been in here for three days, and I have no appetite. Then I see her eating a pizza, and a little while ago I saw smoke coming out from her bed, and I said to myself, 'That woman can't be smoking a cigarette already.' I pulled back the curtain, and, sure enough, there she was smoking a cigarette."

"I joked, "that's because she was hungry, and after eating she always smokes a cigarette."

The lady didn't think this was funny.

My Devices Accepted for the Apollo Program

In 1961 I heard that MIT Lincoln Labs was in charge of selecting suppliers for the Apollo Program to put man in space. I made arrangements to go to Boston and visit the MIT personnel in charge of the program. Dave Hanley headed up the program, and Jane Partridge was in charge of quality and reliability for the program. I went to Boston to convince these people to use Westinghouse as the supplier of ICs. Dave Hanley told me that many companies had been selected previously and were later dropped because they couldn't meet the requirements. "Why is Westinghouse in a better position than Sylvania, Philco, RCA, Transitron, General Electric, and others? The only one that's qualified is Fairchild."

I told them that the method we used for making integrated circuits was better than any of them, including Fairchild. Fairchild's method of fabricating ICs was inferior to ours. They used a triple diffusion process that had low gain, low breakdown voltage, high saturation voltage, and were subject to noise. I asked what I needed to do to qualify as a supplier and was told that if I came back with packaged triple NOR gates that outperformed Fairchild's and they passed quality control, Westinghouse might be qualified.

I called back to the plant at Youngwood and talked to Chuck

Smatlack, who was the technician who laid out the designs, and told him how to lay out a triple NOR gate using our technology. I described the design rules and the critical dimensions with a process like we were doing on Univac.

Two days later, when I got back to the plant, the design was finished, and he even used my initials in the middle of the design. The metal interconnect was shaped as JH. We worked twenty-four hours a day processing the wafers with this triple NOR gate design.

Seven days later, I phoned Dave Hanley and said I have a triple NOR gate that was better than any other supplier. He scheduled me in two days later. I took ten packaged triple NOR gates for the meeting. This was an exhilarating meeting, one of the most exciting events in my life. Dave, Jane, and I sat at a conference table with about eight other individuals. Jane took the devices from me, gave them to a technician, and told him to put them on the curve tracer, see how they look, and come back with the information. Meanwhile I discussed the design with Dave Hanley.

About twenty minutes went by, and the technician came back and whispered something in Jane Partridge's ear. She got up and went out. About five minutes later, she came back and whispered something in Dave Hanley's ear. He got up and went out. Five minutes later, he came back and said, "How did you make those devices? They're phenomenal! They have high gain at all currents; low leakage, high breakdown voltage, and they're matched one to the other."

I told him that the method Youngwood used was a buried layer epitaxial approach, and the devices were isolated by a diffusion that only had to go through the thickness of the epitaxial layer. This meant we had gains of 50 to 70 from low current to high current levels instead of Fairchild's gains of 15 at low current levels. This gave us breakdowns of 25 volts instead of Fairchild's 5 volts. The saturation voltage (which should be as low as possible) was only 30 millivolts instead of the 750 to 1,000 millivolts of Fairchild's devices. The leakage was low because of the superiority of the overall process. Jane Partridge said she would put the devices under high temperature reverse bias life tests to see how they stood up. She would get back to me on the results.

Two months later, Westinghouse had the biggest contract for supplying the NOR gates to the Apollo Program. This was a great victory for Westinghouse, and for me personally.

The introduction of the method used by Westinghouse to produce the NOR gates for this program put pressure on all other suppliers of integrated circuits to develop new processes and techniques to allow them to compete with the Westinghouse method. The low breakdown voltages of the Fairchild and TI type process would no longer be tolerated. Other suppliers would no longer tolerate the limited gains over limited operating currents. The leakage currents at low operating voltages would no longer be tolerated. Our circuits had set a new standard.

The reason Westinghouse had not been recognized prior to this was due to their work on analog-type circuits (ARC 63 radio receiver for the military) and the circuits being demanded for many military and satellite programs were digital in nature. So the digital suppliers had a higher profile. This changed, as we began to supply these NOR logic circuits and the Univac broad range of digital products. Soon Texas Instruments (TI) would convert their process to an epitaxial method with the floating collectors (later to be called buried layers – as were initially developed by Westinghouse.. The floating collectors patented by Bernie Murphy at Westinghouse would be the standard for all bipolar circuits.)

Not only was this method used for the satellite programs and other military uses, but it began to find its way into many industrial, commercial, and consumer parts. Westinghouse's higher allowable voltages and superior operating functions allowed all electronic manufacturers to view this approach as a better way then tubes or discrete transistors to perform their functions.

*** *Added on February 2021* ***

After graduation from the University of Pittsburgh,Pa, I went to the Westinghouse Plant in Youngwood Pa. that made Germanium Power Transistors. I was there only a short time and the Vice President and General manager moved me to head up the Advanced Development Department of the facility. He said, "You know more about transistors than anyone in this plant" This shocked me since there were at lease 50 engineers in the plant that made transistors for a living.

I had stopped eating lunch in 1954 while attending the University since I couldn't afford the cost and I continued this on this job. During my voided lunch hour I ran different materials such as Boron, Phosphorus, Antimony on Silicon wafers at temperatures above 1100 degrees centigrade for varied

times and later cross sectioned them to determine the depths of diffusion versus time (a profile) Then during my lunch hours , using Gold wires to connect different points of the transistors points of the transistors, I connected what I felt were capacitors and resistors and different transistors to make a Video amplifier. I continued doing these rather simple circuits and one lunch hour Dr. Herb Henkle, VP and General Manager came down and asked what I had been doing. I told him. He said "Do you realize our government is trying to put a satellite up in the air to compete with the Russians. The Russians have a more powerful means of injecting a satellite and our small satellites cannot hold the equivalent electrical equipment that theirs does so they are looking for a means of reducing the size of our circuits so our small satellites will contain the equivalent or greater content then theirs. The method you have developed will do it for our country. "I am going to call Arnold Palmer and ask him to fly us to Wright Patterson Air Base in Ohio to present this method to them" He left and came back about an hour later and said "Arnold can't make it but he will have his pilot fly us there tomorrow morning,"

On the flight to Wright Patterson I completely discussed all the things I had done on profiling and making the Video transistor circuits to Dr. Henkle.When we got there there were about twenty five high level government people and he presented the method that Westinghouse had developed. They asked many questions and we answered them and they were impressed.

On the flight back to Pennsylvania Henkles was all excited. He said "watch what they do now". He was right; they transferred thirteen million dollars from the Westinghouse Air Arm Division in Baltimore to the Youngwood Pa. facility with the directions to develop a 300 megahertz video integrated amplifier and I would provide them a monthly report each month on the progress. (I mention this since I did this in 1959 before Fairchild and Texas Instrument ever made a single chip integrated circuit.)

As progress continued on this I took things even further with these people.

In 1961 I heard that MIT Lincoln Labs was responsible for selecting suppliers of Single Chip Amplifiers for the Apollo program. I went up there and met with Dave Handley who headed up the program and Jane Partridge in charge of Quality Control and Reliability for the programs. They showed me a Fairchild Circuit with three MOS devices on it and told me if I could do better than their circuit I would have a chance.. I immediately called on the phone to my plant and described the device I wanted the Layout Man to do. When I arrived back at the plant two days later he had it laid out these devices and the metal connecting the three MOS circuits formed my initials on the device "JDH".

We worked 24 hours a day to produce the chip. In eight days I called Dave Handley and told him I had the device that was better than the one they presently have. He told me to fly up and hey would review it. When I got there I was escorted into a room where Dave Handley and Jane Partridge and several other people were present. I had brought ten packaged devices with me and Miss Partridge gave them to a technician and told him to go and check them out on the Curve Tracer Tester. We talked for a while and soon the technician came back and whispered something in Miss Partridge's ear. She looked excited and went out and soon they came back and said, "How did you do that?" They had found it hard to believe. I told them I had developed a new and better method for making integrated Circuits. I used a "floating collector" (patented by our Burnie Murphy). This was placed on the p starting material at selected places where Collectors of the Transistors would be. An N type Epitaxial layer (invented by Westinghouse) was deposited on the wafer (thickness varies based on what is needed on the circuit being fabricated) , an isolation mask was used followed by etching , and an N type material (Phosphorus) was deposited for the emitter and the topside collector (a first by my group) contact such that when the emitter was being diffused into the base the topside collector would diffuse rapidly through the N type epitaxial layer and make contact with the floating collector. This allows our devices to have topside contacts for Collector bonding later in the process and no other company has this capability in their devices. It also had a Silicon Oxide gate oxide that other companies did not have yet.

The advantages of this approach are many. The Fairchild method gave a gain of five, a breakdown voltage of six , a Vsat of almost a volt; whereas my device gave a breakdown of 50 bolts, a gain of 50 to100 and a Vsat of millivolts - all much better than anyone in the industry at that time. Later in 1962 -63 Fairchild, Motorola and Texas Instruments went this way for their amplifier circuits.

This basic approach is still considered the optimum approach for driving analog circuits.

The Apollo circuits were accepted by MIT and we made them at Youngwood Pa. until the Westinghouse Baltimore Semiconductor operation took the job over.

February 25 2021

As indicated in my presentation, I made this single chip circuit in 1959-60 during my lunch hour.

In 2011 my circuit was recognized as the first Silicon integrated circuit in the world- before Fairchild Semiconductor, Texas Instrument or Motorola had done theirs. They have had all that glory for 52 years as being the first.

In 2012 The University of Pittsburgh awarded me the Distinguished Alumni Award (DAA) for my contributions and a Dinner was provided in my honor along with four other graduates on February 12 2012 in honor of this award.. I am proud of that award and it rests on my kitchen wall a home.

In addition the Epitaxial process with the buried layer and topside collector contact was decided to be used by most semiconductor companies and is still used on most integrated circuits.

The New Plant and the Happenings

Early in 1962, Vice President Knowles told me that all the operations were to be moved to the new plants in Elkridge, Maryland. I told him to leave me at Youngwood with two technicians and ten operators to run the plant until he got the plant working in Maryland. He turned me down, saying, "Don't worry, we'll have the diffusion furnaces up and working in three months." I told him it would take at least six months to get them to specifications, but my argument fell on deaf ears.

Several engineers were to be transferred to Elkridge with pay increases, including me. There was a technician named Vic Mitrisin that I tried to have transferred to Elkridge, but it was not permitted. Mitrisin had had two years of college, found his way to the Youngwood plant in 1961, and was an excellent technician. He was very detailed, and, in many ways, he thought like an engineer. He only made $400 a month, and I tried to get him to Elkridge at $700 a month. They wouldn't go for it. I told Vic to get a job somewhere else and that I would do what I could to get him down to Elkridge. (I mention him here because he is to follow me all my life.)

So a few months after David was born I was in the Baltimore area looking for a house. Fortune followed me in Maryland. I went to a beautiful place on Route 29, close to Ellicott City and across from a beautiful golf course called Allview. This was Allview Estates. They built custom homes there for about $30,000 to $50,000 on one-acre lots. I looked around elsewhere since I couldn't afford those prices, and I found a place that built split-level houses that all looked alike, and they were on quarter-acre lots. They sold for $20,000 and were a great design.

I went back to Allview Estates and told the builder I wanted a house like the ones at this other place but with his custom finishes. I also wanted it built with old, used bricks, and I wanted a bay window in the living room. He found a church that was being torn down and was able to get the bricks for nothing. He built a 3,200-square-foot, three-floor split-level house with air-conditioning on all levels and heated floors in the first floor family room. It cost me $22,000, which I thought was a steal. It was on a 1.3-acre lot not far from Route 29 and an easy trip to the plant in Elkridge. They finished building the house in less than six months, and Peg sold the house in Pennsylvania for $18,000. During those six months, I stayed in a hotel and went to work.

Much to my chagrin, I did not like work for the first several months. Knowles had hired engineers from Motorola to run the production area in building 4, and they knew nothing about the manufacture of integrated circuits. I was in building 2, which contained the engineering development group and was headed up by Doctor Edgar Sack, who had come from the Churchill R&D plant near Pittsburgh. He brought engineers from the Churchill plant, and they led the engineering group in this building. This left me with very little impact on anything at this location. Building 1 was administration and housed Knowles, Sack, and support groups.

Building 3 contained the basic equipment at this time, but a decision had been made to put off any processing in that building until a later date. So it remained inert at the time. After about three months of this organization I was depressed and thinking about a job at the Westinghouse Air Arm Division, which was not far away from the Elkridge plant. Then my fortune began to change. I was called into Sack's office, and he said, "There are seven engineers who have decided to leave the company, but they said they would stay if they worked for you. How would you like to have these engineers report to you, occupy building 3, and be responsible for custom circuits?" I was surprised and elated, since the people he mentioned were excellent engineers, and running custom circuits was exactly what I wanted to do. So life began for me again. With these engineers as a core, I hired other engineers and operators to run custom products in building 3.

Univac was a big customer for this building, as were others in a short time. I went to Knowles and said that Univac was such a big program that we should have an engineer assigned just to handle Univac production and details - a program manager. My wish was granted, and I hired Vic Mitrisin from RCA in New Jersey into the Elkridge plant as the Univac engineer at $900 a month—remember, he was making $400, and they wouldn't allow me to transfer him to Elkridge at $700.

Peg, Jay, Karen, and David joined me, and we moved to Allview Estates in October of 1963. We had just moved and had begun to settle down when President John F. Kennedy was killed in November. My in-laws, Sam and Peg Pool, were visiting us when this occurred. I was quit upset over the turn of events, since I had strong feelings toward this young president and what he stood for. I was depressed watching the preparation for Kennedy's funeral and the replays of the shooting. Also, I remember sitting in the family room with Sam watching TV when Oswald was being transported from his cell and was shot to death. The president's death was a very sad time for all of us. Work seemed a little harder after his death, as a huge energy had left the plant—as it had left the country. It took a few months for things to get back to normal.

Meanwhile, my time with Peg and the kids in our new home was super. It was nice that it didn't snow very much, but it was also very hot in the summer. That made it difficult to spend a lot of summer time outside with the family. But the house was great for playing games with the kids, and it was fun to take them all out to eat. The fireplace in the family room on the first floor extended out into the patio in the back so we could cook inside on the grill when the weather outside was not to our liking, and outside when it was fit.

Taking the family out to dinner always resulted in comments from people on how well our kids behaved (they were six, four, and two years old). Over time, we drove to Annapolis and to Washington DC to look at all the famous building and statues and to enjoy the Cherry

Festival. During the spring, we took rides down to Pimlico, the horse-racing capital of the Baltimore/Washington DC area and one of the locations of the three biggest horse races of the year: the Preakness. We enjoyed the scenery, the stables, and the magnificent horses. We were now living in an exclusive area where the houses cost about twice the one I had been able to secure by looking around and talking to the right people and builders. Peg and I thought it was the best looking and most practical house in the area.

I remember one summer when I looked at the large piece of land that needed mowing, and I thought about how I could make it easier. I had bought a used 1958 Volkswagen and had hooked up the mower to the back of the car and rode around cutting the lawn. The kids got in the car, and away we went. They laughed and had a great time. Every time the grass got a little long, they wanted to ride.

Since Ken, Sherie, and family were back from Argentina and doing well, I talked to Ken about buying a house for Mother and Pap. They had never had a home of their own, and it would be nice for Terry to live in a house instead of an apartment. We decided we could do this, since houses were inexpensive in Monessen. We bought a great house for Mother and Pap for $9,000. It was a stucco house with a basement, main floor, and upper floor. It had a nice backyard and a great front porch that they bought a glider swing to sit on and relax. The back porch set high over the backyard. Mother and Pap were so happy to live in a house where they didn't have someone living over them or below them; they had lived all their lives in apartments. This made Ken, Sherie, Peg, and me all happy.

In the summer of '64, my young brother Terry, who had joined the Navy in 1963, visited us, and we had a great time. Ken and I had talked to Pap and Mother and had told them to send him to the Navy when he was eighteen and he would only have to serve three years. In the meantime, he would be exposed to the rest of the world, and, perhaps, like Ken and me, find a direction for his life. Only time would tell. Only about a year into his time with the Navy, there was already a major difference. He traveled to Monessen every so often for a girl named Noreen, and I thought he was in love. Here again was living proof that a person could change if he or she got out and saw what it took to have a stable and happy life. Terry would later marry Noreen in 1965 and receive a BS degree in business from Rutgers University in New Jersey by attending night school for five years.

Meanwhile, the production area in building 4 was having a very difficult time making circuits that would not leak. They tried various process changes, but the devices continued to show current leakage. They could not sell or deliver units in this condition. This was something I hadn't experienced before, and we weren't seeing it on the devices we made in the custom building. Eventually, the production engineering crew found if they coated the devices with lead oxide at the end of the process and prior to bonding and packaging the units, the leakage went away.

The devices made in my building did not have this problem. Knowles came to my office and told me I had to make all devices in the custom line with lead oxide coating, and I told him my devices didn't leak and didn't require this Band-Aid. He went away grumbling, and we continued to fabricate our products as usual. A few months later, all the devices shipped out of the production building to the Apollo Program were failing in the field and at MIT Lincoln Labs. The lead oxide coating was crumbling. It didn't take long until MIT Lincoln Labs cancelled the program with our company. There went the Apollo Program and Westinghouse's reputation, along with financial losses. It all happened because the products were being made by people who didn't understand how the process affected quality.

Fortunately, we continued supplying Univac and other customers with their custom products. Univac announced their solid-state computer made from our devices in 1964. This was a step forward for Westinghouse and Univac, and especially for the custom products group, and Vic Mitrisin was looking good handling the job of program manager for Univac.

A Better Manager

My diffusion engineer, Paul Kisinko, graduated from Monessen high school the year before I did. I forget where he had gotten his college degree in chemical engineering, but, if he was an example of the school, it must have been a good one. Paul was a great person and a fantastic engineer, but one day he came to me and said he wanted to return to the western Pennsylvania area where his relatives lived. I told him, "Sure, Paul, as soon as you get a good engineer to replace you." He checked around and about a month later said he had located an engineer in the Philadelphia area who was looking for a job. He worked for Philco, and Paul arranged for the two of us to drive up to interview him.

We were on the road about an hour, and I said to Paul, "You know, Paul, I like being a manager, but I like being an engineer. At times I get frustrated with what to do."

It was quiet in the car for about five minutes, and then Paul said something that would affect my life forever. "John, if you are an average engineer, you will get paid an average engineer's salary. If you are a good engineer, you will be paid more. If you are an excellent engineer, you will be paid accordingly. However, there is no such thing for a manager. There is no place for a poor manager, an average manager, or a good manager. You are either a very good manager, or you are fired. There's no place for any manager unless he is very good at managing. If you are a very good manager, they can't pay you enough, since you determine the health of the company."

This sunk in my brain. When I returned to Elkridge, I cancelled all the technical trade journals I received and only kept the ones on solid state devices (transistors, etc.) and started to read books on management style and methods of better management. The rest of my professional career was devoted to being a very good manager of people and technical endeavors. I owe a lot of thanks to Paul Kisinko for that.

Meanwhile, we didn't hire the engineer at Philco, but we hired another person. Paul went back to western Pennsylvania.

Group's Approach Accepted by Philips of Holland

In late 1964, Westinghouse signed an agreement with Philips of Holland, whereby Philips supplied Westinghouse with some of their technology and money in exchange for the rights to our patents and the process on the integrated circuits.

At the time, I thought I wouldn't be involved with Philips. This was incorrect, and it was another interesting experience for the custom products group. As time proceeded, my photomasking engineer, Gene Donavan, and the mechanical engineers had developed methods for handling runs of twenty-five to fifty wafers more automatically, including fabricating four wafers at a time through each of the masking and etching process steps, and for handling loads of up to two hundred wafers at a time in the diffusion operations. The production building had continued working on solving the manufacturing problems and had not advanced their techniques to include multiple-wafer handling.

Jon VonVessen, the head of transistor development for Philips, was sent to Elkridge to secure the patents and processes for running a production line of integrated circuits in the Netherlands at a plant in Eindhoven. VonVessen spent five weeks in the production line at Elkridge, during which time he acquired all the process specifications and became familiar with the equipment for fabrication of these circuits.

At the end of the five weeks, he prepared himself to return to the Netherlands. Vice President Knowles gave him a tour of the engineering building, and then he came to the custom products building. I was introduced, and we proceeded to tour the custom products fabrication facility. As we proceeded, he made remarks like, "This is clever," or "Why aren't they using this technique in the production building?" He asked me questions about why I was processing wafers a certain way. We were only on the line for about fifteen minutes, and he became irate. He turned to Knowles and shouted, "This is production. Why did I spend all my time in that other building? This is what I want to take back to Philips with me!" We were embarrassed and mumbled something like, "You can take back anything you want, Jon." And so it was that

Philips of Holland received the advanced processing of Westinghouse from the custom products line for making their integrated circuits.

During this time, Jon VonVessen and I became great friends. He was a giant of a man (about 6 foot 3 inches, and 240 pounds) with a roar for a voice, and he was always walking around with me. I would look up at him and answer his questions. Going to work for the next several weeks was a joy, showing him the various creations of my engineers.

Analysis of Problem Found by MIT Lincoln Labs

During 1963, I was invited to MIT Lincoln Labs by Jane Partridge to participate in a discussion on what caused some ICs to lose their gains over time. About a week before going to Lincoln Labs, I spent the evenings at home and drew the cross section of a transistor to scale to see if I could envision what was causing this phenomenon to occur. This resulted in a very wide drawing on cardboard of about eight feet wide and only three inches in length. Now when I reviewed the emitter and base of the transistor versus the topside collector contact, I got a view of how the current really flowed inside the silicon and how the electric fields set up. I had always thought of the current as flowing downward from the emitter toward the collector below, but from this perspective, the field was horizontal and the current flowed sideways as well as down. Likewise, when I viewed the bias on the base and emitter of the transistor at this scale, it was obvious how much of the bias was distributed horizontally on this junction and horizontally on the oxide right above the junctions. If the emitter base junction was reverse biased (as it was when checking out the breakdowns of a transistor), an electric field was established in the oxide above the junction of 10^6 volts (million volts) per centimeter, or 1.0 million volts per centimeter.

Now I imagined the reverse voltage being removed from the emitter base junction and the transistor being biased in its normal mode. But to my astonishment, as I reviewed this cross section, I now realized the bias voltage built up in the oxide was still in the oxide above the emitter base junction, and it was a reverse bias. There was nothing to remove this bias instantaneously, because it represented a high impedance to the flow of charge (or current). I felt it was possible there were plus and minus domains in the oxide that built up during the reverse bias and lined up like a magnetic field would cause the oxide to retain this charge and high voltage like a capacitor in this reverse direction. The surface of the silicon next to the oxide would reflect this charge, and that part of the transistor would still be under reverse bias and keep that edge of the emitter base from the current injection that it normally performs. This would reduce the gain.

I went to work the next day with this in my mind and thought about what could be done to bring this junction back to a non-polarized state. I couldn't wait to measure the transistor gain, then reverse bias the emitter base junction, and then measure the gain again. Sure enough, it worked. The transistor I tested had gains of 55, and then I reverse biased the emitter base for half a minute and then measured the gain. It was 44. I repeated this on a couple of transistors and found this to be the case. Having thought about this the previous evening, I had come up with a possible way to relieve the reverse bias in the oxide; it was to take the devices up in temperature. This would provide enough thermal energy to "un-line" these polarized states. These charges would be free to drift and become randomly located in the oxide, resulting in the field collapsing. The devices were put in a nitrogen-filled oven at 175 degrees centigrade for fifteen minutes, and each recovered their original gain. I was happy with the model and prepared to go to Lincoln Labs.

Jane Partridge met me the next day, and we discussed their Apollo Program. I asked her if I could be the last one on the panel to discuss their problems, and she said she would set it up that way. Later, scientists and engineers from nine companies got up and gave their opinions of what was occurring. Jane Partridge had arguments against all of their approaches to the problem. I was very excited. I went to the blackboard and drew a general rendition of the cross section of an integrated circuit transistor, roughly to scale, and went through my explanation of what was causing the phenomenon. They were especially interested in the fact that the high temperature brought the circuits back to their normal state. Neither Jane Partridge nor any of the participants took exception to my presentation. They found it provided a good possibility for what was occurring, and now the discussion turned around as to why some of the transistors didn't show this problem. It was generalized that some oxides behaved differently, and not long after we found out why. (Later, Dr. Bruce Deal of Fairchild was to determine that mobile ions were the culprit, and they were put into the oxide by one of several high-temperature operations that resulted in sodium being incorporated into the oxide. Quartz tubes for diffusion and quartz bell jars for evaporation were the main sources of the sodium. These items had to be specified as sodium free. Methods were developed for steam cleaning the quartz to relieve the problem. Later, Dr. Deal demonstrated that the use of phosphorus glass incorporated in the oxide during the emitter diffusion left a phosphorus-rich glass that gettered the sodium, tying it up so as not to be mobile. This solved the problem for devices that already had been hit with sodium during their processing.)

After this detailing of the sodium issue, all purchase orders for quartz were specified as sodium free.

Suggestion to Bell Labs on Gold Beam Devices

In 1964, I was invited to Bell Labs corporate headquarters as part of a restricted audience to hear a presentation given by two scientists on a method they called gold beam technology. This was an elegant method that provided for the etching of all the silicon between the active and passive devices in a circuit to isolate each and to reduce the capacitance so the circuits would work to higher frequencies. With this approach, all elements of the integrated circuit were left suspended between gold beams, hanging in air, so to speak, like paper dolls. The process was a very complex and costly approach, but it did increase the frequency response of the devices. The one major flaw in this approach was the difficulty in handling each die as it was removed from its position in the wafer.

Each person attending this presentation (there were about fourteen people present, of which five were from Bell Labs) was asked for comments on this approach. When it came time for my comments, I said, "You could use a simplified approach by only etching the silicon away on the outside border surrounding the device, including underneath the leads coming off the device. This would provide a silicon chip with gold beam leads protruding outward, suspended in air and ready to be attached to a package. This would provide the beams for the leads coming off the device, while leaving all the active and passive elements in their normal physical state of being surrounded by silicon. Structurally, the devices would be stronger and easier to handle. By doing this, you would reduce the cost to less than half of your approach, while providing a very valuable and less expensive method for automatic assembly. In addition, the devices would be faster than present methods, but not as fast as the complete beam-lead approach."

The people from Bell Labs took my comment seriously. Shortly after, there was more work done on this method, and Bell Labs essentially dropped their total beam-lead approach. Within years, people were working on methods of supplying either beams or bumps on the outside apron of their chips to allow them to be automatically tested and assembled.

Leaving Westinghouse

The years 1964 and 1965 brought several exciting events. One occurred in early January of '64 on January ninth, when Ken called and told me that Sherie had delivered their third child, a girl named Dana Lee Husher. I asked him, "Don't you know how to put a handle on your new children? We need to keep the Husher name alive and well, and you need a boy to do that." But all kidding aside, I was very happy for them and for our new niece.

They were living in Ohio at the time, having come back to the United States in late 1962 from Argentina. Ken was working on ammonia absorbers for Koppers and had personally made some breakthroughs on the method being used. He had them change the mechanical dimensions of some of the parts of the absorbers, and it worked. Little by little, he was being recognized for his innate capabilities. He had the ability to look at mechanical things and figure out how they work—and why they don't work at times.

In late 1965, I was contacted by the management of Motorola in Phoenix, Arizona. Motorola was one of the three biggest semiconductor companies by this time. They invited Peg and me to their facilities with the hopes of hiring me for a high-level position in their company.

When Peg and I got off the plane in Phoenix, we were overwhelmed by several things: first, the high temperature; and, second, by the elegant way we were treated while touring their facilities. We also were impressed by the large orange orchards that provided a certain beauty to the area.

Peg said she could imagine a home being near orange trees, which would be beautiful. I was personally impressed by the powerful manufacturing and development capabilities displayed at this location. There were several large buildings housing their transistor factories and integrated circuit factories. It made Westinghouse look like a minor player in the integrated circuit business. We spent three days touring their facilities and the orange orchards that surrounded the facilities. All of their management was very professional, and several of the vice presidents, along with their wives, took Peg and I out to dinner and showed us around their homes and the places we might live, if I took the position.

When Peg and I got back home and discussed the situation, we decided that if they gave me an offer that was significantly better than what I had then I would join Motorola. We liked the housing situation and the desert atmosphere in the Phoenix area, and it looked like I could be a significant contributor to their company.

By the next day, I had received a telegram with an offer and position that was to our liking. It only took a couple of days to get back to them and accept their offer. So late in 1965, I committed to joining the Motorola management team, and then something happened that changed everything.

I got a phone call from Mr. Robert Sprague, the owner of Sprague Electric, located primarily in Massachusetts. He wanted me to come and see where they were building a large facility (140,000 sq. ft.) that would eventually build hybrid circuits. He had become interested in Sprague entering the IC business and wanted to see if I thought it was a good place to build integrated circuits. I told him about my commitment to Motorola, and he convinced me that I should leave my options open and see the opportunity that awaited me in Worchester, Massachusetts.

In December of 1965, I traveled to the Worchester facility and was shown around the new building (just a steel frame at the time) by Vice President Ken Ishler. It was going to be a beautiful building and had a large pond out front of the site with several ducks on the water. We also toured their equipment facility (MicroTech), which was to build equipment for the hybrid business and any special equipment that might be needed to facilitate an IC plant. This building housed the hybrid engineers who were to move into the new building when it was built.

On the second and third days, I traveled to the towns surrounding Worchester looking at houses. I saw a house that was only two years old that was located in an exclusive area in Holden, Massachusetts. In 1965, it was expensive at $49,000 for a split-level house with a backyard surrounded by white Birth trees. I knew Peg would like this house and the area. It was only about a mile from the new plant being built. It was a split-level like our previous houses and located on about a half acre.

When I returned and discussed everything with Peg, I told her I was impressed and would see what they offered me. I told her I only had one reservation about Motorola, and it related to valley fever. I hadn't discussed this with Peg. Because the air is so dry in Arizona, there are spores that float around in the air without falling to the ground. These spores are breathed in and can cause a fever and, in the worse cases, something similar to tuberculosis. One in every five people contacts this in the Phoenix area. In most cases it is not severe and acts like a mild flu. However, there is that chance of getting the spot on the lung and the resulting severe case. With five in our family, the chances were that at least one of us would have some problems. This was the only problem I was concerned about relative to Motorola.

Mr. Sprague called me at home the next evening. He said they would offer me the position of general manager of integrated circuits as well as plant manager for the Worchester facility, and the salary was almost double what I was making and competitive with Motorola's offer. I told him that I would accept that position if Sprague bought the house in Holden, and I would buy it back in one year for $29,000. He said, "What do you think you are, a bonus baby?"

I told him I didn't want to have to look for a house; I wanted to dig right in on the design of the new building. There would be numerous changes required to make the facility a clean room-level facility qualified to handle integrated circuits.

He told me he would call me back the next day. The following evening, he called and said, "The house in Holden belongs to you under your specified conditions." This was very exciting, and I told him that I would put all my energy into making this a winner for Sprague.

And so the next few days were consumed with putting in my resignation with Westinghouse and calling Motorola to apologize.

7

Putting Sprague Electric into the Chip Business

Building a Plant and a Professional Team

Peg and I had a station wagon for the family, and I had an old 1958 Volkswagen to travel to work. It was January 1966 when I started driving to Massachusetts, and I knew the Volkswagen was not the vehicle for snow, plus it had many miles on it. Peg needed the station wagon for her and the kids. Ford had come out with their Mustangs the year before, and we went to trade the Volkswagen for a Mustang. At the time, the Mustangs sold for $2,300 with all the latest equipment on it. They gave me $600 for my Volkswagen, plus they threw in a set of studded snow tires. Before I knew it, I was on my way up north in a new, dark-blue Ford Mustang, and Peg stayed back with the kids to try to sell our home.

Jay was in third grade, Karen in first grade, and David was still at home. It was tough leaving them, but I knew it was best for the family. At least we did not have to look for a new home; one awaited us in the beautiful town of Holden, Massachusetts. I hoped Peg like it.

The Worchester, Massachusetts Plant

There were several obvious needs for the new plant. It had been designed well but not to the requirements for a clean-room facility required for the fabrication of ICs. I hired Vic Mitrisin, and he was with me inside two weeks, working on the layout of the air-conditioning, heating, water supply, water filtering, water de-ionizing systems, drains, power, gases, and other requirements for a clean room facility.

I immediately informed Mr. Sprague that the air-conditioning planned for the facility was inadequate. He took steps to have the air-conditioning increased but was somewhat limited by what could be achieved at this late date. But I'll say one thing for him—he tried, and he put the money forth. We ended up with a better system than was originally designed.

When I thought we were fairly well on our way to a satisfactory plant and facility design, I sat down with Vic and John Dannely, president of Thermco, to discuss the furnace requirements for the facility. Thermco was considered the premier supplier of diffusion furnaces for the manufacture of ICs. I wanted something new and better than anyone else had ever used. I wanted all furnaces and equipment under laminar airflow with HEPA filters that filtered out particles greater than one micron in size.

Laminar airflow is like a good rain without any wind blowing. The raindrops would come straight down and each would not interfere with the other and each drop of rain would hit perpendicular to a flat surface without interfering with the other drops of rain. In laminar airflow, this same action is occurring, with the air flows evenly, at a constant rate and straight down, with no interference of any air molecule with any other, and no turbulence. It forms a wall of clean air to prevent entrance of outside air into the work area. In addition, the air flows through holes provided in the work surface so the air is without turbulence at the work surface. This is important because turbulent air results in air flowing in circular patterns at the work station surface and actually pulls in dirty air from outside the work station.

The design we initiated provided these positive advantages in providing clean air to the work surface. A whole plant in laminar flow had not been done before in the manufacture of integrated circuits. I knew Westinghouse made special air handlers and Formica industrial furniture in their furniture facility in Grand Rapids, Michigan. Formica (patented by Westinghouse) would make great air handlers, since the material was hard and did not generate dust. John Dannely, Vic Mitrisin, and I went to this facility and talked to them about the design of laminar flow stations made with their Formica boxes enclosing HEPA filters that would be mounted over each work station in the Worchester facility.

If one were to view one of the stations from the side view, it would be shaped like a C, capable of having a person sitting inside at the work area with the HEPA filter located above the work area. Its air blowers would draw in the air from the room, filter it, and form a laminar flow of air down across the top of the work area through the porous work surface to the bottom of the C and then dump it back in the room below the work surface. Each workstation had speed-controllable fans so that the airflow could be increased or decreased, while allowing a colored gas to flow in the intake and watching the colored gas flow pattern. When the airflow was proper, a colored wall of gas could be seen in the hood with no turbulence. This would go on continuously: pulling the air out of the room, scrubbing and refiltering the air, and dumping it back into the room. As the air circulated back and forth on a continuous basis, it not only provided ultra clean air across the work area, but it continuously made the room's air cleaner.

We spent days working on the design before returning to Worchester. John Dannely eventually bought the rights from Westinghouse to build these Formica laminar flow hoods and provided them to the industry in mid-1966. For now, we were the only company that was designing them to function throughout a new factory: the Worchester IC plant.

I Have a Medical Problem: Five Years to Live

Upon my return from the laminar flow factory, I received a big surprise. Robert Sprague called me on the phone and said that he noticed that my blood pressure was very high from the physical I had taken when I had joined the company. He had arranged for me to go to Massachusetts General Hospital the following Thursday.

I tried to talk him out of it, since they had been finding that problem since I was in the Navy and no one could find the reason. They had found that I had three kidneys but couldn't find any problem with them or relation to the blood pressure problem. I told him that I always ended up with black and blue legs after the hospital got done with me. He said to me, "John, I'm on the board at Massachusetts General. It's difficult to arrange for a physical like they're going to give you. I'm going to call the hospital on Thursday, and, if you aren't there, you no longer work for Sprague Electric."

I knew an ultimatum when I heard it, and I responded with an OK.

After spending one week in Massachusetts General, the top doctor came to my room to see me. He said my blood pressure was 200/160 and that the 200 bothered him. But there was no way of telling how long a person could live with this high reading. It could be to a ripe old age, he stated. Then he said, "However, the 160 is tearing up cells so fast that you'll probably not live longer than five years." This shocked me. I told him that previous doctors had tried to bring both down, but the top one would come down with medicine and the 160 would stay at 160. Since the difference between these is the pulse pressure, my pulse would get so weak I passed out.

He assigned Doctor Starobin to my case, and I was to see him every other Saturday while they tried different medicines on me. He told me the medicine I had been taking for the past few years might as well have been grounded up doorknobs for all the good they were not doing for me.

I remember coming out of the hospital and waiting for Peg to pick me up. I looked up in the sky and said, "No way I'm going to die in five years. I'll stop smoking, stop drinking (I only drank socially anyhow), and nothing is going in my body except what they put in it." This would give them a clean system to work their medical magic. I didn't tell Peg about the five years, only that I would have to go into the hospital every other Saturday.

And so I started to see Starobin every other Saturday. This added another ingredient in the mix of things I had to do. As it was, the building and its facilitating turned out to be a joy compared to finding engineers to fill the plant and trying to beat the blood pressure problem. I had headhunters searching for qualified engineers. I interviewed each of them, showed them the plant, and explained the major objectives for Sprague's integrated circuits facility. But the hardest thing was finding a home for each, once they were hired. Houses were scarce near the plant, and each possible hire had a different set of requirements when it came to a home. I spent days with each candidate trying to find homes. This went on for every day of the week.

Bright Engineers are hard to find.

Slowly, I began having some success in hiring bright young engineers: two from Westinghouse in Baltimore, who were originally from the New England states, Larry Pollock, who was to head up my product engineering and had worked for me at Youngwood and Elkridge; Russ Floyd, a great mechanical engineer from Philco outside of Philadelphia; Al Watkins, a strong process engineer from Philco, Cliff Kile, a strong product engineer from Philco; Dick Forrest, a strong product engineer from Westinghouse, Youngwood; a physicist from Fairchild on the West Coast; and a production control engineer from RCA in New Jersey.

I got two, really solid engineers (Fred Roeder and Andy Durette) from Sprague's transistor facility in Concord, New Hampshire, along with the quality control manager, Charlie Gray). As good as this was, it soon became obvious that I wouldn't be able to hire the number of competent engineers needed to run a new factory, develop a complete set of new integrated circuit technology, as well as design the final product, which included the development of new processes on equipment, installing and debugging the equipment, designing and debugging the circuits, designing and debugging the device technology, developing the process run cards, developing the test circuits and test programs, debugging the test equipment, and establishing the quality control functions.

In addition, there was the fundamental requirement of having all these functions work as a team. Besides these line functions, there were the support functions of human resources, production control, shipping, purchasing, accounting, and marketing/sales.

I visited Mr. Sprague at corporate headquarters in North Adams Massachusetts and described the situation. He said he would supply the purchasing, marketing and sales function from within. He could also supply some of the other support functions but would not be able to provide any of the engineering and production people. He asked if I had any ideas on the matter. I did.

I wanted to go to London and hire engineers from Europe. It would take about three months to properly prepare for this venture. I felt it would take about three months before I could go there with all the things going on. But the seed was planted, and Mr. Sprague accepted the idea. In another three months, the plant would be in pretty good shape except for certain key items that should be finished by then.

———— ~~~∽∼ⓞⓡⓞↄ∼~~~ ————

The method I had previously used at school and work proved to be invaluable in meeting objectives. Each Sunday night I planned for the upcoming week. After some thought, I wrote six priority objectives to achieve during the coming week on a small sheet of paper. I went into work on Monday morning each week and put these six things into motion. This list always helped me be ready for Monday since it is sometimes hard to get "restarted" each week for any person working. Although I sometimes didn't achieve them because other emergencies popped up, they were at least put into motion. This method continued to work for me during my time at Westinghouse, Sprague and later places.

With the plant installation, hiring of engineers, finding them homes, ordering the proper equipment for the plant, and dealing with personal issues relating to my blood pressure and my family, I needed to plan more efficiently. So each Sunday evening I put aside an hour to consider these work-related issues and to plan both my work schedule's objectives and my quality time with the family for the coming week.

This method also allowed for a clear conscience when I did something with Peg and the kids during the week, because I had planned it. It wasn't like I was shirking my responsibilities, since I had included the family in the six priority items planned for the week. Those six priorities did not include the trip to the doctor every other Saturday, since this wasn't within my control. This happened every other Saturday no matter what other plans were required for the business and the family, being a requirement that had to be met no matter what other objectives existed. Besides, it didn't require any thought on my behalf, only to do it.

So the Sunday thinking and planning prepared me for the start of the next day and carried on throughout the week, including my family time. Once written it was on the sheet of paper, I knew how to start my Monday mornings and put things into motion like the weekend had not happened. No surprises (I hoped) and immediately these priorities were put into action for the next seven days.

⟜⟋⟍⟋⟍⟜

The plant activities took me away from the family, but every chance I got I was with them. One weekend we purchased an above-ground pool. It was large and shaped like a figure eight (with the "8" not being closed in the middle) and made so that each half of the figure eight was six feet deep.

We laid out a place for it in the backyard, and I had decided to sink it in the ground. There would be a shallow end that was three feet deep so the kids could play, and the other half would remain at six feet. So we dug a figure eight that ended up being twenty-four feet long. The hole was less than one foot deep on the shallow end and three feet deep on the deep end. The perimeter was dug one foot deep, so the sides of the pool were five feet out of the ground. Then I built a redwood deck around the perimeter, facing the back of our house. I built a redwood staircase up to the deck, which could be folded up and locked so the kids could not get in unsupervised. This protected any kids from wandering in the yard and accidentally getting into the pool.

Our family and the neighbors had many good times in that pool. I have yet to see one like it. It also had a pool pump and filter system like the big expensive in-ground pools, received chlorine each Saturday, and was cleaned every two weeks by the whole family and some of the neighborhood kids.

Before taking the job with Sprague and moving to Worchester, Peg had heard that we wouldn't like it in New England because of the cold attitude of the New Englanders. We found this to be untrue. The day we moved, the neighbors came over and took care of the kids while we moved in. They talked to us like they had known us forever. There never was an issue in entering into their activities or them with our activities. To this day, if we had a second house, we would like it to be in the New England area.

Machine Shop

A machine shop was required on the bottom floor of the plant. It was about finished as far as utilities were concerned. Lighting had been installed throughout the plant, including the machine shop. There was only one problem: in late 1966 you couldn't buy a milling machine, or a factory lathe, or any type of equipment. The demand for equipment was high, and there was a backlog to overcome. Delivery times were two to three years out. We considered buying machines outside of the United States and found the same problem.

We needed Bridgeport milling machines—five of them—that were considered the best milling machine at the time. Its claim to fame was that it was the only machine that could produce itself, but you needed one to start with. My guys found a company in Italy that would sell us a machine that was a copy of a Bridgeport. It was called an Induma milling machine, and one was ordered to be delivered in six months.

Several opportunities for used machines were reviewed, but most were in poor shape. As luck would have it, we found an old machine shop that had been closed for several months. It was located outside of Boston. After imagining what could be done with this dirty, rusty machine shop, I decided we could refurbish most of the equipment. We gave them an offer of $18,000 for the complete shop, without the building. They wanted $23,000 for the total pile of equipment, and I finally got it for $20,000, plus delivery to the Worchester facility—payment upon delivery. It was delivered in one week.

Meanwhile, I had hired two young technicians who had graduated from a two-year technical engineering course from Worchester Tech to refurbish the equipment. Each machine was to be taken apart, cleaned, lubricated, put back together, painted, and installed in the machine shop at locations Vic Mitrisin had established on plant layouts. I remember their comments: "We don't know anything about a milling machine, a lathe, the collets for the Bridgeports. What if we lose some of the parts while we're taking them apart?"

I told them to go and buy bed sheets and to place each machine on a bed sheet, to place they took pieces from the machine on a second bed sheet, and to place the cleaned parts on a third sheet. The two young technicians I had hired from Worchester Tech, Dale Means and Mike Shulty began their education on machines. I checked with them every couple of days, and they were making good progress and enjoying it. Meanwhile, a shop foreman was hired, and he immediately assumed this responsibility.

Several months later, when Mr. Sprague made a tour of the building, he started at the completed machine shop in amazement. "Where did you get the machine shop?" he asked. Our vice president said, "John bought a used machine shop out of Boston and had his techs rebuild them."

As Mr. Sprague looked at the six milling machines, neat bins built to hold the milling machine collets, four lathes, drill press machines, band saws, metal cutoff saws, metal bending equipment, and automatic welding equipment, he asked, "If I give him $100,000, will he buy me five more machine shops like that? The company could sure use them."

We laughed. I was very proud that day and told Dale Means and Mike Shulty they had done a good job.

Equipment arrived in bunches. The laminar air stations for the twenty-four diffusion tubes and the furnaces began to be put in place. The exhaust hoods for the wet etch sinks and other exhausting station along with the laminar flow stations for the Mask Aligner equipment arrived, and installation began. It soon became apparent that we needed more exhaust to balance the many etch and clean stations. In order to have a positive airflow in the clean rooms, the clean air input had to be greater than the exhaust to result in positive pressure. This positive pressure was needed to keep air flowing and to keep dirty air out. Adding more exhaust would unbalance the system, and I had to think the opposite way—somehow reduce the exhaust requirements while retaining all the stations.

A New Approach to Exhausting—Lip Exhaust

After a night of thought I came up with what is now used in the industry as a standard; instead of exhausting the whole hood, I had the workstation designed with "lip exhausts." Each etch or rinse position within an exhaust hood was designed with a stainless steel or polyethylene jacket spaced about one inch around the outside of the position that hooked up to the exhaust underneath each station; with only this "lip" area being exhausted rather than the whole work station. This we called a Lip Exhaust. It reduced the exhaust requirement for each of these hoods by 80 percent. With these innovations, the rooms were now obtaining and maintaining positive pressure. This put the plant in good shape, with complete laminar flow clean rooms, for the fabrication of silicon wafers and their integrated circuits as well as laminar flow for device assembly into packages. No integrated circuit plant at the time had these laminar flow services completely throughout the fabrication and assembly areas, as well as using lip exhausts

Doctor Visits

Each doctor visit to Massachusetts General was an endurance test. Sometimes the medicines Dr. Starobin provided caused me not to make it to the car, and I would have to stay in his office for several hours. These medications were stopped immediately. Some medicines allowed me to make it home, but caused me to be lethargic at work. These would be changed at the next visit. Some caused bowel movement problems, and others caused dizziness.

Then a medicine was found, Aldomet, which dropped the pressure to 180/140. Then a tranquillizer, Librium was found to lower it to 160/120. A year after starting these trials, Starobin tried Aldactone—two tablets, three times a day, along with the other medicines.. The next visit Starobin was surprised. My blood pressure was 127/80, and he almost danced. He asked, "Do you feel good? How are your bowel movements?"

I said I felt fine, and this thrilled him even more. But as I was leaving his office, I told him my left pectoral area was sore. His mouth dropped. He showed me the write-ups he had received, and the warning stated: "In some cases the pectoral area of the male may show pain; if so, take him off the medicine. In some cases the voice of a female patient may drop an octave; if so, take her off the medication." What to do? I suggested that I take one three times a day instead of two, and Starobin agreed.

Two weeks later the results showed 150/110. Starobin was annoyed and said to keep going with this amount to see how it worked out. Every couple of months, my pectoral area would ache again, and he told me to stop the medicine until the pain went away and then to start again. This worked. I went about two or three months, and when the pain appeared I stopped for two or three days and then continued. This was as stable as my blood pressure would get, but this was far better than when he started. (The future would find me visiting the Aldactone again.)it was an improvement.

To England to Hire Engineers

I had contacted Cliff Roe, who had returned to England after spending several years with Westinghouse. I offered him the position of process manager of the Worchester facility, and he accepted. This allowed me to make concrete plans for the trip to London and possibly hire the engineers required for the new plant. Cliff Roe was to set up the interviews at a well-known hotel in London and to place ads in the London papers for positions open at the Sprague plant in Worchester, Massachusetts.

When I arrived, Cliff had set up interviews for forty-nine applicants. We set up for seven to eight interviews per day for seven days running. At the conclusion of these interviews, we made offers for thirteen positions. Of these, eleven accepted, including two from Italy. One turned us down, and one had already accepted a position as a test engineer at an aircraft company in Connecticut. His name was Roy Mullard, and I had offered him the position of test engineer at Worchester. On the day Cliff and I were to leave London, Roy Mullard came to the hotel. He said he had failed his physical due to a heart murmur and had been turned down by the company in Connecticut. He told me he had all his papers completed and intended to go to the United States and seek employment immediately. I told him if he made his way to Worchester, he had a job.

He did come to Worchester as a test engineer and wrote all the test programs for the new products and debugging the first IC tester made by Teradyne out of Boston.

Of the twelve European engineers who came to Sprague, six of them became millionaires over the course of time, including Roy Mullard, though not with Sprague. Roy Mullard became a multimillionaire sixteen years later for his involvement in the creation of the Apple Computer.

And so I returned from London feeling much better about the crew of engineers who would put Sprague on the map of IC suppliers. All

I had to do was find homes for them before they arrived. If not, I had to give them time to find a place of their choosing.

Fun in New England for the family

The area was great for having fun with the family. There was Quinsigamond Lake that extended all along one end of the city. It was long and narrow, being about a couple of miles long and a half mile wide. Vic had bought a boat, and Peg and I went water skiing while the kids swam along the shoreline. We also visited lakes within driving distance with Vic and his boat. Several times we went to New Hampshire to the lakes up there and some more water skiing. Sam and Peg Pool came up one fourth of July week and we went to Maine and went swimming in the cold water of the ocean. Of course we ate lobsters and other good food that we found great in the New England states. People were friendly and we would be invited to cook outs where they smoke grilled clams that were cut into small pieces and cooked and then stuffed back into the shells and grilled. These were great.

It was odd that many people did not take advantage of the lakes on the weekend. They went to the Cape for the weekend and often left the lakes uninhabited. This was fine for us, since there were great eating places around Worchester and along Highway 9 to Boston. We took the kids restaurant hunting on the weekends. Peg and I had more fun in the Worchester area than anywhere we had lived before.

During the following year, the design team had designed fifty-seven circuits of the Texas Instruments (TI) product line called the 7400 series. We thought coming into the market late was to our advantage as a second source to this accepted product line. (A second source refers to a company that makes a similar product to one already being produced and becomes a second source for that product. This gives the user an alternate supplier, which ensures he will have a good supply of the product.) However, this was to cause some problems within Sprague's marketing group. The corporate marketing group out of headquarters had signed an agreement with Signetics of California, whereby we were to second source their product line. We had developed a broad line of their products. We had a fairly large and experienced marketing/ sales group in the plant, and they had made a decision not to push the TI series of products because of the Signetics agreement. I had major arguments with this group that reported back to Corporate. So for several months we had hundreds of thousands of TI products but no push to sell them anywhere.

Fortunately, Mr. Sprague visited the plant to look around the facility and to discuss our reaching our billing dollars of sales. I presented this dilemma to him, and he became irate. He rushed down to the marketing office and directed them to sell the TI as well as the Signetics series.

In the next few months, Sprague began to qualify as the second source of TI part types, and sales started to rise. It didn't take long for top management in Sprague to realize that the yields attained at the plant made us a real contender. The cost of making ICs was primarily determined by the yields of good die on a wafer and at final test. Every device that didn't yield was scrapped, and it carried the costs of material, labor, and the overhead to make them.

Over the ensuing year, young Dr. John Sprague, a recent graduate of Stanford, joined the company at corporate headquarters in North Adams, located in northwestern Massachusetts. He brought with him Dr. Robert Pepper, and they emphasized developing linear circuits intended for manufacturing at the Worchester plant. Linear circuits produce functions in the same manner as everyday functions occur—in a continuous manner, as opposed to digital circuits, which are either on or off. This required different process technology and became an additional load for the plant. So, by 1968 the plant was meeting the dollar billing requirements but was beginning to shift emphasis to linear circuits. This de-emphasized the focus from the TI digital series in the plant and by the field sales force. Their new push was for the linear products, where higher profit margins were available due to higher selling prices and lack of competition.

There was no doubt in my mind that the linear business was healthy, but to obtain short-term billing dollars, the emphasis needed to be on the digital products we were making. I was becoming disenchanted.

Terry Takes a Job in New Jersey

My young brother, Terry, married Noreen in 1965, and in 1967 they moved to New Jersey to take a job with Koppers. He didn't stay long with Koppers, as it was a tough job with low pay. He was hired by Matchbox, the English company that die cast small automobiles to scale and sold them as toys for kids. However, people all over the world were interested in saving these elegant little cars. They became collector's items.

Terry was in production control and eventually went to marketing and sales with Matchbox. They lived in New Jersey, only a couple of hours from our house. The house they had bought was almost identical to my parents' house in Monessen but had cost about a hundred thousand dollars due to the location. Peg and I visited Noreen and Terry a couple of times in 1967. We had good times on these visits. Terry knew his way around New York City, and we went there in the evenings to enjoy ourselves. Meanwhile, Terry had enrolled at Rutgers University and was going to night school. (He later gained his BS degree in Business in 1973. The Navy did it again.)

Resolving Signetic's Problem

During early 1968, Signetics was having a reliability problem with their circuits called Purple Plague. This condition was initiated during the wire bonding cycle, where the combination of heated substrate and the pressure of bonding the gold ball with the aluminum caused a tertiary crystalline compound to form. This compound turned purple over time and became a high resistance contact instead of the low resistance required. As a result of this reliability problem, Signetics was unable to ship their products. Their president asked Mr. Sprague if I could visit their facility in Santa Clara, California, and see if I could find a cure.

I visited the Signetics plant in May of 1968 and spent a couple days reviewing their line processes. I noticed they were using 6,000 angstroms of aluminum thickness for their interconnects. I knew we used 12,000 angstroms (a very small measurement quantity equal to 1.2 microns) in our facility and asked their process manager why they were using a thin metal. They were using a photoresist material from Kodak called KPR, and, if they made their aluminum thicker, the KPR began to break down during the longer etch time for the thicker metal process. It could not stand up to this long etch time and would break down and the aluminum dimensions could not be controlled. I knew we had shifted from KPR to KMER from Kodak when we had established the photomasking process at the plant. It could hold up while etching metal twice as thick as that used by Signetics. I came back to the plant and ran experiments, wherein we split some wafers and used with 6,000 angstroms of metal on one half and 12,000 angstroms on the other half. We found that in order to bond to the thinner metal it took higher pressure at a given temperature or keep the constant pressure constant and a higher temperature to bond to the thinner metal of the bonding. Higher temperatures or bonding pressure resulted in the Purple Plague, whereas the thicker wafers with the thicker metal had no problems since the temperature and pressure both could be kept lower than what was required for the thinner metal. All we had to do with the units that were bonded with the thin metal wafers was put the devices on life test at elevated temperature, and the bonds turned purple in a week.

I wrote a report to Signetics and told them they didn't have a bonding problem; they had a photoresist problem. They needed to change to KMER photoresist and the thicker metal. Mr. Sprague phoned me and gave me two of his emotions: one, that Sprague had helped Signetics solve their problems for which he was grateful we had solved their problem and two, that Sprague did not have the problem that was now rampant in the whole industry and we might be able to take advantage of this reliability issue, since it was now rampant in the whole industry. He complimented me on this.

My Issues With Sprague

In the middle of 1968, Dr. John Sprague moved his office from corporate headquarters in North Adams, Massachusetts, to the Worchester plant.

It didn't take me long to see the writing on the wall. I had hoped to become the president of the company at some time in the future, but seeing him in my plant next to my office gave me a kick out of that dream (turned out it was fortunate for various reasons as you will see.). Before long, Dr. Bob Pepper also moved to the plant, and there was extreme pressure to move Sprague to linear ICs. These moves and the fact that I enjoyed the visit to the West Coast while visiting Signetics started me thinking about moving to California.

Meanwhile, the output of the plant increased dramatically, and we were no longer able to handle all the assembly requirements. Some looking around and we soon found a possible assembly support group in Korea. I sent Vic Mitrisin to Korea to engage with this company to see if they looked legit. The feedback after his first week there, was that it looked real, and he was going to pursue it further.

8

California and Fairchild Semiconductor

Accepting a Position with Fairchild Semiconductor

In the beginning of October, a few things occurred that pushed me over the limit, and I went to John Sprague's office and told him I was resigning from Sprague. I walked out of the office and called Peg and told her to make airplane reservations for me to San Francisco as soon as possible. She was sort of in shock but knew I had been unhappy for the past several months.

The management team that had tried to hire me at Motorola had taken up the management of Fairchild in California, including Les Hogan, who was now the president of Fairchild. I arranged for an interview the following afternoon. I flew to California and stayed at the hotel next to the airport in San Francisco. The phone woke me at five in the morning. On the other end of the phone was Dave O'Brian, an executive headhunter. He said that Steve Levy, the president of Motorola Semiconductor, was in the San Francisco area and wanted to talk to me about a position at Motorola in Arizona. He would meet me for breakfast at 8:30 at the hotel.

So, there I was having breakfast with Steve Levy. At the end of the meal, he said he would like me to accept a position at Motorola. He said he had to run and catch a flight to Florida to view the launching of a space shot that contained many Motorola parts. He picked up a piece of paper and wrote down the salary and stock option they would offer me. He told me to think about it, and he would be in his office in two days and that I should call him. The job offer was almost twice what I had been receiving at Sprague. So there I was going to Fairchild for an interview with a fantastic offer already in my pocket.

Fairchild and California was where I wanted to be. My interview with Fairchild went well, and they offered me the position of director of the South Portland, Maine, plant, the Shiprock, New Mexico, plant, and the installation of a new plant in Singapore. I told them I would take the position if I could have my office in California. I didn't want to go north of the Mason Dixon line again. I was tired of the snow, and I believed that California was the future of the semiconductor business.

Vice Presidents Wilf Corrigan and Gene Blanchette went to talk to Dr. Les Hogan—the president of Fairchild. They soon returned and said it was a go. I could make my office in the new building called the Rusty Bucket, because the outside structure was pre-oxidized and rust colored to prevent it from further rusting. The building's only occupant at the time was Dr. Hogan.

I called Peg and told her I was coming home the next day and that I had accepted a position at Fairchild. She should plan on flying out with me the following week to find a house. Along with a good salary and stock options, I was offered three months' salary bonus and complete expenses for moving; all this to make the move an effortless and rapid one. Peg and I were back the following week to look for a house. We looked the whole weekend, and Peg spent days looking for a place while I was at work.

On the fifth day, she called me and said she had found a house high in the hills of Los Altos Hills, but it didn't have any trees and looked bare. I arranged to meet her at noon to look at the place. The house was as solid as any I had ever seen, built at the highest place in the hills, and we could see forever. To the left I could see San Francisco forty miles away, straight ahead I could see the San Francisco Bay and the whole valley beneath me, and to the right San Jose was twenty miles away. I could see the hangars of Moffett Field in Mountainview, which was one of the Navy air bases that VR1 flew into on their way to Hawaii and Korea.

Across the Bay, we could see the mountain ranges. What a fantastic view. Peg thought the view of the wooded hills out the back were even better. I remembered my brother and I swimming in the river as kids. He had said he wanted to live along the river, and I had said I wanted to live high on a hill so I could see the world. Here was my house, high on a hill, and I could see forever!

The problem was that they wanted $69,000 for the place. We had been looking at houses that sold for $30,000 to $40,000. I bargained with the owner, and eventually we agreed on $65,000. I knew this was going to be a stretch. Only five years later, it cost $40,000 for a lot in these hills, and homes were selling for $500,000. I was excited that at the age of thirty-six, and Peg almost thirty-three, that we would own a house so beautiful and high on a hill in an area so nice.

It was odd that all the other houses had oak trees surrounding them. They also had very sloped properties. This place was on top of the hill over an acre of flat land and with no trees. I told Peg not to worry; I would plant trees. And so we settled on the house. Peg went back and eventually sold the house in Holden for $49,000, so we had an equity of over $20,000 in that house to help us handle the cost of the new place. Later, in November of 1968, Peg and the kids drove to California with her mother, dad, and Vic Mitrisin. The kids took turns riding with Sam behind the wheel in one car or with Vic in the other, driving them nuts singing songs all the way across the country.

They almost drove past the house because by this time I had "adopted" some large, mature trees and they were planted. The place looked totally different to Peg. I had a fence installed along the one side of the lot next to the road and a horse corral up in the far back of the lot. I knew that Karen would want a horse now that she was "out West. I had spent every free evening planting shrubs and spreading grass seed on the muddy backyard.

One night, I spread seed at 2:00 AM while it was raining cats and dogs. The previous owner was still living in the house while her husband was in Philadelphia looking for a house. The lady didn't want me to step foot on the property until she had moved out. So I came when she was asleep and did the things like spreading grass seed.

One evening after work, I drove up to the house and did a few things. After finishing about ten, I got in my car, turned it on, and decided to look out in the distance. It put me in a trance. I had not experienced anything so breathtaking. I was so enchanted by the view that I lost track of time, looking at the beautiful evening scenery of lights.

Then my engine died, and I realized I was out of gas. I pushed the car down the hill. I went down about a quarter of a mile and came to a fairly flat spot. I almost made it up to the next road that turned off onto Black Mountain Road. I was able to push the car to that road and start down again. I went about a half mile and came to another flat area, and it became too much to push any further. It was now about 11:30 PM, and I saw a light about two hundred yards away. I got out of the car and crawled up into a grove of trees and headed toward the house. It was a moonlit night, and I could make out the outline of the house as I moved through the trees. Then I heard a bark and looked up in the direction of the house and could made out a big dog running toward me. Turns out I never was afraid of dogs, and this didn't change that night. As he came toward me with a rush and was, ready to leap up, I punched him in the nose with my right fist. This large German shepherd turned and ran back toward the house. I continued up to the house and knocked on the door, and an older man came to the door and asked me what I wanted. I told him I had run out of gas and wanted to know if he had some gas to loan me. He said he had some out in the horse shed.

As he started toward the shed, he turned around and said, "Didn't my dog attack you or try to stop you?" I said he had, but I had just punched him in the nose, and he had run back to the house. I was never afraid of dogs since I was a little kid and had a dog of my own that used to chase other dogs away. The man shook his head and said,

"You know, everyone who comes to this house gets scared shitless of that big animal, but he's more bark than bite." He laughed and continued down to the horse shed, with his flashlight showing the way. He filled up a gallon can for me and told me to keep the can. "Anyone who can punch my dog in the nose gets a free can." The incident reminded me to watch my gas gauge a little closer.

Finally, the people moved out of the house, and I spent an early evening drawing a pool layout in the backyard. The day Peg and the kids arrived, five men were in the back, putting in an exposed aggregate patio to cover the muddy backyard.

So our family was in California to stay. Jay was ten, Karen was eight, and David was six. They started new schools the following week. It turned out that the part of the hills we lived in allowed the kids to go to the Palo Alto school district, which was supposed to be among the best schools in the state. For the next two years, we had to watch our budget now that we had what was considered a large house payment. (It became a great bargain in a couple of years after pay raises.) The guys at work called me the gentleman farmer, since I spent all my free time working in the 1.3 acre yard surrounding the house.

Visiting the Manufacturing Plants

I reported to VP Gene Blanchette, and my first directive from Gene was to go to the South Portland, Maine, plant and fire the plant manager, John Sussenberger. I asked him why, and he said, "He doesn't know anything about making ICs. He ran the transistor plant in Hong Kong, and he is ignorant about ICs."

Before leaving for my first trip to South Portland, I got a call from Vic Mitrisin in Korea, and he asked me, "When do I start working for you at Fairchild?" I told him that he started when he got here.

So, I was off on my first trip to South Portland, Maine. I met John Sussenberger and everyone else in the plant of about seven hundred people on three shifts. The more I viewed the operation and how John handled it, the more I was convinced he was an excellent production control person who knew nothing about the fabrication of integrated circuits. Returning to Mountainview and talking with Gene, I told him I didn't want to fire John. John knew what it took to run production. What he needed were some product managers who understood ICs, and I could hire qualified engineers to fill that need.

During my stay in Maine and on the plane trip, I had decided what equipment was needed to bring South Portland up to high production and what equipment would be needed for Shiprock, New Mexico, and Singapore. I began to generate a list of equipment that added up to $14 million, which was a huge amount of money in those days. I took the purchase request to Dr. Hogan, the only other occupant of the Rusty Bucket (plus our secretaries). Hogan asked me what I wanted all this money for. I told him I knew what it took to make a great manufacturing facility out of South Portland, and I needed automatic bonding equipment for assembly of packaged units in the new Singapore facility and in Shiprock. He said, "Makes sense to me." And he signed the capital request. This gave me the authority I needed to bring South Portland and the other plants up to speed.

And Now the Mountainview, California Plant

The following week, I was interviewing for the three product managers for South Portland when I got a call from Blanchette. He said, "We just fired John Carey, the manager of the Mountainview Digital operations. We want you to take management of this location immediately. Go and talk to Tony Holbrook, who's the manager of engineering and design for Mountainview. We don't want to lose any of our engineers."

I immediately talked to Tony and settled his mind. With Mountainview as an added responsibility, I was now Director of all digital integrated circuits worldwide.

Within a month, I had hired three professional IC product managers for the South Portland plant—Fred Roeder from Sprague to handle production of new products; Steve Weisch from a company in Palo Alto to handle custom circuits; and John Shea, who was already in

South Portland, to handle standard parts. I inherited three very good product managers in Mountainview—Dave Rossprim, who handled new MSI products; Doug Finch, who handled standard products; and Dave Dierdorff, who handled custom circuits. Now I needed to look for a manager for the Mountainview facility.

During my tour of the facility, I couldn't believe how the epitaxial room was laid out. It had an entrance in one end of a long room with six epitaxial reactors lined up perpendicular to this entrance. When an operator was in the far end of this epi room, he or she had no way out except through the front entrance past all the reactors—and epi is grown in a hydrogen atmosphere. This was an accident waiting to happen, and there was no escape route for the operators of the equipment. I immediately shut down this operation, which also closed all operations for Mountainview, since epi was one of the first steps in the production process.

I told the facilities engineers to tear down the walls around this room and reconstruct them with proper emergency exits. Also, new exhausts were to be installed. Within a day, the accounting people came and told me that funding had not been approved for this task. I told them I was using part of the funds previously approved by Hogan. Besides, this was a safety issue, and funds always needed to be approved for safety issues. They told me that I needed PPA (Planned Project Authorization) approval to spend the $14 million.

I went to the director of finance and showed him the signature of Hogan on the bottom of the approved capital request. I told him, "I only need the approval of Dr. Les Hogan." That ended the discussion for the epi room, and for all the equipment required to make South Portland a major production plant and Singapore and Shiprock, New Mexico, major assembly plants.

Over the next two months, the epi room was completed, the South Portland plant was receiving some of the equipment required, and the three product managers had reported to South Portland. Among the new equipment I wanted to purchase for South Portland was new high-speed test equipment. Up to this time, all testers used in Fairchild were manufactured by the test equipment division of Fairchild located in Sunnyvale. While in South Portland on a visit, I got a call from the Fairchild test division, informing me that I was not permitted to order Teradyne equipment and that I must use their equipment. I told them to shove it and hung up the phone. Soon after, I received a call from Les Hogan. "What are you doing?" he asked. I told him that South Portland would need high-speed test equipment to handle the production needs, and the Fairchild equipment didn't meet those requirements. After a little discussion on the particulars he hung up.

The next day a telegram went out of his office to all management personnel within Fairchild. It stated that each manager was to decide what type of equipment best met the needs for Fairchild's success, regardless of whether the equipment could be supplied by Fairchild. And so, Teradyne testers were ordered for South Portland. Of all the plants that reported to me, the one at South Portland best met my requirements.

The people of Maine were good workers, good thinkers, and they worked until the problems were solved. Sometimes they didn't go home at night because they were fixing a problem. Professionals that lasted a year there ended up staying. They were committed.

Several years later, Fairchild Semiconductor was sold to National Semiconductor, and over a two-year period National closed several of their previous production plants but retained the South Portland plant. So the name of Fairchild disappeared from the semiconductor business. Several years later, the people of South Portland purchased the plant from National Semiconductor and named their company Fairchild. That company became a very successful business and competed against National Semiconductor. This made me feel good, because it turned out to be one of the best production plants in the business.

Shiprock, New Mexico

The plant in Shiprock, New Mexico, was located on an Indian reservation. The plant manager reporting to me was Paul Driscoll. Paul was devoted to making the plant and its people a success. He liked the position of being responsible for helping both Fairchild and the Indian people. I liked visiting the plant. The plant was located in a school, but a new plant was being built and was almost complete when I arrived for the first visit. My tour around the plant made me feel the plant was in good hands, and with a few changes it would be a winner for Fairchild. The new plant was being financed by the government in support of Indian affairs. Soon the new plant was finished, and Peg and I were to attend the dedication along with newly married Julie Nixon Eisenhower (daughter of President Nixon) and David Eisenhower (son of President Eisenhower), as well as the commissioner of Indian affairs Brown, and the Navajo tribal chairman, Raymond Nakai. This was the beginning of a long and successful venture by Fairchild and the Navajo Indians. Peg and I were very proud to be a part of this dedication and the success of the plant as time went on.

Singapore

Obtaining a successful plant in Singapore required a good location in the no trade zone of Singapore. As we searched for a good location for the plant, it became obvious that the good locations had already been taken by companies who had beaten Fairchild to Singapore. This was in spite of the fact that Fairchild was the first big electronic company to build a plant in Southeast Asia in Hong Kong. The tallest building in Hong Kong at that time was the Fairchild Building, and you could see a big F that was about a third the height of the building.

As sites were reviewed (Ed Pausa was the person in charge of this), it became obvious that the best location was just outside the main town, where three tall apartment buildings were being built for the local young people working in the area. This site was checked out several times, and we were told that all space was taken up. However, we asked the builders who owned the land where all the earth-moving equipment was parked. We were told to come back the next day, and the next day they told us that it wasn't taken by anyone. We asked for that space as soon as the equipment was moved, and again they told us to come back the next day. The next day we were told we would be permitted to build a plant there if we finished the roof with a pretty view, so that the people living in the apartments would see a pretty roof top below them. After some discussion, we offered to build a roof that was finished with various colored coral that depicted palm trees. This was acceptable, and that was how Fairchild got the prime location for an assembly plant right next to several hundred potential employees within walking distance. The building was started almost immediately and was ready for occupancy in mid-1969. It would provide Fairchild a great assembly plant for years to come.

Issues with South Portland

By mid-1969, production was increasing dramatically in South Portland; however a major personnel problem reared its head. I got a call from John Sussenberger, and he said the three product managers were driving him nuts. I told him, "John, those are three sharp guys. Never have more than one of them in the room with you. What one doesn't think of, the others will. They'll feed off each other."

He said OK, but a month later he called again with the same complaint. I told him I would do what I could to resolve the issue. Vic Mitrisin and I went to South Portland and stayed a week and looked for alternatives. I recommended that John promote Jim Smaha to operation manager, with the three product managers reporting to him. John said, "Jim is my QC manager. What makes you think he could handle operations?" I told him that in South Portland the test equipment was under quality control's supervision and outgoing quality control was handled by quality control, so Jim Smaha knew more about the products than anyone in the plant.

John said no. I told him that Smaha would be a popular promotion in the plant. He was from Maine and was well respected among the employees. His promotion would be popular, because everyone there thought I always solved problems in South Portland by bringing people from outside the company. Again he said no, and I returned to California.

In less than a month, John called me and said he was going to promote Jim Smaha to operations manager. There were no more issues with the three strong product managers.

Jim Smaha moved up in the Fairchild organization and eventually left Fairchild and joined National Semiconductor. Smaha eventually became president of National Semiconductor in California when Charlie Spork left that position. Several years later, I bumped into Jim Smaha while he was leaving a restaurant. The conversation went something like this: "Hi, John. I hear you had something to do with my promotion in South Portland, which eventually led to my elevation to the president of National."

I said, "Yes, that's probably right."

He said, "I don't know whether to kiss you or kick you in the ass!" He said this with a big smile on his face. He was making a lot more money and living in California. We talked a while and continued on our ways. I was happy he had made the grade.

Peg and Sam Pool Move to California

During Christmas of 1968, Sam and Peg came to visit us for the holidays. I had started to tear down the wall and window in the family room with the intent of making the room twice its present size, extending it out toward the pool in the backyard. As a family, we spent a lot of time in the kitchen and the family room. While working on the room, Sam was amazed at how nice the weather was. He said that back in Pennsylvania his front would be warm and his back cold. I told him to quit his job and move out here. He laughed. "What would I do out here?" he asked. "I'm almost sixty. Who would hire a wire superintendent?" I told him he knew enough about electronics from working on radio-controlled airplanes to find a job easily here. Nothing more was said.

In February 1969, I got a call from Sam and Peg. Sam had quit his job of forty plus years, they had sold their house, and they were coming to California. My Peg was their only child, and I loved Peg and Sam like my own parents. When they arrived, Sam checked out various job opportunities and picked up applications from each. He didn't think anyone would hire a fifty-seven-year-old man who had no experience in the jobs open. I told him to put his age down as fifty-two, but he wouldn't do that. I told him he looked younger than fifty-two, and I filled out his applications for him. He had three offers within a week. He finally decided to take a job as machine shop foreman for Fairchild test systems division. He had his retirement pay from Page Wire, he had this good job and its pay, and within a few years he would be eligible for Social Security. We looked around to find a place he could build a new home, and eventually had one built in Cupertino.

———————

This would prove to be a very good move, as thirteen years later Apple Computer eventually established all their buildings in Cupertino, and the value of houses went up dramatically.

———————

It was great having Peg and Sam only seven miles away. Sam was a good person to talk to about technical issues and things happening around the world. Grandma Peg was a pleasant person to be around. She was also smart and a great companion for my Peg and our children. She was always inviting us down for dinner, and we also would meet Vic Mitrisin on almost every Friday and go to some restaurant. Vic also lived in Cupertino in a condominium he had purchased. We would go many places over the years with Sam and Peg. It was also nice having baby-sitters.

Of course, Sam and Peg wanted to see the Golden Gate Bridge that had provided them an income during the Depression. Sam would look up at the overhanging structure of the bridge and say, "I remember making the cables for this bridge. What a godsend." Sometimes we would drive across the bridge; sometimes we would park and walk across this beautiful structure. Sam never seemed to get enough of this bridge. If I would drive the forty miles from my house to the bridge, he would go every day.

Introduction of the TI Series

Early in 1969, after becoming responsible for Mountainview Digital, I decided I wanted to second source the Texas Instruments product line. There was no room left in Mountainview, and I decided to review the possibilities in the R&D facility located in Palo Alto. This facility was under the management of Leo Dwork, vice president and manager of research and development, who I knew from his Motorola days. There was no space on the main two floors of the R&D plant, but I found a space of approximately 8,000 sq. ft. in the basement and immediately went to ask Leo for the space. He asked me what I wanted to use it for. I told him I wanted to develop and second source the TI product line. He thought that was a great use of the space and granted my request.

Three great engineers were hired to handle this job: Dick Forrest from Sprague; Tom Kloffenstein from Westinghouse; and Colin Knight from Analog Devices on the East Coast. Forrest was the product manager, Kloffenstein was to set up the equipment and establish the processes, and Colin was the manager for the line, which I called the PAT (Palo Alto Fast Turnaround) Line. They were told if one die worked on a wafer, it proved the design was good. The masks and process specs were to be transferred to Fred Roeder at South Portland. Fred Roeder was told each product transferred was his responsibility for making it yield high enough to be economically viable for Fairchild.

Over the course of sixteen months, over fifty products were shipped to South Portland, and Fred Roeder made them yield well. This move to the TI 7400 series started an internal argument within Fairchild. Jerry Sanders, manager of marketing and sales, said that the Fairchild Logic line would be established and outsell the TI line. This subject was taken to the highest levels within Fairchild, and it was determined that both lines could be successful, since there was a major market for both lines. Fairchild's products were faster, but TI's products had been designed into many more functions and looked like it would be the bigger market. Soon after this decision, Jerry Sanders left Fairchild and started his own company called Advanced Micro Devices (AMD). Tony Holbrook soon followed him to AMD..

I had been looking for a manager for the Mountainview operation. In June of 1969, I hired Paul Regan. Paul had been with the West Coast Westinghouse operation and was now the head of custom operations for Raytheon in Mountainview. Paul was a good person to manage the three product managers in Mountainview. Paul handled production, and Tony Holbrook handled engineering, which left me more time for South Portland, Shiprock, Singapore, and the PAT line.

Meanwhile, South Portland kept cranking up production. The combination of John Sussenberger, Jim Smaha, and the three product managers was working well. Singapore was now assembling large numbers of devices. South Portland had an excellent mechanical design engineer from Germany, so South Portland was to design automatic die attach machines and bonding machines for the Singapore operation. Singapore was now assembling large numbers of devices.

Kulick & Soffa, located in Pennsylvania, manufactured certain wire bonding machines that were ideal for assembly of plastic packaging of products assembled in Singapore. I felt great about the accomplishments of all these groups.

And Then I Had None

Early in 1970, Joe Van Poppelin was hired by Les Hogan to take over as vice president and general manager of the semiconductor operations. Hogan had been acting as an interim VP/GM of these operations.

Van Poppelin was only aboard a couple of months when he called me into his office. He said, "You know that you handle 90 percent of my sales. I can't afford for one person to have this much control. I don't like one-on-one management, and I'm going to split up the operations. John Sussenberger will manage South Portland, Paul Regan will handle Mountainview, and there will be a new manager for the Singapore operations. Shiprock may report to Paul Regan. I haven't determined that move yet. All of these people will report to me. I haven't decided how to handle the PAT line yet. I want you to report to Wilf Corrigan, the vice president of discreet devices (transistors in Mountainview and Diodes in San Rafael). Wilf will determine your responsibilities." So, Van Poppelin had essentially replaced me with himself, thus dropping one level of management.

I walked out of his office stunned. Here were all these operations that I had taken from low levels to high levels and new products far in about a year and a half, only to have a new GM come into the company and dump that progress. He felt it would be "one on one," as he put it, since I would have been the only manager of volume ICs reporting to him. At least I had left him with good managers and good equipment for each of these operations, as I had seen to it over that year and a half.

Corrigan didn't know what to do with me. He told me to go to the various plants and determine what could be transferred to one of the other plants. He knew I understood all phases of operations and felt I could be of value in determining which superior methods or operations could be beneficial to one of the other manufacturing plants. He also said, "I'd like to transfer Vic Mitrisin up to South Portland to establish a mask-making operation and run it. It's time for you to let him go on his own." I agreed, and Vic went away for what would turn out to be a great move for him.

I had only worked for Corrigan a couple of months when he told me that Dr. Tom Longo wanted to talk to me. I asked him what it was about, and he said that Longo had been hired by Hogan and was now the vice president of linear operations reporting to Van Poppelin. So I went to see Dr. Longo.

Tom Longo was well known in the industry. He had been one of the founders of a digital product line called TTL at Transitron in the East. This was an interesting visit to Longo's office. Here Longo was a man about ten years older than me with a fantastic mind and well respected throughout the industry. Tom had been given a small stock when he was a young kid, and he had started to watch the stock market from that time on. This proved valuable to him because it brought to his attention many small companies in the United States to his attention. He used this knowledge to determine possible customers for Fairchild's products.

He said, "John, I'd like you to come to the linear products group as the engineering manager. Nine months from now, I'll give you the whole linear operation."

This knocked my socks off. Here was a man I didn't know but somehow he knew me. I said, "Tom, you want me to work for the linear operations manager for nine months and then take his job. The operations manager could make me look bad in nine months, and then I won't get the job anyway." He said to trust him and that he always kept his promises.

I went back to Corrigan, repeated the conversation, and asked him what he thought about it. He said that he didn't know Longo and that I would have to make up my own mind. I decided to trust Longo and accepted the job. I only ran linear engineering for two months, and Longo called me and Gene Lottamoto (the linear operations manager) into his office and announced that he was promoting me to director of linear operations; at last I had met a man of his words. (This would prove to be good move for me and a lot of respect for Dr. Tom as I called him).

About that time, Tom Longo also became responsible for many of the digital product lines. I took him on a tour of the various operations

I had previously run. When we were at the PAT line, he said to me, "It's too late to enter the 7400 TI line of products."

Two years later at a meeting of Fairchild management to review the markets and sales with the field sales personnel, the announcements was made that the 7400 series of products were the biggest revenue producer of all of Fairchild's product lines. Tom turned to me and said, "I guess it wasn't too late. I'm glad you started that line of products." He then addressed the rest of the people in the room and told them to extend the credit to John Husher. This made me feel real good inside.

Work Takes Ken and Sherie to Brazil

After returning from Argentina in 1962, Ken eventually took a job with U.S. Steel. Eventually, he took a position offered to him with U.S. Steel in northern Ohio. He and his family moved to Lakeland, Ohio (just north of Cleveland), in 1970. The job was at first challenging, and what he couldn't find to keep his mind active there, he found while working on the house they had purchased. He kept busy between work and their new house. The house and yard required a lot of work, and within a year the whole family had decided they didn't like living there.

Ken wasn't happy with his job, and Sherie wasn't happy with the cold weather and the wind blowing snow off Lake Erie. When the thermometer read 30 degrees, it was around zero from the wind chill factor. Lori, Gaye, and Dana didn't like the schools they were attending. In addition, Lori and Gaye were heading in a direction that Ken and Sherie didn't like. They had been introduced to drugs and alcohol in an odd community atmosphere that seemed to prevail.

When it became obvious to Ken that he wasn't the only one unhappy, he decided to bring the family together and consider an opportunity that was being offered to him. He had been offered a job with U.S. Steel to go to Brazil with several other consultants and train the Brazilians on equipment that had been erected for a large coke facility that had recently been built there. Ken called the family together and discussed the job opportunity he had been offered. He told them the decision would be up to them. It didn't take but a minute and the decision was to go to another foreign country for a big change. They didn't have to go until early in 1972, so they had time to sell the house and travel to California before leaving. So, their whole family came to see my family.

So the whole family came to see my family. This was a great time, especially for the kids, who were almost matched in age. Lori was fifteen, Gaye was fourteen, Jay was thirteen, Karen was eleven, David was nine, and Dana was seven.

We were all excited by Ken's new job and the move to Brazil, although I had always worried about them when they are gone like when they went to Argentina. While they were gone, it was like a void in my life. When you're born a twin, you're used to turning around and seeing your other half.

(The following section about Ken and family is my paraphrasing things that happened based on letters from Ken and Sherie and every once in a while one of the kids. I also had some inputs from discussions with them later.)

Soon they were getting shots, their passports, and were on their way to Brazil. Only this time they flew in a jet instead of the propeller plane the family had flown in back in 1959. What a difference in speed, noise, and comfort. And this time they took the dog. In a short time they were in Brazil, landing in Rio de Janeiro, Brazil. Ken had left for Brazil three months before, and Sherie had to stay behind and sell the house, the car, and other things they no longer needed.

Ken was at the airport to meet them. This time there was Sherie, three girls, and a dog. He was elated to see them all, and it didn't seem like he could get enough love from all of them, including the dog.

The plant was located two hours from Rio in a city named Volta Redonda.

The years Ken, Sherie, and the oldest girls had spent in Argentina prepared them emotionally for what they would find in Brazil. What they weren't prepared for was the fact that they would live in a small town with the Brazilian people. This was quite different than Argentina, where they lived with Americans in the barrio supplied by Koppers. U.S. Steel believed their employees should live with the people who worked in the plant.

Ken found a house in a small community called Laranjal. Laranjal was located on top of a mountain, a town of 150 homes overlooking the city of Volta Redonda and the steel mill below. The residents represented the upper class of people, and the town was considered private. Most of the family would find this living much to their liking, and they learned to love Brazil and its people.

Ken talked to his kids about living among the Brazilian people. He wanted them to accept the ways of the people they would be meeting: learn their language, learn their habits, and embrace their culture rather than being the ugly Americans. He told them to focus on what it took to be accepted by the people they would meet each day. This was a

Ken and Sherie in Brazil 1973

challenge to the three girls, age fifteen, fourteen, and seven, but they worked on it. Ken was forty, and Sherie was almost thirty-seven. This was a little late in their lives to be learning new habits—but they did.

When eating at home or away from home, he wanted them to speak the language as much as possible. It was a learning period. since it was different for Lori and Gaye who had remembered some of the language from Argentina, but here they spoke Portuguese, which was completely different. Of the two older girls, Gaye found these challenges to be exciting, and she learned everything she could, while Lori was disenchanted with living in this environment, which was more than foreign to her. It was a challenge she didn't relish.

Dana was young, and this was her first experience away from the States. She was happy being with her mother, dad, sisters, and her dog. The palm trees, mangos, and bananas in their backyard reminded her of an enchanted land. There were cobblestone roads and beggars like she had seen in the movies. Soon she too became impressed by the warmth of the people and by the Portuguese language.

The Hushers lived above their previous status. They had a maid named Maria, a cook named Anna, a gardener named Paolo, along with two horses. This was unique living for them. Each of these servants helped to teach them the language and laughed when the Hushers used a word that was completely wrong. Maria was there during the day. Anna came in the morning to prepare their main meal of the day, which was at noon. Paolo brought their horses first thing in the morning and took them back to the barn on his way home from work at the end of day. What a wonderful life for these impressionable young people.

School was a three-bedroom home in the suburbs of Volta Redonda that was provided for the handful of American families. The yearly curriculum was provided by a U.S. company that sent them books and teaching aids for two bilingual teachers and several parent volunteers. School started at 7:45 AM with a tea break from 9:00 to 9:15 AM and finished up at noon. The curriculum included a class on the Portuguese language to prepare them for everyday living.

A four-hour school day was exciting. That wasn't hard to get used to. When they returned back to the States, Dana started fifth grade, but, at a third-grade reading level, she had to spend extra time making up for those four-hour days. So, you always get what you "worked for" in the end. However, Dana told me that living in Brazil made her what she is today. "The experience of that culture was a gift," that helped her throughout her life.

There were other things that impressed them: the bread man on a bike with a large front basket covered with a blanket to keep the hard rolls warm, hollering "Pao!" as he rang his bell. They would run to buy his bread and sit around anywhere in the street to eat the warm bread or run to the veranda of their house overlooking the town of Volta Redonda. Then there was the "ice cream man, who rode around ringing his bell. He was sneaky with the young American girl who didn't know the language well. He would give Dana ice cream without her paying. She thought he was being nice, but at the end of the month he came to their house and handed her folks the bill for the ice cream she had eaten that month!

After eating the main meal when they came home from school, they rode the horses bareback that Paolo had brought in the morning. This was hard on the horse, but sometimes harder on the rider. Dana flew off one day and was taken to the hospital with a concussion.

Volta Redonda is called Cidade de Aco, which means "the Steel City." Volta Redonda was known for steel manufacturing. It was founded in 1941, and the steel mill began construction the following year, with the first steel being produced in 1946. Industry was not foreign to this city, and they looked forward to the coke plant to add to the city's reputation.

The Coke plant had completed construction the year before, and it had been decided that they would contract U.S. Steel to teach the locals how to run the plant efficiently.

There were eleven American consultants like Ken that who lived fairly close that they would shortly befriend. Each of these consultants had a different chore within the plant there in the Brazilian city. Ken was responsible for the training of the locals on how to handle the machines, and how to handle problems, and how to handle themselves when problems arose. He also had to start training selected workers for managerial situations, including problem solving. This was great for Ken since he was not involved in focusing on building a new plant but in building an infrastructure of people to run the place on three shifts for seven days a week, which was his specialty.

It seemed somewhat harder to teach these people than the ones at Argentina, not because they were less intelligent, but because they were less focused. They were more free spirited than the locals in Argentina. They were fun loving, and many of them would get their paychecks and you wouldn't see them until they ran out of money. But there were always a few Ken would find that fit the requirements and who were more mature about their work. Locals who had families seemed to be the ones that care more and used their inherent talent to push to learn more as the days went on. These were the ones he depended on. Like any other place, the cream goes to the top, and it was like that there. It just took time to figure out which ones "were the cream" and to remove the less focused souls from the plant.

Like Argentina, Brazil was a breath of fresh air when away from work. Two hours away, Rio being a two-hour bus ride or a one and half hour car drive was very accessible for the members of the family over their stay in this warm land. Several weekends were spent driving to Rio, with the family and taking in the new sights and beauty of this city.

Ken removed his "pilgrim hat" so to speak and allowed Lori and Gaye a tremendous amount of freedom compared to Ohio and Argentina. It was his way of letting them stay in sync with their Brazilian peers. Since the Brazilians were more carefree in their attitude, it began to rub off on these two older girls. They wanted to go to Rio and have fun with other kids were enjoying. Ken and Sherie encouraged them to take the local transit to Redonda, but they didn't encourage them to take the bus and travel the two-hour trip to Rio de Janeiro and go to the Copacabana Beach.

However, after a lot of begging and noise making, Sherie and Ken finally gave in and gave them permission to take the early morning transit to Rio. Sherie and Ken were a wreck until they returned that evening. They allowed them to go twice. The girls seemed to handle themselves well the first time, so they took a second chance. Lori and Gaye arrived in Rio on the bus and took a cab to the beach. They sun bathed, watched the locals, swam, and drank Fantas (an orange type drink with no alcohol) as the day rapidly flew by.

When their day at the beach was over, they went to one a nearby store and used the bathroom to wash off the sand and change clothes. The toilets in Rio were nicer than the ones in the United States because they were private. When you went in, you locked the door until you were finished. This made it ideal for them since they both went in, locked the door, and made themselves ready to return home. This was a great learning period for them. They even found it exciting to wash off the sand in their "private" dressing rooms and laughed as they proceeded.

Afterwards, they took a cab to the bus terminal and awaited their ride back home.

While Rio presented was a modern city with modern conveniences, the town where the plant was located was not as fortunate. It was a steel mill town and had much less in the way of modern conveniences, however it was a city of about 200,000 people, and therefore was structured to maintain the inhabitants well. It had good schools and hospitals, and reminded one of the steel mill towns in Pennsylvania. Likewise, only a few miles out of the city location, or plant location and you were in a wilderness like no other. Many places could only be accessed by biking or walking. The roads were dirt roads, unless you were on the double lane road leading to places like Rio. All this was to Ken liked the environment. He went with several of the other Americans and a couple locals out into the wild to fish or hunt.

I remember a letter he wrote to me about going duck hunting. It was a laugh. He said they went out in a small boat on a lake early in the morning while it still had its morning fog. The fog was sitting about ten feet above the water, and they blew their duck calls that were made of hollowed out reeds from the area. Then they waited a few minutes, and the ducks (or geese) would fly down below the fog toward their boat. It was easy to shoot a duck that was only ten or twenty feet away from you, zooming toward his fate.

The only problem was getting the catch home before it turned bad. The heat and humidity were so bad that a dead bird didn't remain edible for long. Unlike Argentina, refrigerators were available, but many of them didn't have a refrigerator because they couldn't afford one. This was not so in their little town of Laranjal, where Brazilians and Americans had all these conveniences.

On one duck hunting trip, the wilderness had its revenge. One of the hunters was picking his catch out of the water, and it was still alive and shaking. He reached down to grab it, and while doing so he lost his finger to a piranha. These fish are small but have huge teeth for their size. They normally run in large numbers to attack their prey, but in this case there was only one fish. He got his dinner for the day, and Ken's friend lost his finger. Ken wrote that if one of the locals had come along with them on the trip, it probably would have been avoided, because they were aware of the dangers.

Ken had much more time to himself and his family in Brazil. Where he spent a lot of overtime at the plant in Argentina, this was not the case here. Where previously when there was a breakdown in the plant he would be involved and spent many long hours resolving it, here when there were breakdowns, there was another set of people that took care of these problems.

He did get involved in solving technical problems of a different nature. Whenever equipment didn't work, as they should he would question the locals running the equipment and try to troubleshoot the problem. He was more adept at this than the other consultants who were more specialists. His experience in working up to management helped him to diagnose systematic problems and cures for them. These he taught the locals.

This teaching of the locals on how to solve these problems provided him new avenues for problem solving. Sometimes when he came into the plant and there had been a problem on the preceding shift, the problem been diagnosed and solved by the local, usually with some method taught to him by Ken. This assured Ken that his teaching had worked. However, there were times when the problems were solved solely by the locals using their own methods. Ken would ask what they had done, and this was another way for him to learn. Everyone has something to teach or to learn if one keeps an open mind. Some people have what is called an NIH factor (not invented here) and they think that problems can only be solved by them. Those people normally don't get far in life. Ken kept an open mind, and he worked with the locals like they were part of his own family.

The Hushers became closer as time moved on, emulating the Brazilian families, where kids spent more time with their families. The family spent a lot of their time at private clubs, swimming and hanging out with their new friends.

Ken reserved tables for the family at the carnivals that were celebrated fairly often in Volta Redunda. Some carnivals were five days long, and Ken would not let the family miss any of it. He wanted to participate, and he wanted his family to learn to participate. "Make the best of what's presented to you and see where it takes you," he would say.

He wanted to be a part of the local community, and his Portuguese got better and better. He and Gaye ate up the new language, while Lori was not really trying to learn it. Ken and Sherie became the center of attention at many of these outings as they immersed themselves in the doings of their friends and the other eleven American families. They were excellent dancers and took a somewhat different in their approach to dancing than the Brazilians. Soon there were many Brazilians learning the "American" way of dancing.

As time moved on, Lori became more and more disenchanted with Brazil and wanted to go back to the States and finish high school there. She didn't want to learn the culture or the language or visit historical places around Brazil. So after ten months Sherie and Ken realized that it was probably better for Lori to return to the States and finish high school there. The drive to the airport in Rio was not fun, but they knew it was for the best, considering the circumstances. Lori finished high school and met Dean Coulson, and they got married in 1976. They would give Sherie and Ken their first grandchild in 1978 with a girl named Jamie and two years later a grandson named Shaun. Both of them went on to college and received professional degrees. They recently celebrated their thirtieth anniversary.

During the second year, Ken's job became one of maintenance; he had to ensure that his protégés kept up with their learning and maintained a good operation and insuring that their productivity increased with time. Maintenance in the context that he had to make sure that the better people moved up in the ranks. Secondly, maintenance also meant ensuring that people who left the operation were replaced by well-trained operators. Maintenance in the respect that the operators learned about the way the internal parts of the total plant worked and what could cause problems—helping them to learn how to diagnose problems before they happened or before they became a major problem. (This always reminds me of the movie *Sand Pebbles,* where the lead actor, Steve McQueen, taught a Chinese worker how the steam engine worked, and he took him around the ship and showed him where steam was formed. He called it "live steam," and where the steam lost all it's poop he called "dead steam." I always had this mental picture when I got a letter from Ken telling me about training the locals.)

Good training takes time, but it ends up giving you time. This is what appeared to Ken and his family. The time Ken spent with the training allowed him to go places on the weekends knowing that the crew back at the plant knew what they were doing.

The family vacationed every other month with Ken taking the family to places he had heard of that had some significance about it. His desire to learn more about the culture had them going to places that displayed something new for them to learn. He would read about the place they were to visit: its history and little tidbits, and during the drive he would try to convey this to his three ladies (Sherie, Gaye, and Dana).

They traveled into the wildness of Brazil and saw shrines, waterfalls, and animals they had never seen before. They visited small towns that were historic. Many times they only looked at the magnificence of the country. They looked out over large areas of vegetation, lakes, and streams, and, when they returned to their home, they talked about the exciting things they had seen that day.

Ken and Sherie spent some time teaching Gaye how to drive the Ford they had there, with their three-speed on the column. They gave Gaye permission to drive around the top of their mountain, and eventually Ken let her drive alone to town. She ran errands in the vehicle, and she was only fifteen years old. This is the kind of freedom allowed to Ken's children. He treated the workers at the plant in the same way. As they learned more, he allowed them more latitude in handling their jobs. Delegation was key to his success as time went on.

As time moved on, Gaye became the teacher rather than the pupil. She had learned Portuguese so well that now she began to teach her father. They played word games where the word was given in either English or Spanish and they had to respond with the proper Portuguese word.

Gaye was also the one who gave me much of the information about the events in Brazil and about her dad. She said, "He had so many friends in Brazil, both American and Brazilian. Everyone within the five-mile radius of the plant knew him and liked him. He was the great American rather than the ugly American. Every eager angler (fisher) had my dad on the top of their list to join them on a fishing outing. He went with them to the Amazon where they fished and fought off the piranhas and capybaras (tailless, largely aquatic South American rodents often exceeding four feet in length). I became very proud of my parents."

Before Ken knew it, his contract period was coming to a close. They had spent two years at this location and it was time to start selling things they didn't want to take back to the States. So, Sherie began sorting out their things for sale, the things for throwing away, the things to send as gifts to some of their friends in the States, and some of the things to give to the Americans who were staying as permanent employees.

They sold the car with the understanding that it remained their property until the day they left. There were all kinds of native artwork that Sherie had to make decisions about. Some she wanted to sell or give away and Ken wanted to keep. There had to be compromises and they found them.

Dana was going on ten years old, and Gaye was seventeen. She would go back and finish her last year of school in the States. Ken was going on forty-two and was concerned as to whether he should stay with U.S. Steel or find some other means of employment. This is one of the heavy decisions the returning professionals have to make as they return to the States. If he stayed with U.S. Steel, what would he do? If he found a good position within U.S. Steel, would it be around Pittsburgh and where would they live? These were earth-shaking decisions, especially as Ken became older and the selection process became more and more limited.

However, he was confident of his talents. He had learned a lot about making coke and the way the different parts of a coke oven performed or don't perform. He had become good at troubleshooting.

He removed these thoughts off the top of his mind for the present and thought about other things, like wondering what Lori would do with their return. Where were Gaye and Dana going to go to school?

He felt that Gaye's future was the most important at this time. She was ready for her last year of schooling, and the schools in the States might be foreign to her. Hopefully, her education over the last couple of years would adequately prepare her for the future.

(Gaye went to college and majored in languages, specifically Spanish and Portuguese. She began as an interpreter with the airlines. Later, she went on to gain her master's degree in language and became a teacher.

Dana did well in school, and at the age of sixteen she was selected in a beauty contest as a representative for Pennsylvania in the Miss Teenage America contest. She married Gary Carmen and had two boys and a girl—Colton, Tanner, and Danielle. She has been married over twenty years at this time.)

Before I knew it, they were on a jet plane coming back to the United States to find out what was in store for each of them. They both loved Brazil but were very glad to get the girls back in the States.

Linear Operations Manager

At about the same time that Ken and Sherie were heading to Brazil in 1972, I was heavily involved in taking over the linear operations for Tom Longo and trying to make a more efficient operation. I wanted to make it profitable. Running the linear operations was a challenge. The various groups reporting to linear were spread across Mountainview. Some of my first moves were to consolidate these groups into one new area in the Rusty Bucket. I had Steve Weisch move from South Portland to linear and made him the wafer fab manager. Slowly, the operations in 1971 and 1972 started to increase their productivity.

Sam Pool built radio-controlled airplanes, and one time he had said to me, "I use a voltage regulator made by National Semiconductor, but it only comes in one voltage. I need other voltages at times."

I remembered this and called together my engineering manager of linear, Will Steffe, and his team of designers. I told them I wanted them to design a voltage regulator that would work at voltages from 1.0 volt to 40 volts and drive 1 amp.

They came back a week later and told me this was not possible. I told them I had read an article where the writer showed that with three resistors he could make about twenty resistors, depending on how they were connected. And with five resistors, he could make a huge amount. Why not take this approach and come up with using this technique along with a high voltage-designed regulator and make it a programmable regulator only depending on the last wire bonding selection to connect the resistors at a different point.

The designers went away with this challenge and returned the following week with data they had generated using discrete transistors and resistors. They were able to make a programmable regulator. Now that this had been proven, they went about making an integrated voltage regulator with a string of resistors and, depending on how the resistors were connected with the last metal; they could obtain voltage regulators from 1.5 volts to 36 volts. This was the start of the single-package programmable voltage regulator that operated at currents up to 2 amps.

Several months later, I had them design a smaller version of this device that could fit in a small TO5 package and regulate at currents of 200 milliamps. All of these regulators sold well and became the biggest market in the Fairchild linear business, and over the years other companies picked up methods of supplying multiple voltage regulators.

Changing My Name from Jay to John

Late in 1970, Peg and I talked about the fact that Jay was now old enough to start getting phone calls, and there would be confusion if they were asking for him or for me. We had started to call him JD to differentiate him from me. We thought that maybe as he grew older his peers might start calling him Jaydee, and it would sound feminine. That wouldn't be good. So right then and there we decided to call me John and him Jay. I thought it would be hard for my Peg and Peg and Sam to call me John, but it proved to be no problem at all. Likewise, I never heard anyone call him JD again. So everyone started calling me by my proper name, John. Peg later said that it was one of the best things we ever did because she liked the name John and so did I.

Working on the New Polaroid Camera

In late 1971 and early 1972, linear started to work with Polaroid on five circuits. They were unique circuits, and Polaroid management would not tell us what they were for, only there terminal test conditions. They had a senior-level program manager live on the West Coast while these products were being developed. He was at the plant day in and day out. One of the circuits was a motor drive, one a regulator and three of them were operational amps—each to serve a different function. We were never told how they would be used, even though I got mad at the program manager one day and said, "For all I know we could be making a robotic gun." This didn't sway him.

The pressure to make these circuits work was great, and we were finally being told that they were meeting specifications. But Polaroid wanted them assembled on flexible printed circuit material. This required that bumps be plated on the circuits, so they could be bonded to the flex cable as they called it. We had great difficulty making these products at a yield high enough to produce a profit.

Early in 1973, Wilf Corrigan (now the president of Fairchild), Les Hogan (chairman of the board), and I were invited to Dr. Peter Land's office in Boston. Peter Land was the founder and president of Polaroid. He had invented Polaroid glasses, Polaroid film, and the remarkable cameras sold by Polaroid. After about a half hour, he brought forth a flat, leather-bound object that would prove to be a camera. He shot pictures while we were in the room, and the film popped out in seconds. Remarkable pictures almost instantly.

"Here's where your circuits go," he said proudly. "How long do you think the batteries will last in this camera?" he asked.

Each of us took a guess; we did not think it would not take long at the currents we knew it would require. He threw out his chest and said, "Where are the batteries?"

Each of us took a look at the camera and couldn't find the batteries. Then he looked at Wilf Corrigan and said, "I thought you ran a detective agency in England. You're not much of a detective if you can't find the battery." He pulled out the film pack and showed us the battery. Each pack of film had the battery built into it, so every time a customer bought a pack of film, they were also buying a new battery. Polaroid had built a factory outside of Boston to make this special battery. What a wondrous camera.

About a month later, I got a package delivered to my door, and in it was a custom, leather-bound Polaroid camera—compliments of Dr. Peter Land. As far as I know, I had the only camera like this. He said it was a reward for developing and making the circuits. The sad part was that we could never make these circuits at a profit, as the attachment to the flexible film and the requirements for bumps on the circuits resulted in poor yields for us. Texas Instruments was ahead of Fairchild on the development of flexible circuits and the use of bumps on dies to attach to these unique interconnects. They were able to supply these, evidently at a profit, and they got the volume business.

As time went on, responsibility for the hybrid circuit group, the high reliability business, and the automotive circuit business was transferred to me..

In 1972, linear had been the only business group in Fairchild that made a profit. These various groups were transferred to my responsibility as a "reward" for bringing linear to profitability.

Promotion to GM Analog Division

In mid-1973, while visiting customers on the East Coast, I got a call from Corrigan's secretary telling me to get back to Mountainview as soon as possible. I flew out that day. We had a meeting in President Wilf Corrigan's office. He said, "I'm reorganizing the company into five divisions. Each division will be managed by a vice president and have its own accounting and marketing managers. Roy Pollock will have the MOS division, Greg Reyes will have the discreet division, Van Poppelin will have the LED (light-emitting diodes) division, Tom Longo will have the digital division, and John Husher will be promoted to general manager of the new division called the analog division."

I was elated, but not for long. Wilf then told each of the division heads who their financial controller and their marketing manager would be. When he came to me, he said, "Your marketing manager will be Gus Faeyler."

And I said, "No, he won't. He's a good inside man, but he's an introvert when it comes to the field sales people."

Corrigan remarked that he was the best marketing person we had. Then he said," Your controller will be Paul Synitz."

And I said, "No, he won't. He has a degree in physics, and every time engineers have a requisition signed for a piece of equipment, he thinks he knows more about the equipment than the engineers. I don't want a physicist. I want a financial expert."

Wilf was very displeased with my answers and said the meeting was over. As I left the meeting, I was confused. I could always talk straight to Corrigan, and I knew that I had just irritated him. Thinking back later, I realized that I could talk straight to Wilf while we were alone but not when others were present. This turned out to be a huge mistake on my behalf. Everything became a battle after that.

Meanwhile, I was more concerned about Vice President Tom Longo and how he might feel about me being promoted to his level. Tom called me into his office and said, "John, I'm glad you were promoted. You deserved this, and I'm happy I saw that in you when I brought you over to linear."

Wilf called me into his office and asked me who I thought would be a better marketing manager. I told him Andy Procasini, and he remarked that he had made Andy vice president of marketing and sales a year and a half ago and had to remove him after a year.

I told him, "Wilf, you took Andy from vice president of quality and reliability and made him the vice president of marketing and sales. He didn't know anything about that job, but he's a smart guy. He divided the U.S. market into four sections, and he went and hired a strong manager for each of those sections. Just when he was getting on top of that job, you took him out. I think he would make a great manager of marketing for the analog division."

Wilf wouldn't do this, and there was always a tense feeling between us over this. About a month later, I ran into the vice president of sales out shopping, and he said he would like to have Gus Faeyler as his manager of inside sales. I told him about the conflict with Wilf Corrigan and told him to ask Wilf for this transfer and I would approve it. That weekend I got a call from Wilf Corrigan saying he was approving this but felt it was a big mistake. He also told me I could hire another controller for the analog division, as Jim Hazel (vice president of finance) would like to have Paul Synitz. This was good, but I knew by his tone that he was not happy with me.

I interviewed several people for the controller job, and eventually Jeff Henley became my controller. He was a young man out of college with a very bright attitude, high intellect, and a lot of energy. He and I hit it off well, and he was an immeasurable help to the analog division.

———— ·-·—∙∞∙◦◦∙∞∙-·— ————

Somehow, I knew people. Time and again I would select people, and they turned out to be good choices. I don't know if this was because of the books I had read on management or an innate capability I was born with. Several years later, Jeff became the vice president of finance for Oracle, a big successful software company, and later became the president of Oracle. He would become a millionaire many times over.

———— ·-·—∙∞∙◦◦∙∞∙-·— ————

In the monthly financial reviews that Corrigan held, there would be marketing, finance, and production control along with each division general manager present. Various subject matters were discussed in the war room, and it became obvious after a few months that Andy Procasini would have the best answers to Wilf Corrigan's questions.

229

He stood out as being very qualitative, quantitative, and direct with his answers. They would prove to be right on. He made me proud that he was the marketing manager of linear.

Near the end of 1973, Andy came into my office and told me that the salesmen in Europe thought that they could get a large portion of Grundig's business in Germany if someone would visit Philips in Holland and obtain permission to second source the products being supplied to Grundighe. I told Andy to make plane reservations for me to go on Wednesday and return on Monday. That way I wouldn't miss too much of what was going on in the States.

I got a call from Wilf Corrigan, reminding me that I had been told that there would be no broad siding the European market this year, and I told him to talk to Andy. Later, he called me back to say that he was approving the visit but was not in favor of it. I told him that Andy had said that Fairchild would lose a lot of good salesmen in Europe if someone did not attempt this. The European salesmen, who were on commission, had not been booking any large business and therefore were not making much money,.

And so I went to Europe, first visiting Grundig in Germany. There I was able to get a commitment of half of their business if I could supply the circuits Philips of Holland was supplying. At lunch I asked if there was a place where I could send a telegram to the United States. I sent a telegram to Jim Unruh, vice president of finance (eventually to become the president and CEO of Univac Corp). In it, I stated that instead of his people turning down my requests to have the San Rafael plant converted from two-inch wafer production to three-inch, they should get off their lazy asses and tell me what it took to qualify San Rafael. I told him to be positive and not negative, to give directions and not always rejections.

After lunch I flew to Hamburg, Germany, to talk to the Philips representatives. Arriving there in the late evening, the meeting began with me requesting (and later demanding) the masks and process details for making the products for Grundig as a second source. They refused and couldn't see why Fairchild should gain this capability. I told them that Philips had an agreement with Fairchild, had visited our facilities, and had gotten what they wanted from Fairchild. Why shouldn't they reciprocate?

And so the evening went on and on. I would not allow them to leave without this agreement. At about 11:00 PM, they phoned Tony Opsteltan, the vice president of marketing and sales for Philips, at corporate headquarters in Holland. Tony said he would fly in early the next day. I would not allow anyone to leave the meeting room, and food was brought in. We spent the night there and had breakfast the next morning. I felt if they left the room I would find it impossible to get them all back in the room again and make a commitment..

Tony Opsteltan arrived around 10:00 AM. He asked, "Why should Fairchild receive these designs when it would mean Philips would lose some of our business with Grundig?" I countered by saying that sooner or later the customer would want a second source, and that might mean TI or Motorola would be involved. If Fairchild was involved, Philips would be privy to any improvements made on the Grundighe devices. Philips would not be privy to this information from any other supplier. This argument hit home, and finally the discussion began to move. By late afternoon, we came to an agreement. They said they would send the masks, design rules, and process specifications to Fairchild within two weeks. I told them I was going to stay there until they boxed it all up and put it on the plane with me. Several hours later, they agreed. The next day, a large wooden box was put on the flight I took back to the States. This guaranteed Fairchild their biggest piece of business in Europe.

Back at Mountainview, I expected to be received well for what I had accomplished in several days. However, I was called into Wilf Corrigan's office and reamed out for the telegram I had sent to Jim Unruh concerning the three-inch conversion in San Rafael. There was not one mention of what I had accomplished in Europe. The European sales force now saw corporate support from the States, went after the Grundig business as a cohesive team, and eventually got half the business. It became the biggest market for linear in Europe, until later when the voltage regulators from linear overtook those sales.

As much as I respected Wilf Corrigan and what he was doing with

Fairchild, it was obvious that we were not seeing eye to eye on a daily basis. It was no surprise to me when he called me into his office and said he was pulling me out of that position and that Tom Longo wanted to have me back with him. So I was back with Tom. He now had a huge part of the Fairchild's large scale integrated circuits business; since Roy Pollock had left the MOS division, Tom had taken over the MOS as well as the other digital groups he had.

Tom wanted me to do several things that were a pain to him at the time. Mask making in Mountainview (now under Vic Mitrisin) was getting blasted by general managers and operations managers at all the plants, concerning the quality of the masks being received and the time it took to receive them.

The MOS division was having terrible yield and cost problems, and Tom wanted me to consult with the manager of that operation on a daily basis. The bump process for automated bonding of the die led to packages having technical problems. Tom told me to take the mask-making facility under my wing, as well as managing the bump process to see what could be done to bring the yields up.

Meanwhile, Wilf Corrigan had cut my pay, and I decided to resolve this with him. I told Wilf that when he promoted me I had turned down a raise and had told him not to give me a raise until I had handled that position to his satisfaction for a year. Since I had never accepted a raise, why should I take a pay cut when I was removed from that position? He said, "That's what I think your new job is worth." That was the end of the subject as far as he was concerned.

Mask-Making Issues to Solve

I reviewed the mask shop and the flow of material through that area with Vic Mitrisin and came to two major conclusions: the proper equipment was in place to do the job and the ordering and supplying of masks needed better interdivision communication with the mask shop. I had the paperwork system for ordering masks changed and the production control method slightly altered. Then I invited all of the general managers and operation managers to the buildings to have them meet the people running the buildings, to review how masks were ordered and shipped (new paperwork system), and to review the excellent equipment the company had at its disposal. I felt the equipment was second to none and felt that major progress would be made in the quality and on time deliveries to each of them. Now they at least knew who the players were and were impressed with the equipment and what it took for each of their group's mask needs to be satisfied.

After three months, the comments in the war room changed from derogatory comments about the masks to praise of the on time deliveries and the quality of the masks. One general manager commented that I had done a great job in hiring the right people for bringing the mask shop up to this kind of performance. Tom Longo looked over at me and winked, knowing that I had not hired anyone for the mask shop, just changed some paperwork.

MOS Issues to Solve

A review of the MOS process allowed me to make certain recommendations that resulted in improved yield. One suggestion was to drop the standard technology and go to a technology that was similar to the isoplanar process patented by the bipolar memory group of Fairchild. This was tried on one device with a six-day turnaround and displayed superior results. After this, each major production device type was converted to this modification of the isoplanar process with the use of nitride in the processing. Yields were impacted dramatically. I spent considerable time on the line and was able to recommend the elimination of process steps that were not needed and to modify other process steps slightly to obtain improved performance of the finished product. I had never had any experience with MOS, and I found the process, techniques, and technology to be more exacting than the bipolar processes used in linear products. This experience helped me for the rest of my professional career.

Bump Process Technology Issues

The bump process was very crude, consisting of etching the oxide over the bonding pads to expose the aluminum bonding pad. At this point, a bump was formed by establishing a plating action on the aluminum pad and eventually ending up with gold bumps in these locations. The crudeness related to the use of fairly dirty chemicals relative to what is primarily used to manufacture Integrated Circuits and the fact that each device required a different printed circuit to be placed on the flexible printed circuits.

My approach was to clean up the chemical methods being used through improved purchasing specifications and qualified suppliers that would ensure better reproducibility from one batch to the next. In addition, we worked on the standardization of the bonding pads location so that the flexible printed circuit material could be standardized to work with various die sizes.

Therefore, more and more products fell within the same requirements for automatic bonding as the flex material and the packages receiving these flex circuits. My progress on this task was not satisfactory, and I couldn't put my heart and soul into it like I did with other projects. But it was an improvement.

One day, early in 1974, there was a knock on my office door and in walked Andy Procassini. He said, "John, I just found out from Corrigan the trouble you went through to get me the marketing job. I just want you to know that Corrigan told me I was the best marketing manager in the company, and he offered me the job of vice president of European marketing. I accepted it. I want to shake your hand." I got a lump in my throat and told him he deserved the new job and that I was happy for him.

A couple of years later, Andy was promoted to marketing vice president for the Far East. He did a great job for Fairchild, directing us into the right markets and pushing his sales personnel to penetrate the Eastern market. After a few successful years, he was approached by the newly formed American Semiconductor Industry to be their president. In this position, he was the lead person struggling with Japan to allow American companies to sell their products in Japan. At that time Japan had frozen the purchasing of any semiconductors from outside the country. Here was a growing market, and the U.S. suppliers could not penetrate it. Andy demanded that 20 percent of all semiconductor sales in Japan be American products. His argument was that the United States didn't freeze Japanese products in the United States, so he wanted reciprocity.

It took him about five years, but he gained this market share for U.S. semiconductor manufacturers. This allowed the markets to grow for American companies and served as an example to other industries that had also been receiving the same "frozen out" treatment. If some of the older industries in the United States had taken this same kind of stand earlier, their businesses would have prospered instead of eventually losing the markets to Far East countries. Andy's success was another example that I knew people. I was a "people's person" and it seemed that I always had competent people working for me.

From Fairchild to Advanced Micro Devices (AMD)

In March of 1974, just after celebrating my forty-second birthday, I was approached by AMD (Advanced Micro Devices) to join them. Jerry Sanders, the president, wanted me as the managing director of bipolar memories, which had become a big business for Fairchild and other companies. AMD was building a new building, primarily to produce bipolar memories.

By early May, I had decided to go to AMD, reporting to John Carey, the vice president of operations. On the day I was to leave Fairchild, I was called into President Wilf Corrigan's office, where I was to receive the best compliment I ever received from a professional. Wilf asked, "Why do you want to leave Fairchild? Everything is going well for you."

I said that since I didn't drink or take drugs the only way for me to get a high was to run a production line. He said, "I hate to see you go. The moment you don't like what you're doing, you call me, and you have a job. You're the only one I know who I could give you sand and tell you to make something and you'd make it." Wow! I told him he should have said that to me while I was working for Fairchild.

At the time, AMD was about one-tenth the size of Fairchild and still operating like a small company, but growing fast. Jerry Sanders told me my job was to develop a product like the Fairchild isoplanar bipolar RAM. I told him I was not privy to how Fairchild made that RAM but felt confident that we could develop a process/product to compete in that business.

A month after joining AMD, I was attending an AMD marketing and sales meeting in Honolulu. The meeting was supposed to be a week long, but, after three days, Jerry Sanders called us together and said the data was showing that a recession had begun, and it was important for us all to get back to work and stop spending the company's money.

Back at the Santa Clara facility, Jerry called me into his office and said that he had changed his mind about moving bipolar memories into the new building. It would now be an MOS (Metal, Oxide, Semiconductor) facility, since he saw this was the direction the business was moving (This later proved to be correct. MOS transistors have low gain, but require low power and are ideally suited for use in Memory products. Bipolar on the other hand has higher gain, higher power and is ideal for functions which require greater drive and power handling capability)). In order to reduce costs, he wanted each managing director to take on two jobs. Besides running the bipolar memory directorate, he wanted me to also run all the wafer fabrication in the main fab. Tony Holbrook (from Fairchild) would run all testing besides the interface directorate reporting to him. The three other managing directors had similar double duty.

At first, running the wafer fab operation was difficult due to the many products being made for all five of the directors. They each had engineers in the area, and there was no order of priority. It was chaos. I called the directors together and told them that I wanted one engineer from each of the directorates to be assigned to the wafer fab area.

The masking line had an engineer from MOS, since their masking requirements were more difficult than the other technologies. The metals area had an engineer from bipolar memories (my group) because this technology had tougher requirements for metal. The diffusion area had an engineer from the digital Schottky directorate. Tony Holbrook's interface group had an engineer responsible for the implant area.

In addition, a stop/start system was established. Any time a run stopped due to a step being out of spec, the operator would initiate a stop slip. These stop/start slips came in five different colors, each representing a product line. The slip was placed in colored slots in a small clean room between the main wafer fab area and the outside area. In this way, the engineers could see if any of their products were on hold and take an action on that run without entering the clean room of the wafer fab area.

The engineers were happy to see this procedure, since it meant they didn't have to smock up to find out how there products were doing. If there were no gold cards in the stop/start room, the engineers running the gold-diffused devices knew there were no problems with their products and that they could continue working on their other priorities. Things began to run smoothly, and the yields of each product kept improving.

To compete in the bipolar RAM market, a new technology was developed using an all implant and oxide-isolated process that we called IMOX. The group also developed a new approach for programming a PROM (Programmable Read Only Memory). Both of these developments advanced the products made by AMD. However, the IMOX process yielded high at times and zeroed at times. This left us missing shipping commitments Jerry Sanders had made to his top customer priorities for Bipolar Memory products. We could not figure out why some runs ran so high a yield and some runs ran zero yield.

(Later, we found that implanting equipment was unreliable when programming large areas. The implanters would build up charge and destroy random bits of the memory device. Two years passed before this problem was recognized, and it wasn't while I was at AMD. I found the problem several years later at Fairchild.)

Meanwhile, I was learning a different mode of operation that I found at AMD. Everyone from the president down was direct and confrontational when observing any act they didn't personally agree with. So no one took it personally if they were told they were screwing up some step in an operation. This taught each individual to not be defensive, sensitive, or emotional when being criticized.

This directness provided a very positive and open atmosphere throughout the company. This approach grew on me, and I became more aware of other people's experiences. I would carry this technique with me from this experience.

During the recession, AMD laid off operators and professional people. It was very difficult to walk up to a foreman or engineer and tell them to pick up their belongings and to walk them out. We had to say something like, "Sorry to have to let you go. Your personal belongings will be boxed up, and you can pick them up on Saturday at the main entrance." The walk from there to the door was very quiet and emotional.

During this recession, the remaining people took a 10 percent cut in pay but were expected to work on Saturdays. As a director, I was expected to work the normal shift and also the night shift on every third week, during which time I went between buildings to make sure everything was going well in areas not normally reporting to me.

I remember going over to the new building in the evening and finding the lights on. Only small crews of workers were in the production line. On my daily report, I commented that it reminded me of the *Titanic*, and of the band playing music while the ship was sinking. The next day, the building lights were out except in the production space being used. Jerry Sander's objective was to work doubly hard during this recessional period, and, when the recession was over, AMD would come out firing. He was right. During this down period, the company designed many new products, debugged processes, debugged procedures, and became emotionally stronger. When business picked up, AMD was ahead of the other companies and picked up market share. Business began to grow rapidly.

Having Fun with the Family

From 1973 to 1975, Peg, the kids, and I went to Lake Tahoe on several occasions to enjoy the snow and to get away from work. We took our dog, Meggie, along with us. Skiing was a lot of fun in California—compared to New England—because it wasn't as cold. You could actually enjoy the weather as well as the skiing. Peg wouldn't go skiing but took Meggie on some of the small hills and rode a sled with Meggie alongside her. I took the kids up the ski lift on the low hills and taught them to ski. We had a lot of fun.

Soon, they all were able to navigate down these smaller hills, and I decided to take them up to the higher hills. Jay would ski like he learned to ice skate back in Worchester: he sort of stood straight up in his skiing stance. Karen was more cautious than David. David was too young to fear anything and zoomed all over—falling, getting back up, and going after it again.

One time in 1974, it had turned cold overnight, and the weather was a little more violent than it had been the day before. I was concerned for the kids' safety. I told them to wait while I went to the top of the hill and skied down. I wanted to make sure everything was OK. I got to the top and things looked good, and I started down the hill. As I traversed the hill, I got close to the tree line on the left side of the slope. Unbeknown by me, the sun had melted the snow along that line and during the night it had frozen into ice. When I hit that ice, I lost control and rapidly began my descent down the slope.

Soon I had fallen, but I still continued down the slope on my belly with the sharp ice cutting into my ski sweater on my chest, arms, and at times my face. By the time I was within shouting distance of the slope I was pretty cut up. I gained control and skied to where the kids were. I told them to wait there while I went to the first-aid station. First aid got my sweater off, and they provided medicine, gauze, and bandages to the various areas.

Afterward, I told the kids that I would stand at the bottom of the slope while they went up, warning them to stay away from the tree lines. About fifteen minutes later, I saw them making their way down the slope. They had fun, and later we picked up Peg at the sled area. She was in shock when she first saw the bandages. This was a lesson learned, and all of my family benefited from my mistake by making sure to watch out for ice.

We also went to Lake Tahoe in the summer and went water skiing or swimming.

As the kids grew older, Peg and I spent some evenings in the gambling joints while they went to a movie. I played Blackjack, and Peg liked to play the quarter slot machines. She would win money, and I would lose money. Sometimes she won enough to pay for our visit.

It used to amaze me during February or March when returning home from Tahoe. Here we had been skiing in deep snow for a couple of days, and within an hour we could be in warm weather. People use to say that we could go skiing on snow or water on the same day in northern California. We sure loved it (and still do).

Early in 1975, we got some bad news. My mother became ill and was taken to the hospital with a high fever. I flew out to see her for a few days. She had a fever similar to the flu, but the doctors didn't know what was causing it. They were never able to diagnose the reasons why. In June of 1975, my mother passed away. A later autopsy showed that she died of valley fever, an illness unique to the Southwest where the humidity is low and spores remain airborne. One of these spores is the source of valley fever, so named in Phoenix where it is prevalent. If my mother had been living in the Southwest, they would have diagnosed her illness almost immediately and resolved it. She had never been in that part of the country.

Ken Gets a Promotion

Later in 1975, having been in pain for about a year with a kidney stone too big to pass, my doctor decided to operate on me. In this operation, the doctor would cut from my stomach area all the way around the left side to my spine. Here's a cure that was almost as bad as the illness. With the muscles cut in this direction, it would be difficult to behave normally for some length of time. Everything from picking up the newspaper to having a bowel movement was a task. I only missed nine days of work but was weak for a couple of months. It killed my golf game for several years.

While I was in the hospital with the kidney operation, I got a call from Ken. He said he was coming out to handle a problem for U.S. Steel. He would be in Fontana, California, for two days and then would come up and visit us. I was glad to see him but had to warn him not to make me laugh because it hurt to laugh. I asked how he ended up in Fontana. This story he told was why I was so proud of him all my life.

Ken said, "When I arrived back from Brazil this past year, U.S. Steel didn't know what to do with me. They told me to take an office on the thirteenth floor of the U.S. Steel building in Pittsburgh. Then one day they called me to the main office and told me that the president of Fontana Steel had been calling the president of U.S. Steel for a couple of years about the poor efficiency of the Coke Ovens U.S. Steel had designed and installed. They didn't know who to send, and someone told them to send the guy on the thirteenth floor since he wasn't doing anything. So, that's how I got chosen.

"Gort, I spent two days there, and they have all kinds of problems. I could walk in the mill and smell things that were wrong. I'm going to go back down to go through their whole mill and write up their problems."

We talked awhile and Ken went back to Fontana before returning home. A couple of months went by, and I got a call from Ken. He said, "Gort, the president of Fontana Steel sent a letter to the president of U.S. Steel that said, 'Mr. Husher, who you sent down, told us to make some changes on our coke ovens that are saving us twenty-two thousand dollars a day. Then Mr. Husher went through our whole plant and wrote down suggestions for us to change, and we're doing them, and they're working. We're very pleased and want a special commendation placed in his personal file along with this letter.' Well, Gort, they decided I knew more than they thought, and now they're sending me to Detroit to look into some problems they're having there with U.S. Steel installations."

I was happy to hear this. Ken continued this role for U.S. Steel, and in 1977 he was named chief consultant worldwide for U.S. Steel on coke ovens and coke by-products." He ended up with twenty-four other engineers, and they solved problems all over the world: Austria, Australia, Germany, France, and throughout North America.

My Brother Terry and Noreen Have a Baby Boy

Another good thing happened in April of 1975. My brother Terry and Noreen had a child. He was born at Hackensack, New Jersey, and named Justin Max Husher. I called Terry and told him I was happy he had a boy so the Husher name could carry on. All he needed was to grow up, get married, and have some more Hushers.

Terry laughed, as did Noreen, and said that Justin was going to have to do it because they weren't able to have any more children. I was happy for them and happy that Terry had used his college education. He was the marketing manager for Matchbox and was being interviewed by a company in Kentucky for another job in children's toys. The business degree from Rutgers and his hard-working intensity was paying off.

Terry had made toys his avocation as well as his vocation, collecting old toys in excellent shape that had reached an antique rating. Things were going well for them. I was very proud of one move he had made while at Matchbox. They had come out with a Model T Ford, but it was not black like the original. They didn't sell well, and Terry later talked them into selling him the molds for making the car. Years later, Terry made a number of black Model T Fords. He was able to sell them at an elevated price since there were many Matchbox car collectors who wanted a black Model T Ford. It was a good move.

Our Kids Become of Automobile Age

In April of 1974, Jay was sixteen years old, and I took him down to the DMV to take his driving test. He passed and immediately wanted to get his own vehicle. I remembered what I had promised myself in the Navy: When my children were old enough, I would get them a vehicle so they could expose themselves to the opportunities that surrounded them. I would also hold them responsible for being home on time, since they would have no excuses.

So I began looking through the paper to see what was available in used cars. I found an ad for a 1972 Volkswagen Beetle and took Jay to look at it. It was in good shape and reasonably priced. So Jay had a vehicle. In 1976, Jay was admitted to California State University at Chico. He traveled to and from Chico State in that Beetle and was as happy as a young man could be.

In 1976, Karen was sixteen, and she passed her driving test. We went through the same deal with her, only this time I didn't have the spare money to buy her a car. Peg and I each had a car, so Karen drove around Peg's station wagon as though she owned it. One weekend when Jay was home from school, he had a large load of clothes and other things to take back to school, so we decided he should use the station wagon and Karen could drive his Beetle until he returned the following week. Karen drove to and from school in Jay's Beetle. At the time, her school friend, Mary Demolle, was staying at our house. Mary's mother and father, who was a lawyer, were getting a divorce, and Mr. Demolle asked us if Mary could stay at our house until this was over.

Each day Karen drove herself and Mary to school and back. On Thursday of that week, we got a call that Karen had been in an accident and was in the Stanford Medical Center. I drove immediately to the hospital, and when I arrived they were taking Karen in to operate on her arm. She told me how the accident had happened and that Mary had a compound fracture of her leg. The Beetle was dead. Karen's arm was broken badly in a couple of places and required a metal plate in her arm. I went and picked up Karen's and Jay's things that were in the Beetle.

Wouldn't you know, Mary Demolle's dad, who had asked us to keep Mary with us until his divorce was final, sued us for Mary's injuries? The insurance company ended up paying him over $70,000. I felt that as a lawyer, he was looking at how to take advantage of his position.

Now I had to find Jay another car for when he came back with

Peg's wagon. I found a 1974 pea green Fiat sport coop that was a great-looking used car, and in good shape.

When Jay came down and saw it, he was happy but thought the green color had to go. I had practiced painting cars around that time and had gotten fairly good at it. So Jay and I went out and found a color he liked. He chose a metallic gray, and I got the garage cleaned up to paint it while he was away to school the following week. I taped the car off in preparation to paint it and gave it a double coat of lacquer. Then I lightly sanded it and put another coat on it. I kept doing this, and eventually it had about a dozen coats of paint on it. I rubbed it out real good until it shined like a "new nickel," and, when Jay came home that weekend, he was really surprised. He loved the color and the car.

And so, when 1978 rolled around and I took David to the DMV for his driving test, I remember him pulling out with the DMV test driver in the car and me thinking, "This is my last child to get a license. This only happens once in a lifetime for each child. I wonder if they know how lucky they are and how lucky I am." David was my last child to get a license, and I got tears in my eyes and a lump in my throat. David was different than the other kids; he wanted a truck. So I looked around and found a used 1974 Toyota truck. It was in good shape being only four years old, and I bought it for $1,900. This was before trucks became a big item for young people and older people or I wouldn't have got the truck for that price. He drove that truck to school and back everyday, and Peg and I were always telling him to wear his seat belt.

He and Greg Dronkert used to ride to school together in David's truck. One Saturday afternoon, he and Greg took off down the hill, and after five minutes I got a call on the phone. It was David. He had rolled the truck under the highway overpass, and he was calling from a nearby house. "Could you please come and get us before the police come?" I asked him if he had gotten hurt, and he said that he and Greg had both had their seat belts on, and, when the truck had rolled over, they had been hanging upside down by their seat belts. They had kicked out the back window and crawled out of the truck. I drove down the hill and, when I came to the site of the wreck, there was the wrecked truck and David and Greg standing there waiting for me.

David had also called his friend who had a Jeep, and the three of them rolled the truck back upright. The truck wouldn't start, and we hooked up a cable to the Jeep and pulled it to the house before the police arrived. So now we had a truck that needed about everything replaced on it. Over the next several weeks, I went to the junkyard to find parts for the truck. I got two fenders, a hood, one back fender, a wheel, two doors, and finally I found a wreck that had a good cab. I cut the cab off of David's truck with a welding torch and began putting everything back together.

After getting the body in shape, I worked on the underside of the truck, replacing many parts. Then I bled the brakes and replaced the brake fluid, and the brakes worked fine. When this was finished, I got a new window for the front, and, while a friend of mine and I were putting it in, it cracked on the driver's side, about ten inches down and twelve inches across to the edge. I left it alone at this point.

Finally, I applied the finish. The only part of the body that didn't get replaced was the truck bed and rear bumper, which were not damaged. The front bumper was bent on the driver's side like a person holding his lip in the air, and I couldn't find a replacement for it or straighten it. So I left it alone.

It drove well, except it sort of went sideways down the road. I took it to the garage to have it aligned, and the garage wouldn't align it. So I drove it home and told David that he had to drive it like it was. That was his punishment for rolling it. He drove it everyday, and he came down the road it looked like "John Wayne in a Western movie, where he sort of walked a little sideways.

This went on for a couple of months, and finally Peg told me to get him another truck. I put an ad in the paper for this truck and went and found another 1974 Toyota because David thought they were the best trucks. I paid $2,000 for this blue truck, and it had 61,000 miles on it. A couple of days after the ad was in the paper, a Mexican man came up to look at the repaired truck. I had advertised it for $1,000. We talked a while, and I told him what the truck had gone through. He said he would pay $900 for it, and I told him that I would paint it for him, any color he wanted. By then I had painted about ten vehicles and could do a fairly good paint job. I told him if he bought it, he should have the brakes checked and get the front end aligned. So he gave me a check for $900 and off he went. Two years later while shopping in a plumbing store, I ran into this man and asked him how the truck was running and if he had the front end aligned. He said, "No, never had to do anything with it. Drove my wife and son down to Mexico City to_see some relatives, and it ran fine. The brakes are fine, and I got a friend of mine to paint the truck." He said that I'd done a good job priming it. I shook his hand and walked to where he said he had parked the truck. I laughed out loud. The truck was painted gold with little red flecks in the metallic finish, the front bumper was still sticking up like a hair lip, and the front window still had the cracked glass in it. I looked at it and kept laughing.

On the way home, I couldn't wipe the grin off my face. I was so happy that he had not had any problems with it. When I got home and told Peg about bumping into the guy who had bought David's truck and described my discussion with him, we both had a laugh. She was also relieved that he hadn't had any problems with it.

In the meantime, I leased a red 300Z for Karen. She drove it for two years and then wanted a red truck. She still drives a truck to this day. It's odd to see this truck driving up and a good-looking girl getting out of it. She liked a stick shift and was a great driver after her one accident.

In 1980, David was accepted to Cal Poly (California University at San Luis Obispo) and drove back and forth with that blue truck for two years before Sam and Peg Pool bought him a new truck, and I inherited the blue Toyota. Several years later, David and I did an overhaul on the truck with 140,000 miles on it. When we took the engine apart, we found the cylinder rings were still in spec like a new truck. Several years later when the truck had 242,000 miles on it, I traded it for a new truck in 1997.

Buck Shutterly Passes Away

In mid-1976 I got a call from Ken to tell me that Buck Shutterly had passed away. He was upset because he had really liked Buck. He had made a great father-in-law, always there to help Ken and his family. After hanging up the phone, I called Sam. Sam was shocked and said, "It's hard to believe that someone that strong could pass away at the age of sixty-four. It seemed like only yesterday that we were on his motorcycle riding out to Denver. I can still see him holding onto that old lady's car with that strong arm of his until we got to his aunt's. I will never forget that."

I missed him too but was glad that Sam was still around.

As hard as I worked and raised the levels of AMD's bipolar memory products and improved the wafer fab yield, and as much as I liked AMD, Jerry Sanders found my inability to meet the bipolar memory requirements unacceptable, and in late 1976 I was told to leave the company. They gave me a severance pay and allowed me to exercise my stock up to the end of the year.

I made about $150,000 on the stock, which was a nice sum of money before taxes, but I was very disappointed in having to leave a good company. I had learned many things in my three years there, including a strong management style and that I no longer wanted to be president of a company. I knew I wanted to run the heart of a company. I wanted to run the operations: the engineering, the production, the line maintenance, and the facilities.

Back to Fairchild Semiconductor

I immediately called Wilf Corrigan and was hired back to Fairchild several weeks later. I told Wilf I wanted a job running a production area. I no longer wanted to be the president of a company. I never ate lunch, didn't like going out with customers in the evening, didn't drink and didn't enjoy taking customers out for a drink, and these qualities made me unqualified to be the president of a company. I just wanted to direct engineering and production. I was sent to be the operations manager of CCD (Charge Coupled Device) operations in Palo Alto, reporting to Gil Amelio, GM of CCD operations. Charge coupled devices are like transistors except they received signals that form a charge bucket and the charge is moved along the silicon surface like a "bucket brigade" fighting a fire. As each signal is received the bucket of charge is moved down to the next position to allow space for the new bucket of charge just received. This makes them valuable in storing information. While running this operation, I did everything I could to avoid the upper management. I wanted to learn more about the details of making MOS and CCD devices. I wanted to get back to engineering and directing production. If I saw Wilf Corrigan's car or Tom Longo's car at the plant, I would come in the back entrance. This worked for about five months.

One day, I was invited to the Palo Alto Country Club for a lunch meeting, even though I did not eat lunch. When everyone had eaten, Gil Amelio went up to the microphone and made an announcement. He had been promoted to vice president of the newly formed MOS and CCD division. He announced that John Husher would be the new general manager of CCD. I couldn't stay away from top management even when I tried.

My Medical Problem and Golf

In mid-1976 the doctors tried a new medicine to control my blood pressure. It was called Catapresso, and after a few weeks I noticed that I got leg cramps. I thought it might be the new medicine.

About that time, Peg's dentist wanted to golf against me since Peg had told him I was a good golfer. My handicap was about 6 at the time, but I always wanted to play with friends for the joy of the game, and the dentist didn't fit this description. So I kept telling him I was busy.

Finally, one day after her dental visit Peg said I should go and play with him. So I decided to go, and we were on his course the next morning. I was feeling pretty good, and away I went to golf. Several hours later, I returned home in a bad mood.

Peg asked me, "What's the problem?"

I told her, "I was beating the dentist's pants off when I got to the thirteenth hole, and my legs gave out. I had to quit when we finished fifteen." I told her it was the new medicine they were using on me, and I was quitting it immediately. She argued that stopping medicine cold turkey could kill me. She advised me to go to the family doctor. I said, "What good would the 'local yokel do for me? I've gone to the best specialists in the country and they couldn't fix me."

She said that he had gotten his license from Holland and had then gone to the Mayo Clinic in Minnesota. His name was Adrian Dronkert. His son Greg was David's best friend. Once, Mrs. Dronkert had called me on a Sunday because a pipe had burst and it was flooding the cellar. She hadn't known who to call on a weekend. I had gone over and fixed the broken pipe. Later she had sent me a bottle of wine. So, that's all I knew about the Dronkerts. I told Peg to set up an appointment with Dr. Dronkert."

I got an appointment to see Dr. Dronkert, and he looked at my history and saw what medicine I was taking. He said, "How can you function with all this medicine in you? How do you handle your work?" I told him I ignored those feelings as long as I could do my work. Anyhow, he said he was going to wean me off of those medicines and on to others he thought would work better and would relieve any pressure that the nerve medicine had placed on me. He told me he wanted me to still take one of the Aldactone tablets in the morning but to ignore taking them any other time of the day. I asked him why. He said, "There's a small gland on the kidney that controls your blood pressure. Many times people take medicine for their blood pressure, and the pressure drops. After a while, this gland sees that the blood pressure is lower, and it makes the blood pressure go back up. I want you to take one Aldactone in the morning to fool that gland and keep it busy. Aldactone is a diuretic/hormone, which keeps the kidney and that gland busy doing what I want it to. I think one a day should do the trick."

He was right. My blood pressure went down, and six months later I was able to obtain life insurance without a premium. So it was good that I went golfing with Peg's dentist and went to the right doctor.

I have continued taking Aldactone and the two other medicines he prescribed since 1976.

Running CCD Operations

Managing the CCD group was interesting. It was the only technology where the finished product basically showed you the technical problems within the product. A CCD array is like having a small television set built into a chip. The finished die and its array would be displayed on a television display with its thousands of pixel sites. With voltage applied, one type of problem showed up as streaks, while another showed clouds, while yet another showed missing columns or rows.

Essentially, these pictures told us what needed to be corrected in the process, or where defects were entering the process. There was no other technology that displayed failures and the reason for the failures. Most were caused by random defects, but the random defects were tractable. A review of the finished product on a monitor screen displayed the results of these random defects in a curve that pointed out the type of problem.

Week by week, these problems were eliminated. The large area array was on a piece of silicon that was a centimeter by a centimeter square for each die. You could only fit less than ten die on a wafer. This was a large die in 1976, and one of the major markets for this area array was the military. An array of this type could be hooked into the periscope of a submarine, and it allowed the target to be seen at night with its ability to see infrared heat targets.

Using the information we learned from CCD troubleshooting gave us information on the problems that must occur on MOS devices and EPROMs at this location. These lessons would help me with future responsibilities.

The CCD array eventually became a major market in cameras. By the year 2000, almost all cameras had a CCD array on the back of the camera that let users decide if they wanted to keep the picture or not. CCD arrays became a common display for printers and many other electronic items.

Happy Times with Peg

During 1975 to 1978, Peg and I went to a restaurant called the Monterey Steak House each Friday night. They had entertainment that consisted of two young guys named Rick and Craig. They played the guitar and sang. We enjoyed listening and dancing to their music. Peg was a great dancer, and sometimes we were the only ones dancing. Rick and Craig enjoyed seeing us on the floor enjoying their music.

On many Fridays, Vic Mitrisin would meet us there. When Ken and Sherie came out, we always made a trip to the Monterey Steak House to have a good meal and a lot of dancing. Ken and Sherie enjoyed them as much as we did. We became good friends with Craig and traveled to other places where they entertained. Craig had graduated from California University at Chico where Jay attended college from 1976 to 1980. So we had something in common to talk about, since Chico was a nice, small agricultural town. Craig was intelligent, and we talked to him about getting a job based on his education rather than his hobby. Eventually, he came up to the house and told us he had accepted a job with Xerox and was going to school in the East for a few months. We were happy for him, but now we had to find some other place that played good music. We figured all that exercising on the dance floor also helped to keep us in shape. Every once in a while we would hear a song on our stereo that reminded us of Rick and Craig, and we would want to find a place to dance.

Peg and John 1978

Ken Gets a Better Opportunity

In mid-1978, I got a call from Ken, and the conversation went something like this: "Gort, you know I do jobs all over and I'm always getting job offers from different companies. I just let them go in one ear and out the other, since I like doing this job for U.S. Steel. Well, yesterday I got an offer from a small company named Furnco. They offered me a large share of their company if I would go there and put them in the coke oven repair business. They do repair work on blast furnaces, and they have another small division doing environmental work. If I go there, they'll provide me with a new car every two years, a great salary, and a bonus if I beat their goals each year. What do you think?"

I told him I didn't know why he was calling me to talk about this; I would be out there working for Furnco right now. "You should be calling from a Furnco phone." He laughed and said that's what he thought. He left U.S. Steel as a pioneer on coke oven repair work and went to this small independent company.

That night I said to Peg, "You know that money we were saving because I was worried about Ken in South America and that he might be in financial problems? Well, you can go and spend that money. He's going to be just fine." And then I told her about Ken's new position.

We were both happy. Ken had finally reached the point in his career where he was going to benefit from all that experience he had gained around the world. Here was a man who had experienced every part of the making of coke; as a laborer, as a supervisor, as part of a team installing a complete coke processing facility, as a teacher in training operators in a new plant in Brazil, as a troubleshooter, and as a consultant on solving coke oven problems. Ken had worked his way up the ladder by being smart and ambitious and working hard.

It was also nice that Ken would be back in the Pittsburgh area. He had grown up there, and his children and many relatives lived within a short distance. It was nice for me too, because when I visited I could stay with Ken and his family. Peg liked it too, since she and Sherie got along great. For her, it was like visiting her sister.

Semiconductor Problem Solving

Over the course of a couple of years of running the CCD business, a 64K CCD Memory (64,000 bit locations for storing information on a single chip of silicon) was developed and transferred to the South San Jose facility for production by the MOS division. At first the product was yielding in production, but then yield issues began to plague the 64K MOS RAM and the 64K CCD RAM. Tom Longo asked Gil Amelio to send me down to determine the cause of the issues.

On my first visit, I spent two weeks reviewing the 64K RAM (Random Access Memory), which was a huge market product used in the computer industry and the main revenue producer for the South San Jose plant. It took priority over the 64K CCD. My review indicated that there were shorts occurring in the gate oxide. I had two runs of fifty wafers each held at gate oxide, and I had engineering measure the breakdown voltage of the oxide at various locations. It showed breakdowns of approximately 1 volt instead of the 30 volts expected for oxide rupture. This indicated that there were pinhole-type problems or some other problem affecting the gate oxide. I told them to stop all production and to carry the wafers though all the process steps until they got past the gate oxide and poly silicon deposition, which is deposited over the whole wafer and is located above the gate oxide and the rest of circuitry on each device.

Normally, at this point in the process, the poly receives a masking that defines where the poly gates are located and all the other poly is etched off. However, I decided to instruct production to leave the poly on the wafers and use the scribe-line mask on this poly, which is normally the last mask and is used to etch the oxide between die to prepare them for scribing and separation. Using the approach, I recommended the sheet of poly be etched on this outside location where the scribe line would normally be etched. This essentially separated each die from one another, since the poly was etched around each die at the scribe line location using this technique. Each die now existed with poly completely over it but separated from neighboring dies by this scribe-line etch. This leaves each die separated with the oxide portion of the die as the thinnest layer beneath the poly coating each die. Engineering was then to measure the breakdown voltage of each of these poly patterns, which should show the weakest oxide spot on each die. This should be at least 30 volts, since the gate oxide was the thinnest oxide and should be the oxide that ruptured with this voltage applied.

I also indicated that the line should be stopped in production until at least 20 volts were realized at this point of the process. With this line stoppage being enforced on the production line, the place was essentially out of business. This put a lot of pressure on everyone to get the problem solved. All engineering was doing everything possible to determine why the breakdown voltage was so low. The first measurements using this technique showed breakdown voltages of about 1 to 2 volts and kept the line stopped. To improve the integrity of the gate oxide, we found that the gate oxide needed to be removed (called a sacrificial oxide in today's processing) and then re-oxidized. This removal step removed nitride and any contaminants that had previously been under the oxide. This new oxide brought the average breakdown to approximately 20 volts, and the line could then start moving.

After this, we found several cleans that raised the breakdowns to the 30-volt level. The neat thing about this "invented" (although

I never applied for a patent and I still do not see any other company doing this to determine their process viability) approach was that once the scribe line mask was used to electrically separate the die and this measurement made, the wafers passing this test could then receive the normal poly gate mask—since all the poly remained over each die—and the wafers could proceed on to completion as if nothing had been done to them. So, it was a non-destructive test. After a couple of weeks of using this method, the scribe line mask was eliminated, since the major problems had been found and eliminated. This unique defect analysis method was used many times during my professional career. I should have patented it.

A short time after solving this problem, Tom Longo asked Amelio if I could go to the South San Jose plant to look into the inability of the production line to make a full 64K RAM. Random defects were causing several bits of the RAM out of 64,000 bits to not be operative. If a bit failed, the whole die failed, and the failure was called a single-bit failure mode. After several months of trying to solve the issue, I was accused of changing the process that had been developed and transferred by R&D. I took exception to this comment. I felt there was a systematic failure mode causing this problem and began to suspect the ion implantation process as the problem. I decided to take processed wafers to ion implantation at the San Jose facility and have them implanted at Palo Alto R&D and returned to San Jose for completion of the processes. At the same time, I took wafers from Palo Alto R&D and had them implanted at San Jose and returned them to Palo Alto for the completion of processing..

The wafers processed at San Jose and implanted at Palo Alto yielded well, and the wafers processed at R&D and implanted at San Jose failed. The R&D implanter was a low-current implant machine versus the high-current implanter at San Jose. It was then found that the high-current implanter used for fast throughput at the San Jose plant built up an internal charge and placed a high voltage spike on random bits. This was the supplier of the implanter's fault, and the correction improved implanters throughout the industry. I also realized this was the reason why the IMOX process I had installed at AMD had high and low yielding runs of the bipolar memory that Jerry Sanders had relied heavily on. I wish I had known this back then; I would have been a hero at AMD. But things happen for the best.

On another occasion, I was asked to review the yield problems of the MOS line in general, but now leakage current was appearing across all products. This line previously yielded. A review was started whereby a wafer would be pulled from the lot at various operations as a lot of 50 wafers proceeded through the process steps. Each of these wafers would have the oxide etched away, and a special

Stacking fault etch was used to delineate the stacking faults occurring in the silicon. (Stacking faults are imperfections in the crystal structure and they show up under microscopic examination like small crow's feet or little "V's. When you see these they indicate some sort of abnormality with the crystal structure. Silicon has the same crystalline structure as diamond. They are in the same chemical family as diamond. Diamonds would make an excellent transistor but would be too expensive.) It was a known fact that if you have stacking faults in the silicon that these will be sites of leakage. Huge amounts of stacking faults were found from the beginning of the process up to one of the last steps, where the wafers were doped with phosphorus, and the stacking faults dropped precipitously after this step. However, there were still significant amounts of stacking faults remaining, and they were enough to cause the leakage.

After further review, I noticed that a step early in the process flow had been changed months ago. Originally, after an early nitride deposition, the wafers were oxidized, and this oxide was etched in select locations to form an oxide mask used to etch the nitride (a nitride etch has little impact on etching of oxide). With new plasma-etching equipment, the wafers did not need an oxide mask to etch the nitride in the select locations, and the oxide step had been dropped.

I asked the senior engineer, Lloyd Walsh, to split a run into two 25 wafer lot sizes instead of the 50 wafer lot size presently being utilized, and to conduct an oxidation on one half (25 wafers) and not on the other half. Then he was to perform a stacking fault etch on a wafer from each half of the split and count the stacking faults to compare the ones with oxide to those without oxide.. He told me he was going on vacation that Friday for two weeks and didn't have time to do the experiment. I told him if he didn't do it that I would have management reject his vacation. That was Tuesday, and on Friday around noon I heard someone running up the steps to my office. Lloyd rushed into my office and said the stacking faults on the present method were in the thousands per square inch, and there were no stacking faults on the half that had been oxidized. We both jumped for joy, and his excitement was probably more than likely because he could now go on his vacation.

The following week, we found out that the oxidation cycle relieved the stress in the nitride silicon interface. That was why there were no stacking faults. We tried doing the same annealing procedure with nitrogen at 800 degrees C, and it also worked to relieve this stress. In the meantime, I had set up another experiment for wafers.

I set up an experiment at poly silicon deposition, since previous data had shown that there was also stacking faults generated at this step, which added to the ones acquired at the nitride step. The split at this point was to add hydrogen in the poly deposition step to the one half run and not on the other half.. Stacking fault data showed us that this hydrogen in the poly also reduced the number of stacking faults generated.

I wrote a technical paper called "Stacking Fault Generators and Stacking Fault Eliminators" and submitted it to the R&D library. This showed that wafers receiving the original process had stacking faults added at all the high-temperature steps and that approximately 10,000 faults per square centimeter were removed at the phosphorus step.

If we used both the anneal after the nitride and the hydrogen in the poly process to reduce the level of stacking faults, the phosphorus gettering step further reduced the stacking faults to levels that eliminated leakage. My paper was well received and selected to be presented as one of the top five papers for presentation at the Key Man seminar that year. Solving problems like this was like a doctor finding a cure for a deadly disease. This always excited me and made me feel good inside.

On February 19, 1981 Peg and I were presented with our first grandchild, Bren Lyndell Husher, the daughter of our oldest son Jay and his Wife Rebecca.

9

Big Gamble at the Age of Fifty

Vice President of a Small Company: Micrel Test

As excited as I was with things at Fairchild, a job opportunity presented itself that made me think twice. A professional recruiter out of Sunnyvale called me several times to line up an interview with a small test company called Micrel Test that was trying to establish a production wafer fabrication facility in Sunnyvale and was looking for a vice president to run this operation. I was attending an evening class on microprocessors in Sunnyvale. I finally told him I would look into the opportunity after school the next Tuesday.

So that Tuesday evening I visited with Micrel Test and met Ray Zinn, the president of the small test company. He took me over to a small fab that he had just obtained from Siemens of Germany. The fab provided CMOS metal gate die (a type of transistor that uses two complementary MOS transistors that works at no power when inactive and medium power when activated. The most popular transistor technology used today.) to its subsidiary, Litronix, in Sunnyvale. The operation was a very small one; the building was only 10,000 sq. ft., and the wafer fabrication clean room facility inside was only about 4,000 sq. ft.

Mr. Zinn walked me around production and then the surrounding area. Behind the building were the process gases in the tank farm. This tank farm had a tank of liquid nitrogen, the water neutralization system, the de-ionized water-making system, the air-condition heat transfer fans, and a computer system that monitored various functions out on this pad and inside the plant.

Mr. Zinn realized this was not a state of the art facility and downplayed it, but he did sound positive about growing the facility. As I reviewed the plant and its wafer-making facility, I thought of Westinghouse at Youngwood some twenty-three years earlier. This plant had been about that size and capability. It also ran a process that was quite similar to the one I had run, with several of my patents being applied. It made me feel at home. We discussed a salary and stock options that would make my leaving Fairchild and coming to Micrel worthwhile.

As I drove home, I thought about the place and my previous experiences. This would be quite different than Fairchild, where I had responsibilities at the edge of technology, where many of the biggest problems were with debugging new equipment rather than producing the product. Micrel Test would be a dramatic change. It was not at the edge of technology, and the equipment was similar to the equipment used at the Westinghouse facility in Elkridge, Maryland. It was about fifteen years behind in making integrated circuits. But I did believe there was a place for a business supplying old customer's products to their older designs. Most of the "chips" in use in the world were made many years ago and were still running. Soon replacements would be needed. Also, many of the companies didn't want to redesign something that was working and expanded their production lines with these older designed chips.

When I got home, Peg asked me what I thought about the interview. I told her my impressions but said, "If they give me a good stock option and the proper salary, I probably would take the job. It would be like starting over at the age of fifty."

This was the gamble. However, although I had always gotten paid well, I had never made a large sum of money through stock options. I had almost no retirement funds, so this was my opportunity to take a small, unknown test company to a successful position and hopefully cash in the stock option for Peg and my retirement. It was a gamble. After six years at Fairchild, I left to join this small test company in early 1982.

Micrel Test Company

I joined Micrel in May of 1982 as vice president and general manager of the wafer fab division. Warren Muller, one of the founders of Micrel, was the vice president of the test division. We reported to Ray. The company was essentially privately owned by Ray and Warren. They had taken a loan against their houses and had started the test company in 1978 with one fairly high-speed tester purchased through loans from Bank of the West. The company's expansion after this small start was financed through profits made by the test division. This would remain true for several years until the wafer fab started to make a profit. Each year since 1978, as profits fell into place, Micrel Test would add additional testers, allowing for taking on additional business.

When I joined Micrel in 1982, they had revenues of about $2.5M a year and a profit of a million dollars. They knew that the growth of the company was quite limited, since most new business—and therefore growth—was due to test limitations of their customers. If Micrel's customers' businesses were good, the companies would need extra test capacity and come to Micrel to test their added output. This was therefore a passive business, which is what resulted in Ray Zinn discussing the purchase of the small LSI wafer fabrication business owned by Siemens. Ray knew to make a big company; he had to be in an active business where we made product and not services. Ray pursued the purchase, wanting Siemens to come down in price and to provide a guarantee to Micrel of a certain level of business supplying Litronix's (a Siemens subsidiary) wafer requirements. Eventually, he was able to negotiate conditions that were satisfactory, such as the purchase price of the wafer fab and a contract to supply a certain amount of our output to Litronix, including supplying them at least 50 percent of their total requirements for the first two years.

Upon completion of these negotiations, Ray sought out an experienced person to run this part of the business. He initially hired one person and this didn't work out after a couple of months. That's when I was contacted, and now it was my chance. It was a gamble at the age of fifty, but I felt good about it. This would be quit different than heading up the big divisions at Fairchild with annual revenues of fifty to one hundred million dollars.

I had told Ray Zinn that if I took the position of running the wafer production he would have to fire the sixteen engineers who were presently running the place. He asked why. I told him that they had antagonized their only customer, Litronix (a subsidiary of Siemens), by supplying devices that didn't meet spec or they didn't ship enough for Litronix to satisfy their end customers. Conditions were at the point where Litronix didn't believe in LSI (the wafer fab) and wanted to go to other semiconductor manufacturers to be supplied. I didn't want to start with this handicap. I felt that with new management and new people to work with, Litronix would gain confidence in our ability to provide their needs. Ray agreed with this approach, even though he expressed his reservations that I would be able to run the fab without engineering support until I was able to hire engineers. The day I was receiving my initial papers with Micrel, they were walking out fifteen engineers from LSI.

I went to the plant, and there was one engineer still there, Pete Stylianos. How he got to stay I never did find out, but it turned out that he was young and had a good attitude. He also turned out to be malleable—malleable in the sense that I could teach him rapidly about how to produce a product, and he carried these instructions to completion, freeing me up to look into other issues.

As it turned out, Ray Zinn had negotiated with Siemens to sign a contract requiring that we receive a minimum of 50 percent of Litronix's needs for the first two years' products, and more if we supplied satisfactory products to schedule. So, as a lone engineer, I started reviewing the process being used to manufacture the metal gate CMOS (a very slow cmos device technology) being supplied to Litronix. There were some neat steps being done to stabilize the circuits that I was not aware of, so it was a learning curve for me also. By the end of the first week, the manager of production control, the manager of purchasing, and the manager of quality and reliability had left.

I desperately needed someone to handle these functions. I decided to call my son, Jay. He had double degrees in accounting and in agriculture machinery. He had graduated from Chico State College in 1980 and was working for a company named DeLaval in Oakland. They designed and built the power drives that propelled ocean-going vessels. I told Jay I needed someone I could trust to handle purchasing, production control, and quality control. After some discussion, he agreed to work for me—if he could eventually get into engineering. In two weeks I had Jay doing all these jobs, and he was designing a computer-generated purchase order, a shipping invoice, and a production control system, allowing me to concentrate on the production problems. It didn't take him long to shorten many processes, install computer methods for purchasing and shipping using a small computer he had a home. Jay made my life and my job easier.

Progress continued in the right direction over the next six months in supplying Litronix their metal gate CMOS product, and Pete and I had developed a Darlington power transistor to aid Litronix in completing some of their jobs in a better manner than the single transistor device they previously were being supplied. This helped Litronix to gain some confidence with the operation. They could see that we had good experience and wanted to satisfy them. The process was a simple one like I had done at Youngwood Westinghouse some twenty years earlier.

In September of 1982, I got a call informing me that the computer system used for security had sensed a temperature problem and that a fire truck had been dispatched to the plant. I hurried to the plant at 2:30 AM, and there was a fire truck and about ten firefighters at the scene. The chief took me around back, and we looked in the rear door. Inside the plant and off to my right was a sprinkler system spraying. This implant system was composed of a thick lead shield built around the whole outside of the implanter, and this metal shield was in meltdown as a result of an internal fire inside the implanter.

Looking ahead, I could see the red glow of the diffusion tubes full of wafers looking like nothing was happening. I turned to the fire chief and said, "This reminds me of the *Titanic*. They were playing music while the ship was sinking. Here the diffusion tubes are diffusing wafers while the implanter is melting down." He asked me if they should blast water at the problem area, and I told them to hold off as long as the sprinklers kept the situation in control. I was concerned that spraying with the fire hoses would ruin other equipment and put us completely out of business.

By morning, the fire was completely controlled, and we could walk around in the area. We had insurance to cover such a problem, and the insurance company was quick to order an implanter to our specifications. By January 1983, we had a new implanter, much more capable than the one it replaced. However, our yields had dropped considerably, and we reported to the insurance company. These were the secondary effects of the fire, since we had suffered air contamination throughout the clean room facility from the smoke and other airborne contaminants. The insurance company didn't want to settle at the large amount of money we were asking. I kept yield curves and continued supplying the insurance company these curves and doing verbal battle with them. We took them to court. It took a couple of years, but we eventually received the equivalent of four million dollars, which was concluded by a large check for several million dollars that definitely helped keep Micrel financially stable.

During the year, we had put the recipes for each step of the various processes on a small computer. We maintained this computer in the quality control area, and as we added new products and new processes to our computer library of processes.

During these early years, when we received a new job, we would print out the processes that we felt provided us the flow for the new process. These recipes were cut out like paper dolls and pasted on standard 8 1/2" x 11" sheets of paper in the order we felt the new processes should be processed. Month after month, we added new products and new processes to our computer file using this paper doll approach. My goal was to add technology to this little company so we could broaden our business base. All of these products were foundry products, which made wafers for customers or for Micrel Test Division, with the test patterns provided by our customers. As we added the test patterns to our library of processes, we were building up a powerful variety of technical capability for eventually designing Micrel's own proprietary products.

A stop/start system was installed that required a test at the end of each recipe step. This test was done on a test site designed into the wafers and monitored the result of the previous process step that had been completed. If the wafers passed the test limits, they moved on. If the wafers failed the test limits, the run was stopped for review by the product engineer and he would make one of three decisions – scrap the run, provide a revised process, or allow the run to move on with no changes. The product engineer would then sign the stop/start sheet with one of these dispositions for the run to be scrapped or allowed to proceed with the actions noted. The stop/start slip was made up of four copies. One remained with the run, one went to quality control, one went to process engineering, and one to the product engineer signing off the stop. From that day on, all run would be started by quality control, since they had the latest recipes stored for whatever process we had run and would run. Meanwhile Rob Hurlston was named as the new manager of Quality Control.

As the years went on, we developed many new processes and continued making wafer starts out of quality control (Jay Husher and Rob Hurlston). No other company started their runs from quality control. The main reason I wanted this to be the control point is that we were running a true foundry business—we were making what the customer wanted, rather than our standard process. We would be running a special process for each company from which we would receive our orders, and I wanted to ensure that we were on the same page as the customer. Each company we were to supply would be unique in their technology and the related processes. Each would want a different transistor technology (bipolar, MOS, CMOS,

BCD, DMOS, etc.) with different parameters and limits than other customers. No other semiconductor company ran multiple processes like those run at Micrel. Since we weren't running the same process in production day after day, I wanted the control of all wafers being done by the quality control department, which retained the customer's specifications.

Also, on occasion, each of these companies would made changes in their process while we were already in the process of fabricating their products. We might have had wafers that were halfway through the process when these changes would be made. We wanted quality control to receive the documentation from those companies on their requested changes and the date of change. Since we were responsible for duplicating their process, it was important that all changes went through QC "real time" and that the recipes were updated, the Wafer runs in line captured, and the changes made in the paperwork, thus ensuring the processes were updated.

At times, the lots had already progressed beyond change, and the lots had to be scrapped. When this happened, the customer had to pay Micrel for the scrapped wafers. The key was to be able to do a variety of processes while maintaining complete real-time control of these recipes. It would take years to develop all the new technologies and their related processes, but this was a start. The key was having a computer to record all the updated recipes and to call upon when new runs were started for a customer. We had a very simple computer at the time.

On November 23, 1983 Peg and I became grandparents again. Cinnamon Rose Husher was born to Jay and Rebecca.

New Capabilities—People

During 1983, several significant steps were taken to make Micrel a more diversified producer of ICs. Martin Alter was hired in March of 1983 to be the director of engineering. He was a bright guy who had been serving as a consultant in the industry. He was very knowledgeable, had many contacts throughout the industry, and most of all he had a lot of energy and knew how to focus it. He would serve me and the company well for years to come.

Carmen Pena had joined the company in July of 1982 as the manager of production. She was a very dynamic and focused individual. In addition, she had years of "hands on" experience that would allow her to train operators and foremen the proper techniques required for reliable production of integrated circuits. Martin and Carmen would be my best acquisitions over the years. Not only did they provide a strong technical base, they were two people dedicated to the success of Micrel. Both had very good stock options with the company. During 1983 Martin added to the engineering staff, and Carmen strengthened her foremen positions.

The Last of Our Parents Passes Away

Late in March of 1983 I got a call from Ken. Pap had died. This was sort of expected; he hadn't been the same since Mother died and suffered from senility. I flew back to Pittsburgh the next morning. Funny what I thought of when I was sad and alone on the airplane. I thought about how good my dad had always been. He never drank alcohol, rarely swore, and only smoked about half of what Mother had smoked. He was a good man. Why, I asked myself, should Uncle Bud, who drank and beat his wife and was always getting in trouble, be allowed to live and not my dad? This didn't seem fair. Uncle Bud was two years younger than Pap, but he looked wore out from the terrible life he had lived. I caught myself having these bad thoughts and decided it was not right for me to think that way. How people were chosen was always a mystery to me.

Upon arriving at the Pittsburgh airport, Ken met me, and we drove home. We had only gone about five miles when Ken said, "Did you hear about Uncle Bud?" I shook my head, and he said that Uncle Bud had died today. I got quiet and thought about the airplane ride. I made a promise to myself to never think about people the way I had. It was a sin. Ken and I went straight to the funeral home, even though it was late, to look at Pap. He looked like he always had while sleeping. I thought about how Pap and Mother were back together again.

Back to the Battle

During 1983, Micrel approached Fairchild in South San Jose, seeking to second source their p-channel silicon gate product line. This would require us to develop a p-channel test pattern. Fairchild was happy to find someone who wanted to second source their products, and we started to receive business from Fairchild. They supplied us with p-channel test patterns, and we were on our way to establishing another new process within Micrel. We would supply p-channel technology to other companies as the years proceeded, as well as using some of the lessons Fairchild taught us to provide additional processing power.

One of our biggest customers in the early days was LSI Computer in New York. They designed products around several technologies, and each design had a small test pattern on the active die. This company was very easy to work with, since they provided yield information on wafers continuously. Between their engineers and ours, we were able to determine steps that could be modified to provide them improved products. LSI Computer had two top people named Al: one was Al Kaplan the president and engineering guru and the other was Al Musto, the original president who still maintained control of the company. These people would work with Micrel and me to provide each other the needs for business for many years to come. Likewise, we were able to provide technical information about their products that would allow them to yield higher. The bilateral workings between the people of these two companies were significant in allowing both private companies to succeed over the years.

In 1983, Fairchild Automotive visited our facility seeking someone to supply them bipolar integrated circuit products for their automotive line of products. These bipolar products were required to work at high voltage, which was an added ingredient we wanted to acquire as we built up our library of technologies. Not many suppliers of integrated circuits provided them at high voltage. Most products were working at only three or six volts. We eventually received a limited test pattern for their bipolar process and proceeded to supply them with completed wafers. Eventually, we also received added business to test their wafers. This was called wafer sorting, and our Test division picked up that business. This experience added medium voltage bipolar to our arsenal of technologies.

In 1984 we also added other regular customers for foundry wafers: CDI for metal gate CMOS products, AMI for PMOS metal gate products, ASTEC for bipolar wafers, and other smaller orders for these technologies. In early 1984, we were contacted by Cherry Semiconductor of Rhode Island in search of a supplier of high voltage, high current DMOS (double diffused MOS) technology. The president of Cherry was Al Budnick, who had worked for me as a product manager while at Sprague. We didn't have this technology, but neither did anyone else. Lateral DMOS technology was available in the industry, but no high voltage vertical DMOS had been developed for ICs. We negotiated a contract to develop a high voltage DMOS (double diffused metal on oxide) technology for Cherry Semi. They would pay for us to develop a set of DMOS test patterns, which would become their property as well as ours. In addition, we were given a $450,000 contract to supply them samples of a high-voltage DMOS gate and amplifier as well as supply them with the design specifications for our silicon gate CMOS technology. This initiated our business on DMOS. A recipe was designed for each step of the process. It would take approximately eighteen months to supply the first successful products to Cherry Semiconductor. The combination of silicon gate vertical DMOS and silicon gate CMOS would provide Micrel the basis for developing our own proprietary product lines in the near future.

In 1986, Micro Power, a company located in Sunnyvale, tested our capability by giving us a small order for their unique products. These devices used a moly (molybdenum) gate structure, which no other IC supplier produced. We were able to work hard and engineer a process capable of providing them working models of their devices, and shortly afterward we received production orders. Besides establishing a moly gate technology, work on these products provided us experience on the use of silicon nitride as well as the capability of using nitrogen gas blankets within quartz furnace tubes to process materials that could not otherwise take high-temperature processing without being consumed by oxidation (such as Molybdenum). This added another level of recipes in our computer files, along with the additional business from Micro Power for needed revenue.

In 1985 and 1986, Micro Linear, a small company that produced linear ICs, came to Micrel to have us develop a digital Silicon Gate CMOS (as differentiated from our normal metal gate CMOS, this technology used Poly silicon for the gate) circuits to be used in arrays. Here again was a company with a different approach. We would process the wafers through metal deposition and test the wafers to determine if they passed process specifications. Wafers that passed were then sent to Micro Linear, and they would customize the circuits by patterning the metal. This company had no quality control, and we worked with their engineering to provide them specifications for accepting wafers and for processing the metal in their facility. We worked with their engineers and provided both companies (Micro Linear and Micrel) with a quality control manual that Micro Linear used as their bible. This turned in to betrayal. When we got the wafers yielding and Micro Linear's internal specifications established, they took their business overseas to be produced. However, during this exercise we became a stronger company in establishing improved control specifications for ourselves and improving our CMOS capability while providing Micro Linear their requirements.

I would not take on any business just for the financial justification. Each new piece of business had to add to our capabilities. With each new customer, we added to our repertoire with things like new technologies, technology test patterns, new processes, new recipes, some new techniques, new procedures, new higher voltage capability, higher and lower current capability, and a better means of testing our device structures—all to seek a broader range of foundry business and to eventually provide us the technical strength to produce our own proprietary products in the near future.

Our new equipment was hard to come by. Each required an argument with Ray Zinn and thorough justification, requiring months of discussions before he would finally sign paperwork authorizing their purchase. This was understandable from Ray's point of view. He was running a company on limited resources, and Micrel was still considered a test company. We had yet to establish ourselves as a viable supplier of profitable integrated circuits.

All the business the wafer fab division received was second source and overflow business. Eventually, Ray would approve equipment that gave Micrel a viable advantage. Ray had a quality background, and it was easier to have equipment approved that allowed us to improve our quality, which included such equipment as:

ffi   An electron microscope to physically see the cross sections of the structures we built, to verify structural results, to find faults, and to improve upon them. This was the first expensive piece of equipment authorized, and it was in 1983.

ffi   An advanced CV plotting machine, which allowed us to better characterize our processes and to analyze our products for mobile charges and fixed charges. This was another piece of quality control equipment.

ffi   A projection aligner, which allowed us to produce smaller geometries with lower defect densities, which improved our yield. It took months of arguing with Ray Zinn before the aligner was approved because the business we had at the time did not require a projection aligner. All of our aligners were contact aligners, which could handle the critical dimensions we required on the product we were producing but resulted in defects on the wafers as a result of the contacting method. My argument was the chicken and egg: first you get an aligner and then you get the business. Eventually, we were able to obtain new business from companies that had projection aligners and could supply us the masks. This equipment allowed Micrel to pursue business that had not been previously available to us. Many projection aligners follow this original piece of equipment.

ffi A Perkin Elmer sputtering machine to replace the evaporation system. This gave us added capabilities of back sputtering to clean certain surfaces. We were able to improve the thickness control of our metal deposits. It also reduced sodium as a mobile charge, which affects reliability.

ffi A Coyote plasma nitride system, which gave us improved control of plasma oxide depositions and provided us the ability to deposit plasma nitride, which was a fundamental requirement for advancing our technologies. As our capabilities broadened, the demands also broadened. We replaced liquid etchers with plasma etchers. This brought improved controls of critical dimensions on devices within the chips.

Another Husher at Micrel

In 1983, my youngest son, David, was home for the summer from California State College at Polytechnic Institute in San Luis Obispo. He was majoring in industrial technology and was eager to gain experience. My manager of facilities and maintenance, Guy Barrett, was looking for some temporary help for the summer, and he interviewed David and gave him the summer job. Guy later said that David became the best technician on building the sources for the evaporators and sputter machines, and he brought David in whenever he was home on weekends or on holidays.

Several years later, Guy offered David a full-time job as a facilities technician. I was happy for my son. He had an innate intelligence when it came to machines that I think he inherited from my dad and Peg's dad. I also liked to have him around because he laughed as he did his work or talked to people at lunch. I could be in my office doing something on a Friday, and I would hear this laugh from the back of the building in the tank farm, and a smile would come across my face.

Jay Becomes a Diffusion Engineer

In early 1984, Paul Boon had an opening for a diffusion engineer. Paul's candidates from outside the company did not qualify above Jay, and Jay was given a lateral transfer as a diffusion engineer in 1984. Shortly after, we made the decision to convert our product line to four-inch silicon wafers instead of the three-inch we had been running. This adding capacity to the operation without having to add new management or move into another facility. There were more than twice as many die on this size wafer, which actually resulted in yielding greater than twice as many good die per wafer. This process of crossover, while maintaining control of the three-inch wafer business, was very touchy. We had to continue supplying customers with die off the three-inch wafers while doing this conversion. We had to change masks to accommodate this conversion, but the biggest shift related to the diffusions. Slowly we converted various furnaces based on the business we had and which furnaces would be available for the shift.

The four-inch conversion of the diffusion area was handled completely by Jay. Each furnace to be converted had to have their elements, blocks, collars, and quartzware changed, and the new temperature profiles had to be determined. The temperature profiles had to be changed since the bigger quartzware and larger wafers resulted in added thermal loads on the furnaces. This required experiments and empirical data on each separate tube for each process it was to maintain. This was more significant for Micrel than for any normal semiconductor company, since our foundry business required temperature changes of the furnaces on a daily basis. It was not abnormal for an oxidation tube to be changed four times to a different diffusion time and temperature during a twenty-four-hour period, versus any other semiconductor company that set the tube to a temperature and kept it there for years.

So Jay had to not only convert the furnaces, but each furnace's new temperature and time had to be determined per tube. This total conversion of twenty-two tubes and all their cycles—plus the addition of four new furnace stacks containing eight additional tubes—resulted in thirty diffusion tubes, and all their requirements being completed by late 1985. Four of the new tubes contained silicon carbide liners instead of quartz. This was to allow us to go to higher drive temperatures to shorten the process time. The added advantage of these tubes was that they held their temperature profile better than quartz liners. A key feature determined by Jay was to find the proper recipes for both three-inch and four-inch wafers on some furnaces as we proceeded through this major conversion since many of our customers only had masks for three-inch.

In late 1984, I put out a letter to all our customers that we were converting to four-inch wafers and would require that they have all their masks changed by early 1986 or we would not be able to supply them. All customers conformed and not one customer was lost and all of them responded by letter after the switch that they were receiving at least twice the yield on the wafers we were supplying. This was good news/bad news situation. The good news was that the customers were happy with the higher good die per wafer. and the bad news was that this resulted in their needing fewer wafers from us. We overcame this by increasing the sales price of the wafers by a factor of 1.5. This capability also allowed us to address more customers.

Martin Alter had established a new operating procedure, whereby, when we received new masks from a company, we had one of our very experienced operators review the masks via microscope with instructions to point out the smallest dimension on the mask sets. This was then compared against the critical dimensions that the customer had stated as their smallest dimension or spacing. This method was to point out a fault in almost every new business we took on. A good example related to National Semiconductor in 1985. The product was a circuit that controlled the air-conditioning in an automobile and was supplied in high numbers to several large auto manufacturers. Two days after receiving the masks, we advised National Corp., located in Santa Clara, that there was a design rule violation on one of the masks that resulted in a short circuit. We told them we would not run this product until that was corrected. The next day we got a call from the manufacturing manager in National's Connecticut plant. He told us that he had been running this product for three years, and there was no problem with the masks. They had been running a good number of die per wafer and were making money on this product.

Engineering responded by pointing out the location of the problem. The very next day we got a call from Connecticut verifying the error and apologizing. They said they had been running the product for so long that they had a hard time believing what we found, and said they would provide a new mask to replace the one mask. It turns out that this product could yield with this imperfection if certain other parameters fell within certain limits. Needless to say, in five months we were providing National wafers that yielded approximately twice the yield they had been experiencing.

The Anti-Fuse and Three Patents

In 1985, in order to encourage more people to work with Micrel, I told our marketing people to spread the word that Micrel had a great strength in technology, and companies working with us might take advantage of this great technical capability. In return for any patent we applied for and received while working on a customer's device or product, the customers would have the patent transferred to them with Micrel retaining the ability to use the patent transferred to them without paying royalties. In return there would be reciprocity received from them on their patents which they would be required to share with Micrel. With this approach a customer could take advantage of Micrel's technical strength to solve some of their problem. This almost immediately brought opportunities to work with two companies on a process called anti-fuse. In a normal fuse process, a metal link is burned to program circuits and provides a certain function. In the anti-fuse, the opposite action takes place. By shorting metal fuses the circuit is programmed to perform a function.

A start-up company named Actel came to us with this technology in late 1985, early 1986. This was mainly developmental work, and Actel sent us a young engineer to develop their new technology at that time. Over a year, a good deal of progress was made on new masks and processes. After a year I found a better way to make their anti-fuse and applied for a patent. The patent was awarded fairly rapidly, and Actel decided to take advantage of this patent. However, they were concerned that Micrel might use this patent against them on their array business. Their array business used the anti-fuse to program custom circuits for customers.

I was invited to visit with their management and to discuss how Micrel intended to use Actel's patents. I told them that Micrel didn't want to use this patent or any of their patents but might in the future to make programmable voltage regulators. They felt this would not endanger their markets, and we signed an agreement. Over the next year, Actel's engineer and I received two additional patents on modifications of this original approach, and these were used by Actel. Actel grew quite fast in this business.

Micrel also worked with a company named Altera for a short time on their approach for programmable arrays. They also grew quite rapidly and eventually sent their production business overseas.

In 1987 Micrel worked with the engineering personnel of Analog Devices to produce their silicon gate CMOS products. They had developed this process and products in R&D but had been unsuccessful in placing it in high production. They were a bipolar supplier, and the CMOS technology was foreign to their production people. I told them I would install the process and supply them wafers if they supplied the test patterns and we were then permitted to use these test patterns for any silicon-gate CMOS business we might take on. They agreed, and we were soon shipping wafers to Analog Devices. Our process worked so well that in nine months Analog Devices put us on hold because they now had more good die than they needed. This business had provided us needed revenue, and we now had an improved silicon gate CMOS technology, which had become the most popular technology in the IC business.

We had added additional computer capability in the wafer fab division and no longer needed to cut out paper dolls to generate a new specification or process flow sheet. Through a computer we were able to review the various recipes that controlled each step and selected ones were printed out in the order we believed would provide the proper flow for a new product.

Meanwhile, the added computer provided our stop/start system some major advantages. It provided us improved step-by-step control within the production process, and helped us identify problems or potential problems.

Now It's Micrel Semiconductor

One day I ventured over to the test plant and talked with Ray. I told him that Micrel Test was no longer a viable entity. Most of the testing they were doing was for wafers manufactured by my Micrel fab division. We so completely loaded the test area with work that it was almost impossible for them to free up capacity for outside test services. I told him, "We no longer are Micrel Test and should change our name."

He said, "What name do you suggest?"

I said, "We are now a Semiconductor company." He said, "How about Micrel Semiconductor?" I said, that would be great since this name would tell people what our business really is."

Ray didn't think about this for more than a minute or even take issue with this. He said, "That's a good idea and a good name. Micrel Semiconductor it will be." The next day, he got everything started for changing the company's name, including changing the letterhead of our letter paper. New personal cards were made and issued for the various managers. A major new sign was erected outside the wafer fab and test buildings: Micrel Semiconductor. This was thrilling to everyone in the company. This was a step up, and both our people and our customers knew it.

I Establish a New Rule for Oxide Thickness

We proceeded to work on establishing rules to improve quality and reliability for the CMOS silicon process. There had been a recent scare in the business whereby many people were complaining about products failing in the field. They called this phenomenon time-dependent breakdown (TDB). I had seen enough data on life tests we had run at elevated temperatures and high reverse bias to realize there was some fundamental weakness in the basic oxide process that could be causing this TDB. I had engineering set up some high-temperature tests on devices with varying degrees of oxide thickness. Data from these tests allowed me to come to the conclusion that there were random imperfections in the oxide, resulting in oxides being thinner in random locations that resulted in failure mechanisms.

Theory and tests done on the rupture voltage of the oxides showed that the theoretical rupture voltage should be 1 volt per nanometer (a billionth of a meter) of oxide thickness. However, the data we had derived on these oxide tests showed that there were three types of structures:

ffi   Oxides that ruptured at very low voltages like 0.1 volt per nanometer. These turned out to not be a reliability issue, since they would fail immediately upon our testing.

ffi   Oxides that showed rupture voltages of approximately 0.6 volts per nanometer. These were the reliability problems, since devices made with these random problems passed electrical test specification but over time failed in the customer's application. These were later to be verified to be time-dependent breakdown (TDB) failures. Evaluation of cross sections were characterized by a specified oxide thickness over 97 percent of a given area, but having small random areas in which the oxides were about half the specified thickness. These random areas were the places where the failures would eventually occur.

ffi   Oxides that passed the rupture voltage between 0.9 and 1.0 volts per nanometer of oxide thickness. These proved to be the high reliability devices. Cross sections of these oxides were characterized as having the specified oxide thickness over the entire test area.

ffi   Over time, we determined that these random, thinner than expected oxides were stacking faults or cleaning faults that resulted in slow oxide growth in these areas.

ffi   From this data, I generated a rule within the division. All devices would be specified at maximum operating conditions that were one-third the theoretical rupture voltage of the oxide being considered. For example, if a product had an oxide a hundred nanometers thick and a theoretical rupture voltage of 100 volts, we would specify the maximum operating voltage of the device to be 33 volts. In this manner, Micrel's devices would stay away from TDB failure. At one-third the theoretical rupture voltage, the voltage would also be below the 0.6 volts per nanometer that resulted in time-dependent breakdown. Also, at this low operating voltage, the electrical field in an oxide would be lower than that required to have mobile ion drift should the oxide have sodium or some other mobile ion within the oxide. No other company that we knew of established this tight rule within their operations, probably because they were unaware of the oxide-related time-dependent breakdown issues.

This rule on specifying Micrel products would prove to be valuable in that no Micrel product ever evidenced failures due to TDB or mobile ion issues. This was significant for a company with limited resources. We could not afford any major quality or reliability issues with customers returning products at our expense. We also could not afford to have irate customers missing their shipments to customers because of any issue that could come back to haunt us.

The Rule Pays Off—Genie Garage Door Openers

The engineers and management responsible for Genie garage door openers visited our facility to determine if Micrel should produce the IC chips for their garage door openers. We looked at their design and told them they would eventually have problems with field failures.

Obviously, they could not afford to have garage doors that wouldn't open or close at the touch of a button. Their devices were designed with an oxide that was not thick enough to operate at the specified voltages and prevent eventual TDB.

They disagreed with Martin Alter and me. saying, "We have visited other design and fabrication facilities, and they believe there will be no problem with these oxide thicknesses will be fine." I asked them to give me the name of one of the potential suppliers, which they did.

I then called a friend who headed up design for the company they were referring to and allowed the Genie people to listen to the conversation. I told him, "I understand that Genie was in to see you, and you said that you see no problem with the oxide thicknesses that would be employed." He said that this was true. I then said, "I believe these thicknesses will eventually see TDB problems and failure in the field. How can you quote that these oxide thicknesses were satisfactory?"

The reply was that they quoted it to be responsive and competitive with other quotes Genie had received. "So then you agree with me that these oxide thicknesses will eventually cause field failures?" I asked. He said that this would probably be true.

After hanging up the phone, the engineers from Genie gave Micrel the job of supplying their products. This was a piece of business that would last for years with Genie using our chips in their garage door transmitters and receivers for years. Genie never returned any product to Micrel for reliability problems over the many years Micrel supplied the product. I made sure I got a Genie garage door opener for our house. Genie was the biggest supplier of garage door openers in the U.S.

Genie was not the only beneficiary of Micrel's conservative rules. More and more of Micrel's customers being supplied by Micrel were happy with the results and the reliability of the products they received.

A Home by a River for Ken and Sherie

Ken had always wanted a house by a river, and Sherie and Ken kept looking. Every couple of weeks they would look along the river for houses for sale. But the house was not to be found. Then one day early in 1984 while Lori was visiting, she told her dad that her friend's parents were looking to sell their house along the river and move to a place where they could have horses. She called her friend and asked where the house was located and the address. That weekend, Sherie and Ken planned to go and visit friends who lived south of where this house was located and on their way back they would see if the house was worthwhile.

As they drove back, they stayed on the main road that wandered alongside the river. All the houses looked typical of western Pennsylvania houses – two or three stories high with cellars, mostly brick but some of wood. Then, there before them was a low, California-style ranch house. They checked the address and were excited as it matched the slip of paper they had brought with them. They rang the doorbell and were greeted by a nice-looking woman with the friendly smile. They walked around the house and then walked the fifty yards to a sloped hillside that ran down to the river. Ken kept hoping that he wasn't dreaming and hoping that they wouldn't find something wrong with the house or the location. After an hour of looking, they found nothing wrong.

Ken was ready to buy the house within fifteen minutes of seeing the inside and outside. He could envision building a wharf out on the river and having a boat tied to its side. This was the house by the river he had always thought dreamed about. They discussed the sale price with the lady and bargained a little and came to a suitable conclusion that both parties agreed on. Ken made out a check as a down payment, and they were on their way to home.

For the first fifteen minutes of driving home, they were almost in an unconscious mood. Almost like being hypnotized, and not knowing where they were driving because their minds were on the house by the river. Finally, the silence was broken and they began talking in an excited manner. They could hardly wait to get home and call the kids and tell them about the house. They were "thrilled to death" as Sherie later described the trip home to her friends. Ken couldn't believe how much the house looked like Gort's house in California. He knew this was forty-five miles from his work, but it was open highway most of the way. He was willing to take that drive to have this perfect prize.

It wasn't long before they were moving. And it wasn't long until they were both enjoying their new house and putting energy into it. Ken was surprised that there were fish in the river. "When Gort and I were kids, nothing could live in that river," he said. However, that was in 1947 and thirty-eight years had passed, along with legislature to clean up the river by eliminating industrial sites from dumping of various organics and solvents into the river by the steel mills, the zinc mills and other industrial sites. Even the sewer water went through some central river water processing procedures in many of the towns along the river. Here was the Monongahela River that flowed out of West Virginia to meet the Allegheny River, to form the Ohio River at the confluence of the two rivers at the Pittsburgh "point"

Ken was only there a day when he wet his fishing line, and not many days before he had caught a variety of fish in his backyard. He would catch a fish, patiently remove the hook from its mouth, scrape some lesion from its side, and gently slip the catch back into the water— sometimes with a kiss before throwing them back.

This was not only a great house in a great location, but it was the kind of thing that took up his time. They added a boat house and a wharf shaped like an upside down L. Coming home from work in the summer while the sun was still out allowed him the chance to drop a line in the river before eating supper.

Here he was, finally by his river. Many was the time he would think about the time he and Gort had sat by the river and he remembered telling Gort, "When I grow up, I want to live by the river," and Gort saying, "Not me, I want to live high on a hill so I can look out and see the world." He thought about where they were living. "Gort is living high on a hill out by San Francisco, and here I am by my river." Here we were, by a River, on a Hill. Life was good.

———— ⁓⁓ ∽ ⦿ ⦿ ∽ ⁓⁓ ————

Over the years this house and the river itself would be an attraction for Ken and Sherie's family and all their friends. Every Fourth of July Peg and I would go east to visit them and have fish fries and other outdoor entertainment at this delightful location. Every holiday would find this place loaded with family and friends. As the grandchildren grew older, they would come to swim and fish all day, collecting their rods from Ken's boat house, walking down to the river, and dipping their lines in search of fish.

Boating was also fun. The boat set at the dock, and every once in a while there would be additional boats at the dock visiting the Husher family. After visiting there one summer my son Jay said, "That place is a party waiting to happen."

Micrel Begins to Produce Proprietary Products

By 1987, it became apparent to Ray Zinn that Micrel had several advantages over other suppliers in certain areas, mainly in high-voltage and high-current applications developed by the process engineers at the wafer fab division. We had also gained a significant knowledge on analog circuits. Ray contracted an outside design company to design a chip with these significant advantages. Since we had no commercial product line and were not established as a supplier of proprietary products (designed and made by Micrel), the management decided the chip would be an Analog custom array, designed by customizing the metal mask to a customer preference. The customizing would occur with the last patterned metallization on the device to provide a special custom circuit to the customers specification.. If successful, it would be the first analog array designed for high-voltage and high-current applications.

The design group was located in the test building, which was about five miles from the wafer fab building. The general block layout of the product was initiated by Ray Zinn and several design engineers, with the final layout details being done by the contractor. It was a smart approach that took our major advantages and implemented them. The design was to have an option for ten output DMOS (a technology that used "double diffused MOS structures that, uniquely provided high power, high voltage devices) devices around the outside perimeter of the die, each capable of operation at high voltage and high current.

These output devices could be connected as individual high output drivers or in parallel to provide an even greater capability single output device with approximately ten times the operating current, or in many other combinations using these as the outputs.

The internal structures of the design provided various voltage references and had various op-amps (operational amplifiers) that could be connected in a multitude of ways to form functions. There was a significant amount of logic within the design that could be connected to provide many functions. The design also contained level shifters that could shift logic level outputs to the levels required to operate other devices that required different drive and supply voltages within the chip. This was a large and fairly complicated chip. It would take approximately a year and a half to provide the design, using process specifications established by my engineers in the wafer fab division.

While this proprietary design was proceeding, Martin Alter took on the responsibility of designing a super test pattern. The test pattern would consist of four quadrants, each optimized for a given type of technology, thus allowing quadrants to be used for all of the technologies we had developed to date and for those we felt we would work on in the future. This test pattern would eventually provide Micrel wafer fab an avenue into many technology improvements and innovations over the years. Martin had to think ahead to any future potential devices or needs for making measurements to confirm capabilities that could not be measured on the devices themselves. This was like inventing before an invention and it worked.

The test pattern needed to preempt any future processes that Micrel might invent or be supplied by other manufacturers' designs over the next several years. This included different technologies such as vertical DMOS, lateral DMOS, bipolar, CMOS, BiCMOS, and BCD (bipolar, CMOS, DMOS). This required an immense effort and fantastic creativity by Martin Alter. Martin Alter long hours until late in the evenings almost every day of the week for months. I would estimate it took a year of fourteen-hour days for Martin to complete the design of this test pattern. Some aspects of it were of immediate use, but other aspects of it would serve us well into the future. Since

Martin was to spend so much time on this design, I took over the day-by-day monitoring of the process group, headed up by Paul Boon, and personally directed the process development during that time.

Finally the day came when we were processing this analog array. There were many steps to this large and complex analog array, and early yields on the product were low. However, analysis on the test structure showed the major problem as defects—mainly masking defects. Slowly the yield improved as we attacked the various defect causes and we were able to start sampling the device.

We never had any large production orders for this device, but it brought many potential customers to Micrel's doorstep and allowed us to initiate dialogues with many companies. We did require smaller volume orders for our customers to work out the best use of the device and to optimize the metal interconnects. This put Micrel on the map for companies considering analog solutions for their systems. We were now being considered a viable supplier of complex integrated circuits. The biggest business that came out of this array was a special circuit supplied to Xerox, which used the fundamental technology of the analog array.

Shortly, we began to supply Elantec with high-voltage devices. Along came Hewlett-Packard, and we were left with an opportunity to supply them with decent volumes of bipolar medium voltage devices. Both Elantec and Hewlett-Packard were second source business, with these two companies supplying the masks and test patterns. But they represented business and the revenues that come with the business, and they kept Micrel profitable.

Micrel had now run for twelve years making money on every quarter (forty-eight quarters) during that time period—the first few years as a test company and finally as a semiconductor company. This included tough times when the economy was in recessions and periods where the whole semiconductor industry was hit hard. During those periods, Micrel did not lay off people. We went through pay cuts of 10 percent and periods where the operators worked a shortened workweek at accordingly reduced pay. Carmen Pena did a great job of multiplexing her operators to these shorter shifts, and the outcome was good. Ray was a very good financial manager, and among Ray, Warren, and Me, we found ways to reduce our costs dramatically during these recession periods.

Ray was also responsive at revising the pay cuts as soon as it was practical. He was good at analyzing business data, talking to the right people, and determining early when things were going wrong and when it looked like business was about to pick up. He would preempt these businesses going both ways and we stayed on track.

Micrel Gains a New Design Team

In 1989, Ray hired Larry Sample from National Semiconductor to head up the design department and add new proprietary products to Micrel's product line. Here was a very experienced and talented person who was drawn to Micrel because of its potential. High-level people were paid well and given good, substantial stock options.

Micrel not being a public company provided us some advantages in hiring key people. These added people thought that Micrel would eventually go public, and they would be rewarded accordingly through their stock options. Compared to other new companies started by venture capitalists who acquired very large percentages of the companies they started, Micrel stock was not diluted by outside concerns. The stock was held by internal people from Ray Zinn and Warren Muller down through the ranks. So potential hires felt they had a better opportunity of making significant money when and if Micrel went public, and they became Micrel employees. Micrel stock was valued internally at between $0.10 and $1 in those early days. Bottom-line, we were able to hire good designers and marketing people, which was where the company needed to add horsepower.

How Micrel - Started in the Regulator business

Larry Sample and the design team started to design a test vehicle that they called FRED. This was to be a chip containing transistors, diodes, resistors, capacitors, and DMOS to characterize the process being manufactured in the wafer fab division.

This FRED design continued for about six months, and one day I called Larry Sample. I told Larry I would like to have an operating device put on the test device that would allow my people not only to evaluate the process required by his design people, but also to see how well our process functioned toward making a finished product.

Larry asked me if I had a product in mind. I told him I didn't. and thought he could think of a product in high production at National that we could purchase and analyze. The next day he said that one of his designers was going to buy a high-volume voltage regulator, made by National Semiconductor and sold through several distributors. The device was called a 2950. We took the device apart and analyzed the cross section, the transistors, and resistors. We knew our process was different, but we were experienced at meeting varying parameters and felt even though our device would look different than theirs that we could produce National's parameters with our technology. This would require a different design based on our approach. Soon, Larry's designers began to lay out the device according to our process capabilities and design rules. A few weeks had passed, and I called Larry. The conversation went something like this:

"Larry, can we add some unique properties to the new device we're designing?"

"Sure, John. Do you have something in mind?"

"Yes, I do. I'd like to see an over voltage dropout and over current dropout designed into the device My previous experience at Fairchild with voltage regulators showed me that many people would like to see these functions included in a voltage regulator."

"Sure, John, we can come up with something fairly easily."

And so the design included several capabilities that no one else had designed into their regulators up to that time. We received the design masks for the test pattern for this simple regulator in about three months. We included these test patterns on six sites on each wafer.

The processing flow sheets were awaiting these masks, and wafers were started in the wafer fab line. The wafers were split up at several key operations and held in line so that if we had problems with wafers that were processed further, we could go back and bring some of these wafers forward. The stop/start system ensured that wafers held at positions met parameters up to any point in the process.

After about eight weeks, the most advanced wafers came off the production line. Tests at parameter test showed that they met our process specifications. We were also able to make some simple tests that left us confident that there would be life on the new product, and wafers were sent to the design department for their evaluation.

After several weeks, I got a phone call from Larry Sample. The conversation went something like this:

"John, we tested those 2950 equivalent die, and they beat National's devices in every respect. In fact, these are the best voltage regulators I've ever seen. Besides, the over-voltage protection and over-current protection work great. If you increase the voltage, the device soon turns off and isn't destroyed. The same is true for the over current protection. When returned to the normal operating conditions, the devices work like they've never been taken out of specification range. They're bulletproof!"

This floored me, and I said, "So are you saying we have a product we could sell as a proprietary product?"

The answer came back, "You betcha!"

And so the first proprietary product was born out of a test vehicle. It was called the MIC2950. We had several hundred assembled and put on high-temperature life tests. The results were very good, and we began to make this device in large volumes to send samples to potential customers. In order to satisfy most companies, we needed to supply them with enough units to put through their life tests, to put in samples of their finished product, and enough to be sure that we were in fact a potential high-volume supplier.

Soon we began to receive orders on this product. One major cellular phone supplier in Europe took 1,000 of our devices and 1,000 of their present supplier's devices and fabricated something less than 2,000 finished phone boards. The feedback through our salespeople was that Micrel's product finished up with 1,000 finished phone boards out of

1,000 started that passed specifications, and the competitor's product did not fare as well. They told us that they found our devices were not vulnerable to the normal fallout caused by handling in the production line. They were not destroyed by voltage spikes and other random events that occur in their assembly line. Nor were there any losses due to noise, voltage spikes, poor voltage regulation on their printed circuit boards, inserting of devices backward in the sockets, static charge and discharge, poor handling, and other random events. Because of this improvement in their line yield, they increased the orders to Micrel, and within months we were their major supplier.

Eventually, their original supplier realized Micrel's design advantages and redesigned their products. They got most of their business back, since they were volume suppliers on other products to this customer and could leverage Micrel out with pricing or as a broad product supplier. But the die had been cast, and Micrel became a major supplier in the voltage regulator business. We were in the volume proprietary business and were there to stay. I guess lighting can strike twice, I brought Fairchild into the regulator business and I just helped Micrel get into a different kind of regulator business - a better one. This device got Micrel into many phone designs, power supply designs, control circuitry, dot com new business, and many other electronic circuit supplier's products. We were off and running.

In fairly rapid order, the design group came up with new devices for us to process through the wafer fab production line. We soon had a broader proprietary business as a result of these designs.

Key Advantage—Development on Production Line

A key advantage held by Micrel was that new products never went through a research and development cycle in a separate area. All development was performed on the production line. This resulted in less time from development to production and no need to transfer products from R&D to production. The production line ran by individual recipes, calling out the details for each individual step in the sequential flow.

In addition, tests were conducted at the end of each step to ascertain the step had been completed in compliance. The operators followed the recipe and never knew if they were running a new product, a research product, or a standard product until the product got to the wafer testing at the end of the processing.

All new designs were handled by product managers and their engineers, reporting to Martin Alter – my engineering manager.. We had established excellent product managers over time. Marty Garnett handled these new products with his engineers, including making up the initial process flow run sheets that drove the product through the line. Many new products did not work the first time through because they might involve new processes and the recipes and flow sheets might have had an error in judgment or interpretation by the operators on line. Garnett's engineers would debug the processes and come up with solutions. He was also responsible for any new technology developments being established for the line.

Another product manager was Bob Rumsey, who handled all products known to meet specs and were to be run in production volumes. Bob would pick up the products that met specifications from Marty's people. Bob detailed the reasons for any fallout of the transferred product and made sure it was improved upon. He took products from low to high yield by definitive attention to detail and took them to high volume as these details were ironed out.

Kirpal Atwal was responsible for taking products that had reached maturity and high yield in Bob Rumsey's product list and maintain them long-term. This took the load off Bob Rumsey so that Bob had the time required to take another new product from Marty Garnett.

Kirpal was also very good with customers. His products were required to meet varying conditions, depending on the customer and the customer's requirements. He had to handle these varying conditions such as increasing orders, or decreasing orders, or changing of specifications. In many cases the customer we supplied gained new business where their customer wanted some slight changes. These were negotiated by Kirpal, and he handled them well.

I should interject something special about Kirpal. When I arrived at Micrel, Kirpal was an hourly operator on the production line, a very good one. He was moved to harder and harder jobs within the production process. Eventually, he was in the parameter test room, where I spent considerable time ensuring that wafers were looking good and being shipped to customers. I forget the exact incident, but on one occasion a particular problem came up in the test room and Kirpal corrected the problem. I went to Carmen Pena, who was my production manager, and asked her about him. She told me he had a degree in mathematics from a school in India, but it had not been recognized in the States. In the not too distant future, we added a third shift to the wafer fab operation and were looking for a foreman to run the difficult shift that went from 11:00 PM to 7:30 AM. This shift requires someone with an analytical background, good line experience, and the qualities of a good leader. Carmen and I discussed trying Kirpal in this position. She was more than happy to do so, since she liked to see promotions from within. So Kirpal became the third-shift foreman. He did a great job. He hired many Indian operators who looked up to him, and the third shift was a success.

Several years later, we were considering taking some load off of Bob Rumsey, which would require hiring an engineer. Sure enough, we turned around and promoted Kirpal to product engineer under Bob. Eventually, as production increased and we wanted to install new processes and products, we thought about adding a third product manager to handle the high production line products and to take this load off of Bob Rumsey. After reviewing our alternatives, Kirpal Atwal was promoted to product manager of established product lines. This was indeed a great story and what America is like.

Kirpal went from an hourly operator to a high-salaried product manager. This also turned out to be a successful venture for Kirpal and Micrel. He handled his job well in his quiet, analytical, and natural way. This is a good example of the American way—of being able to rise depending on your abilities and not your social status.

1989 Earthquake, Almost a Disaster

In late 1989, an event occurred that could have been a disaster for Micrel, but the company proved its mettle again. It turned out that the San Francisco Giants and the Oakland Athletics baseball teams in the area won their league's championship and would meet in the World Series.. The first two games were played in Oakland, and my son David and I had tickets for the Giants' home games at Candlestick Park in right field, as high up and as far as you could go in the stadium.

While waiting for the game to start, David went to get a beer on the deck below. He was only gone about five minutes when all of a sudden I heard a noise like a train coming and looked off to my left. The stadium is made up with concrete slabs hanging out in cantilever fashion and forming the finished, closed circle around the top of the stadium. These slabs must have been about fifty feet in length, and twenty-five feet in width, and approximately a foot thick. The inner edge of each is attached in pivot positions like the hinges of a door. The extended edge of each of these foot-thick slabs rests on a metal bar by gravity. The train noise I heard came from the left of me and as I looked in that direction, I saw each of these slabs, one by one, rising in the air while pivoting on the inner pivot points and each slab movement lifted the next slab in such a way that it was like a deck of cards being flipped sequentially toward me and moving around the top of the stadium in a counterclockwise direction. This was what sounded like a train.

In the meantime, the outside walls of the stadium were swaying like they were ready to collapse. I knew immediately I was experiencing an earthquake. I knew the seats where we sat extended out over the outside of the stadium, and if the stadium collapsed, I would fall about sixty feet to the concrete outside the building. My mind immediately remembered the auto accident I had experienced some years before and I hadn't felt the pain. Now I said to myself, "Is this how it's going to end? Will I feel any pain?" And then I sat down and decided to relax while it was happening. Within seconds, the train noise stopped and the stadium ceased swaying. Young kids in front of me, thinking it was like most earthquakes around here and would not cause any harm, immediately began hollering, "Even the Lord's behind us. The Giants will win." Little did they know?

I was happy that only some concrete pieces fell about ten feet away and caused no harm. The ballplayers from the two teams had run onto the field to be away from the swaying stands. I had brought a portable, battery-operated TV with me and immediately began to see reports on the TV about damage in the Bay area as we sat there. I hollered that there were fires in San Francisco, the Bay Bridge had collapsed, and there was a collapse of the concrete structure of an overpass in Oakland. Now I realized that this was not one of the many small harmless earthquakes that hit the area each year.

About five minutes later, David returned with his beer. I told him we were leaving this place, but he wanted to stay and watch the game. I told him that when we got to his truck, if the radio said the game was on, we would come back.

Leaving the stadium and looking back we could see the stadium emptying without any rush or panic. It was like an anthill, with the ants flowing out of their home. When we got to the truck, David said, "Dad, I want to see the game." Again, I told him if the radio said the game was on, I would turn around and come back. However, as we tried to leave, the police stopped all cars until the stadium was emptied. We sat there for over an hour before moving toward home.

When we reached the house, I noticed that the driveway was wet, but everything else looked OK. I went in to see Peg and get a report. Peg said that when the quake hit she had run to the sliding back door to the backyard, and then the quake had thrown her against the metal siding of the door. Her arm was bruised. She said as she was getting through the door, the water in the pool leaped out. It dumped about half the 22,000 gallons of water toward the gate leading to the driveway. Now I knew how the driveway had gotten wet. Two televisions sets had leaped from their stands and landed on the floor, and some of the dishes in our china closet had fallen to the floor.

Now it was time to check the factory. I called but got no response. I called Bob Widas, the line maintenance manager, at his home, and he said that the power had been cut off at the plant and soon after firefighters had entered and told them to evacuate to their homes because they had detected a gas leak from the EXAR plant, which was about 100 yards behind our plant. I said, "Call the service that monitored plant security computer and tell them to keep watching for signs that show the computer's on. This means power has been restored to the plant." "Establish a plan with the monitoring service, whereby they keep monitoring the readouts from the computer and when they get a reading, have them call you at home. "When you receive verification that the power's on, call Guy Barrett and me. Proceed at that time to the plant. Put on gas masks and other required gear that provide oxygen, enter the plant, and turn on the exhaust systems. Then leave the plant for half an hour to allow any possible fumes in the plant to be exhausted, and then go back in and check for leaks on all the gas systems. If they're all found to be sound, then you can start turning on the power to the equipment. Don't turn on any application gases, such as phosphorus, until you get the OK from HAZMAT."

I got a call from Widas at 4:30 AM signaling that the power was back on, and I proceeded down to the plant. By the time I got there, Widas and his guys had everything under control. Everything was operational, and we were ready to turn on the process gases. I was excited, believing we would be the first plant to return to operation in the Valley. But we had to wait for the HAZMAT person that was responsible for our site. He had to check out what we had done and the status of the building. If it met with his approval, we would be allowed to turn all the gases on and prepare for operation.

Soon our HAZMAT representative arrived at the plant. He was excited and out of breath. I told him to relax that everything seemed to be in operational shape. He took Guy Barrett and Bob Widas and entered the plant to make a survey of the facilities and equipment. About an hour later, he completed his survey and came out. He said, "You don't have an emergency backup power system, and I'm going to write your company up for noncompliance to ordinance."

I asked him how long he had been our representative, and he said about three years. I then stated, "You've been our representative for three years and not once have you instructed us to install a backup power system. If you write us up, I'll complain to HAZMAT and to the city and write you up for negligence. I want you to give us the OK for start up today and write me a letter in a couple of days instructing me to add an emergency back up power system by some future cut off date. I also want a backup system, but they cost money. The president of Micrel needs to know that it's required." He stared at me for about 15 seconds and then said, "OK, I ma giving you the acceptance you need to start your operation, but I will come back with a demand for the backup system. At that time we will determine the amount of time you have to install one. You have to excuse me for over-reacting, but this thing is overwhelming with all the plants I have to cover. I told him I understood. He left without writing us up. Meanwhile, we started to turn on all the operation gases, and an hour later our operators arrived and business was started again. I still believe we were the first plant that was operational after that quake.

Several days later, I got the letter from HAZMAT requesting Micrel to install a backup power system that would run the exhaust and other safety equipment in the plant should we run out of power. I took this to Ray Zinn, and he immediately approved buying the system. Guy Barrett and I reviewed the various systems available, which were run on gasoline, diesel, or natural gas. We didn't like the gasoline or diesel systems, since they required a large holding tank in the plant, which took up space and were dangerous. We ordered a system with natural gas, which was available via underground piping, and sent the drawings of the system along with its system specifications to HAZMAT and to the city engineering. The system and its specifications were approved in about five weeks. We installed the system in approximately four months, including the electrical power switching system that automatically activates the system when power is interrupted. We checked the operation on a Saturday when the workload was light and found it working fine. HAZMAT and the city were advised that it had been checked out and was available for inspection.

One day, a HAZMAT person arrived to check out the system, and Guy Barrett took him to the back pad for the checkout.. They were only gone five minutes when Guy returned and told me that the representative was not going to approve the system because the ordinance called out that the system have a self-contained energy source for running the equipment. Later, the representative arrived at my office and relayed this same information to me. He said he had tagged the system as not approved.

I told him, "We sent the drawings and specifications for this system to your office over five months ago, and it was accepted. We have an infinite source of underground natural gas connected to that back up system. We will not change the system, and you had better do one of two things: remove the tag from the equipment and place an approval tag on it or return later when you have checked things out with your people and take the tag off and approve it."

He left.

Several weeks later, Guy Barrett came to my office and said the tag had been removed and an approved tag was now on the system. We never had the occasion to use this emergency system for anything as violent as an earthquake, but over the course of eight years the system came on about four times during power outages in the area. The system worked great during these occasions, allowing the main exhausts and several critical pieces of equipment to remain on. The 1989 earthquake had been a test of our mettle, and the growing company continued to flourish.

In 1990 Micrel had a design team for adding new proprietary products to our product list and a marketing team that assessed the needs of the analog market so we could come up with new products as the industry needed them. Our foundry business remained healthy with new capabilities, new capacities, and new customers. This combination started to bring in more business, and the revenue for Micrel was on an upward slope.

In 1990–91 we picked up foundry business with several new customers. Unitrode gave us orders for bipolar products in high volume; NCR with business on p-channel silicon gate products; Thomson (in France) with p-channel silicon gate products; Rockwell for PMOS metal gate products; Maxim for CMOS metal gate products; EXAR for high-voltage bipolar products; and new orders for CMOS silicon gate products from Analog Devices.

We also worked on special circuits for Hughes for use in outer space. I used to laugh and made a comment, "If the Russians were looking for who's making these special circuits for Hughes and they found out it was Micrel, they would drive by our building and laugh. They would say there was no way that this little company could make these special circuits for Hughes."

A New Semiconductor Facility

Late in 1990, Ray had asked me to look around for a bigger facility than the small building we were in. I didn't feel too inspired to look for another plant, since history showed me that finding a new plant was left for Ray to do. On previous occasions, Ray had asked Bob Flint, the facilities manager for the test plant, to look for a new place for the test business, and everything that Bob found, Ray would find something wrong with it. Ray eventually went out and found a new building to house both the corporate headquarters and the test facility. They had moved into that facility around 1987, and it showed off well for the company.

Anyhow, I convinced myself to look around one day a week for several weeks. My early surveys of the local area didn't raise my hopes, but one day I l found a nice facility that presently housed Seeq Semiconductor in San Jose, on the border of the city of Milipitas, California. They had one large beautiful building that housed their top management and their wafer fabrication production line, and another building that handled peripheral services. Seeq was building a new facility without a wafer fabrication line and would import wafers from services overseas. They wanted to sell the wafer fabrication equipment in the building in addition to dropping their lease on the building.

I called Ray and told him about the building sometime in October of 1990. Time went by and I sort of forgot about Seeq, their building, and equipment. In late December I got a call from Ray, and he said he had visited the Seeq building and liked what he saw. He said I should pursue it further. This was exciting to me and I went that week and talked to the people responsible for selling the equipment and the building and made appointments for mid-January after the holidays were over to start further discussions and negotiations.

We negotiated with a representative for Seeq about selling the equipment and with the landlord of the building about taking over the lease. We wanted to purchase much of the equipment that was in place, since it would allow us to be up and running without installing new equipment and the resulting debugging. The building also contained equipment capable of fabricating six-inch wafers, and I wanted to move in that direction. I had made an agreement with the landlord of the building that he would loan Micrel the money to purchase any equipment in the building. This served two purposes: he would be able to have Micrel as a tenant in short order, and I wouldn't have to seek financing to purchase the equipment.

However, I soon found a problem that would complicate the situation. There was a hang-up between Seeq and the landlord. Seeq felt the laminar flow hoods in the facility belonged to them, since they had purchased and installed them. The landlord felt they belonged to him because of the lease that had been agreed to years before: any equipment tying into the air-conditioning (that was considered a part of the building) became a facility improvement and the property of the landlord. This disagreement went on for months. There were over 120 laminar flow systems in the building worth approximately one million dollars when purchased. Seeq also wanted money to pay for moving into their new building and began to auction off the equipment that I had wanted. I tried to have them maintain a certain amount of patience while we worked out the details of our taking over the building, but they kept selling equipment out from under me.

Meanwhile, Ray got involved and looked over the expenses that Seeq had incurred while running the building. He called me over to his office and discussed his concerns. He saw the electrical service bills that Seeq had incurred month after month and it averaged $127,000 a month. He said he couldn't afford this kind of power bill and expect to make money. I told him I would look into it and see if I could find a way around this high power bill. I reviewed the power bill for the corporate/test building and my wafer fab building. Together they ran about $55,000 a month. I looked through the Seeq building and told Ray I would be able to cut the Power Bill in half at Seeq.

He didn't believe it was possible, and I reviewed with him the many places I could reduce the power consumption. The whole air-conditioning and airflow system could be completely changed. They had three, 100-horsepower motors on the roof used to push and direct air into the place just to control the pressure in one room versus another that I felt I could eliminate. They brought their cold air through ducts directly to all the laminar flow stations. In order for the operators to work under those laminar flow stations, they had to preheat the air to a comfort level. This meant they had a large number of heaters in the ducts to control the temperature at 70 degrees into these workstations. They had differential air pressure sensors throughout the various operating levels that would control louvers in the main air input to the plant (those three big motors) so as to provide a positive pressure in the masking area relative to the other processing areas. They also completely exhausted all the air instead of recirculation of some of the clean, cold air for makeup.

I would eliminate the large motors with their huge power drain, turn off the differential air pressure sensors and replace the ducts so the cold air would be dumped directly into the masking rooms, which would automatically provide positive pressure in the masking area relative to the other working areas. Air would be ducted from the masking area to the other areas. This would automatically provide the masking area as the most positive. The air would be dumped directly into all the rooms, rather than going through the laminar flow hoods. This would allow us to remove the heaters in the ducts and reduce that power use. The laminar flow hoods and their fans would draw the air from the room and would just circulate clean air in each of the areas, making the air cleaner and cleaner each time it recirculated. This would eliminate the heaters in the ducts. The ducting would be rearranged to provide 50 percent make up of clean cold air rather than the 100% exhausting that was being done. This would reduce the demand for air conditioned air. With these main changes and several other small ones, I told Ray I could cut the power cost to about what was presently being paid by the two buildings that we would be leaving. He reviewed this and felt it was a viable plan and gave me the go on this.

After several months of trying to acquire the rights to the facility and getting stonewalled by different issues I decided to call a meeting with the responsible people. At the same time, I was losing several pieces of equipment that I had wanted in the plant to other companies who were buying them from Seeq. I asked that a meeting be held between Seeq's management, the landlord, Ray Zinn, and me to see if we could come to some kind of mutual understanding. The discussion kept going back to the laminar flow hoods and who owned them. I asked Ray to step out in the hall. I suggested to him that we go back in and suggest the following: "Micrel will put up $300,000 (I believe that is the amount) for the laminar flow hoods. If later on it was decided that the laminar flow hoods belonged to the landlord, the money would be returned to Micrel. If it was determined that the laminar flow hoods belonged to Seeq they would receive the $300,000, and the landlord would reduce the lease cost to Micrel by $300,000 over a certain time period."

After some discussion, this was accepted. and the meeting continued. Then came the shock of the meeting. Out of nowhere, the landlord said, "I want to tell you gentlemen that I have declared bankruptcy today, and I will not be able to bankroll Micrel on the purchase of the equipment." The room became quiet. Ray looked at me in disgust and pointed toward the door and out we went into the hallway. He was very disturbed and kept walking around in circles. "Do they think I need their money? I could make a call this afternoon and have the money. Let's go, John, we're going to get this building today." And so we went back into the room and discussed the equipment we wanted and reiterated our stand on the laminar flow hoods and our lease. Ray told them he didn't need the landlord's financing. The meeting came to a conclusion in less than an hour, and we went out of the room—the future owners (lease of twenty years) of this great building.

We were moving from about a 25,000 square sq. ft. corporate/testing building and a 10,000 square sq. ft. wafer fab building into a 125,000 square sq. ft. modern building that was made for making wafers and serve as a great building for corporate headquarters and the marketing center for Micrel Semiconductor. The other thing that would become apparent as time passed is that the building alone brought some business to Micrel. Potential customers, who used to come to the Wafer Fab building on Pastoria, take one look at our old building and walk away without giving us the business, now came to this building and we got their business. The name of the location was almost enough to bring customers to the new plant. It was located at 1849 Fortune Drive, and people that know any history of California remembered gold was discovered in California in 1849.

But there was a lot to do to make this a functional plant. Seeq had established production in the plant on six-inch wafers, while all the wafers we now produced were four-inch. If we were going to make a viable production plant out of the Fortune Drive facility, we needed to shift everything to six-inch silicon wafers. But I had wanted to go to six-inch wafers anyhow. The race was on.

Another Medical Problem Appears

The year of 1991 began in a dreadful manner. Sam Pool had a massive hemorrhage and died the next day in the hospital. He was seventy-eight and still in good shape physically, so this came as a shock. My daughter Karen moved in with Peg Pool to share the house and to help Peg. It was nice having my lovely daughter around, and her sense of humor made life happier. Karen and Grandma Peg got along great together. It was also nice having Karen close to her mother. This was the only good thing about Sam dying—having my daughter around more. Life would be a little less exciting with him gone but life went on. Later, I said to Peg, "This is the way your dad would have wanted to go. He was out working in his garage and died doing what he loved. I sure will miss the guy. He was a pleasure to be around."

Meanwhile, I had another medical problem bothering me. In 1985 I started to lose taste on the right side of my mouth. By 1986 I had lost all taste. In 1987 I was sent to a neurologist, Dr. Jay Hess, and he ran MRIs on my brain to see if a tumor was causing the problem. He said there was no tumor, but there were bright spots that his cohorts called UBOs (unidentified bright objects). They didn't know what they were, possibly arthritis he said.

I went every other year to see him, and when I went in December of 1991 he checked me and arranged for another MRI. As I was leaving his office he said, "Do you have a hard time remembering things lately?" I told him I was having a problem like that. He said, "I heard something when I was listening to the blood flow in your neck, and I want you to get an ultrasound at the hospital." He said he was going somewhere for Christmas and wouldn't be around for a couple of weeks, but he would get in touch with me to let me know how I made out. So the next day I went to the El Camino Hospital and had both an MRI and an ultrasound. The following day I got a call from Dr. Hess, and he said he wanted to see me in his office. I went over, wondering why he wasn't on vacation. When I got there, he showed me the MRI of my brain and said it looked about the same. Then he discussed the ultrasound. The carotid artery on the left side of my neck was about 80 percent blocked with plaque caused by cholesterol. He said I should have it taken care of as soon as possible. It would involve cutting the neck at the carotid, putting a bypass around the artery, clamping it off, and then opening it and cleaning it out.

I told Dr. Hess that Ken was coming in early February to celebrate our sixtieth birthday and I would have it taken care of after he left. Hess said, "Oh, no."

And then, realizing he considered it dangerous in its present condition, I said, "Oh, no, then how about today?"

He said, "Are you serious?"

And I said, "Certainly. If it's that important, do it right away."

He called two surgeons and then said he had scheduled for me to go to the El Camino Hospital the following Monday, where they would do an angiogram, which entailed putting a catheter into a blood vessel in my inner thigh and sending it up to the position of the carotid artery to determine the exact location of the blockage.

Then they would operate the following day. This was accomplished on that following, which was Tuesday. After the surgery, I began to remember short-term things immediately and couldn't wait to go and thank Dr. Jay Hess. However, my taste did not return.

I lost my taste for seventeen years, during which time I gargled after each meal and before going to bed in hopes that it would help. I not only lost my taste, but eating ice cream burned like fire. The only advantage to losing the taste was that nothing ever tasted awful. This included the medicine they had me swallow to look at my esophagus. Then in 2002 I started to taste a little on my left side of my mouth. By 2003 I had about 75 percent taste on my left side and 25 percent on my right side.

When I talked to the doctor about my gaining my taste back, he said, (now that stem cells were the big thing) "The body is a wonderful thing. When you lose a capability like taste, it's due to some loss of function in the brain and the body tries to rebuild another way to the brain via the use of stem cells. This probably happened over the last seventeen years." Maybe the doctor was right. All I know is that I began to eat ice cream once a day with a few cashew nuts. They tasted great.

Strategy for the New Plant at 1849 Fortune Drive

There is a definite advantage to running six-inch wafers over four-inch wafers. With no change of management and resources, a six-inch wafer has approximately 2.5 times as many die on a completed wafer. For the same number of die required a month, we needed only to run about 40 percent of the number of wafers we were presently fabricating. This gave us the capacity to expand, as well as allowing us to reduce our selling prices and be more competitive with our proprietary products.

It was a great cost reduction without having to establish a new plant or add new overheads.

I gave a great deal of thought to the method of turning on the 1849 plant on with six-inch wafers and shutting down the Pastoria plant with four-inch wafers. My final conclusion was that I would turn on four- and six-inch wafers at 1849, starting with processing four-inch wafers from the last steps of the process and work my way toward the early steps in the process. In this manner, we could run all wafer starts at Pastoria and, as the backend processes were qualified at 1849, we could finish the wafers there. Eventually, as we approved processes earlier in the process flow, we would work our way closer to starting the wafers at 1849. We had three metal deposition systems that could deposit metal on four-inch or six-inch. We had at least one alignment machine that could handle four- and six-inch wafers. So I would transfer one metal sputtering system to 1849 and one masking line. My first strategy was to prove that we could deposit metal and pattern four-inch wafers in 1849 as well or better than Pastoria. This could be accomplished by splitting a run of wafers processed in Pastoria up to the metal deposition step and metalizing and patterning half in Pastoria and metalizing and patterning half at 1849 and see how they yield at Wafer Sort Test. The wafers yielded well at both facilities. This meant I could transfer all the metal systems to 1849 and no longer deposit metal and pattern the metal on four-inch wafers at Pastoria. Thus the 1849 facility then relieved Pastoria of processing from metal to shipping all wafers. At the same time, we could qualify the metal and metal masking for six-inch wafers at 1849 on this transferred equipment. For topside passivation(an operation where a glass or nitride layer is deposited on the surface of the completed wafers to protect them), all these wafers would have the topside deposited at Pastoria and patterned at 1849.

Since the test division was to be located at 1849, this meant that after this last step in the wafer process the test division would pick them up at 1849, sort them, and send them overseas for packaging, and returned for final test and ship to customers. So, essentially, all four-inch wafers would receive their backend processing at 1849 and be shipped from 1849. This established a four-inch capability immediately at 1849 and helped to turn on the test division's capabilities immediately. It also turned on shipping, accounts receivable, and accounts payable of Finance located at 1849. So we were establishing all this backend experience on four-inch wafers in this six-inch facility while also debugging these process steps for six-inch wafers by depositing metal on blank six-inch wafers and patterning them, followed by tests of the metal's resistivity, continuity, spacings, thickness control, and the grain size. The key goals were to duplicate the capability of the Pastoria fab on four-inch wafers so we could transfer the four-inch products to 1849 and remove ourselves from Pastoria, while qualifying the equipment at 1849 for a six-inch capability.

The hardest steps were the diffusion processes on four- and six-inch wafers in new diffusion tubes with new software controllers and new boat pullers (wafers are loaded in slots cut into a quartz boat that is placed in and pulled out of the furnace by the automatic boat puller). This task was given to Jay Husher, who ran the diffusion processes at Pastoria, and he was also the only one with software programming experience. Jay was transferred to 1849 earlier than any other engineers to handle this difficult task. All the tubes at 1849 were computer controlled versus the ones at Pastoria, which were done by hand using digit switches. This meant that all the processes run by hand in Pastoria had to have software programs written to run them automatically on the forty diffusion tubes at 1849.

This required approximately 250 software programs written for four-inch processing and at least the same number for six-inch. What made this additionally difficult was that we had no experience with six-inch wafer processing. The same process run on six-inch as on four-inch wafers required a completely different software program because the larger six-inch wafers represented a different loading on the diffusion tubes. The same number of six-inch wafers occupying the larger quartz boats weighed approximately 2.7 times as much as four-inch wafers. In order to handle this bigger load and to obtain the same diffusion depths and profiles in the silicon, the furnaces had to supply a significantly greater amount of heat. We had to obtain data empirically for each diffusion process and, when successful parameters were obtained, to convert this data into software programs.

Here again, I had engineering start with the last diffusion process. Let's say that this was a phosphorus process where we wanted a certain sheet resistivity. A full boatload would be processed to emulate the normal production process. The time and temperature would be programmed into the furnace computer, along with the estimated rate of entrance of the loaded boat into the hot zone and the rate of withdrawal when the process was completed. This was done with a boatload of four-inch dummy wafers to qualify the furnace for four-inch first. After some tweaking of the time and temperature, the target parameters were exact duplicates of Pastoria. This provided data for Jay, and the next four-inch wafer run at Pastoria that was to receive phosphorus to a given specification, was split and half run in each plant and compared. When 1849's data duplicated Pastoria's, Jay advised production (Carmen Pena) that the 1849 diffusion tube was qualified and should be used for all four-inch processing.

Meanwhile, a boatload of blank, six-inch silicon wafers would receive a similar program, taking into account the different loading and the boat puller had to exit from the furnace at a different speed since the greater surface area of the six-inch wafers cooled much differently than the four-inch wafers. When processed, the wafers would be measured to determine if the six-inch parameter data duplicated the four-inch. When this was accomplished, the furnace number and its tube site (top, bottom, and center, since each furnace stack contained three tubes) were entered into a program listing this furnace tube as a qualified six-inch furnace for phosphorus diffusion of a certain sheet resistivity and junction depth. If another product required phosphorus with a different sheet resistance and/or depth for this furnace and tube, then empirical data had to be obtained through the same method to provide data for the software programming for that recipe.

Over months, the diffusion tubes would be qualified as four-inch and then six-inch for all the recipes to be used at the 1849 facility. Working backwards in the flow of the process, establishing the last diffusion process step first and the first diffusion process last, four-inch wafers would be processed at Pastoria up to this point, transferred to 1849, and the subsequent process steps completed and the wafers shipped. Eventually, all four-inch process steps were qualified at 1849 and four-inch wafer starts and all process steps were completed in this facility. As steps were qualified at 1849 on four-inch wafers, these steps could be shut down at Pastoria. This method allowed us to reduce the power and other facilities at Pastoria and transfer the operators and foremen to 1849. The process of shutting down Pastoria took considerable time since we were also in the process of qualifying all six-inch wafer processing at 1849. Our purpose was to not interrupt shipments of products made from four-inch wafers while transferring four-inch processing to 1849 and at the same time to establish a six-inch capability at 1849.

When the six-inch process steps were completed on each of the technologies that were on Micrel products, the four-inch wafer starts on a given technology would be stopped on that technology and all new starts would be on six-inch wafers. If that technology was also a process used for customer foundry wafers, the customer was informed well ahead of time that they should change their masks and that they would benefit from the larger wafer's reduced die costs.

Ray Zinn complimented me and my team of engineers, comparing this successful transfer and establishing Micrel as a supplier of six-inch wafers, to changing trains while both are in motion. Ray didn't give out many compliments.

Six-Inch Wafers for Production

Being able to run six-inch silicon wafers required a new mask set (ten to seventeen masks made up a set determined by the technology), and a certain listing of diffusion tubes for a given technology such as Bipolar Technology. Each technology would require certain diffusion tubes at given temperatures to be qualified as discussed.

Six-inch dummy wafers were required to emulate the full load the furnace would see when running production wafers. Considering the cost of dummy wafers, it would cost approximately $2,000 for each of these dummy runs. This adds up when we consider approximately 250 process steps in the diffusion area to cover all the various technologies. This being the case, as much information as possible was calculated by Jay's computer models in advance. The idea was to be able to meet the parameters on the very first dummy run. Fortunately, each technology might only require six of the total tubes to be qualified.

To determine the order in which we would qualify the forty diffusion tubes and approximately two hundred recipes, a listing of products was made based on customer demand, marketing inputs, backlog, die size, and cost effectiveness. Once this list was compiled, it showed us the order in which each product should be selected. Furnaces would be designated, target dates were established for masks to be made, and the starting and completion date for the first run of wafers on that technology was established.

Product test results determined the compatibility of the finished wafers. This was followed by reliability life testing. Once three runs and their resultant packaged units passed these tests, the product was considered a qualified six-inch product and no more four-inch wafers were started at either Pastoria or 1849. After this first product qualification on a given technology, the next product of that technology was selected and run. In the case of a second product on a given technology, we were only qualifying the new mask sets and not re-qualifying the process. This meant they had to pass electrical test over temperature range since the process had been proven reliable by life testing. Using this approach usually meant we didn't have to have more than six tubes qualified for each technology. It also meant that other technologies that might run a common process automatically qualified a given tube for more than one technology.

We had several Stepper Aligners that could run four- or six-inch wafers. After qualifying four-inch wafers through these, the exposure time was determined for six-inch wafers by running oxide dummy wafers through and qualifying the stepper for each of the masks in a set. This was rather inexpensive, since the oxide masking could then be stripped from the wafer, re-oxidized, and used over again. So, the masking exposure time and cycle for oxide or metal patterning, or metal patterning etc. were consistent from one technology to the other technologies for six-inch wafers.

Fortunately, the ability to implant six-inch wafers was essentially established by buying a high- current six-inch implanter from Seeq as part of the initial purchase. Likewise, the equipment for other operations such as depositing oxides and nitride of various types was executed by equipment capable of handling six-inch wafers that we had either purchased from Seeq or elsewhere.

On February eighteenth, 1992, Peg and I became grandparents again for the third time. Samantha Carol Husher was born to David and his wife Sue. This was their first child.

On May thirteenth, 1992 Peg and I became grandparents for the fourth time. Collette Elizabeth was born to Jay and his wife Kathy.

Micrel, a Powerful Analog Chip Supplier

While transferring technologies to a new plant and establishing a new six-inch capability, business kept picking up. We increased our foundry base to our growing customer list, while at the same time designing and developing new Micrel proprietary products (products where Micrel was the primary, and sometimes only, supplier) for a growing market. Micrel was now being considered a powerful analog chip supplier with its six-inch capability on new proprietary designs.

Our foundry base for wafers included additional business from analog products for CMOS silicon gate wafers; from Unitrode for high-voltage bipolar wafers; Xerox for analog circuits using high-voltage DMOS off our proprietary analog array; Micro Linear for silicon gate wafers; HP for medium-voltage bipolar wafers; Elantec for high-voltage bipolar; Cherry Semiconductor for CMOS silicon gate and high-voltage DMOS; and continued business with the Genie Company using silicon gate CMOS.

Micrel was selected by other companies to provide devices with characteristics quite different from the standard analog circuits. Among these were special solar cells supplied to companies like Amonix. Amonix was one of the leaders in the field for remote power stations where power is supplied by solar cells. Their designs and Micrel's processing provided them with high-efficiency solar cells, especially when used with offset magnifier lenses to concentrate light and focus it onto the solar cell, as Amonix did.

Micrel continued to supply solar cells to Amonix but now on six-inch wafers. Six-inch wafers were a major step forward in providing Amonix with an improved cost structure and in making more cost-competitive products for the general consumer. Solar power was beginning to be used in the home. As solar cells became more efficient and the cost of other fuels went up, there would be a greater demand for this approach provided by our sun on a daily basis around the globe—some places better than others.

As we moved into the new building at 1849 Fortune Drive the company drew more candidates for business mainly because we no longer looked small. A professional building of 125,000 sq. ft. and a growing reputation as being unique in our product lines drew customers with established reputations. We were the only company that used a mixture of technologies to perform a function rather than being an MOS house or a bipolar house. We used whichever technology or combination of technologies would provide us the superior product for a given function.

One of the new big customers was Motorola Semiconductor, whose business had increased to the point where they were looking for a second source supplier for their bipolar wafers. They visited the plant and began providing us with business in late 1992. Doing business with Motorola was interesting, since they used SPC (statistical process control) and wanted us to use this technique. Micrel had very little success with SPC as a methodology. The reason we had little success with this approach was due to the fact that we didn't run enough volume of any one process to obtain a credible database that is required for statistical control. To use statistics, one needs a high volume of related data to the process being monitored. Motorola has some of their plants devoted to one technology and in some cases have a locations devoted to one product type and more specifically had each piece of equipment locked into doing one process step only. A Memory product running high volume can consume a complete plant. Therefore they could lock in their furnaces at given temperatures and diffusion times for a given step in the process flow and did not have to change anything and therefore expect little drift on any given parameter making up that product. These plants ran like a smooth-running automobile.

On the other hand, Micrel had to change times and temperatures on each furnace three to four times a day to service their multiple technology customers. When this was explained to Motorola, they wanted to know how we intended to maintain control of their processes. We described for them our stop/start system, which automatically stopped any run of any technology at any process step when it doesn't meet the targets and distribution for that process step. Further distribution of this run was determined by the product managers for their products. This was real-time control, and Motorola accepted this method as long as we re-established our SPC program and began to show results within six months.

As we began shipping wafers to Motorola, they visited our facility and were actually impressed with the control obtained on our stop/start system. Over the course of several months, we began to show them data on SPC. They were a good customer to work with, sending engineers to our facility to work with us on maintaining control of their process.

Micrel continued to supply solar cells to Amonix, but now on six-inch wafers. Six-inch wafers were a major step forward in providing Amonix with an improved cost structure towards making more cost competitive products for the general consumer. Solar power was beginning to take hold for the average consumer for use in the home. As solar cells became more efficient and the cost of other fuels went up, there would be a greater demand for this approach provided by our sun on a daily basis around the globe—some places better than others.

Impetuous for a Big Move on New Products

Relocating the design department and my product engineering department in the same building began to pay off big time. They were now sitting in cubicles or offices right next to each other in 1849 Fortune Drive, and this allowed for closer communications between them in debugging a new design or a change required in the process to center the process or characteristics of a product. In addition, the product engineering group continuously worked on reducing the cost of making a die (or chip as consumers called them) and a finished product. Costs were coming down, and business was going up.

New products in a design called Low Drop Out Regulators (LDOs) became a big item in our business. These are used in every design and application in the electronic world: telephones, TVs, car radios, computers, communication, automobile controls for braking, automatic controls for controlling emissions in autos, music CD players, DVD players, games, and the list went goes on. Almost every electronic system requires some type of voltage reference and voltage regulation. This applied in the computer world, the digital world, the instrumentation world, the analog world, the automotive world, and many more.

Another big business was in USB (universal serial bus) applications. Micrel was one of the first companies to initiate voltage and power control for USB products. The elegant thing about our product was that it didn't matter what the voltage requirements of the product were, our product automatically handled that product's voltage and integrated it into the computer. As more computers went to USB inputs, the demand for these chips grew. External memories, printer inputs, and scanner inputs were sent through USBs.

Although many of Micrel's products were considered Analog Products, they were used in every digital product in one way or another. Micrel also enjoyed markets where high voltage, high current, or high power was needed for driving motors, making things move, making sounds, printing, and many other everyday functions..

The Production of Circuits for Ink Jet Printers

Early in 1993, we had visitors from Lexmark. Lexmark is located in Lexington, Kentucky. Their business was a spin-off of the printer division of IBM. Lexmark's people were looking for someone to make the electronic chip for their inkjet printer head. They had tried several other semiconductor manufacturers but found no one capable (or willing) of processing their chip, or the other manufacturers did not consider it good business. The main reason being, most semiconductor suppliers do not have the technical capability and they don't want to move away from their prime process capabilities and develop a new one.

They were the first company to approach Micrel and ask us to have the capability to deposit silicon carbide (SiC) and tantalum (Ta) and to etch these materials. We discussed their chip design. They used the silicon carbide because it isn't etched by their corrosive inks, and the same thing was true of the tantalum. We advised them to leave their test chip and to come back in two weeks. We would show them whether we were able to process the chip, or more specifically, the processes around SiC and Ta.

I had a very good masking engineer named Hui Ip, and he took on the responsibility of finding a way to etch the tantalum and the silicon carbide. Jay Husher would be responsible for finding how to deposit silicon carbide and tantalum or for finding an outside service company that would provide the service for Micrel. Within a week, Hui Ip found a way to change one of our plasma etchers to etch both the SiC and the Ta. Meanwhile, Jay found an outside service to supply us with SiC and Ta, and he also worked on trying to have the machine we had for depositing silicon nitride changed to deposit SiC and our sputter machine to deposit Ta. Without a Ta target it was impossible; however when working with Actel several years earlier, they had purchased a pure tantalum target, which became our property after their exit from Micrel. So this resolved our problem, and we had a tantalum target worth about $30,000.

When Lexmark came back, we had deposited and etched the test pattern they had left us. They wanted to give us an order for a small amount of devices, but I didn't want to work on something so out of line with our standard processes without receiving a large purchase agreement that, when supplied, would make a good profit. Discussions went on for a month; the two companies agreed on a program whereby we worked with them on the design of the product and the test pattern to go with it. In addition, Lexmark was to provide us additional monies to purchase equipment that would provide us the capability and capacity to allow us to supply them in large numbers without burdening our normal production equipment's use. This is called stand-alone equipment, since I did not want to use up valuable capability and capacity that might keep us from our main thrust of business.

Near the end of 1993, we received the first small order. The process time on this product at the time was around four months, so it took most of 1994 for us to turn their product several times and gain some sort of handle on how we could produce it. During 1994, we received new equipment that made it possible to provide most of the steps in their process, but we lacked the equipment (that was on order) to deposit SiC with the control needed to supply this product reliably and on a routine basis. There also was other equipment ordered for Lexmark that hadn't yet arrived.

We received a new deposition system in late 1994 and began debugging the equipment to produce silicon nitride, silicon carbide, and silicon dioxide on a routine basis at volumes that Lexmark would require.

—————ᴡᴡᴏꙆᴇᴛᴏᴑᴛᴇᴏᴏᴡᴡ—————

It's worth a general discussion of how an ink jet printer works for the average person to understand how technically difficult making this product, it's worth a general discussion of how this product works. It should also be interesting for people who have a printer to know how it prints text and pictures.

The chip is made up of digital logic for decoding information supplied to it as to which letters to print, the colors to print, and in which sequence. This requires part of our repertoire of standard processes for making digital logic circuits, so we didn't see a problem supplying this capability—only the capacity at Lexmark's volumes.

The digital logic decodes the letter and colors to print, and the proper ink is released from the multiple inkwells that are part of the print head and is usually contained in a triple-bottle container attached to the printer head. This ink flows down channels (like enclosed tubes) formed in the SiC toward a Ta plate built into the chip.

Meantime, the Ta plate has received a signal to heat up. The tantalum plate very rapidly reaches a temperature of approximately 600 degrees Fahrenheit and a controlled volume of ink spills out of the SiC channels onto this hot plate. This then has a reaction like your mother gets when she is checking out whether her skillet is hot enough by dropping a little water on it. The water explodes off the skillet in little balls, having reached well beyond the vaporization temperature. This same action occurs in the ink head. As the ink hits the hot tantalum, it flies off the plate at a terrific speed in the form of a ball. This is how the inkjet system works. As the ink hits the plate and flies off, the heat of evaporation results in the plate cooling rapidly to operating temperature, and the plate is ready to heat up for the next drop of ink.

This ink ball release takes one microsecond (a millionth of a second). This is immediately followed by numerous cycles like this to keep forming ink balls that are in flight. The total cycle is 1,100 microseconds (or 1.1 thousands of a second) with the ball being formed and ejected in one microsecond and the remaining 1,099 microseconds consists of cooling the hot plate and preparing to release the next ball of ink. Every 1,100 microseconds (in this example), an ink ball is released to begin construction of a letter. If you were to observe this action in slow motion, you would see one ink ball flying from the printer head toward the paper it is printing on, followed by another ink ball in the air only .001 seconds behind. This happens too fast for one to observe, since a printer puts out 1,000 balls of ink in a second from a single-headed system, which appear as ink dots on the paper being printed. This is a typical sequence of events.

In more advanced systems, several of these are done at the same time. It is like a machine gun that shoots ink. The dot size is determined by the amount of ink released down the SiC channels in each cycle. If you were to take one of the ink heads off a printer, you would see an electronic chip on the front of the head attached to a film-like material that makes up the printed circuit. It would be sitting on three bottles of ink that make up the primary colors.

Electronic signals in the chip determine the colors and the letters to be formed. This chip has to be rugged, since it handles ink that is highly corrosive and has huge fluctuations in temperature cycling. It's a wonder of science and electronics that this not only works but does it reliably over long periods of time. The ink head rarely fails, but after a while it runs out of ink. Some companies will take this old head and refill the ink at a reasonable price. Print heads sell for about $25 to $50.

It's a wonder of electronics and materials that allows printing from your computer and in some cases directly from a digital picture print system. These true to form pictures from digital cameras have detail that matches the old methods of picture development and printing. It also allows a huge number of people to enjoy taking pictures, printing pictures and sending them by email or fax to their friends, relatives, business associates, or others requiring a print of data or of a picture.

Solving Problems Associated with Inkjet Circuits

By late 1994, we had provided several thousand chips to the Lexmark specification, and their demands went up. However, we still received some services from outside, and we didn't like their control or in some cases their quality. So we limited the amount of wafers for Lexmark and advised them that upon receiving the last piece of equipment required, we could eliminate the outside service and up our deliveries to them with better quality. We were able to start a large increase in wafers starts and carry them to this point in our process where we were limited by the equipment, to be purchased by Lexmark. There we would hold them, gambling on the fact that we would receive the required equipment and it would resolve the last problems where we sought improved control as well as cutting down on the production time. However, this was a race in time. First the equipment had to arrive, be installed and, debugged, and pass all the electrical tests required. Until that time, the large number of wafers started would be carried about 70 percent of the way through the complete process and held. We will come back to this subject later and describe the solution.

On June third 1994 Peg and I became grandparents for the fifth time. This time it was a boy (I was beginning to believe the Husher's couldn't have a boy. My twin had three daughters, and the first four of Peg and my grandchildren were girls. Girls are great but I wanted someone to carry the Husher name forward). Zackary Husher was born to David and Sue. Their second child.

10

Micrel Goes Public
December 1994

Ray Discusses Taking Micrel Public

Near the middle of 1994, Ray Zinn decided to begin discussing the possibility of taking Micrel public. Ray made contacts with various financial firms to ascertain what it took to take the company public, as well as the feasibility of doing it successfully. He received inputs that ranged from "Don't do it now," to "Do it right away." or "wait until later."

Regardless, he began taking the steps to ensure we could go public successfully if we wanted. Ray was a very detailed person and had very good command of the financial aspects that related to going public. However, sometimes he was very sure that now was the time, and at other times he felt it wasn't a good time. His emotions started to wear on him, and he decided one day to hold a meeting with his top executives to see where they stood on the subject. The meeting was held in the boardroom with the vice presidents of finance, the test division, the wafer fab division, marketing and sales, design, along with the managers of reliability, production control, and two other managers.

Ray started off by saying that there was no financial need for the company to go public. We had plenty of cash in the bank, ample inventory to handle our level of business, high accounts receivable and low accounts payable, and our short- and long-term loans were in good shape. He also indicated that he personally did not need the money. (Ray Zinn and Warren Muller held about 70 percent of the company stock between them, and going public would make them rich if the IPO was successful. It would also make me wealthy.) However, he realized that many of the people in the company had made commitments over many years to Micrel based on the promise that one day the company would go public, and they would be rewarded for their good efforts in carrying the company forward to this point by selling some of their stock.

Ray stated that maybe we should wait a little longer until we saw more clearly that we were going to be successful in this move, also indicating to each of us that going public took some of the authority away from each of us individually (including himself). We would not have the freedom of choice that we had previously possessed since there would now be a board of directors making some long-term decisions. We would be going from a company that was completely owned by its people to one where a large share of stock would be sold in this public offering to others outside the company. People would be added to the Board of Directors and would participate in making some of the major decisions in the future.

With this general discussion as background, Ray asked that each person give his or her opinions on this move. He began soliciting each person at the meeting starting from his left and moving toward his right. He received positive feedback from the initial four people but nothing specific until he came to me. I said, "You indicated you might not have enough information to make the decision to go public. I'm going to tell you a short story that happened recently. Tom Longo's private company was going to go public seven months ago. At the last moment, Tom decided to hold off because a new product was being manufactured and he felt that when it was announced it would have a positive effect on the public offering. So they decided to hold off for four months until this product came out. As fate would have it, the first runs found a problem, and they weren't able to use these as bait. They hurried some changes to the product process and design, and, when they came out, they again did not meet their expectations. Now they decided the time would be bad for them to go public and felt, with this result, that the timing would be bad. They didn't go public, and things have deteriorated to where they are now considering going bankrupt. We have enough positive information to know where we stand. We don't know what will happen in the future, but we do know what's happening now. Let's go public."

Ray didn't solicit any further inputs. He said, "Tomorrow I'll begin to take us public."

A Medical Problem for Ray and Micrel

Ray's word was good, and he began to take all the steps necessary, including going out and talking to the financial community. This trip took several months and a great deal of energy that was loaded on Ray's shoulders. By the time he arrived back at the company, Ray was having problems with the sight out of one eye. Years before, Ray had a problem with one eye and essentially lost sight in that eye due to a genetic problem. Now he was having problems with the remaining eye. Doctors were confused, since they had never seen this problem occur in both eyes of an individual. I would like to discuss the medical things that happened to him over the next several months, but I would not do them justice. Needless to say, he went through difficult tests and experiments.

Surely though, he was under duress, and the partial loss of sight in his functioning eye resulted in loss of his ability to drive a car and to fly his airplane. He was forced to depend more on his wife for certain chores and on people in Micrel to handle things that he normally handled. He had a machine put in his office that magnified print on paper by a large factor so he could make out some of the paperwork, and he depended on his hearing more and remembering what he heard instead of what he saw or read. He stubbornly fought his way through these issues and continued his work on taking the company public. And through it all we progressed toward the golden goal of going public.

Ray had contacted a company on Sand Hill Road in Palo Alto that was considered one of the top firms in taking companies public. Their top people had discussed this with Ray on several occasions, and he had finally decided to go with them versus other top-notch companies. These people went back to the president of their firm and said they wanted to take Micrel public.

"Take who public?" the president asked.

They said Micrel.

"And was does Micrel do, and where is Micrel located?" he asked.

They said Micrel was a privately held semiconductor company located in a very large professional building in San Jose.

"You're kidding me, right?" he asked. "There's no company in any large building on this peninsula that I don't know about, let alone one you want to take public. Where did they get the money to become as big as you say they are?"

They said that Micrel had grown by making profits and committing them to the company growth over the last seventeen years. Micrel had been profitable every quarter in those seventeen years—sixty-eight quarters of profitable business.

"Well, I have to see this Micrel for myself," he shouted. "Tell me where it is."

They sheepishly gave him the address and told him to go and talk to Ray Zinn. The president drove down to 1849 Fortune Drive in San Jose and arrived at Micrel. He got out of his car and went in and spent an hour talking to Ray Zinn. Upon leaving, he walked to his car and looked back at the building and got in his car and started it. He turned off the car, got out, and looked at the building again. "I can't believe it," he said to himself. "If I didn't see this for myself, I wouldn't believe it." And with that, he drove back to his firm and told them, "Take Micrel public."

I think this story is a wonderful picture of how unknown Micrel appeared to the venture capitalist community.

And so on October 28, 1994, Micrel Semiconductor Inc. offered several million shares of their stock as well as additional shares from some owners and went public. The market opened at $9.50 a share, and in a couple of days was at $14.50 a share. This was the beginning of a rise in the stock price for Micrel that would occur over the next seven years.

The First Challenge for Micrel after Going Public

Micrel proceeded into 1995 with great hopes of running with the big dogs. Sales in 1994 had been $60M. Here was a company I had entered the company thirteen years before when it was a $2.5M test company, and here it was a semiconductor company with more than twenty times the sales, a significant amount of cash in the bank, and worth over $150M based on the stock price.

Almost immediately there was a problem. My division had delivered large numbers of Lexmark's devices but had not received the equipment needed until it was too late to make the deliveries forecasted for the first quarter of 1995. If we missed this billing by any significant amount, the first quarter would be a disaster, and it would dramatically affect our stock price, since it was the first report of a full quarter after going public. I called my staff together and discussed the steps we needed to take to meet the sales to Lexmark for this first quarter. Sales to Lexmark had been forecasted at $1.5M for this first quarter, but the way things were going, we would be lucky to make a tenth of that amount. I realized that this being the case, this might be the first quarter in the history of the company where we weren't profitable. This would kill the stock price and would come at the worse time, with the public looking. It was serious.

We finally received the equipment for deposition of silicon carbide and some etch equipment and by mid-March had made some depositions on runs and analyzed the results. They were perfect, but there was no way for us to ship enough products at the price we had negotiated with Lexmark to make the quarter billings required. We put a bull rush on runs for Lexmark, and I decided to fly to Lexington, Kentucky, and present the problem to Lexmark. I explained my situation with Lexmark's top management. I stated that part of the problem was due to Lexmark's delay of signing off on the equipment they had to buy to make their products. They understood this. I presented a short-term proposal whereby they would analyze the most recent couple of thousand units I had sent them and if these units met with their objectives they would allow me to ship the remaining units from March at ten times the agreed-to price.

In the meantime, we would rush the rest of the wafers we had been holding to complete them as soon as possible. But they would not make the deliveries in March (the first quarter ending month). This would serve their purpose by showing that we were capable of supplying products to specifications with our latest equipment and serve mine by providing Micrel the short-term revenue required to make our first quarter's forecast. The proposal indicated that in the second quarter I would make up the total units of the first two quarters and ship the second quarter units at approximately one tenth the negotiated price. So over the course of the two quarters they would end up receiving the total units they had ordered and pay exactly the total price we had negotiated. This would provide them all the units to their specifications over those two quarters, and I would be able to meet my billing in the first quarter. In return, if they would accept this, I would reduce the price of the units shipped over the remaining two quarters of 1995 at a 10 percent lower cost to them then our present purchase order called out. If they would accept this, with the extra new equipment having been installed, I would be able to pick up other business on our proprietary products to make the year's billing targets.

At the conclusion of this presentation they told me they would get back to me, and I returned home. It was now the twentieth of March, and time was of the essence. We were working around the clock to make as many units as possible for Lexmark short-term and for the second quarter. We had several discussions on the phone. They liked the units we had shipped, and they were talking to top management about the requested agreement. Of course Ray Zinn was very nervous as we approached the end of the quarter, and we were very far from our billing goal for the quarter. The test division was working overtime to test and ship our proprietary units to our other customers and to our distribution dealers and hopefully make up any short fall of my division.

This was a race against time. With several days left in March; I received an OK from Lexmark with a new purchase agreement. We shipped the units to Lexmark at this agreed-to price, and Warren Muller (vice president of test division) shipped a significant number of units of other products over the test division's target, and Micrel's first quarter after going public was a success. This was a good example of two companies working together to achieve success on both sides.

As for Lexmark, we shipped the extra number of units in the second quarter to meet the requirements for the two quarters as promised. This began a great relationship between the engineering and management of Lexmark and Micrel for years to come.

Micrel Supplies the Dot-Com Business

Business continued to grow for Micrel during 1995 and 1996 with a mixture of new products. We continued to make major strides in new markets. In addition, we were being accepted by the stock market as a viable company, and our stock kept going up.

New big markets occurred in the dot-com (mostly related to the rapid growth and acceptance of the Internet market) growth of small companies with new products from entrepreneurs supplied with seed money from venture capitalists. These new dot-com (as they were generically called) businesses popped up all over the States. The Internet sprung up and introduced new suppliers of sales of products that were as unique and new as the company that introduced them. Each thinking their new business would be the "Next Microsoft" or Amazon dot-com. As these companies came to being, they brought other companies into business that would either supply to, or use parts from that new company.

Nowhere in the States did new businesses occur more frequently than in Silicon Valley, where the venture capitalists were salivating at the possibility of it all. Each of these new companies was a possible customer for Micrel, since our products were used in every business. The power supply systems in every product are a basic requirement and an opportunity for Micrel.

One big market was the LDO (low dropout regulator), where the voltage or power regulation was controlled down to very low levels before losing control. That their product continued to run, was of prime importance for our customers that had product that ran off battery supplies. As the battery loses its voltage over time, Micrel's LDO regulators would continue to work down to lower levels than our competitor's products under these low voltage conditions.. Micrel continued to lead in this area.

Large market growth was occurring in the cellular telephone marketplace and Micrel continued to supply products for this market. This market was growing dramatically, not only in this country, but also all over the world. Can you imagine India and China, where normal telephones are scarce, and who had been considering putting huge amounts of money into putting in telephone poles and cables and all the systems like those established in the U.S. over a long period of time? Now, with the acceptance of the cellular phone, they could forget about that expense and go directly to cellular. No earth digging, no telephone lines, no telephone poles, no large switching stations, etc. All of a sudden, third world countries could install amplifying/transmitting stations and use cellular phones at a much swifter rate and lower cost. We are now talking about countries with populations that are four times those of the United States.

At the same time, there was huge growth in the CD music market, the game market, total communication market, the television market, the computer market, the automobile electronics market, and the medical market, with new equipment like the SCAN systems, heart pacers, and better hearing aids.

But the biggest new growth was the communication market and the related dot-com companies that were to, in one way or another, revolutionize communications. It was a wonderful time for growth in the semiconductor marketplace with chips being supplied to these amazing new growth markets.

Life for me was meeting new demands and new deadlines. Micrel added equipment and people—both professional and hourly employees. The number of people employed by Micrel would approach 1,000 in the States, with assembly being performed by many people overseas.

In the midst of all this growth, there were openings for engineers in many new companies. My son, David, decided to leave Micrel and took a position with Linear Technology, which was a semiconductor company—and Micrel's chief competitor in some markets. Linear Technology was a good choice for David. It was about four times the size of Micrel in terms of sales and provided David with new challenges. He joined the facilities group with Linear. This group was responsible for installing new wafer fabrication equipment and providing for all the equipment utilities, such as gas, water, power, exhaust, cooling, air-conditioning, mechanical hook ups, as well as establishing new facilities for different wafer sizes. His experience at Micrel prepared him well for issues that would face him at this new company. I believe it is a good experience to just work for a new company and see how you fit in and face new challenges, some of which are the new people and management to work with and for. In some cases one finds they have something to offer that they did not previously recognize. In some cases a person has made some errors and these sort of stick with them. These stick to them like "crosses." Sometimes when you move you lose the "crosses." The new company and its people don't see the "crosses" obtained while gaining experience. If a person learns from these experiences and benefits from them, he/she has matured and the new company benefits by those experiences.

This brought mixed emotions for me, since I hated to see him go but knew it was good for him. Linear Technology was located in the immediate area, so Peg and I didn't lose touch with our son, his wife, and our four grandchildren.

Ken Has a Medical Problem, 1995

While at the office one day in 1995, Ken felt a problem in his back that reminded him of the kidney stones he seemed to pass every so often. He tolerated it for a couple of hours and then told the secretary and others he was heading home to drown a kidney stone. They laughed, knowing that he believed when you have a kidney stone you should drink some beers to drown the stone out. One of the guys asked Ken if he needed to be driven home, which was forty-five miles away.

Ken said, "No, I'll go home and drown this out, as I've before." As Ken drove home, his back began to hurt more and more. When he got about ten miles from home near the town of Washington, Pennsylvania, he passed out. The car went off the road and into a field before coming to a halt. Luckily, there was a car about a quarter mile behind him that saw what had happened. The driver stopped his car and ran out into the field. Ken was passed out and leaning forward with only his seat belt holding him. The driver went to his car and called 911 with his cell phone. There was a hospital only two miles down the road toward Washington, and they were directed to go to the site of the problem.

So within about fifteen minutes an ambulance had come to the site and taken Ken to the hospital. On the way they gave him two baby aspirins, in case it was a stroke or heart attack, which was the procedure being followed at that time for anything that looked like this. Upon arriving at the hospital, Ken had gained consciousness and told the doctor that he had passed many kidney stones in his recent history, and that they should give him a shot of Demerol and call his two daughters—one to come and get him and the other to go and get his car.

The doctor said he didn't like what he was seeing and told him that he would like to run an ultrasound. Meanwhile, the administration secretary took his daughters' phone numbers and told them what was happening and advised Sherie about what was going on.

So Ken was taken for the ultrasound and the doctor began to look at his stomach area. Almost immediately, the doctor turned and shouted out instructions urgently, "Call the helicopter and have this man taken to Allegheny Hospital in Pittsburgh immediately." With that, he had Ken shifted to the rolling bed and wrapped him with warm blankets, even though it was not cold outside. Ken was in a stupor. "What the hell is going on?" he thought.

Meanwhile, the doctor and an assistant rapidly rolled him out onto the helicopter pad and the bird was already coming down for a landing. As they moved Ken into the helicopter, the noise of the helicopter sounded like a war was going on, and the doctor yelled into his ear. "If you feel something like a grenade going off in your stomach, you start yelling no matter who's around or wherever you are." With that, the bird took off for Allegheny Hospital, thirty-five miles away. As they approached the roof of the hospital, the pilot could see the hospital aids waiting for them on the roof. They landed, and he was whisked away to the elevator and then down he went to the bottom floor and out the elevator, and rapidly rolled in a direction down the hall. They had only gone about fifteen feet when Ken felt the problem the doctor had indicated—the grenade went off, and the pain was excruciating. He yelled as loud as he could yell.

The next thing he knew, Ken heard Sherie calling him, "Ken. Ken? Ken, do you hear me? Wake up, Ken."

He slowly opened his eyes and saw Sherie. "What happened?" he asked. She told him to relax and get some rest. He hurt from his stomach to his toes, and he wanted to know what had happened. Sherie told him that during the ultrasound the doctor at Washington, saw that he had an aneurysm of his aorta. A blood sack had swollen to the size of a grapefruit and was wedged between his stomach and his spine. He was sure it was going to rupture, and he was not equipped to handle anything like that. He decided to send him to Allegheny Hospital where there were specialists that handle that kind of problem. They had cut open his body from his privates, past his bellybutton, to his chest to get in and work on him. During the operation, he received nineteen units of blood, and they clamped off his aorta and cut out about four inches of his aorta. They replaced this portion with a piece of hose made of Gore-Tex, which duplicates the structure of the aorta. It is a material that is waterproof and breathed, and the body doesn't reject it. This same material is used to make sneakers and shoes for working or playing in wet areas, like hunters or golfers, since it is waterproof and allows air to circulate.

Sherie told him the doctors said he would be OK, but it would take some time for him to heal and gain any energy. The point of the aneurysm block had also caused very little blood to get to his femoral arteries that lead to his legs, and so his legs were not properly nourished for some time. This would cause discomfort and require the strengthening of his legs when he got out of the hospital.

Sherie called me the next day and told me about this event I was shocked. I was the one who always seemed to have the problems with my health, and Ken had always been the strong one, free of disorders. I asked her how long he would be in the hospital, and she said about ten days. So the next day I scheduled a flight for Pittsburgh and got a flight leaving in a week, since I had some things to clear up at work before leaving. When I arrived at the hospital, Ken was looking good for what he had gone through during this dramatic event. We spent a few hours each day for a couple of days talking about the past until they gave him his release to leave. When they rolled him out in a wheelchair, the doctor came and told him to take it easy for a couple of months. He gave him some instructions for people who have survived this type of operation.

As we were leaving, Ken asked, "Hey, Doc, how close was I to the pearly gates?"

The doctor looked up at the ceiling for a moment and then looked down at Ken. He said, "Eleven seconds. If that aneurysm had broken while you were coming down that elevator, we wouldn't be talking today. You would have bled to death."

While we were going to the car, Ken looked up at me and said, "Fortunate for me that doctor in Washington didn't give me the Demerol and sent me home for kidney stones like I asked him. I have to go and thank that doctor when I get well enough to travel." When we got to Ken and Sherie's house, he told me to help him walk down to the riverbank so he could look at the water passing by. We walked slowly down and he looked out at "his river."

I stayed for a couple more days and returned home. I sent emails to Ken, and he sent emails back bringing me up to date. After a few weeks, he was walking down the street and back. His legs hurt, but he was happy to be walking and smelling the air.

One email said, "I'm lucky the guy behind me on the road from work that day was close enough to see what had happened. If he would have come along a half minute later, he would have seen the car sitting out in the field and figured that some drunk had driven off the highway the night before and landed in that field. He probably would have drove right by."

A few months later, when Ken was able to drive, he drove over to the Washington Hospital and spent a few minutes thanking the doctor for his competent action that day. The doctor was happy to see he had survived and was well enough to drive. He was fortunate that all the events occurred in the order they did and how they did: the guy in the car behind him, the Washington doctor, the helicopter flight, the medics on the roof, the fact the doctor had called Allegheny and told the doctors there what he had seen so they could be ready, the speed of the medics to the elevator, down the elevator and to the emergency operating room, the good surgeon, the blood they had on stock and all the good people helping him since. He was fortunate.

Some good news – on May 19th 1997 Peg and I welcomed two twin grandsons born to David and Sue Husher. Lucas (Luke) and Jacob (Jake) were the happy arrivals. I knew that somewhere along the line that another set of twins would appear like Ken and I appeared many years before this. David and Sue's sons sounded like the cowboys were coming – Zack, Luke, and Jake – quite a nice crew. Now the Husher name will be carried on.

Micrel, We Have an Implant Problem

Early in the second quarter of 1997, I got an emergency call from Bob Rumsey, the product manager on standard products, telling me that all the products going through the parameter test, which was the last test before packaging and shipping, were failing. He described the failure as a constant failure on two-thirds of each wafer. It was 4:22 PM, and I told him to have all the product managers, Martin Alter, and Carmen Pena meet me in the downstairs conference room at 4:30 PM to discuss the issue.

The discussion of the issue centered around what was causing the wafers to be working on one-third but not on the other two-thirds. The data indicated it had to have been the implanter's fault on the one implanter that all the wafers and runs had gone through. Wafers that had been implanted on another implanter didn't show the problem. The data also indicated that whatever the problem was, it occurred for six days and then disappeared. We were able to track down the exact date the problem occurred and when it stopped by reviewing the lot run sheets on these failing wafer lots. Now the discussion shifted to what would cause that implanter to form a pattern like this. It seemed to be something in the way of the beam of the implanter as each was implanted. We checked the maintenance book on that implanter, and it showed that each new shift operator over six days had done their check off on the machine to show that it was set up correctly. One of the machine checks is to do a horizontal scan and vertical scan and to arrive at a certain pattern on the oscilloscope screen during these scans and these had checked out.

One hypothesis was that a partial wafer had got stuck such that the beam would block the bottom two thirds of the wafer being implanted. This seemed unlikely, but we would check it out further. Another was that somehow partial wafers had gotten behind the target where they were not supposed to be, and we didn't see how this could physically be done. It was now around 6:00 PM, and the second shift maintenance technician was in the building. We called him over the loudspeaker, and he arrived in the meeting. Interrogating the technician brought out some interesting information. I asked if he had ever cleaned behind the target, and he said he did. He had gotten into this habit while working elsewhere. His data showed that he had been called to the implanter for service on the night before the problem disappeared. He cleaned the machine and removed thirteen allen bolts to clean the back of the target area. He said he had found parts of wafers back there, and he had never seen them in this location before. He vacuumed them away. The problem we were stuck with was the timing. His action occurred and the problem fixed on the evening before the problem had shown to disappear. Why didn't we see some good wafers on that second shift? Closer examination of data showed he finished around ten-thirty that evening and told the second shift operator not to run anything on the machine because third shift would be running the system in short order. So wafers were run after midnight and therefore would have showed as the day we hypothesized the problem cleared up. We brought the supplier of the implanter in to check things out, and they never found a problem. We asked the insurance company to compensate us for this accident. This started a four-year battle with the insurance company to compensate Micrel for the accident. The insurance company brought in implanter consultants who could not duplicate the problem. My engineers tried to put wafers in front, but they would not stay in the vertical position. We placed partial wafers behind the target area and could not duplicate the problem. A legal battle was initiated in late 1997 and I was called for depositions by lawyers representing the insurance company, as were all my engineers. Whenever the consultants for the insurance company came up with an issue possibility, it was soon shot down empirically by trying their recommendation or they soon found that it could not hold up. This incident had caused a loss of over a million dollars and was not to be taken lightly, and so the battle began. (I will cover this issue in a subsequent portion of this book.)

Why Not Retire?

In early 1998, Ray Zinn called me into his office and told me he was bringing in Bob Whelton, a long-time friend of Ray's, as the executive vice president. His reasoning, as best I could make out, was that Warren could never be the president of Micrel due to some shortcomings, and I could never be the president because he and I had argued too much over the past sixteen years and this could be cause for future issues. Besides,

I was sixty-six years old, and Ray felt this was too old for a job that would show up in the future. Ray was about five years younger than I.

Warren and I would report to Bob Whelton. I was sixty-six years old and had always wanted to work until I was seventy. But this new arrangement meant that I would be spending the next year trying to provide Bob Whelton with the information he might need to run an operation that was not deep in management; i.e. the operational General Foreman, Line and Facility Maintenance, Engineering all reported directly to me without any cushioning of management in between. It took a strong technical manager to take over this position and handle it well.

Bob Whelton had worked for me as a product engineer in 1969 while at Fairchild. He had eventually moved up in National Semiconductor's management to head up their linear operations and eventually went to Micro Linear the year, before where I don't think he provided any improvement in that organization. In my opinion, he didn't have broad enough experience or enough hands-on management experience to handle Micrel and its thin managerial organization (my opinion). At his other places of employment, he had inherited a large organization that buffered him from day-to-day technical problems and production problems and worked out the problems for him. I thought he might work out for Micrel in about five years.

In the meantime, I would be spending my time teaching him how to run many aspects of the company that he had never experienced. I didn't want to go through that again and decided to retire. I put in for my retirement that day.

When Bob arrived at Micrel, he talked to me about staying another six months while they found a replacement for me. He said that he didn't have the right experience to run the place as it stood, and, since I had a lot of stock in Micrel, it would behoove me to work with him over the next six months to ensure the stock remained viable. Micrel's stock price was quite good at the time and he had a good argument. He also wanted me to help find a substitute for my position and to eventually succeed. His argument made sense to me, (so he at least showed some management skill at that point) and I agreed to stay on for six months.

While providing help for Bob Whelton, the other project I was given was to resolve the implant issue with the insurance company. The insurance company had come back and stated that not all the runs that failed were due to the implant machine, and some runs had in fact been shipped to customers and internally to the Test Division to supply our proprietary products and second source products to customers. So Ray told me to review this as best I could, and I began doing that in February of 1998.

Meanwhile, Ray had Robert Barker, vice president of finance, out looking for companies to purchase and broaden Micrel. Robert Barker called on me to review each of the potential companies from a technical standpoint as he weeded them out. This was interesting work, which allowed me to visit these companies and review their approach to their marketplace and their production capability. My extensive experience in reviewing monthly profit and loss statements for Fairchild and for Micrel over the last sixteen years paid off as I reviewed these company's financial books.

An interesting situation cropped up early in 1998, as one of the companies Barker and I both found interesting. He had reviewed their worth and I reviewed their technology and their financial status. Barker and I both recommended that Ray Zinn purchase the company and this resulted in a disparity between Barker and me. Barker felt that it would take $90 million to purchase this company. I felt we could purchase them for $40 million. When this was presented to Ray, he wanted to know why I was so optimistic that the company could be purchased for so little. I told him that in reviewing their books it became apparent that they owed a significant amount of money to three companies who had helped to finance their company. The money backing was based on this company supplying a certain amount of unique timing devices to each, and they had not been able to supply them. Since three years had passed and this device had become less important to these companies, they were essentially stuck without the product or the money involved. Because three years had gone by without these three companies being compensated, I believed that they had probably written it off their books. We could purchase the company and pay each of these three companies about ten cents on the dollar. They had probably written this money off their books (especially with new management at each company), and any new management would consider receiving any amount of money as a gain. Ray did not believe I was correct on this assessment and Robert Barker, who I have a great deal of respect for, just didn't see this the same way. With this deduction, Ray felt they were not worth $90 million and passed on making a bid for the company. I kept bringing this subject up to Ray, and finally Ray put out a memo to his staff and said that if he ever heard the name of that company mentioned by John Husher again, he would fire him immediately. This was Ray's way of cutting off any more discussions.

Several months later, while having a discussion with several engineers in my office I got a call from Robert Barker. He said, "John, do you know that company you wanted to buy?"

How could I forget? I said, "Yes."

"Well, Maxim bought them for $40 million."

I almost laughed over the phone, but there were people in my office. Maxim was one of our major competitors. "Wouldn't you know?" I thought to myself. I asked Bob if Ray knew. He said, "No, but I'm going to tell him now." I told Barker not to mention my name while he was in there. I hung up the phone and smiled to myself.

11

Becoming a Philanthropist— Now We Are High on a Hill

Becoming a Philanthropist

As Micrel's growth continued, the stock advanced with it. Micrel allowed officers to sell stock four times a year. For example, Micrel's earning for the year 1995, along with all the details, was released late in January 1996. Executives were permitted to sell stock one month after this release. In this manner, executives could not take advantage of information they might have had before the earnings were released. So in mid-1996 I sold some stock. Peg and I had talked about how to use the money. I had wanted to give some high school graduating students a scholarship toward college. As Peg and I investigated the situation at Monessen High School in Pennsylvania, we found scholarships ran between $500 and $1,000, and there were not many of them. We wanted to do more than this. I had to work hard while going to college, and I felt it deprived me of the proper time to study and absorb all that I should have absorbed. We wanted to remove that problem from some students. We decided to provide a scholarship of $40,000 to be used at $10,000 per year for a student that we would select. We told the school what we wanted to do, and an application was made for students interested in the Husher Scholarship. This scholarship would be awarded each year for as long as we could afford it.

In 1998, we selected Christopher Josay to receive this scholarship of $40,000 and decided to award a $5,000 one-year grant to Deborah Zerone, who wanted to go to school and work with young people who had speech impediments. We would continue providing this amount each year till she got her degree.

———⁓⁓⁓⁓———

Josay graduated from Washington and Jefferson in Pennsylvania and went to work for a small development company in West Virginia. After two years of work, they decided to send him to West Virginia University on a full scholarship towards his doctor's degree. He got his master's degree in 2005 and decided to return to work for a year or two before earning his doctorate.

Deborah Zerone was given a grant of $5,000 each year, and when she graduated she had all A's. She was named Woman of the Year at California University of Pennsylvania. We provided her $6,000 per year for the next two years until she got her master's degree. She went on to accept a position at the Greensburg Pennsylvania hospital in the department of speech repair. Peg and I were very happy.

———⁓⁓⁓⁓———

During early 1998, I was able to sell some additional stock, and Peg and I initiated an irrevocable Husher Scholarship Fund. Our initial deposition was to put in over a million dollars in the trust to establish a long-term plan with the understanding that we would add another million in the near future.

The plan was to establish the fund with Renaissance Charitable Foundation, where the fund is expected to earn money from stock selections handled by my financial advisor. Each year, Peg and I would select the persons to receive the various awards with the intention of providing between $80,000 and $100,000 for graduating students from Monessen High School each year. They would have to attend a school in Pennsylvania. Peg and I would select the students each year. The target was to earn from stock investments in the Trust approximately the amount provided for the students each year from the Husher Scholarship Fund. Peg and I thought of it as giving a "Noble Prize" to deserving graduates from the High School each year. If this could be maintained at its current rate, it would go on for at least a century and be worth over ten million dollars. Our main goal was to turn Monessen back into a healthy city like the one we knew as young people. At one time, the town had 22,000 occupants, but now it was down to 8,000 since the steel mill closed. All the stores on the main streets were boarded up, and people had to go to other cities to shop. The scholarship fund stated that the students selected had to go to a university in Pennsylvania and earn a Bachelor's of Science degree. It was hoped that many of these students, upon obtaining their degrees, would live close to or in Monessen and work to provide new industries to the area.

I always said I wanted to live high on a hill. Now Peg and I not only lived physically high on a hill, but mentally we felt high on a Hill with this scholarship achievement.

———— ᴍᴏᴏᴇᴛᴏᴏᴛᴇᴏᴏᴍ ————

The $40,000 scholarship given in 1999 to Melanie Vrable resulted in her graduating with a BS degree in biology from Juniata University in 2003. Her grades and energies were so well respected that she was given a full scholarship by Carnegie Mellon University in Pittsburgh towards a doctor's degree in chemistry. This scholarship was worth $29,000 per year, and she was also paid $6,000 per year for teaching undergrad labs. So another recipient of the Husher Scholarship was awarded an outstanding opportunity. At this writing she has already obtained her master's degree and moving toward her doctorate.

———— ᴍᴏᴏᴇᴛᴏᴏᴛᴇᴏᴏᴍ ————

Early in 1998 I decided to write this book because I felt my twin brother and I had each lived exciting lives and reached difficult goals through hard work and creativity. I felt it was a story worth telling, and perhaps some young person might read it and be encouraged to reach a goal. About the time I started to write, a friend at work encouraged me to go to Maui, Hawaii, and look at a house he saw for sale. I had never thought about having a house in Hawaii, but the more I thought about it the more I liked it. It would be quiet and provide me the proper ambiance to write. I talked to Peg, but she was not interested in our having another house since it would put a load on her to rent it and to keep track of the finances. She had had enough of that when we had purchased houses in Chico, California, where Jay went to college. Anyhow, I convinced her to go and look. We would fly over on a Friday and come back on Sunday evening.

It was a nice trip to Maui, and Peg liked the house, since it came with another building called an ohana. Hawaiians have ohanas for their parents, and some people have them for servant quarters. We decided the house would not be rented out, but the ohana would be. She liked the idea of no one sharing the house we would occupy when we were there. Our kids and their families could go there on vacations. The house was located in Napilli Bay, which is in the northwest corner of Maui. This was the ideal spot to live, since the trade winds brought breezes there all year and kept it cooler than towns like Lahaina, which is only six miles south of Napilli Bay but, it is usually ten to fifteen degrees warmer than Napilli. Peg liked the people she met, the fact that we didn't have to get dressed up to go to a restaurant, and the cool breezes. So we decided to buy the property.

I would make trips to the house to work on things. I built a workshop in the garage and made many changes to the house even though it was only two years old.. I was so busy working on the place that I never wrote one page of this book there. Even though we were right next to the ocean, I only went swimming one time when I happened to be warm from working. In addition to our children and their kids making trips there, Ken and Sherie went there with us on several occasions as well as their children and grandchildren. Terry and his wife go there every year for about two weeks and tour the whole island. They found a place that makes great cream puffs. They make this one of their stops each year. All in all, it has been a nice addition for the family.

Micrel Purchases Synergy

Meanwhile, Barker and I recommended we purchase another small company called Synergy. An offer went to Synergy for around $83 million sometime around April of 1998. Synergy refused this offer, thinking they were going to receive better offers. As we watched the market go down for one of their high-selling devices, Micrel decided to offer them approximately $60 million in July. They turned that down.

In October, as their market continued to drop, Ray asked me up to his office. He asked me why I still thought it was a good company to purchase. I gave him four reasons:

ffi   They have a nice fabrication area for processing six-inch wafers.

ffi   Their product line is made up of high-frequency devices and a unique process, which could provide Micrel with a future improvement in technology.

ffi   They had already taken steps to reduce their headcount, and I had given Barker other cuts that should be made to reduce their monthly costs.

ffi   They had twelve design engineers. You know how hard it is to get design engineers. Here was a staff of twelve to be plucked, and from what I knew they were good designers.

Ray felt that my fourth reason was a very good one. He offered Synergy approximately $14 million, including relieving them of some outstanding debts and some other considerations.

I can't honestly say I know how much money was actually involved but Synergy accepted this offer. So we now had a new small company.

(This is an example of how a company sometimes thinks too highly of itself and doesn't know when they are getting a realistic offer like the one initially extended by Micrel.)

Bob Whelton called me into his office and asked me to take charge of Synergy beginning in November and run the company's operations, engineering, and facilities. I told him I would do it until February of 1999, which was only a few months away, because I had plans for February. He was not happy about that, but it at least gave him four months to find someone.

Meanwhile I was excited about running a new company again and forgot about retiring for the time being. I had always wanted to work till I was seventy years old. I loved the engineering and production that go together to make a winner. I love the everyday battles that go on. There are not many better feelings in this world than solving a problem whether it is with engineering or production or people. They are all everyday challenges. The best learning period is when there are problems. Having a problem normally relates to whenever something is running borderline to an unknown problem, and it fails. You never know you are on the precipice of a huge problem until it occurs. Then you realize the limitations you were working under and know how tentative the "every day" processes are. This is true for engineering problems, production problems, and people problems. Solving the reason for the failure teaches you what you didn't know before. If there were no problems, there would be a lot less learning and a lot less progress in this world. No one wants problems, but the winners in this world are the ones who meet problems with as much enthusiasm as they do success.

Running Synergy's Business

Here was a small company, Synergy, that had shown sales of $6 to $8 million a quarter in 1997 and during 1998 had shown a total of $6 million for the year. This drop in sales was mainly due to the loss of the market for a device used to make "High Speed Testers."

The Tester market had dropped dramatically in 1997 and 1998, and so did the required devices from Synergy. They were one of the victims of the early dot-com busts, whereas many of the new companies that were involved with supplying product to the Internet companies went down the tubes, so to speak. There were also many dot-com companies that intended to use the Internet to support their new company. Many of these new businesses didn't work out and went bankrupt. All of these companies were buying chips of one sort or another, and this affected the semiconductor business dramatically. The drop in business was reflected by the offers Micrel had put forth for Synergy over the past nine months. Micrel's final offer was about one sixth of the original offer. Synergy's management had been naïve when they thought they could obtain a much better offer than the initial or second offers from Micrel. They surely must have seen the way the business had decreased.

As I arrived at Synergy, I was expecting to see the company I had seen several months before. My reviews had allowed me to provide Robert Barker where and how much money we could take out the company with cutbacks in several areas. So I arrived at Synergy with this plan in mind. I was in for a shock. Two months earlier, they had started to reduce their headcount. They had fired Larry Pollock, one of their founders, and the same Larry Pollock who had worked for me at Westinghouse, Sprague, and Advanced Micro Devices. Larry had been in charge of advanced development for Synergy. In addition to Larry's release, they had cut the vice president of finance, they had dropped the second and third shift operations as well as the weekend shift.

What I found was an advanced development group with Ron Schlupp in charge. This was no problem, since I had worked with Ron at Advanced Micro Devices and had great respect for his fantastic mind. He had only two engineers working for him and one technician. In engineering, there was only a senior engineer in charge named Peter Hogarth and four young engineers under Peter. In production I had one general foreman (Dave Pulizzi) six operators, and no one on the off shifts to run production. The facilities manager reported to me along with maintenance. To say the least, this was down to a skeleton crew.

I reported back to Ray Zinn and Bob Whelton. Ray told me to do whatever I could to obtain sales of $6 million over 1999 and break even (no losses), with my P&L (profit and loss) statement also being stuck with the amortized monthly cost of the purchase of Synergy by Micrel. As was my normal mode of operation, I reviewed what Synergy was doing in their production line to see where the yield problems were occurring. I talked to Ron Schlupp, Peter Hogarth, and Dave Pulizzi to assess the capability we were left with. It became obvious that they were running their equipment right up against the edge of its capability on their high-speed products. They were working with one micron line and space dimensions in the design of their products, and this was at the limit of their masking equipment. I knew that I could improve the yield and the throughput performance of the company just by adding one piece of equipment—if possible.

After one week, I went back to Ray and asked him to agree to purchase a "used" 5X automatic stepper tunnel from Integrated Device Technology (IDT). IDT was closing one of their plants in Sunnyvale and was moving to a new plant in Washington. They were selling off some of the equipment. Ray asked me why I wanted a 5X stepper. I told him that my assessment of Synergy was that all of their designs were at the edge of what their technology could handle with their present equipment. It was a one-micron technology at best, and that was the best their equipment could produce. I believed that with one piece of equipment we would be able to raise the yield of Synergy's products dramatically through improved line dimension control and faster throughput. I told him I could purchase one for about ten cents on the dollar, since IDT was moving. I could probably earn that much extra money from the yield improvement to pay it off in a year.

He agreed, and we purchased the 5X stepper tunnel. This was an automated machine where you placed a cassette of twenty-five wafers in the input and it spun these up with resist on two spinners located in the tunnel portion, automatically aligned and exposed the wafers, automatically developed the wafers on two developers built into the return tunnel and the wafers were delivered to the output in the original cassette, ready to have the patterns etched into the device. This tunnel could process approximately a hundred wafers an hour, ready to be etched. In addition to the stepper, IDT allowed me to interview and hire the woman engineer who knew how to run the machines. She had previously worked at Micrel when we were at the Pastoria location and had left in 1985. She didn't want to move to the new IDT building, and she was looking for a new job.

This was the only engineer I added to Synergy from the outside. She reported to Ron Schlupp and made sure the 5X stepper was operating properly, as well as developing a short process test mask and converting one of the high volume product's masks for the 5X stepper.

Ron was so happy to see the 5X stepper system arrive that he jumped right into his work, realizing it would take an inordinate amount of time to achieve what I wanted.

Synergy Business Starts to Pick Up

Early in February of 1999, Synergy started to pick up, and, as I reviewed business with the small marketing group, I began to get a feeling that things were picking up in the telephone and Internet markets. The dot-com market looked like it would be a boomer. There were little companies popping up all over the States believing that they had a new super thing for the Dot Com Market.

By mid February, I went to Ray Zinn and told him I believed we would do $26 million in 1999 and make a lot of money. I believed the business growth would start showing itself immediately, and we should be on a ramp for each of the quarters in 1999. He had a hard time believing this and again pointed out my optimistic nature. I told Ray I wanted to add some second shift operators and wanted to start to fill my third shift. Business had slowed down at the 1849 location, and he told me to wait a couple of months. If things looked as I had said, than he would transfer some operators from the 1849 second shift to my operation.

I also informed him that I had reached the end of the commitment I had made to run Micrel Synergy. A week later Ray sent Bob Whelton to talk to me about staying and running Micrel Synergy. They asked me what I was going to do that was so important. I told him my twin brother was coming, and he and I were going to celebrate our birthday by going to my house in Maui for a week with our wives. They said that was OK, and how about running the place when I got back? I told them I would return if I could run Micrel Synergy on a four-day week, working from Monday through Thursday, with no fires to fight. They agreed.

So Ken and Sherie arrived that month, and we had a great time in Maui. I was also happy because I really wanted to turn Synergy around to making money. I felt it was a jewel in the rough. I don't know if I enjoyed Maui as much as I did knowing I was going to come back to work. After returning from my short vacation, I jumped into making Micrel Synergy a winner.

One day in April of 1999, Ron Schlupp walked into my office with a grin, and I asked him why he was smiling. He said, "You remember when we built the test die to go on the product die for the 5X stepper? We included in the test die some critical dimensions that went down to two-tenths of a micron. Well, we've run the first product die with these test structures, and the 5X stepper hit within the two-tenths of a micron like a plane landing on an aircraft carrier. No sweat."

That was great news. Now we could really roll on making the products hit new yield levels—all because of that 5X stepper.

As the year proceeded, we began to be qualified by the biggest telephone companies in the business along with those in the Internet market. These included Lucent (used to be Bell), Marconi in England, Alcatel in France, Nortel (Northern American Philips) in Canada, and other big local companies in the Valley. Business was picking up.

As 1999 proceeded, the second shift operators were transferred from the 1849 facility. Ray was beginning to believe me. These were experienced operators, but we had to retrain them to handle the tougher process requirements of Micrel Synergy. We had to add people on the third shift and a couple came from 1849, but the bulk of them came as new hires. By the end of the year, we were ready to start bringing the weekend shift on.

During the year, Peter Hogarth lost his diffusion and deposition engineer. He liked the work that Jay Husher had done at 1849 and asked to interview him. In a short time, Jay transferred over to Micrel Synergy. This was a good move, since we had started to rebuild the fabrication area clean rooms to make them Class One (maximum of one defect greater than one micron in one cubic foot of air) operation areas. This involved pouring a significant amount of money into the facility to improve the air-handling capacity and quality, converting some additional products to the 5X stepper, adding updated diffusion tubes that had computer control throughout, improving our deposition equipment, and knocking down walls to allow for an improved flow of product as it moved through the process steps. Ray Zinn supported the upgrade. Ray always liked the facilities to have what it took to upgrade them and supported these with capital dollars.

Micrel Synergy Has a Big Year

As predicted, we did quite close to $26 million in 1999, and everyone was excited about the Micrel Synergy contribution to profitability that Micrel achieved for the year of 1999. But if 1999 was good, I felt that 2000 would be even better. It was completely different than running 1849, where there was a broad range of products going to thousands of small volume users. Here we had very large communication companies each using large amounts of product.

The key difference though was the selling price of the Synergy products. The technology was so advanced and the speed of the product so fast that each product brought top dollar—approximately five times those of our 1849 products. These were small chips with large numbers of them on each wafer out of the Fab line. The key was to yield well and we didn't have to start many wafers. In order to improve the yield, we had meetings once a week. Attending those meetings was Ron Schlupp, Peter Hogarth, Tom Wong (vice president of design, a great technical man, and a good, honest man), and my wafer fab manager, David Pulizzi, who was as good as I ever had, especially with the computer and the data he derived from it. He also kept the line balanced well and trained new operators through experienced operators. At times we had the facilities manager attend if the subject matter related to equipment and facilities. We also occasionally had a design engineer involved when the product being discussed was his design.

These were all powerful and knowledgeable people who contributed to the increase in yield that continued to occur. The surprising thing was that we never cornered one process or design rule that was causing the yield to suffer. We just found little things to correct or improve upon: cleans, etches, handling methods, slight changes in a resistor on a product, thicknesses of silicon that we were planarizing, steps that could be dropped, better methods, slight changes in diffusion, slight changes in depositions, a shorter waiting time between operations, and so forth. Maybe the yield improved because we were paying attention to the details; whatever the case, the yield kept improving.

At the end of the first quarter of 2000, I made some dramatic changes that would turn out to benefit all the products on the 5X stepper. The alignment was so good that I believed we could drop doing a develop check on all wafers coming off the 5X stepper. For one thing, this eliminated rework. One should only do rework if the effort resulted in a large improvement, otherwise forget it. From what I could see, we could forget it on anything going through the 5X tunnel system. My staff thought this would be a mistake, except for Ron Schlupp, who saw how well the 5X stepper was aligning. Dropping this step freed up the operators who were performing them and freed them up for other operations where we needed additional help.

Next, I dropped final inspection after etch using the same rationale. By the third quarter, I felt we were hurting ourselves by 100 percent probe testing the die on each wafer. This is called wafer sorting and consists of probes coming down on the pads leading out of each die on the wafer, the test voltage force functions being applied and the transfer functions being tested. If the results were bad on a die (they failed the transfer functions), an ink dot was automatically applied to that bad die, after which the probes rise and step to the next die. The wafer sorter stepped from one die to another until a wafer was completely tested. There could be anywhere from 500 to 1500 gross die on a wafer and this probing would test each. This testing was expensive, since it took several hours to test a wafer at a high cost per hour. Bad die tested on a wafer were inked as mentioned and the wafers were sent to our assembly plant in the Far East. This ink dot was to allow our assemble plant service to recognize bad die and only assemble the non-inked die. The wafers are diamond scribed between die and the wafer is expanded and the die come apart. The inked die are pulled out as being defective.

I had a feeling that we might be losing good die during the wafer sorting process due to fundamental wafer-sorting equipment problems. So the test area was told to wafer sort only half of the wafers in each of the next four runs and to send them all to our assembly and test area. This meant that approximately a hundred sorted wafers and a hundred unsorted wafers were sent overseas from four lots of 50 wafers each.. These lots of sorted and unsorted wafers were to be kept separated in assembly so that when packaged units came back we knew which ones were off the sorted wafers and which were off the non-sorted wafers.

The results were astounding. From the gross number of dies on a wafer we were able to ship 76 percent of the packaged units from the sorted wafers and 94 percent of the packaged units from the unsorted wafers. This was a huge improvement achieved by dropping an expensive step. If this could be done on a repetitive consistent basis, it was a win-win situation.

Further investigation of the reasons for this discrepancy showed that some die didn't have all probes hit properly on the die during the wafer test sorting, and so a good die would be inked as a failure. Some poor maintenance of the inkers resulted in ink splash such that good die would be inadvertently inked and be considered as bad. In some cases the power being supplied to the probes would result in a slight arcing as the probes were pulled up from the a die just tested and moving to the next die to be tested. This would result in the good die that had been tested being zapped and, after packaging, it failed the final test. There were other reasons. Needless to say, we stopped the expensive step of wafer sorting on wafers using the 5X stepper. All wafers that were fabricated using the 5X stepper went without develop check, final inspection, and wafer sorting. This resulted in a compound advantages such as; dropped process steps to reduce cost, improved yields resulted in significant cost reduction (losses due to yield dropout carry with them the cost of material, labor and overhead as losses), reduced manufacturing time, and reducing the number of operators needed to be added from the outside as our demand for product increased. These improvements all resulted in higher productivity and lower costs.

During 2000 I suggested to Bob Whelton that we buy several other 5X steppers for the 1849 facility and eliminate many operations. The use of the 5X stepper tunnel would eliminate many of the operations, equipment, and people from 1849 as well as improving the yield and freeing up additional clean room space for any future expansion.

If business continued to grow, we wouldn't have to look for additional manufacturing facilities, since this increased efficiency provided additional unused capacity. This suggestion was met with deaf ears. I did convince Ray to buy another 5X tunnel for Micrel Synergy from IDT's used equipment. We found, however, that some other company had already purchased the tunnels on the input and output side of the only 5X stepper remaining. This resulted in the loss of the double spinners and the automatic developers that were included in the tunnels.

We purchased this 5X stepper and immediately begin to look for the missing two tunnels. Engineering found these pieces with a parts seller, and we were able to purchase them and now had the original parts returned to the stepper thus providing us a complete stepper and related tunnels. This was important because new 5X steppers were selling for $5 million. We looked at the used equipment market, and they wanted $5 million for a used stepper. It turns out that this equipment was now in big demand. Not everyone was convinced that the tunnels were beneficial, and therefore the demand was looking for the "naked" 5X stepper. This latest purchase provided Micrel Synergy with a stepper and all the parts to make up a complete tunnel for about $750,000. This 5X tunnel system was not needed immediately at Micrel Synergy, and I again tried to convince 1849 management to assemble this one in that building and free up many costs. Nothing happened, so I shut my mouth and went about the business of making Micrel Synergy a big winner.

The addition of operators to fill the shifts was completed, and the place was humming. All changes were made to the facility, making it a Class 1 clean room (very clean room with less than one particle the size of a micron in a cubic foot of the room air) with improved flow of processing, due to the improved layout of equipment.

The year 2000 ended quite well from a business and profit level. Micrel Synergy did approximately $108 million in sales (remember we had just done $26 million in 1999) and provided a huge profit for the company. Micrel in total did a little over $346 million, with profits of almost $80 million, and Micrel Synergy provided a significant amount of those profits.

Micrel's stock was flying, and all the people at Micrel Synergy, including myself, were benefactors of this stock improvement. The financial review of the Micrel Synergy's operation for the year 2000, as presented to Bob Whelton in January 2001, showed the fantastic drop in cost to produce a product and the resulting profits. I remember Bob Whelton asking the production control person giving the presentation, "Is this what John has been talking about relative to the advantages of going to the 5X stepper?"

The answer came back, "Production of wafers was achieved at a higher yield while moving faster and with better throughput than at any time in the history of Synergy or Micrel Synergy. It is obvious that there was a huge increase in productivity."

I had told Bob Whelton that I would no longer run the Micrel Synergy business at the end of the year. So as the year 2000 came to a close, Bob had selected a person to run Micrel Synergy and relieve me of this duty at the beginning of 2001.

2001, a Time for Thinking

Bob Whelton had asked me what I wanted to do. I still wanted to work until I was seventy, but I would feel embarrassed if I wasn't actively involved in some way. I told him that I would like to have time for thinking in 2001. I had some good ideas for patents and hadn't had a chance to think in that direction for forty years. I asked him to let me come in four days a week and sit in my office and think. Meanwhile, so I didn't burden Micrel with my salary, I told him to pay me $100 a month. This would about take care of my medical insurance and other things they take out of the pay. He agreed. It was funny receiving a $26 check after deductions each month, and being happy.

Each day, I went into the plant and walked straight to my office without asking anyone, "How's shipping doing? Are there any machines down? Did we have any yield problems? How many orders did we receive this past day? How's our operator attendance? Do we need any more operators? What's the line inventory of wafers look like? Is the inventory evenly distributed? Did we have any yield busts? What's the booking rate?"

I just went into the office and closed the door and thought. During the year 2001, I submitted sixteen patents: Some were for ways of fabricating wafers using a different method than Micrel Synergy, and would actually cost less and provide additional advantages over competition. Several were for device changes that would provide improved functions. A couple of patents were submitted after visiting my house in Maui, Hawaii. At the Kahalui airport in Maui was a huge map of the world hanging on the wall that showed the amount of carbon dioxide being produced per capita by each country. The United States had the highest amount per capita. However, China was close to our total output, due to their much larger population.

The thought came to me that if solar cells had an improvement in efficiency and were used instead of fossil fuels that the air would be much cleaner. So, when I went back to the plant, I worked on new approaches to solar cells. I submitted two patents for unique approaches to improving the efficiency of solar cells to levels that I thought would allow them to reach levels of efficiency that would allow them to compete against fossil fuel energy on an economic basis.

The year of 2001 was rewarding to me for the time I was able to spend thinking about technical things rather than about engineering, production, and people problems. The year had some other significant events. I had continued to pursue the insurance issue we had due to the implanter accident in 1998, which Ray Zinn had told me to pursue? I did continue to pursue this while running Micrel Synergy.

During 2001, I was called for another deposition on the implant issue. During the deposition they kept bringing up the fact that neither Micrel nor the consultants for the insurance company had been able to duplicate the way in which it was hypothesized the event took place, and they asked me why this wasn't duplicated. I told them it was an accident. They wanted to know why the accident could not be duplicated, why not this one? Like a flash, the crash of the British Concorde came to mind. It hit me right then and I said, "Remember the flaming crash of the British Concorde? According to experts, the accident occurred, when a piece of cowling fell off a plane that took flight just before the Concorde flight. It was a small piece of metal, about a yard in length and two inches in width and a quarter of an inch thick. They found this in the wreck.

"Anyway, they theorized a wheel had hit this small piece of aluminum, causing the tire to rupture, and a piece of the composite rubber from the tire had flown up and struck the wing where the fuel was stored with such pressure that the compression caused a rupture in the fuel line. This alone would have not caused the fire that almost immediately burst over the engine of the plane. They believe that as the piece of rubber flew up, it caused a cable from the wheel to be broken, and the metal cable whipped in the air and struck metal, causing a spark—and the rest is history. Further review of flights taking off from that airport showed the flight that had taken off before the Concorde, and, when they found this plane, the piece of metal was missing off the structure. The experts who reviewed this situation stated that this was an accident that could not be duplicated. It was a once in a lifetime accident."

I stated that this was what happened in a true accident, where statistical events occur that would have to be tried over and over millions of times to cause the same results.

Later in the year, the insurance company sent Micrel a check for $2,500,000. A plaque was sent to me with a silver copy of that check mounted on it. This was in reward for the work I had done to achieve this payment. I took the plaque home and hung it on the wall in my workshop.

During February, Ken and Sherie came to visit Peg and our family and to share in the celebration of our birthday on February second. They gave me a statue of a sailor for my birthday. Along with the statue was a "certificate of authenticity" stating this was an official statue called "The

Lone Sailor", authorized by the United States Navy Memorial Foundation in Washington D.C. It was a beautiful statue that set by our TV. On the back of the certificate was a note from Ken, dated Feb 2, 2001.

"Gort"

I know how much the time (1950 – 1954) spent in the Navy meant to both you and me. I also know, because of the Navy we're the benefactors of the G.I. Bill. Your 4 years & My 2 years set us off in the direction that would eventually place us onto the path of success. When you look at this statue of the "Lone Sailor" --- Remember that success.

Your Twin Brother
Ken

I would look at that statue almost every day. In the evening when some lights were on, the statue cast a shadow on the wall and it looked like my brother would walk out.

The Navy had been good to my brother and our younger brother.

The year of 2001 had its issues too. On 9/11/01, terrorists flew two airplanes into two skyscrapers in New York City and another plane into the Pentagon. There was another plane intended by the terrorists to crash into the Capitol building of United States in Washington DC. The terrorists on this plane had their plans disrupted by some heroic citizens and eventually crashed in Pennsylvania, not far from my hometown. There is a memorial located at this spot. The president of United States declared war on terrorism as a result of these violations on the citizens of the U.S.

A week after 9/11, my mother-in-law, Peg Elizabeth Pool, died. She was eighty-eight and had lived a very full life. Peg, the kids, and I will miss her.

Karen, who was living with her at the time of her death, continued to run the house in Cupertino, which was willed to her. Karen looked young and beautiful at the wake for Grandma Peg, as if time never passed by for her. Having a daughter was a fortunate event for Peg and me. Having an exceptional daughter was extra happiness thrown in.

Retirement for All

Early in 2001, Ken had retired at the age of sixty-nine. He had put in many rewarding and profitable years in his profession, and he and Sherie were in excellent financial shape to allow them a rewarding retirement. Ken had started to restore a 1961 four-door convertible Mercedes in 1998, and this would now give him more time to complete the job. He had purchased a second one to use for parts. He tore the car completely down even to the screws and bolts, and, as he rebuilt it, he would only replace parts with the original part type, even if he had to order it from Germany.

When the car was finished, it was better looking than the original. He took it to many shows and won first ribbon at the shows. It was cherry red, and all the chrome parts had been re-chromed. He painted the engine with a high-temperature epoxy paint, and it looked clean enough to eat dinner off it. After finishing this, he purchased an old 1953 convertible Ford like he had had he got the last year in the Navy. He wanted to do a complete renovation job on it: a new cloth top, special mufflers to sound like the ones he had in the Navy, and a brilliant red paint job. And so he started this job in 2001.

As I approached the year 2002, I knew it was time to finish my life's work. I would be seventy years old on February second and would be fortunate enough to have reached this goal. It turned out that February the second fell on a Saturday, so I couldn't leave Micrel on my birthday and had to wait until Monday the fourth. This was a good date for me also since Peg and I had been married on the fourth of February, forty-six years earlier.

The company planned a New Year's party and combined my going away celebration on that date. Ken and Sherie were here and invited to go to the party with Peg and me. It was a wonderful affair, and I was given some thoughtful gifts—one being the sign that denoted my parking space at Micrel Synergy. Eventually, I was asked to give some comments, which I was happy to do. After thanking everyone for this night and expressing my appreciation for being able to work with a wonderful company for twenty years, I made this closing comment.

"After working for Micrel for about five years, Ray Zinn told me that he had made a bet with Warren Muller. This bet was made on the day I accepted the position with Micrel in 1982. Warren had bet that I would not last three months working for Ray, since he was so hard to work for. Ray had bet I would last six months. Neither of them knew the street smartness and toughness of a kid from western Pennsylvania who would last twenty years."

Everyone clapped and howled about that comment. Then I made the comment that Ray Zinn recently told me that if he had to go fight a battle with someone, and he was allowed two people that I would be the other person. That was the second best compliment made to me in my professional career. (Wilf Corrigan had once said I was the only person he could give sand to, and I would turn it into what he wanted.)

I had a very rewarding few moments after the dinner. Kirpal Atwal came up to me with his wife and thanked me for all that I had done for him. He was wearing his Indian turban, and he took my two hands and placed them on his chest and closed his eyes and spoke in a quiet voice as if saying a prayer that lasted about a minute. Then he gave me a hug. I had goose bumps. I appreciated that more than the dinner and gifts I had just received.

Retired

My retirement found me at my home doing a lot of work on the yard, fixing things, painting things, writing this book, and enjoying Peg. There we were, high on the hill looking out with no more deadlines to meet. It was odd but I still liked my weekends better than the weekdays, just as I had while working. It's like that was the only time for a vacation, besides all the good sports were on the weekends.

Peg and John's house high on the hill

Peg and I had fun visiting places. In 2003, Peg and I went to Nags Head, North Carolina, and met with Ken, Sherie, and all their family. My brother Terry and Noreen were there, and we had a wonderful time. Ken would go fishing like he always does, and I would watch as I always do. All the guys played billiards on the pool table in the evening. We went to Kitty Hawk, where the Wright brothers flew their first flight at Kitty Hawk, and went through the museum there. This was quite interesting and they were celebrating the birthday of the one hundredth flight of the Wright Brothers. Here are some pictures taken while we were there.

Ken, Sherie Gaye, Dana, Lori

Peg and John at Nags Head

Some more good news, Eugene Durbin McClay was born to Cinnamon and Craig McClay. This was Peg and my first great grandchild. Wonderful little boy and it was hard to believe that Cinnamon was already 20. Seemed like not too long ago she was running around in diapers.

On November 12, 2004 Hannah Gabriela Husher was born to Jay and Anca Husher. This brought the total up to eight grandchildren and one great grandchild. They were all great for Peg and Me.

My retirement was great. I found it quite interesting for several reasons. The sixteen patents I had applied for while at Micrel took almost three years to clear through the two legal companies that Micrel employed. This included emails back and forth correspondence with patent attorneys to correct drawings, wording, and providing critiques of similar applications by others to the U.S. Patent Office, and the Patent Attorneys applying and reapplying.

By 2005, I had received fourteen patents (that became Micrel property), and there were two patents still being worked between these services and the U.S. Patent Office. One of the patents I received was for a unique solar cell that I had thought of when I had seen that world map in Hawaii showing the amount of carbon dioxide released to the atmosphere by the various companies. The second solar cell patent is still in the works between the lawyers and the U.S. Patent Office.

The other thing that kept me busy was taking on the responsibility for the development and building of a new house in the Los Altos Hills. It was a speculation build, whereby the house was built to designs by an architect with my inputs in the hopes of selling the house to someone wanting to own a home in the Los Altos Hills area. It consisted of 6,750 square feet of living space and 8,000 square feet total, counting the garage, a wine cellar, a cabana, and some space in a half basement.

The house was built on a little over an acre in the hills of Los Altos and gave spectacular views of the Silicon Valley, the Bay area, and the western hills. It took three years to build, but about half of that time was fighting with the town of Los Altos to put a sewer line up to this area where other houses had septic tanks that weren't working properly. I had vowed not to start building until I got the sewer permission. Eventually, I won the right from the town of Los Altos and the county, and I paid $360,000 (counting the engineering, the architect's time, and months presenting proposals to the town of Los Altos) to build a sewer main to an area where I hoped all the other people living in those hills would be able to hook into this service.

Meanwhile, I purchased a 2.9-acre piece of land not far from my home in the hills. It was a spectacular property with views of Silicon Valley, the Bay, and the east and west hills. I spent a year working with an architect on the design of the house to be built there. I was counting on selling the first house and then building on this property, but the first house did not sell in the time I wanted, and I ended up selling this property. I didn't feel too bad since working for a year on the design provided the exercise my brain needed when one retires from their primary occupation. I had fun designing and looking at materials that would go into these houses. The colors and ideas that go into a new large house are exciting and keep one's mind wondering actively. It was also rewarding to be able to use some of the engineering skills I had learned at the University of Pittsburgh, such as surveying, strength of materials, and mathematics.

12

Tough Years for the Hushers

2005, a Tough Year for the Hushers

The year 2005 started well. Peg and I went to Ken and Sherie's house in late May to attend Awards Day at Monessen High School. By now the Husher Scholarship was well known and well attended. Because of this, they devoted one day for the Husher Scholarship awards and held the other awards two days later. Peg and I had selected some outstanding students for awards and decided for the second year in a row to give out $1,000 to all the applicants who did not receive a grant or scholarship. We had received thirty-one applicants.

All in all, $93,000 was awarded that day, and Peg and I received much thanks from the parents and students attending. They held breakfast for Ken, Sherie, Peg, and me early that morning before the awards, and most of the previous year's awardees attended breakfast with us. This was a very pleasant and eventful day. What was most rewarding was the response on the Awards Day held two days later. While there were only a handful of awards the first year we initiated our scholarships, the awards had grown due to the publicity associated with the scholarship awards. There were articles in the local papers about our scholarship, and this seemed to provide awareness of what was needed for many potential students who wanted to go to college and couldn't, due to lack of finances. Previous graduates of Monessen High seemed to come out of the woodwork and gave $500 to $1,000 toward helping graduates. More and more organizations participated in giving scholarships, including the Army, Navy, and Marines. Representatives of these services each awarded $1,000 scholarships, and the awards for scholarships totaled approximately $240,000.

Vic Has Throat Cancer

When we arrived back from Pennsylvania, we found that Vic Mitrisin had been diagnosed with trachea cancer and had entered the hospital. They did a tracheotomy on him, put a valve tube in his neck, began feeding him through the stomach, and proceeded to treat the tumor. This consisted of radiation treatments and chemotherapy.

Peg Has Lung Cancer

Meanwhile, Peg had complained coming back from Pennsylvania that her chest and neck bothered her. They took X-rays of her chest and scheduled her for special scans. However, it was a month before she could be scheduled for a scan. Meanwhile, her face became swollen, and, by the time she had the scan, it was obvious she had a major problem. She was diagnosed with small cell lung cancer, and there was a tumor the size of a tennis ball extending from her lung and pressing against the vena cava vein in her neck. The blockage of the vena cava was what was causing the swelling in her neck and face, since the blood flow was being blocked. She received heavy radiation treatment on the tumor and surrounding lung for two solid weeks. After this, she began chemotherapy treatments that consisted of six cycles and lasted eighteen weeks. Each cycle consisted of chemo for each day of the week and then two weeks without chemo, and another cycle started until eighteen weeks had passed. Her white count went down dramatically, and they decided to give her white cell shots the following Wednesday, Thursday, and Friday after each week of chemo. This helped improve her white count immediately. After two cycles, they saw that her red cell count was down and decided to give her a red cell shot the following Wednesday after the week of chemo. This helped to improve her strength. The chemo was tough to live with. It caused Peg to lose her hair and to have deep depression until they found a medication that relieved that stress. She also suffered with weak legs and shortness of breath. It was no wonder, since they had taken a large part of one lung away with the heavy radiation. Little by little, I saw the depression go away, and then her hair began to come back in. She gained strength and endurance.

After eighteen weeks of chemotherapy, in December they gave her a body bone scan and a scan of her lungs. The tumor had been reduced from the size of a tennis ball to the size of a grape, and the doctors were happy to see this dramatic progress. In the middle of December 2005, they told her to come back on February 21, 2006, and have a complete scan again. Things looked like they were progressing well.

Ken Has Pancreatic Cancer

The bad news continued. We got a phone call from Ken in June telling us that he had been diagnosed with pancreatic cancer. The doctors gave him five to six months to live. If he had treatments, such as chemotherapy, they told him he would live nine to twelve months. He thought about the quality of life with these treatments, and only extending life for a short time. With this in mind he told them that he wanted his remaining days to be quality days, and therefore he decided to refuse the treatments.

Ken knew his son-in-law, Gary Carmen (the husband of his daughter, Dana), had been diagnosed with cancer years before and had started to taken NONI juice from Tahiti on a regimented schedule. and he was later diagnosed as being clear of cancer. There was information around that this juice did wonders for cancer recovery when taken religiously. Ken immediately began this program.

At the time of his original scan, the tumor on his pancreas was 4.5

cm in diameter. On January 20, 2006 (about seven months later), the tumor had only increased by a quarter of an inch. The doctors were happy with this progress and began soliciting information from other doctors on NONI juice. Fortunately, his daughter, Dana had collected significant data on NONI juice and was actually buying and distributing it at no profit to her. She provided the doctors with all this information.

Ken and Sherie Celebrate Their Fiftieth Anniversary

There was some good news during the year. Ken and Sherie had their fiftieth wedding anniversary and celebrated it with their family and many friends in their large backyard by the river. Both Ken and Sherie looked wonderful. Sherie always did look good, and Ken didn't show any signs that the cancer was a problem. They renewed their vows in the shade of their pavilion down by the bank of the river. As always, Ken was happy to be by the river—his river. See the pictures taken at this affair.

A Letter to Ken

Knowing that my brother was living on borrowed time, I wanted to send him a letter to tell him how I felt about him. I sent the following letter to him on August 13, 2005.

> My Twin,
>
> Ken,
>
> There is something I have wanted to say to you for a long time. I just never got around to it. I don't know how much time you have left, and I am not trying to be patronizing.
>
> I have always been proud of you both as my brother and as a person. When we were growing up, I could not

stand for anyone to say anything bad to you or about you. If they did they were in for a fight.

Growing up with you was fun. Always something for us to do together. I didn't even need another friend. I had a built in one thanks to Mother and Pap.

When we went to the Navy, I was proud of both of us. When I was transferred to Patuxent Maryland, it was a glorious day. I loved being there with you and doing things with you and your friends. I was proud of your job with the Link training.

When we got out of the Navy, I was proud you went to college and did well. I was proud of your selection of a wife and proud of you when you decided to give up school to work for your family.

Your trip to Koppers plant in Argentina gave me something else to brag about you and your family. The follow up trip to Brazil was just another thing to make me proud. Proud you were striving for the best for you and your family. Proud that you were able to remember what you did learn in the short time in college, and how to use it along with your other inherent talents.

Probably the proudest I was of you was when you went to Fontana and proved to U.S. Steel that they had a winner in you. Follow that up with the advancement to Chief Consultant World Wide for U.S. steel in coke and coke byproducts. I bragged to everyone in shouting distance. When you left and went to Furnco, I came home and told Peg, "You know the money I was saving in case my brother got in trouble? You can spend it now—he could buy me." I was so proud.

And you continued to impress me as time went on with the various companies that bought Furnco and found you to be their ace in the hole.

Looking back, I am so happy that you got that home on the river. It was there waiting for you. You earned it and deserved it and wanted it. It became a place to vent your energy when not at work. It provided a place for Sherie to be proud of and love. The work done around there was a labor of love for you.

Each time Peg and I visited you and Sherie, we felt at home and enjoyed the ambiance of your home and the beautiful setting by the river.

The thing that you and I both enjoyed due to someone in our family tree was the lack of fear of failing. At no time did you or I back off of any challenge. We did not fear making a mistake. Somewhere in our family tree, there was that confidence. I knew where I stood, and as time went on I watched and saw you display this gift given to you. I was fortunate that I got my education to help me. You did it the hard way, and in many respects I sometimes felt envious of you—being able to do that without the educational background; but as time went on I felt, "It was only right to be—it was in the genes—the twin genes." We were fortunate for that.

Now you have made another tough decision, and I am proud of it. You saved your family the agony of a "long selfish hang on desire" to have you around longer—but not under the best of conditions.

I think about you being the friend I have had the longest

and the best. I was born lucky thanks to being a twin—
and especially with you.

Take care, have fun.

Love always,
Gort

Ken and Sherie renew their vowels on pavilion by the river

Ken and daughters at fiftieth anniversary

Ken and I celebrated our seventy-fourth birthday on February 2, 2006, and hoped to live a significant number of years beyond this birthday. He had gone eight months without medical treatment for the cancer, but he did have two hernia operations during that time span. These caused him more pain than the cancer. The battle now consisted of fighting the pancreatic cancer while recovering from these two hernia operations. He was on fairly high daily dozes of morphine to reduce the pain. Ken continued to handle this battle with a smile on his face and didn't allow anyone to feel sorry for him.

Vic Mitrisin's cancerous tumor was eliminated, but he continued to be unable to swallow food. The heavy radiation he had to endure over two months nailed the tumor, but it also damaged other parts of his throat. He suffered from the lack of saliva, which is the result of the salivary glands being damaged. In order to take in nutrition, he had tubes in his stomach and bags of nutrients fed to him though these tubes. This included medication needed to fight infection. He had contacted staff infection in the hospital and spent over six months in the hospital. He then went home to recuperate, and they gave him exercises to help him gain back his ability to swallow. Each evening he must insert the tubes in the stomach and allow the contents of the external bag to provide him his daily diet of food and medicine. He had to take the bag off in the morning.

Vic lives just seven miles from us, and the kids all call him Uncle Vic. Over the years, he has made it a habit to come up to the house every weekend just to talk. He has spent almost every Christmas and New Year's with our family. It was odd not having him around this past Christmas and New Year's as he recovered from his illness. We have a horse stall and two small barns in the backyard that Vic and I built. I keep yard work equipment in them, and over the years when they needed some maintenance, Vic helped me with them. I sometimes think about the time he was hired some forty-five years ago at Westinghouse and all the places he worked for me over the years. He has been a good friend from western Pennsylvania in the early 60s to the present here in California—a good worker friend and a good everyday friend. You don't get many of those in a lifetime, maybe only one.

Jay left Micrel and moved to Sonora with his wife, Anca, and their little girl, Hannah. He took a job with MRL, which is a Swedish company that makes the diffusion systems used in the semiconductor industry. Jay's experience on the use of these systems and working with the software programs that steer them was something that this company was looking for. Sometimes when you're making a product, it pays to have someone working in your company who has experienced the use of your product. Jay fit this bill.

Peg in 2004

Sherie at her fiftieth class reunion

John 2006

2006: A Year of Good and Bad

Peg and I Celebrate Our Fiftieth Anniversary

On February 4, 2006, Peg and I celebrated our fiftieth wedding anniversary. I bought her a necklace with three diamonds on it for the three diamonds she had given me (Jay, Karen, and David), and a gold chain that is the length she likes to wear with the diamond mount. I also spent the better part of a month rising early each morning when she wasn't up and putting together a neat photo album. I found an impressive, black leather binder that holds pictures up to 12" × 12" and has "Memories" written on the leather in script sewed with white thread. I used an Adobe software program that allows me to work with a computer and achieve photos of different sizes, shapes, and improved color and contrast. I searched through all the pictures Peg had saved on CDs. I was able to modify and print select pictures on the computer printer all the same size and insert them in chronological order, starting with our wedding, and moving to our wedding reception, honeymoon, each of the kids' birth pictures with her holding them, a picture of each of the kids after they are one and two years old, and recent pictures when they were forty-seven, forty-five, and forty-three years old, and then each of eight grandchildren, one great grandson, and finally pictures of Peg and me taken recently.

The last page is a picture of our dog, Jack. Putting this album together was like reviewing my life. It gave me a lump in my throat each morning as I quietly made up the album. Life would be nothing without a family and kids to grow up together. It was not one life but a life of each and every one and the whole bunch of us together. How wonderful!

The fiftieth anniversary party and my birthday were combined in one party at Karen's house. While working on this album I was happy to see Karen's pictures going back to her birth. What a beautiful woman she has grown to be. Not only beautiful on the outside but on the inside too. She would give her body away if it would help someone. She is one of the few people I have met in my life who is completely unselfish – like her mother. I don't say that because she is my daughter, only because it's true. She would give whatever she had away, even if it caused her some personal difficulty.

Peg and Karen were more like sisters than mother and daughter. Karen always says that her mother is her best friend. I know that Peg has to talk to her on the phone each day or her day is not complete. I guess my mother was right about a daughter; they never leave home. I only have to look out the backyard of our house, and I see Karen everywhere. There are many plants growing that she planted.

She is one of those people that likes to work in the evening. She would come up around dinnertime and start working on the yard, and when it got dark she had big lights that allowed her to work till early morning. It was not infrequent that she would be out there till 4:00 AM working on the yard. I had a habit of sleeping on the floor with the TV on. I would lie down around one-thirty in the morning and fall asleep and wake up around four and go to bed. Many times she was still working in the yard, and I had to holler at her to go home. "Tomorrow will be another day."

And she would holler back, "Just a little longer, and I'll go home." It always made my heart beat a little faster when I would see her coming. She always beams, and it rubs off on everyone around.

Karen with Jack 2004

On the weekends or when my grandchildren were out of school or on the weekend, they would be with Karen. She has a neat truck with two rows of seats so she could have up to three passengers with her. Most of the time it would be Samantha (Sam, who is fourteen and named after Sam Pool) and sometimes it would be Collette (soon to be fourteen) with Sam. She has been great with them because she doesn't spoil them and directs them when helping her with yard work or work in the house. My sons say she has a good influence on them and is not selfish in providing her time with the kids.

Jay Karen David—my great children

369

Parallels

It was always nice to think about the parallels that Ken's life and mine followed. We each married the only daughters of two good friends who went west on a motorcycle to find a job during the Depression.

Sherie and Peg were within a month and a half of being the same age and treated each other like they were sisters.

Sherie and Ken had seven grandchildren—four boys and three girls. Peg and I had eight grandchildren—five girls, three boys, and one great grandson.

Our fiftieth anniversaries were celebrated within six months of each other.

How good both Sherie and Peg both looked good at seventy years of age.

Each of us got to work in our chosen professions for many enjoyable years and retired within a short time of each other.

Each of us got our wish. His: to live by the river, and mine: to live high on a hill.

Peg's Cancer Is in Remission

On February 21, 2006, we went to the oncologist to review what Peg's scans had shown. The news was great. The oncologist, Dr. Wu, told Peg her cancer was in remission. She scheduled the next scan for the middle of May, to make sure everything was still under control. We quietly left her office, but both our hearts were beating wildly in relief. We gave each other a hug. She is a good woman, a good wife, a good mother, and I was happy.

Ken's Cancer Becomes Worse

On March 10, 2006, I went to see Ken. He had gone downhill over the past two weeks, and Sherie told me the prognosis was not good. I took the flight overnight to Pittsburgh, and Dean Coulson met me at a little after six in the morning, and we drove to Ken and Sherie's home on the Monongahela River. We arrived about 7:30 AM, and everyone was asleep. We awakened Sherie by calling her cell phone number. I went in and saw Ken asleep on a bed they built up for him in the family room. The bed was up on concrete blocks so Sherie could get him in and out of bed more easily.

I couldn't believe this was my brother. He had lost so much weight. He was down to about a hundred pounds. I wept to myself as I looked at him, not wanting Sherie to be caught up in my grief.

Gaye had arrived a couple of days earlier and she was up, and we discussed his situation. She said that her dad had a drastic downturn about ten days before and had become bedridden. He had to be put in a wheelchair to do anything. He refused to use bedpans, so he had to be lifted up to his feet, turned around, set in the wheelchair, and wheeled to the bathroom. They had constructed his couch in the family room as a bed so he could watch or listen to the TV and to make it easier to get in and out of the bed and into the wheelchair.

Later, when I had a chance to talk to him, it was obvious that his mind was still in great shape, but his voice was just above a whisper. He would be wheeled out to the breakfast table each morning, and he ate a bowl of cereal and drank a small glass of apricot juice. He didn't eat anything else until supper, and then he only ate a bowl of wedding soup that Dana had made for him. He told everyone to not eat his soup so he would have it until Dana made some more.

Two weeks before this, when Sherie was driving Ken home from a doctor visit, she had to stop in the Giant Eagle to pick up some food. When she came out she told Ken that they had king crab legs for $5 a pound. He told her to go back in and buy twenty pounds, and they would have a Crab Day for the family. Ken had called me at home and told me he was having this special meal on the twelfth of March to celebrate St. Patty's Day that falls on the seventeenth. He didn't know I was going to be out there on that day. Later, when he was bedridden and knew I had planned to come out, he called me and told me to make it for that feast.

So here I was, and he was down and not able to enjoy the Sunday feast that everyone in the family was there for. My brother Terry and his wife, Noreen, came from Ohio, along with my nephew Justin and his girlfriend, Sara (soon to be married). All three of Sherie and Ken's girls were there, along with Lori's husband, Dean, and their two kids, Jamie (from Toronto) and Shaun, Dana's husband Gary and their three kids, Colton, Tanner, and Danielle. Gaye was up from Florida with her two children, Tori and Lane.

There were seventeen people there for the feast, and each of the girls had brought some good things to eat. Ken was happy to see everyone but was not able to eat any goodies. It was fun talking to everyone and enjoying the ambiance and the great food. It turned out Ken was right—twenty pounds of crab legs were finally finished by Colton, who ate more than everyone there. They all stayed the whole day, and it got quiet about 11:00 that night.

Jamie had come down from Toronto where she works for an advertisement firm. I had taken the only bound copy of this book (before it was edited and sent for publication), and she said she wanted to read the whole thing. I had a memory stick in my pocket that contained the book. She got on Ken's computer and sent it to her email address in Toronto. She was excited to read it all.

The days I spent there were good ones. The weather was great for this time of the year. I went up to Dean's shop, and he was loading his newly built warehouse behind his shop. He had purchased an old forklift, and he was picking up pallets that held five boxed lawnmowers and maneuvering them into the warehouse. Shaun was standing on a storage area built about twelve feet above the floor level to receive the crated boxes. He would remove two as Dean raised the pallet to that level and then would lift the pallet and sit it up at this level. They had to do it this way because this high shelf could only take three boxes and a pallet without hitting the roof. Back and forth they went until about 130 mowers were stored. Then they began to store the boxes of lawnmower oil. I stayed for a couple of hours and then went back to help Sherie. She wanted some food from the store, which I picked up for her in Ken's truck.

I went to Dean's shop the next day, and he had cleared out his old shop and was putting up firing strips along the walls so that when the new shelves were moved in they wouldn't hit the new walls that had been put in. I helped Dean as we snapped a chalk line and installed the firing strips. Dean mentioned that he was usually the one helping me in California. Well, now I was returning the favor. It was fun work.

On my way back to Ken's, I stopped and looked at the house that Peg and her parents had lived in. It looked exactly as it had looked all those years before. It set there on the knoll of the yard with a fresh paint job looking regal. I had spent many good hours in that house with Peg and the cellar gang. I got a lump in my throat and continued my drive. Then I drove down past where my mother and Pap had lived and looked at their old home. It also looked like it hadn't aged a bit. I drove down and toured the town of Monessen. It was depressing to see this town that had once been alive with work and people and great stores to shop, and now was like a ghost town. All the shops on the main street of Donner Ave. were closed and boarded up. It was almost as bad on the other main street of Schoonmaker Ave.

I drove past the site that used to be American Chain and Cable (Pages), and it was gone. I drove the length of town, which used to be paralleled by the huge Pittsburgh Steel Mill, and the steel mill was gone. This was sad. I thought to myself that this was why Peg and I had set up the scholarship fund for Monessen graduates to attend college and perhaps one day bring Monessen out of this tomb. This proud town once held 22,000 people and now was down to about 8,000 with no large industry to support it.

I drove back to Sherie and Ken's house and was happy to be there. Gaye helped to bring the spirit of the house up during her visit, which would end on the eighteenth for her and the kids. Fortunately, Dana and Lori visited every morning to help Sherie with her chores and to lift Ken's morale. Ken and I would watch basketball, which was approaching March Madness, and there were various tournaments being played.

I stayed five days, and the day I was leaving I bought a quiet pump to pump the rainwater off the pool cover. I just wanted to do something for Sherie before leaving, and I didn't want to sit in the room and become depressed watching Ken. A large plastic ball about three feet in diameter had been placed on the pool water, and the pool cover set over this and over the pool. There were about 1,000 gallons of water captured in the droop of the cover and stretching it. I hooked up the pump and placed it in an area on the cover that didn't have any leaves and began to pump. I figured it might take an hour, but the hose running from the pump could only handle about ten gallons a minute. It took me almost two hours to drain it and clean up the cover.

Afterward, I knew I had to go pretty soon and decided to put off talking to Ken until about fifteen minutes before leaving. When the time came, I sat next to him and told him how much I loved him and how much I had always loved him while kissing his cheek. The tears were running down both of our cheeks. He whispered to me to move so he could get his arm around me and then he hugged me with his weakened arms. He still had a lot of hugging power, and he pulled me close and said, "This is the last time I will see you, Gort."

I whispered back, "I will see you somewhere again." We both had tears running down our faces, and I took my right hand and softly wiped the tears from his cheeks. He pulled me close one more time and kissed me on the lips. I repeated, "I will see you somewhere again." And then I left the room and had a good cry. Later, Sherie told me that Ken said this was the hardest thing he had to do in his life.

Lori drove me to the airport, which was about an hour and fifteen minutes away. We talked about her dad and how strong he had been. She said that Gaye was disturbed because she knew her dad didn't want to put the family through this kind of thing, but he had made a strong and conscious decision to live a quality life as best he could. I told her that even though he was in this condition he was happy to see his family each day and to enjoy them. Every once in a while someone would make him smile, so I know he was enjoying the presence of those around him. Like always, he was strong until the end.

My Twin Passes Away

On April fourth, Sherie called me and told me that Ken hadn't eaten for six days and the girls and she didn't know what was keeping him alive.

He no longer could talk, but she knew he could hear them because his breathing rate changed as she viewed his chest while talking to him.

They each had whispered in his ear that they loved him and asked him to go with the Lord. He hung on, and the reason she was calling me was to say that she and the girls believed Ken was waiting for me to give him my love and ask him to be with the Lord.

She said she would hold the phone up to his ear. I heard her say, "Gort is on the phone and wants to say something to you."

I said to him, "I have always loved you and always looked up to you. I have always been proud of you and your family and your achievements. It's time to leave us and free your family. I know that is what you always wanted, not to be a burden on your family. Go with the Lord and I will see you somewhere again. God Bless you."

I then had tears flowing down my face and had to softly hang up the phone. About five minutes later, Sherie called me back and said he had heard me and the tears had run down his cheeks. I thanked her for giving me this chance to say good-bye to him. Each time I heard the phone ring I thought it would be Sherie to tell me he had passed on.

On Friday morning, April seventh, she gave me the call. This call and the one I had received from Sherie a few days before are the two saddest messages I have received in my life. Five minutes later I was already missing him. It is hard for me to conceive of any person being closer to another than I with my twin. Time spun around in my head, and I thought of many things we had experienced together: growing up, the Navy, the projects at his house, projects at mine. I remembered the dialogue between us during these times, like special gifts. We had a way of pitter-pattering with words that flowed with respect one for the other—an experience I shared with no other person. It's amazing that two people—so different, though twins—could have things so much alike while engaging in some function. All these things filtered rapidly through my mind as Sherie continued talking on the phone. She said she was sorry that he had passed away on David's birthday. I told her that I was sure that David would be proud and softly told her that I had to hang up.

Later, when I was wishing David a happy birthday over the phone,

I mentioned what Sherie had said. He said, "Dad, I am proud of Uncle Ken and proud that he passed away today. Now when I have a birthday, it will mean more to me. Uncle Ken was the first person ever to take me fishing when we lived back in Pennsylvania and later he sent me a fishing rod for my birthday. Eventually, he sent me three good fishing rods that I still have and I think of him often." I smiled and was glad that David had those three rods from Ken. Ken always loved fishing, especially by a river, next to his home.

I flew back on April twentieth to attend Ken's wake, which was being held at Rhome's Funeral Home on Saturday, April 22, 2006. An obituary had appeared in the *Valley News* and the *Pittsburgh Post Gazette* relating his passing and that friends would be received at Rhome's Funeral Home from two until four and in the evening from seven until nine on the twenty-second of April.

On the twenty-first, I went with Sherie, Dana, and Gaye to see the house that Sherie was buying. Ken and Sherie had decided several months before his passing that their house was too big for Sherie to live in alone, and she should buy a home close to Dana and Gary's place about twenty miles away from the river home. It was a good choice of a home for Sherie, and it wouldn't be finished for occupancy till July twenty-seventh.

I had known about this and couldn't see that house by the river going to anyone. It was like a magnet that pulled all the family members to it on each holiday and many a weekend. I thought that I would buy it, but I knew I didn't want to rent it to anyone. The more I thought about it, the more I realized that the only way I would buy it is if Shaun Coulson (Ken's grandson and the son of his oldest daughter, Lori, and her husband, Dean Coulson) would live in it. So I mentioned this via an e-mail early in April to Lori. The subject hadn't come up yet.

The wake on Saturday was a sad but wonderful experience for Ken's family and me. There were many people there that were our classmates at Monessen High—those that still remained. There were the students, many with their families that had received Husher scholarships and grants over the last eight years. There were Ken's fishing buddies and people who had worked for him over the years.

One man and his wife traveled by car from Chicago. I talked to him and asked him how he knew Ken. He said he worked for him for over twenty years, traveling all over the States and overseas. One time he had him go to Birmingham, Alabama, where he met a woman who became his wife. She was there with him. He said he would go to hell for Ken.

Another man and his wife traveled from Indiana, and their story was similar. Since Ken had been cremated, there was no casket. There were personal things like his fishing jacket with things sticking out the pockets, a half-size fishing boat with oars inside along with his picture. There were various other paraphernalia displayed on the wall or alongside the little boat.

On one wall was a fantastic colored photograph of my brother that contained a story in itself. The original picture was taken in 1994 while Ken was in Venezuela. He had gone down there to fish for a fish that is indigenous to one lake and not found elsewhere. It was a fish that is about two feet long and about one foot around and has a yellow stripe around its middle. To go fish for this one prize, he had to take shots—to prevent malaria—and other precautions were taken to provide him some safety. He caught a fish, had its picture taken, kissed it, and threw it back in the lake. The picture taken of him (sans the fish), Sherie's favorite, shows the upper half of him with his thumb raised in the air indicating his success. He is very handsome in this picture. A friend of the family had called Sherie and asked for a good picture of him and something that Ken said many times in life. He took the picture and printed an enlargement on a material-like oilcloth. It was about three feet tall and four feet wide and near the bottom was printed "Red skies at night, sailor's delight," something that Ken said all the time when he was going fishing. It had been brought to the funeral home before anyone arrived and hung on the wall. When I arrived and saw it, I thought my brother was going to jump out and shake my hands. It was both handsome and beautiful. Everyone who came in the afternoon or the evening admired this handsome rendition and made comment after comment.

Ken—Venezuela 1995

Ken's granddaughter, Jamie, had made a DVD containing 320 pictures taken over seventy-four years that were displayed in slideshow on an iMac computer, with its twenty-one-inch screen. Twenty-one songs that Ken loved played as the pictures flicked through a long and happy life: from ones showing each member of his family, pictures of the twins at various stages of our lives, Ken fishing, Sherie and Ken's fiftieth anniversary, and Ken and his fishing buddies fishing in Canada. They covered a long and happy life.

There were twenty chairs set around the screen so that visitors could sit down and watch them. As soon as anyone moved on, the seats would immediately be filled again. The pictures told a story of an integrated life of one man across a long time period, and each photo pulled in all the other participants into that life. For me to watch was like seeing some of them happening again before my eyes. They were unbelievable, but believable. This was not a funeral; this was a celebration of a good man's life. It was a relief. People left, not crying and not laughing, but happy to have been there and been a part of his going away.

Buying Ken and Sherie's Property

That evening, Dean talked to me and wanted me to know that he had mentioned the house to Shaun and got a positive answer. He asked me if I had discussed it with Sherie at all. I hadn't and told him I would do that this evening. I did, and she was somewhat confused. She was depending on receiving enough from the sale of the home for her to pay for the new house and have enough left over to provide her a full and happy life. She had planned on that and said she would think about it.

The next day was Sunday, and Sherie's daughters and the rest of the family had planned a dinner as a completion to the wake. There were all kinds of good food to eat and later, Dean said that he would like to have a meeting with me and the rest of the family to discuss the possibility of me buying the house and Shaun living in it..

Later, I started the conversation by saying that I didn't want to see anyone else living in this house except someone in the family. My brother had loved this place and out of respect for him and love of this property that I would buy it. But I wouldn't pay for it completely. I wanted Shaun Coulson to own half and to live here. I wanted him to earn the place by taking on approximately half of the cost via a mortgage. I felt he could sell his house, and, with the money, pay down the mortgage remaining on this house so that he would have a monthly payment close to the one he presently had on his house. Then, when I died, I would pass my half down to him.

Sherie expressed a concern that an assessment made by an outside assessor was much less than she had felt it was worth and wanted to know how this would be handled.

Shaun was twenty-seven years old, and he said that he would love to live in this house. He would keep it neat and clean and maintain it just like his GP (Grand pap). He would not bring in large groups of youngsters or do harm to the building. He gave his house as proof that he was a responsible person who cared about the house he lived in. He said he had two concerns—one that he could afford it, and the other concern was how others in the family felt about it. He wanted to hear how each person in the room felt.

So one by one each member of the family spoke up. Each had a favorable opinion, and Shaun's older sister, Jamie, said she would be happy to see Shaun live in this house. She thought it was wonderful and felt she was more mobile than Shaun and, living in Toronto at present, could not determine where her work would take her. She said that Shaun worked here and deserved to have this place. He also liked to fish in the river like his GP. She felt it would be wonderful that the house would be in the family and that we could come there on the holidays just as they had since she was born.

Happy with what I heard, I asked Sherie how much she thought the house was worth and that we would pay that for it. That ended the discussion. The next day I flew back to California. I thought about how to handle this with loans and mortgages. Finally, I decided I would put up the money for over half of it and let Shaun make the decision on how he would handle the mortgage. His mother, Lori, had said that she would talk to her lawyer and figure out what was the best way for Shaun to handle the finances from his end.

After a few days I got the following email from Sherie.

Gort and P.A.,

What on earth can I say, and how do I thank you making it possible for Ken's dream home to stay in the family? The tears are pouring down my face as I write to you. I can see him up in heaven smiling and so happy that his grandson and fishing buddy will live here and continue to fish in his beloved river with the fishing poles he left for Shaun.

You have also lifted a burden for me and made it so much easier to leave this beautiful place. Just knowing that I can always return is a blessing and a gift. I will have to knock on the door. Ha, ha. That's ok.

Love you both so much.
Sherie

This relieved me and I sent this to Shaun. I received the following email back from him.

Uncle Gort,

I got all your emails. Everything is looking good so far. My mom is working on the lawyer, and I am still figuring some things out. Just want you to know that we are getting things together. The email you forwarded from Grandma was very nice to hear.

We have such a great family!

> Thank you, thank you, thank you
> I'll keep in touch
> Shaun

So I made arrangements for the finances from my side to be taken care of. In a few months, the house will be Shaun's and mine; his to live in for the rest of his life and me to be happy knowing that someone who reminds me of my brother when he was Shaun's age will be living in it. And it will be there for all the family to visit when Shaun gives the word.

Ken's favorite date each year was May first. He waited for that date like it was very special. This was the day he looked forward to, since it was the beginning of planting season for him. He loved to plant tomatoes, beans, squash, cucumbers, zucchini, peppers, radishes, and others, starting on that date by placing seeds in small, dirt-filled containers he kept inside the sun porch until the nights became warmer.

His most favorite rewards came from the great tomatoes he grew. He and Terry used to have contests where the rest of the family tasted their tomatoes and picked the winners. Ken always won. So every year on May first, many folks whom he had befriended over the years called and asked him if he started his planting yet. He always had.

So, this May 1, 2006, Sherie and the family sprinkled his ashes and a handful of soil from his garden into the river as it flowed by his house. These were two of his favorite pastimes. Some of the sprinkles will come to rest there next to their home, some will flow down the Monongahela River past Monessen, and some further on to the point in Pittsburgh where it joins the Allegheny to form the Ohio River and continues flowing on its journey till it reached the Mississippi. Ken would enjoy that trip.

On May second, I got an email from Dana, Ken's youngest daughter.

Uncle Gort and Aunt Peg

The day was beautiful, unlike the rainy days when Mom and Dad met, got engaged, got married, Dad died, and his funeral. Mom could not get over it—how on all of these occasions had it rained? We couldn't wait till May 1st to see what would happen. As we hoped, it was a beautiful day to let Dad go. It really completed all of us. You were there with us. The dirt was a great idea. The kids were so excited to let their GP go. Tanner was 1st, then Colton, then Danielle, then Jamie, then Shaun, then Lori, Gaye, and I all went out, then Gary and Dean (Dean did the dirt and ashes), and then mom by herself. What a wonderful closure! We can finally have closure. It's been hard, but we can all still talk to him like we've been doing daily. I keep finding myself imagining him there answering my questions when I have something to ask him. I hear his answers—seems odd huh. And sometimes when I go to do something—like making a decision on something—I will say to myself, OK, Dad, you're right, it would be better to do it this other way. God, I just hope I don't talk out loud in the store or something. Crazy but peaceful to me. Next time you come in—WE HAVE EXTRA ASHES OF DAD—you will have to take some and let them go on the river yourself. Aunt Peg too! If you do it, I want to watch, if that is OK.

Thanks again for all you have made possible in our lives. You have touched so many lives, and we recognize that. You two were 2 peas in a pod. Always thinking of how you can help someone. I want to grow up and be just like you guys and my mom. If I could have a fraction of that recipe, I would be on top of the world. I am—in a different way. We have health for right now, and that is everything.

Thanks again for taking us under your wings.

PS. Aunt Peg, I think of you often. How are you feeling? We missed you so much during the funeral days. It did not seem right without you. My mom had us, but it would have been more special with you there. You both have been such a great part of their lives—even from two ends of the country. My dad always talked of you fondly. He loved you so much. He told us that Uncle Gort couldn't have picked a better partner. He said the same about our mom. He was so lucky.

WE were so lucky! Thank God we still got Mom. She is truly a gem in life. We love her so much.

> We love you,
> Dana

The 2006 Husher Scholarship Presentation

On May twentieth I went back to Monessen to award the Husher Scholarships to the graduating class of 2006. Twelve scholarships were to be given out, bringing the total to forty-eight Peg and I had provided over the past eight years.

I always gave a talk to the students of the eleventh and twelve grades on my presentation day. However, Randy Murino, the principal of Monessen High School, decided to have all the students from seventh to twelfth grade present this year since he felt the message was worth their hearing. In the previous years, while I was giving the presentation, he had it sent via closed circuit television to all the classrooms. There were approximately five hundred students present in the auditorium.

I directed most of my talk toward the students who weren't going to college in the coming year. I tried to inspire them to find a way to take advantage of several opportunities to finance their schooling or to go to junior college or perhaps go into the military, since it provided educational benefits. The military has excellent schools for teaching trades and many times preparing them for after service. There are also still educational bills to provide for those leaving the military service.

As part of the talk, I told them that this drive to attain betterment reminded me of the book and Broadway play *The Man of La Mancha* and the main song in that play—"The Impossible Dream." It is a story about an older man, Don Quixote, who thinks he is a knight, and goes traveling around on the back of his donkey and swinging his sword, chasing after windmills and trying to do right, trying to achieve the "Impossible Dream." I told them that every once in a while when I felt down, I would take out this song and play it. Listen to the words (and I had the song played over the loudspeaker system). I paused as this song played throughout the auditorium, with a lump in my throat as I thought about my brother.

Afterward, I said, "We don't know what's inside each of us until pressured, and then it seems to creep up on you. Many times a single event in our lives changes his/her whole life. Don't let this pass you by. I just completed a book, writing most of it over the past year while Peg was being treated for lung cancer. It just completed being edited and I hope to have it published this year. The name of the book is *By a River, On a Hill*. When my twin and I were about fourteen years old, we would sneak down to the river and swim. This was not allowed in those days because the river was so polluted. We found a bush that we could rub against our bodies and clean ourselves. We used to do this so our parents wouldn't know we were in the river.

"One day while soaping up, Ken said, 'When I grow up, I want to live by the river.' I said, 'When I grow up, I want to live high on a hill so I can look out and see the world.' These were our impossible dreams" that we made possible. The book is about our fight to gain these dreams. I want all of you to fight for your dreams. For those going to college, be a winner. For those fighting their way to college or to a trade remember what Abraham Lincoln once said, "Whatever you are, be a good one."

Reflections and Conclusion

Every once in a while I wake up in the middle of the night and think about the past and how fortunate I have been: wonderful parents, wonderful brothers, a wonderful wife, a wonderful family, being able to reflect on the various fantastic jobs I have held in various parts of the country, the various trips overseas to support those jobs, and being able to work on new, creative technologies that are now being used all over the world. Wow, how fortunate I have been to live my dream.

Then I look over on the wall by the bed and the nightlight helps me to see Peg's face framed in a picture. The picture was taken by her uncle during our wedding. It has always been my favorite picture. She is not smiling in it. She looks like she is thinking about what the world is about to bring us. She never could have imagined what life had in store for us. What a great ride it has been. I smile and go back to sleep.

—John Durbin Husher

CPSIA information can be obtained
at www.ICGtesting.com
Printed in the USA
LVHW091447050322
712718LV00002B/5